Coding, Communications and Broadcasting

ELECTRONIC & ELECTRICAL ENGINEERING RESEARCH STUDIES
COMMUNICATIONS SYSTEMS, TECHNIQUES AND APPLICATIONS SERIES

Series Editor: **Professor P. G. Farrell**
                       University of Lancaster, UK

1.   Sequence Design for Communications Applications
      Pingzhi Fan *and* **Michael Darnell**

2.   Communications Coding and Signal Processing
      THIRD VOLUME ON COMMUNICATION THEORY AND APPLICATIONS
      Edited by **Bahram Honary, Michael Darnell** *and* **Paddy Farrell**

3.   Coding, Communications and Broadcasting
      FOURTH VOLUME ON COMMUNICATION THEORY AND APPLICATIONS
      Edited by **Paddy Farrell, Michael Darnell** *and* **Bahram Honary**

Coding, Communications and Broadcasting

FOURTH VOLUME ON COMMUNICATION THEORY AND APPLICATIONS

Edited by

Paddy Farrell
University of Lancaster, UK

Michael Darnell
University of Leeds, UK

Bahram Honary
University of Lancaster, UK

 RESEARCH STUDIES PRESS LTD.
Baldock, Hertfordshire, England

RESEARCH STUDIES PRESS L
15/16 Coach House Cloisters, 10 H

and

325 Chestnut Street, Philadelphia, PA 19106, USA

Copyright © 2000, by Research Studies Press Ltd.

Marketing:

UK, EUROPE & REST OF THE WORLD
Research Studies Press Ltd.
15/16 Coach House Cloisters, 10 Hitchin Street, Baldock, Hertfordshire, England, SG7 6AE

Distribution:

NORTH AMERICA
Taylor & Francis Inc.
47 Runway Road, Suite G, Levittown, PA 19057 - 4700, USA

ASIA-PACIFIC
Hemisphere Publication Services
Golden Wheel Building, 41 Kallang Pudding Road #04-03, Singapore

UK, EUROPE & REST OF THE WORLD
John Wiley & Sons Ltd.
Shripney Road, Bognor Regis, West Sussex, England, PO22 9SA

Library of Congress Cataloging-in-Publication Data

Coding, communications, and broadcasting / edited by Paddy Farrell, Bahram Honary, and Michael Darnell.
    p. cm. -- (Electronic & electrical engineering research studies. Communications systems, techniques, and applications series ; 3)
  Includes bibliographical references and index.
  ISBN 0-86380-259-1 (alk. paper)
  1. Digital communications. 2. Coding theory. 3. Digital audio broadcasting. I. Farrell, Paddy. II. Honary, Bahram. III. Darnell, Michael. IV. Series.

  TK5103.7. C63 2000
  621.382--dc21

00-020868

British Library Cataloguing in Publication Data

A catalogue record for this book is available from the British Library.

ISBN 0 86380 259 1

Printed in Great Britain by SRP Ltd., Exeter

Editorial Preface

It is with great pleasure that I introduce the third volume in the Series published by Research Studies Press on Communications Systems, Techniques and Applications. The aim of the series is to publish timely and authoritative texts featuring subjects in Communications and related areas where theory and practice have interacted beneficially. The third volume is an excellent example of this. Most chapters in the three sections of the book, on Coding and Decoding, Communications Techniques, and Digital Broadcasting in the LF, MF and HF bands, are concerned with topics which have recently advanced precisely because of the beneficial and close synergy between their theoretical and practical aspects.

This third book in the Series is also the fourth in the set of books which have emerged from the International Symposia on Communications Theory and Applications, held regularly at Ambleside in the English Lake District. The Symposium held in July 1999 achieved a particularly relevant, balanced and timely programme, from which key presentations have been expanded and edited into this volume, for the benefit of all those unlucky people who were not able to attend the event! The Editors are to be congratulated on putting together excellent, coherent material which will inform and stimulate the research and development community. On behalf of Research Studies Press, I am delighted that it has been possible to include this outstanding volume in the Series.

P.G. Farrell

Lancaster,
February, 2000

Contents

Introduction

This book consists of chapters on recent research topics in three important and related areas of digital communication theory and practice: coding for error control, communication systems and techniques, and digital broadcasting at frequencies below 30MHz. All the chapters are updated, expanded and edited versions of selected presentations made by outstanding and well known international researchers from academia and industry at the 6th biennial International Symposium on Communication Theory and Applications, held in July 1999 at the Charlotte Mason College in Ambleside, Cumbria, UK.

The three Sections of the book conform to the three areas of digital communications listed above. The first Section, on Coding, is the largest, reflecting the fact that the Symposium has succeeded in achieving an enviable reputation for the quality, timeliness and relevance of its presentations in this area. Chapters in this Section contain the latest theoretical and practical results on turbo and low density parity check codes (including a particularly interesting chapter on Gallager codes), on iterative and low complexity decoding algorithms, on optimal source coding and uniquely decodable codes, on public key cryptography, and on several additional topics.

The second Section, on Communications, is also quite large, reflecting the way in which the Symposium has been able to attract an increasing number of excellent presentations in the area of systems and techniques for digital communications. Highlights of this Section include chapters on frequency domain and biosemiotic equalisation, on robust image transmission, on the synchronisation of coded modulation schemes, on complementary and chirp sequence design, and on signal processing for communications. In particular, the two related chapters on the complex finite field Hartley transform and on orthogonal multilevel spreading sequence design are of considerable interest.

For the first time, the 1999 Symposium included a half-day special session on a current "hot topic". The chosen topic was on digital broadcasting below 30MHz, currently of great interest because of the opportunities opening up to convert broadcasting in the LF, MF and HF frequency bands to digital operation. Almost all the presentations given in the special session have been developed for inclusion in the third Section of this book, together with an additional chapter on channel coding for digital video broadcasting. The review chapters by Jurgen Lindner (who ably organised the special session) and Jonathan Stott set the scene, which is then supported by chapters on signal processing, modulation, coding and robust hierarchical techniques for broadcasting. Of particular value is the chapter on MPEG audio standards and developments.

The Symposium was made possible by the generous support of the IEE, the IEEE and HW Communications Ltd, for which the organising committee is most grateful. The editors are most grateful to all the authors for their enthusiasm, dedication and hard work in revising and submitting their chapters, and also to everyone else who has contributed to the creation of this book. It is a real pleasure to see this volume emerge as a result.

Paddy Farrell
Mike Darnell
Bahram Honary

Lancaster, February 2000

SECTION 1

CODING

An Efficient Method for Servo-ID Synchronization with Error-Correcting Properties

Mario Blaum, Bill Kabelac and Steven Hetzler

IBM Research Division

Almaden Research Center

650 Harry Road

San Jose, CA 95120, USA

Abstract

The servo sector of a disk has a field dedicated to servo identification (SID). The purpose of this field is to provide synchronization and also a limited amount of information, like determining if the field corresponds to an index field or a data field, if it corresponds to an even or odd sector, and others. We present a method that allows for efficient SID in the presence of a limited number of errors.

1 Introduction

In a magnetic recording disk, there are two types of sectors: data sectors and servo sectors. Techniques to protect data against errors are well known. That is not the case with servo sectors, that have control and addressing functions allowing for correct reading and writing of the data. This error-protection is important since typically servo sectors represent around 8% of the disk surface. As data densities increase with increased frequencies, servo sectors must match these increases in densities, therefore they become more prone to errors. In this paper, we give a general description of the method. Implementation details can be found in [1].

The servo sector in a magnetic recording disk consists of the following fields:

1. An Automatic Gain Control (AGC) field, that can be represented as a string of ones;

2. A Servo Identification (SID) field, that consists of a pattern of zeros and ones, combining synchronization properties, error-correcting (ECC) properties, and a certain amount of information, like index, non-index, odd or even sector, etc. After the SID has been read, we need to have perfect synchronization with the next field;

3. A Track Identification (TID) sector, generally Gray encoded, containing bits identifying the track where the head is on, together with a certain amount of redundant bits for error correction and detection;

4. A Position Error Signal (PES) field, consisting of four different bursts (that can be represented as strings of ones) whose function is setting the head on track through an integration process of analog information.

In this paper, we concentrate on the SID field. In particular, we consider the issue of adding reliability to the SID. The basic concept is the use of SID patterns having a specified minimum Hamming distance against the patterns encountered during a SID search. This process can be viewed as follows: as stated above, the AGC sequence is assumed to be ...11111.... This AGC sequence (or preamble) is used to set the head read amplifier gain and servo bit clock phase and frequency. The AGC sequence is concatenated to the SID sequence, which has length, say, n. This SID sequence is slided over the concatenation of the received AGC and SID sequences until a match is found, in which case, synchronization has been achieved. If the distances obtained during this process are above a certain threshold d, there is a robustness that allows for a certain correction and/or detection of errors.

In the description that follows, we denote vectors or sequences by underlined letters, like $\underline{u}$, and scalars (numbers) by regular letters, like n.

A typical embodiment proposes one such $n = 9$ bit SID pattern with minimum distance $d = 5$ (i.e., it corrects up to two errors). A similar embodiment was proposed in [4] for servo. For synchronization in data using partial response, see [2]. We will extend this concept to multiple SID patterns. There may be multiple SID patterns of a given length n giving a minimum distance d against the search. Among these multiple SID patterns, there are some that are also at distance d from each other. This means that it is possible to distinguish each of the patterns from both the search *and* each other, to the same degree of robustness. Formally:

Definition 1.1 Consider an AGC sequence $\underline{t}$, like $\underline{t} = \ldots 11111 \ldots$. We say that $\mathcal{C}$ is a code of *size m*, *length n* and *sliding distance d* if

$$\mathcal{C} = \{\underline{u}_1, \underline{u}_2, \ldots, \underline{u}_m\},$$

where each $\underline{u}_i$ is a vector of length n, and the (Hamming) distance between $\underline{u}_i$ and any vector obtained by sliding a window of length n over $(\underline{t}, \underline{u}_j)$ $((\underline{t}, \underline{u}_j)$ denotes the concatenation of $\underline{t}$

with $\underline{u}_j$) is at least d, except in the case in which the slided vector is $\underline{u}_i$ itself, in which the distance is 0. We say that $\mathcal{C}$ is an (n, m, d) code.

As in the theory of error-correcting codes, the sliding distance d determines the tolerance to errors of the scheme.

Example 1.1 Let

$$\mathcal{C} = \{0000010\,,\ 0010111\}.$$

$\mathcal{C}$ is a (7,2,3) code. In effect, it is clear that the two codewords are at distance 3 from each other. If we slide 0000010 over $\ldots 111110010111$, the set of distances we obtain is described in the following table:

Distance	... 1	1	1	1	1	1	1	1	0	0	1	0	1	1	1 ...
6	0	0	0	0	0	1	0								
6		0	0	0	0	0	1	0							
5			0	0	0	0	0	1	0						
6				0	0	0	0	0	1	0					
6					0	0	0	0	0	1	0				
3						0	0	0	0	0	1	0			
5							0	0	0	0	0	1	0		
3								0	0	0	0	0	1	0	
3									0	0	0	0	0	1	0

Similar results are obtained when sliding 0010111 over $\ldots 111110000010$, 0010111 over $\ldots 111110010111$, and 0000010 over $\ldots 111110000010$.

A code of size 2 as in Example 1.1 may not be enough. The price for larger size is a larger value of n.

Here are some suggested uses of multiple codewords for the SID. Consider a code of size m. Then, for different values of m, we have:

m=1 Generic servo SID (only choice). Therefore, in this case, the SID has synchronizing properties only, which is the traditional use of the SID.

m=2 Index, non-index (now index is robust to d also! Very powerful) The index denotes the first sector in a track, all the other sectors are non-index sectors, therefore, it is essential to determine the index reliably.

m=3 Index, even or odd data sectors.

n	m	d	n	m	d	n	m	d	n	m	d
4	1	2	6	1	3	7	1	4	9	1	5
5	4	2	7	4	3	8	2	4	11	3	5
6	7	2	8	5	3	9	3	4	12	5	5

Table 1: Parameters of optimal (n, m, d) codes

m=5 Index, and 4 servo mod 4 values, e.g., encode 2 least significative sector numbers in SID.

Of course, there are other possibilities.

2 Main results and decoding algorithm

It can be readily verified that the following is an (8,5,3) code.

$$\mathcal{C} = \{00000010,\ 00010111,\ 00011001,\ 00101000,\ 01001111\}$$

Table 1 gives the optimal (n, m, d) codes for a variety of parameters. Essentially, for each choice of the length n and the sliding distance d, we found a code with a maximal number of codewords m, i.e., the table states that there is an (n, m, d) code but not an $(n, m + 1, d)$ code.

Next we give a decoding algorithm that allows for correct identification of the stored SID symbol when an (n, m, d) code $\mathcal{C}$ is used. There is a tradeoff between error-correction and detection. Assume that we want to tolerate up to s errors and detect a situation in which more than s errors have occurred but no more than $s + t$, where $2s + t \leq d - 1$. Let $\underline{u}_1, \underline{u}_2, \ldots, \underline{u}_m$ be the codewords in $\mathcal{C}$, and $\underline{t}$ the AGC sequence (for instance, $\underline{t} = \ldots 1111 \ldots$ or $\underline{t} = \ldots 1010 \ldots$). Assume that $\underline{r}$ is a received (and possibly noisy) version of the stored sequence $(\underline{t}, \underline{u}_i)$. The decoder keeps shifting a window of length n over $\underline{r}$. For each shift, it makes one of three possible decisions. Explicitly:

Algorithm 2.1 (Decoding Algorithm) Let $\underline{v}$ be a vector obtained by sliding a window of length n over $\underline{r}$, and let l_j be the distances between each $\underline{u}_j$ and $\underline{v}$, $1 \leq j \leq m$. Then, we have three possible decisions:

1. If $l_j \leq s$ for some j, then output $\underline{u}_j$ and stop.

2. If $s + 1 \leq l_j \leq s + t$ for some j, then declare an uncorrectable error and stop.

6

3. If $s+t+1 \leq l_j$ for each j, $1 \leq j \leq m$, then go to the next shift and repeat the process.

The second step in the algorithm above is omitted when $2s = d-1$, that is, the algorithm is used for correction only. The procedure can correctly determine the stored SID vector even in the presence of s errors. Moreover, if more than s errors occur, but no more than $s + t$, these errors will be detected and wrong identification cannot occur.

Example 2.1 Consider the (10,5,4) code

$$
\begin{aligned}
\mathcal{C} &= \{\underline{u}_1, \underline{u}_2, \underline{u}_3, \underline{u}_4, \underline{u}_5\} \\
&= \{0000001001, 0001000111, 0001101100, 0010110101, 0010111010\}
\end{aligned}
$$

Here we have, $s = 1$ and $t = 1$, therefore $\mathcal{C}$ can correct one error and detect two. Assume that we receive $\underline{r} = \ldots 11110101101100$. Decoding Algorithm 2.1 slides a window over $\underline{r}$ and measures the distance to each codeword. It keeps shifting while these distances are at least 3, and it stops when some distance is at most 2. Identification occurs when the distance to a codeword is at most 1, error detection when the distance to a codeword is exactly 2. As we can see, in the last step we find that codeword $\underline{u}_3 = 0001101100$ is at distance 1 from the vector $\underline{v} = 0101101100$ obtained by sliding the window. The algorithm stops here: it concludes that $\underline{u}_3$ was the stored SID pattern (one error has been tolerated) and at the same time, synchronization has been achieved.

3 Conclusions

We have presented a method for correct synchronization in the servo field of a magnetic recording disk. The method allows, in addition to synchronization, the storing of a certain amount of information and it is tolerant to a limited number of random errors. Let us point out also that the method can be extended to other types of errors, like burst errors. In that case, the code an be optimized by using the burst distance introduced in [3], as opposed to the Hamming distance.

References

[1] M. Blaum, S. Hetzler and W. Kabelac, "Disk Drive Using Multiple Servo Timing Marks that Form a Code of Unique Interrelated Bit Patterns," US Patent 5,903,410, May 1999.

[2] J. Hong and R. Wood, "Method and Apparatus for Determining Byte Synchronization within a Serial Data Receiver," US Patent 5,448,571, September 1995.

[3] S. Wainberg and J. K. Wolf, "Burst Decoding of Binary Block Codes on Q-ary Output Channels," IEEE Transactions on Information Theory, pp. 684-686, September 1972.

[4] R. S. Wilson, "Fault Tolerant Index Patterns and Decoding Means," US Patent 4,933,786, June 1990.

Correction of Single-Byte Errors by the (16,8) Nordstrom-Robinson Code *

I. Boyarinov[1], G.Markarian[2] and B. Honary[2]

[1] Institute for High-Performance
Computer Systems
Russian Academy of Sciences
Nahimov ave. 36/1,
117872, Moscow, Russia

[2] Communications Research Centre
Lancaster University
Lancaster LA1 4YR
United Kingdom
E-mail: b.honary@lancaster.ac.uk
g.markarian@lancaster.ac.uk

Abstract – A simple decoding algorithm for nonlinear (16,8) Nordstrom-Robinson code suitable for implementation in combinational circuits is described. It is proved that the Nordstrom-Robinson code can correct simultaneously single and double random errors as well as 4-bit byte errors. The proposed decoding algorithm is modified to allow the correcting of such 4-bit byte errors.

Index Terms – **Nordstrom-Robinson code, Preparata code, Nonlinear code, Coding and decoding, Burst-correcting coding**

1   Introduction

Several decoding algorithms for nonlinear (16,8) Nordstrom-Robinson (NR) code have been proposed [1]–[5]. However, these algorithms are not suitable for applications in computer semiconductor memories as they are relatively complex for implementation in combinational circuits. It is known that the decoding algorithms of Preparata codes can be used for decoding of the NR code [6]–[8]. Although these algorithms are simple to implement, they do not use the full error correcting power of the NR code. In this paper we consider a modification of the decoding algorithm [7] such that correction of 4-bit byte errors becomes feasible.

2   The Decoding Algorithm for Random Errors

We will consider the Nordstrom-Robinson code as a Preparata code of length 16 and use the simple description of Preparata codes given in [9]. Let $\alpha_i, \beta_j, i, j = 0, 1, ..., 7$ be the

---

*The work was partially supported by the Royal Society, UK

elements of $GF(2^3)$, $\alpha_0 = \beta_0 = 0$, $\alpha_{i_l} \neq \alpha_{i_k}$ and $\beta_{j_p} \neq \beta_{j_q}$ if $l \neq k$ and $p \neq q$. For a binary word $v = (a_0, a_1, \ldots, a_7, b_0, b_1, \ldots, b_7)$ we define

$$F(v) = (F_0(v), F_0^*(v), F_1(v), F_3(v)) \tag{1}$$

where

$$F_0(v) = \sum_{i=0}^{7} a_i, \quad F_0^*(v) = \sum_{j=0}^{7} b_j, \quad F_1(v) = \sum_{i=0}^{7} a_i \alpha_i + \sum_{j=0}^{7} b_j \beta_j, \tag{2}$$

$$F_3(v) = \sum_{i=0}^{7} a_i \alpha_i^3 + (\sum_{i=0}^{7} a_i \alpha_i)^3 + \sum_{j=0}^{7} b_j \beta_j^3. \tag{3}$$

The Nordstrom-Robinson code consists of the code words v for which $F(v) = 0$. We consider a modification of the decoding algorithm for Preparata codes [7]. Let $v = (a_0, a_1, \ldots, a_7, b_0, b_1, \ldots, b_7)$ be a code word of the Nordstrom-Robinson code V, $e = (\xi_0, \xi_1, \ldots, \xi_7, \zeta_0, \zeta_1, \ldots, \zeta_7)$ be an error-word and $v' = (a_0', a_1', \ldots, a_7', b_0', b_1', \ldots, b_7')$ where $a_i' = a_i + \xi_i$, $b_j' = b_j + \zeta$, $i, j = 0, 1, ..., 7$. If $e = 0$, then $F(v') = 0$. For convenience $F(v')$ is called the syndrome of v'. As V is a nonlinear code, $F(v')$ may or may be not equal to $F(e)$. Nevertheless knowing $F(v')$ we can determine e if the weight $wt(e) \leq 2$. In addition to $F_3(v')$ we will calculate $F_3^*(v') = \sum_{i=0}^{7} a_i' \alpha_i^3 + \sum_{j=0}^{7} b_j' \beta_j^3 + (\sum_{j=0}^{7} b_j' \beta_j)^3$, $S_1(a') = \sum_{i=0}^{7} a_i' \alpha_i$, $S_1(b') = \sum_{j=0}^{7} b_j' \beta_j$. Furthermore, for convenience we will write F, F_0, F_0^*, F_1, F_3, F_3^*, S_1, S_1^* instead of $F(v')$, $F_0(v')$, $F_0^*(v')$, $F_1(v')$, $F_3(v')$, $F_3^*(v')$, $S_1(a')$, $S_1(b')$, respectively.

The decoding algorithm for random errors is described as follows.

1. For the received word $v' = (a_0', a_1', \ldots, a_7', b_0', b_1', \ldots, b_7')$, calculate the syndrome $F(v') = (F_0, F_0^*, F_1, F_3)$.

2. If $F(v') = 0$, there are no errors in v'.

3. If $F_1 = F_3 = 0$, then the errors are $\xi_0 = F_0$ and $\zeta_0 = F_0^*$.

4. Calculate $\delta = F_0 F_0^*$ and F_3^*.

5. If $\delta = 0$, then locators α_i and α_j of errors ξ_i and ξ_j are $\alpha_i = F_1^2 (F_3^*)^2$, $\alpha_j = F_1^2 (F_3^*)^2 + F_1$, if the trace $Tr(F_1^4 F_3^* + 1) = 0$, and locators β_i and β_j of errors ζ_i and ζ_j are $\beta_i = F_1^2 F_3^2$, $\beta_j = F_1^2 F_3^2 + F_1$, if $Tr(F_1^4 F_3 + 1) = 0$.

6. If $\delta = 1$, then locators α_i and β_j of errors ξ_i and ζ_j are respectively $\alpha_i = S_1^* + (F_3 + F_1^3 + (S_1^*)^3)^5$ and $\beta_j = S_1 + (F_3 + F_1^3 + (S_1^*)^3)^5$.

7. In all other cases the errors in the word v' are detected but are uncorrectable.

From (1)–(3) it follows immediately that the decoding algorithm for random errors is correct. The algorithm is suitable for combinational curcuits as follows. We will represent elements of $GF(2^3)$ in the basis $\alpha^2, \alpha, 1$ where α is a zero of the polynomial $x^3 + x + 1$ over $GF(2)$. Then every component of locators $\alpha_i, \alpha_j, \beta_i, \beta_j$ is represented as function of components of the syndrome $F(v') = (F_0, F_0^*, F_1, F_3)$ and F_3^*. It can be easily implemented as a combinational circuit, containing XOR and AND gates.

10

4-bit solid byte error	$F_3(v^{(i)})$
$e^{(1)}$	$S_1^2 + S_1 + 1$
$e^{(2)}$	α^4
$e^{(3)}$	$S_1^2 + S_1 + \alpha^3$
$e^{(4)}$	α^2

Table 1: The syndromes $F_3(v^{(i)})$ of the words $v^{(i)} = v^{(*)} + e^{(i)}, v^* \in V^*$ and $e^{(i)}$ is a 4-bit solid byte error.

3   Correction of Single-byte Errors

In some applications it is required that the memory array chips be packaged in a b-bit-per-chip organization. A chip failure or a word-line failure in this case would result in byte oriented errors that contain from 1 to b erroneous bits. Byte errors can also be caused by the failures of the supporting modules at the memory card level. We will show that the (16,8) NR code can be reconfigured to correct 4-bit byte errors. The reconfiguration involves the transposition of the bit positions of the original code.

Let $v = (a_0, a_1, \ldots, a_7, b_0, b_1, \ldots, b_7)$ be a code word of the Nordstrom-Robinson code V. Locators of symbols a_i, b_j of the word v are $\alpha_0 = \beta_0 = 0$, $\alpha_i = \alpha^{7-i}$ and $\beta_j = \alpha^{7-j}$ for $i, j = 1, \ldots, 7$. Transpose the bit positions of the word v as follows:

$$v^* = (a_0, b_0, a_7, b_7, \quad a_1, a_2, a_3, a_5, \quad a_4, a_6, b_2, b_3, \quad b_1, b_4, b_5, b_6). \tag{4}$$

If the same transpositions are produced in all codewords of V we receive the code V^* equivalent to code V.

Lemma 1 *The code V^* corrects single, double and 4-bit solid byte errors and detects triple errors.*

As the code V^* is equivalent to the code V it is sufficient to show that the code V^* corrects all 4-bit solid byte errors. Let $e^{(1)} = (\xi_0, \zeta_0, \xi_7, \zeta_7, 0, 0, 0, 0, 0, 0, 0, 0, 0, 0, 0, 0)$,
$e^{(2)} = (0, 0, 0, 0, \xi_1, \xi_2, \xi_3, \xi_5, 0, 0, 0, 0, 0, 0, 0, 0)$, $e^{(3)} = (0, 0, 0, 0, 0, 0, 0, 0, \xi_4, \xi_6, \zeta_2, \zeta_3, 0, 0, 0, 0)$, $e^{(4)} = (0, 0, 0, 0, 0, 0, 0, 0, 0, 0, 0, 0, \zeta_1, \zeta_4, \zeta_5, \zeta_6)$. If $\xi_i = \zeta_j = 1$ for $i, j = 0, 1, \ldots, 7$, the error words $e^{(1)}, e^{(2)}, e^{(3)}, e^{(4)}$ are 4-bit solid byte errors. Let $v^{(i)} = v^* + e^{(i)}$ where v^* is a codeword of V^* and $e^{(i)}$ is a 4-bit solid byte error. Calculate $F(v^{(i)})$ for all $i = 1, 2, 3, 4$. Note that $F_0(v^{(i)}) = F_0^*(v^{(i)}) = 0$, and $F_1(v^{(i)}) = 0$ for all $i = 1, 2, 3, 4$ and any $v^* \in V^*$. The results of calculating $F_3(v^{(i)})$ for all $i = 1, 2, 3, 4$ are given in Table 1. As traces $Tr(1) = Tr(\alpha^3) = 1$, the equations $S_1^2 + S_1 + 1 = 0$ and $S_1^2 + S_1 + \alpha^3 = 0$ have no roots in $GF(2^3)$. Therefore $F_3(v^{(i)}) \neq 0$ for all $i = 1, 2, 3, 4$ and $v^* \in V^*$. Let $v^{(i)} = v_i^* + e^{(i)}$ and $v^{(j)} = v_j^* + e^{(j)}$ where v_i^*, v_j^* are codewords of V^* and $e^{(i)}, e^{(j)}$ are 4-bit solid byte errors. Then $F_3(v^{(i)}) \neq F_3(v^{(j)})$ for all $i, j = 1, 2, 3, 4$ as the equations $z^2 + z + \alpha^5 = 0$ and $z^2 + z + \alpha^6 = 0$ have no roots in $GF(2^3)$. On the other hand, for $v' = v^* + e'$, $v^* \in V^*$ and $wt(e') = 1$ or 3 we have $F_0(v') = 1$, $F_0^*(v') = 0$, or $F_0(v') = 0, F_0^*(v') = 1$. For

11

Byte error	Error pattern of the weight 3	F_0	F_0^*	F_1
$e^{(1)}$	$\xi_0\zeta_0\zeta_7$	1	0	1
	$\xi_0\xi_7\zeta_0$	0	1	1
	$\xi_0\xi_7\zeta_7$	0	1	0
	$\xi_7\zeta_0\zeta_7$	1	0	0
$e^{(2)}$	$\xi_1\xi_2\xi_3$	1	0	α^2
	$\xi_1\xi_3\xi_5$	1	0	α^5
	$\xi_1\xi_2\xi_5$	1	0	α^4
	$\xi_2\xi_3\xi_5$	1	0	α^6
$e^{(3)}$	$\xi_4\xi_6\zeta_2$	0	1	α^4
	$\xi_4\zeta_2\zeta_3$	1	0	α
	$\xi_4\xi_6\zeta_3$	0	1	α^5
	$\xi_6\zeta_2\zeta_3$	1	0	α^3
$e^{(4)}$	$\zeta_1\zeta_4\zeta_5$	0	1	α
	$\zeta_1\zeta_4\zeta_6$	0	1	α^2
	$\zeta_1\zeta_5\zeta_6$	0	1	α^3
	$\zeta_4\zeta_5\zeta_6$	0	1	α^6

Table 2: The syndromes of the words $v^{(i)} = v^* + e^{(i)}, v^* \in V^*$ and $e^{(i)}$ is a 4-bit byte error of the weight 3.

$v'' = v^* + e'', v^* \in V^*$ and $wt(e'') = 2$ we have $F_0(v'') = F_0^*(v'') = 0, F_1(v'') \neq 0$ or $F_0(v'') = F_0^*(v'') = 1$. Thus, every word $v^{(i)}$, containing a 4-bit solid byte error, has the nonzero syndrome $F(v^{(i)})$ that differs from the syndromes $F(v')$ and $F(v'')$ of the words v' and v'', containing single or triple and double errors, respectively.

Theorem 1 *The NR code V^* corrects single, double and 4-bit byte errors.*

By Lemma 1 the code V^* corrects single, double and 4-bit solid byte errors and detects triple errors. Therefore for proof of theorem 1 it is sufficient to show, that any two words, containing distinct 4-bit byte errors of the weight 3, have distinct syndromes. As shown in table 2 all 4-bit byte errors of the weight 3 have distinct syndromes.

The decoding algorithm for random errors given earlier may be modified for the correction of single-byte errors. After the step 6 the algorithm would continue as follows:

7. If $F_0 = 1$, $F_0^* = 0$, $F_1^3 \neq F_3^*$ or $F_0 = 0, F_0^* = 1, F_1^3 \neq F_3$, there is a byte error of the weight 3, that is corrected according to Table 2.

8. If $F_0 = F_0^* = 0$, $F_1 = 0$, and F_3 is equal to anyone from Table 1, there is a solid byte error, that is corrected according to this Table.

9. In all other cases the errors in the word v' are detected but are uncorrectable.

12

4   Conclusion

A simple decoding algorithm for (16,8) Nordstrom-Robinson code suitable for implementation in combinational circuits has been described. It has been proved that the Nordstrom-Robinson code can correct simultaneously single and double random errors as well as 4-bit byte errors. The proposed algorithm requires a low complexity implementation and is suitable for application in computer memory systems.

5   Acknowledgment

The authors would like to thank The Royal Society, UK, in their support of Dr. I. Boyarinov during his stay with the Communications Research Centre at Lancaster University.

References

[1] J.P. Robinson, "Analysis of Nordstrom's optimum quadratic code," *in Proc. Hawai Inter. Conf. System Sciences,*, pp. 157-161, 1968.

[2] F.P. Preparata, "An alternate description and a new decoding procedure of Nord-strom - Robinson optimum code," *in Proc. Second Princeton Conf. on Information Sciences and Systems,*, pp. 131-134, 1968.

[3] V.A. Zinov'ev, Y.P. Pyatoshin, and V.A. Tuzikov, "On decoding of nonlinear (16,8) code (in Russian)," *in Proc. VI All-Union workshop on computer networks, Moscow-Vinicha*, ch. 4, pp. 30-33, 1981.

[4] A. Vardy, "The Nordstrom-Robinson Code: Representation over $GF(4)$ and Efficient Decoding," *IEEE Trans. Inform. Theory.*, vol. IT-40, pp. 1686-1693, 1994.

[5] G. Markarian, and B. Honary,"The Nordstrom-Robinson code is a (8,4) GAC over Z_4," *in Proc. Third UK–Australian Symposium on DSP for Communication Systems, Coventry, UK,* pp. 45-46, 1994.

[6] F.P. Preparata, "A class of optimum nonlinear double-error correcting codes," *Inform. Contr.*, vol.13, pp. 378-400, 1968.

[7] I.M. Boyarinov, "Parallel decoding of Preparata codes (in Russian)," *Voprosy Kibernet.*, no. 135, pp. 170-179, 1988.

[8] A.R. Hammons, P.V. Kumar, A.R. Calderbank, N.J.A. Sloane, and P.Sole, "The Z_4 Linearity of Kerdock, Preparata, Goethals and related codes," *IEEE Trans. Inform. Theory,* vol. 40, pp. 301-319, 1994.

[9] R.D. Baker, J.H. van Lint and R.M. Wilson, "On the Preparata and Goethals codes," *IEEE Trans. Inform. Theory,* vol. 29, pp. 342-345, 1983.

Optimization, Neural Networks, and Turbo Decoding

M. Eoin Buckley and Stephen B. Wicker
School of Electrical Engineering, Cornell University
Ithaca, New York 14853

October 28, 1999

Abstract

Neural networks can be trained to predict the presence of errors in turbo decoded data. They can also be trained to predict convergence during decoding. The inputs to the networks are samples of the cross entropy of the component decoder outputs at two or more iterations. An examination of the connection weights of the trained networks indicates that the networks are monitoring the rate of descent of the cross entropy. Such networks can be used to substantially reduce decoding complexity and delay while maintaining a high level of data reliability.

1 Introduction

In this presentation it is shown that neural networks can be trained to predict errors and convergence during turbo decoding. The inputs to the network are samples of the cross-entropy of the component decoder outputs at two or more time instants. Error detecting neural networks can be used as triggers for retransmission requests at either the beginning or at the conclusion of the decoding process. Convergence detecting neural networks can be used to halt the decoding process, providing the same reliability performance as classical turbo decoding at a significantly reduced level of complexity.

An examination of connection weights for the trained convergence detecting network indicates that the network is monitoring the rate of descent of the cross entropy, indicating a possible connection between turbo decoding and greedy search optimization algorithms.

2 Cross Entropy

Cross-entropy (also known as the Kullback-Leibler distance) is a measure of the distance between two probability distributions. Let $q^{l,i}(\hat{u}_k = a|\bar{\mathbf{Y}})$ and $p^{l,i}(\hat{u}_k = a|\bar{\mathbf{Y}})$ be the estimated *a posteriori* probabilities (APP's) generated by two component decoders at the lth iteration of the decoding of the ith frame. Assuming that the information bits in a sequence $\{u_k\}$ are independent $\forall k$, the cross-entropy of the two decoder outputs is computed as follows:

$$D^{l,i} = \sum_{k=1}^{N} \sum_{a\epsilon\{0,1\}} p^{l,i}(\hat{u}_k = a|\bar{\mathbf{Y}}) \log \frac{p^{l,i}(\hat{u}_k = a|\bar{\mathbf{Y}})}{q^{l,i}(\hat{u}_k = a|\bar{\mathbf{Y}})} \tag{1}$$

15

$D^{l,i}$ can be interpreted as the total information passed between the component decoders during iteration l. Hagenauer et al. [2] have suggested that the cross-entropy be used as a means for detecting decoder convergence. In this presentation we show that by using $D^{l,i}$ or $log_{10}D^{l,i}$ for several values of l as a multi-dimensional input for a neural network, a practical method is obtained for predicting the presence of decoder errors and for detecting decoder convergence.

3 Design and Training

We can design a neural network that approximates, to any desired degree of accuracy, a given piecewise continuous function [4]. In the case at hand, we wish to approximate three indicator functions using two-layer networks. The first indicator function accepts as inputs the cross-entropy for the first k iterations of the turbo decoding process (i.e. $\vec{x}_i = (D^{1,i}, D^{2,i}, ..., D^{k,i})$) and indicates the future presence (or absence) of errors when decoding is completed. The associated neural network is referred to here as the "Future Error Detecting Network" (FEDN). The second indicator function accepts as inputs the cross-entropy throughout the entire decoding process and provides an indication of whether or not the decoded data contains errors. The associated network is referred to here as the "Decoder Error Detecting Network" (DEDN). The third indicator function accepts as inputs the log of the cross-entropy and the number of different hard decisions for the first k iterations of the turbo decoding process (i.e. $\vec{x}_i = (\log_{10}(D^{1,i}), \log_{10}(D^{2,i}), ..., \log_{10}(D^{k,i}), C^{1,i}, C^{2,i}, ... , C^{k,i})$) and indicates whether the two distributions have converged. The associated neural network is referred to here as the "Decoder Convergence Detecting Network" (DCDN).

The training set for the error detecting networks was generated by simulating the transmission of a rate-1/3 turbo code with information block length N=1023 over an AWGN channel. E_b/N_0 was randomly chosen between 0 and 0.8 dB for each of 300,000 sample frames. The cross-entropy and the number of errors per decoded block at each of the first 10 iterations was recorded.

The training set for the convergence detecting network was generated by simulating the transmission of a rate-1/2 turbo code with information block length N=4000 over an AWGN channel. E_b/N_0 was randomly chosen between 1 and 1.5 dB for each of 50,000 sample frames. The cross-entropy, the difference between the two component decoder outputs and the difference in hard decision decoder output from the previous iteration was recorded at each of the first 10 iterations.

FEDN, DEDN, and CEDN neural networks were super-imposed onto turbo decoders with two different stopping conditions. In the first case the turbo decoder executed a fixed number d of iterations and halted. These decoders are denoted by an integer suffix that denotes the value selected for d. In the second, denoted by the suffix "CE," a cross-entropy threshold was used as the stopping condition [2]. Let s be the iteration at which the CE threshold ($0.01 \times D^1$) is passed. A five-dimensional input $\vec{x}_i = (D^{1,i}, D^{2,i}, D^{s-1,i}, D^{s,i}, s)$ is provided to DEDN-CE. If s= 2 or 3, then some of the inputs are duplicated. If the CE threshold is never reached, then decoding is halted at the 10th iteration. FEDN-CE was designed to accept $\vec{x} = (D^{1,i}, D^{2,i})$ as an input vector. The vector $\vec{x} = (D^{1,i}, D^{2,i}, D^{s-1,i}, D^{s,i}, s)$ was provided as an input to DEDNpost-CE, a neural network trained to catch any errors that remain after FEDN has accepted the packet.

The performance of the various error detecting neural net-assisted decoders is listed in table 1. A "0" denotes the event in which a decoded frame contains errors, while a "1" denotes error-free decoding. $P(0|1)$ is thus the false alarm while $P(1|0)$ denotes missed detection. K is a design factor that can be viewed as a relative emphasis of test frames with errors during network training. Higher values of K result in lower undetected frame error rates and increased false alarm rate.

These figures show that error weights that escape detection by the neural networks have far lower weight

16

ARQ trigger	K	$P_{Test}(0\|1)$	$P_{Test}(1\|0)$	Avg. errors per missed detection frame
DEDN-10	20	1.1×10^{-2}	3.2×10^{-4}	26.2
FEDN-10	0.03	4.8×10^{-3}	0.39	28.5
DEDNpost-10	5	7.2×10^{-3}	8.0×10^{-3}	
crc-10				110.1
DEDN-CE	20	1.3×10^{-2}	4.8×10^{-4}	8.2
FEDN-CE	0.05	7.7×10^{-3}	0.68	26.2
DEDNpost-CE	20	7.1×10^{-3}	8.6×10^{-3}	
crc-CE				118.1

Table 1: Neural network performances on test sets

than those that escape detection by a CRC code.

The performance of the convergence detecting neural net-assisted decoder is listed in table 2. A "0" denotes the event in which a decoded frame has not yet converged, while a "1" denotes convergence. A high $P(0|1)$ results in increased complexity while a high $P(1|0)$ results in an increased BER.K is a design factor that can be viewed as a relative emphasis of convergent test frames during network training. Higher values of K result in a lower increase in BER but greater complexity.

The underlying characteristics by which the DCDN determines convergence are clear from table 2. Defining $w_{i,j:k}$ as the weight from node k in level $i-1$ to node j in level i, and $b_{i,j}$ is the bias term in node j level i. Weights $w_{1,1:1}$ and $w_{1,1:2}$ or $\log_{10}(D^{s-1})$ and $\log_{10}(D^s)$ indicates that the rate of descent of the cross-entropy is a strong indication of eventual convergence. By assuming zero mean, unit variance normalization for all input dimensions, the corresponding weights for an equivalent DCDN, $DCDN_{Norm}$ can be obtained and are shown in table 2. Since DCDN is effectively a linear network, this clearly demonstrates the dominance of the rate of descent as a reliability measure.

4 Conclusions

The apparent use by the neural network of the rate of descent of the cross entropy as a reliability measure allows for the interpretation of turbo decoding in terms of a local search. The search space is defined in terms of the distance between the information probability measures initially generated by the component decoders. There are problems with this interpretation - the existence of cross-entropy cycles during nonconvergent decoding operations indicates that, if the local search interpretation is appropriate, the search itself is far more complicated than a greedy search algorithm. The local search perspective does, however, lead to useful results. Additional experiments at the Wireless Multimedia Laboratory at Cornell have shown that a well-timed randomization of the information exchanged by the component decoders, can force rapid convergence during turbo decoding. This "heating" of the exchanged information is used in simulated annealing to prevent the termination of a search in local (suboptimal) minima. It is expected that other local search tools can be used to improve the performance of turbo decoding algorithms.

Performance							
Network	K	$P_{Test}(0\|1)$	$P_{Test}(1\|0)$				
DCDN	100	0.43	7.6×10^{-4}				
Hag(-2.5)		0.61	1.7×10^{-2}				
Weights							
Network	$w_{1,1:1}$	$w_{1,1:2}$	$w_{1,1:3}$	$w_{1,1:4}$	$b_{1:1}$	$w_{2:1,1}$	$b_{2:1}$
DCDN	-2.34	2.59	3.2	-0.31	3.52	-0.99	1.0
$DCDN_{Norm}$	-2.13	3.57	133.7	-0.41	67.7	-0.99	1.0

Table 2: Neural network performance and weights

References

[1] C. Heegard and S.B. Wicker, *Turbo Coding*, Boston: Kluwer, 1999.

[2] J. Hagenauer, E. Offer, L. Papke, "Iterative Decoding of Binary Block and Convolutional Codes," *IEEE Transactions on Information Theory*, vol 42, No 2, March 1996.

[3] M.E. Buckley and S.B. Wicker, "The Design and Performance of a Neural Network for Predicting Decoder Error in Turbo-Coded ARQ Protocols," submitted to the *IEEE Transactions on Communications*.

[4] T. Fine, "Feedforward Neural Networks," *Wiley Encyclopedia of Electrical and Electronics Engineering*, 1997.

Two Stage Decoding of the Nordstrom Robinson Code Based on the Twisted Squaring Construction.

J. Castiñeira Moreira
I. Martin.
B. Honary

Department of Communications Systems,
Lancaster University,
Lancaster,
UK.

Abstract: A two stage decoding scheme for use with the Nordstrom Robinson code is proposed which partitions the code into a number of subsets.The subset containing the codeword can be found using a simple Reed Muller decoder. Soft decision decoding can be performed at both stages of the decoding using a trellis. The result is a sub-optimum decoder with near maximum likelihood performance but complexity of about one third that of a full decoding. The performance of the decoder is also compared to that of the 15,7,5 BCH code and is found to be comparable but with approximately half the complexity.

1. Introduction.

Decoders, particularly decoders with soft maximum likelihood performance, can be complex devices. There are often a large number of calculations required in order to extract a small amount of information. As codes become more powerful and bit rates increase the demand placed on decoders becomes very high resulting in expensive hardware and complex software. One method of alleviating the implementation problem is to use a powerful code but perform a sub-optimum decoding. By trading correcting ability for a decoder complexity reduction it is possible to significantly reduce decoding complexity whilst maintaining near optimum performance.

19

Non-linear codes have the potential to be more powerful than an equivalent linear code. As they are free from the strict structure governing linear codes it is possible to design a linear code which has more codewords or a greater distance than an equivalent linear code[6]. For example the Nordstrom Robinson[1][6] code has length 16 and 256 codewords with minimum distance 6. The closest BCH code has 128 codewords, length 15 but only has a minimum distance of 5. Traditionally, non-linear codes have been used only infrequently due to their lack of a strong mathematical structure. The Nordstrom Robinson code, however, contains enough structure to allow us to construct a regular trellis and to perform Viterbi decoding as we can for any other block code. The regular trellis of the Nordstrom Robinson code is of a form suitable for a type of low-complexity decoding known as two stage decoding. By performing a low complexity decoding on a Nordstrom Robinson code it is possible to achieve better performance than by performing full soft maximum likelihood decoding of an equivalent BCH code.

Viterbi decoding is widely used for the soft decision decoding of convolutional codes due to its maximum likelihood performance and low complexity. However, for block codes of any useful length the complexity of the algorithm is such that its use is not practical. A solution to this problem is to use a low complexity, sub-optimum variant of the Viterbi algorithm where not every path is searched. Paths which are unlikely to contain the correct codeword are discarded early. Although the performance is reduced to slightly below the level of soft maximum likelihood decoding the complexity is reduced by a large amount. If the complexity can be reduced to a level comparable to a hard decision decoder an improvement in performance is possible by switching to a sub-optimum soft decision decoder.

If a regular trellis[2] (with a similar structure to Figure 1) can be constructed for the code then a good method for achieving this is to use two stage decoding [3][4].

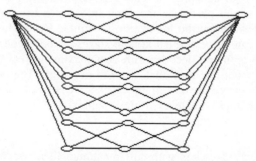

Figure 1 Regular Trellis

The aim of the first stage is to determine which sub-trellis or sub-trellises are most likely to contain the correct codeword. The second stage is to decode the selected sub-trellises using a standard Viterbi [7] algorithm. The performance of two stage decoding depends on the accuracy of stage one. If the correct sub-trellis is discarded then stage two can never return a correct result. It is possible to trade performance against complexity by changing the number of sub-trellises decoded in stage two. This paper concentrates on a technique for selecting sub-trellises of the Nordstrom Robinson code.

2. Squaring Construction.

The squaring construction, introduced by Forney in 1988 [5], is a method for constructing a code from a smaller code. Long codes can be built up in an iterative fashion by repeating the squaring construction.

Let S be a set of codewords of a linear code, then the partition S/N divides the set into the subset N and a number of cosets of N. The partition S/N itself is the set of coset representatives of N in S. Each coset is identified by a label which is the coset representative from S/N of that coset. The order of the partition $|S/N|$ is the number of cosets or the number of members of S/N.

Consider the partition of the Reed Muller code $R(1,2)/R(0,2)$. $R(1,2)$ is the first order Reed Muller code of length 4 and dimension 3 (a single party check code) and $R(0,2)$ is a 4,1 repetition code. The 8 codewords of the $R(1,2)$ code are partitioned into 4 cosets with 2 members each.

Figure 2 shows a trellis section which demonstrates this partition, the paths are grouped in to 4 cosets of two codewords each.

Figure 2 Partition of $R(1,2)$ Reed Muller Code

The Cartesian product of two sets R and S, $R*S$ is defined as the set of elements (r, s) where $r \in R, s \in S$. The order of $R*S$, $|R*S|$ is given by $|R||S|$. We can also define the Cartesian square as

$$S^2 = (s_1, s_2)$$
$$s_1, s_2 \in S$$

(1)

The squaring construction of the partition S/T, $|S/T|^2$ is formed by taking the Cartesian square of the set of coset representatives and concatenating the members within the coset in all combinations.

Returning to our example of the $R(1,2)/R(0,2)$ partition. We form the Cartesian square of the set of coset representatives $R(1,2)/R(0,2)$ resulting in four vectors of length eight. This partition can be represented by the trellis shown in Figure 3.

21

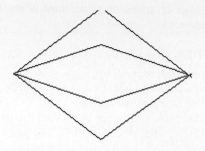

Figure 3 Trellis of $R(1,2)/R(0,2)$

We also concatenate members of $R(0,2)$ in all combinations such that there are $|R(0,2)|^2$ codewords in each coset. Figure 4 shows the trellis representation of this concatenation.

Figure 4 Trellis of $R(0,2)^2$

Figure 5 shows the trellis diagram for the whole code which is the $R(1,3)$ Reed Muller code. Note the that the trellis is built up of 4 sub-trellises corresponding to the 4 cosets. The trellis is the Shannon product [8] of the $R(1,2)/R(0,2)$ trellis and the $R(0,2)^2$ trellis.

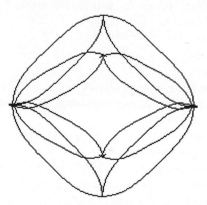

Figure 5 $R(1,3)$ Code Trellis Generated Using the Squaring Construction.

22

In this trellis, the cosets in the first half connect to the corresponding coset in the second half. The codeword U is given by (2)

$$U = |S/T|_a + T_b \cdot |S/T|_a + T_c \qquad (2)$$

where a, b and c are labels representing the codeword, · indicates concatenation and addition is binary exclusive or.

An alternative construction is possible where cosets connect to some other coset in S/T given by a function $f(x)$.

$$U = |S/T|_a + T_b \cdot |S/T|_{f(a)} + T_c \qquad (3)$$

This is known as a twisted squaring construction as the connections in the square are given a *twist* which is defined by $f(x)$. $f(x)$ is known as the twisting function. In some cases it is possible to obtain a better minimum distance using a twisted squaring construction although the result may not necessarily be linear.

3. Nordstrom Robinson Code Construction.

The Nordstrom-Robinson (NR) [1] code consists of the union of the codewords of the $R(1, 4)$ Reed Muller code and seven translates of the code which are in $R(2,4)$ [6].

The $R(1, 4)$ code may be formed by the squaring construction $|(1,3)/(0,3)|^2$ which generates codewords of the form(4).

$$\mathbf{c} = (a_1 G_{(0,3)} + \mathbf{a} G_{(1,3)/(0,3)}), (a_2 G_{(0,3)} + \mathbf{a} G_{(1,3)/(0,3)}) \qquad (4)$$

where $G_{(1,3)/(0,3)}$ is the generator matrix of the $R(1,3)$ codeword with the row corresponding to the all ones codeword deleted and $G_{(0,3)}$ is a generator matrix consisting only of the all ones codeword so as to generate an $(8,1)$ repetition code. $\mathbf{a}$ is a vector of 2 binary values, a_1 and a_2 are single bit values. a_1, a_2 and $\mathbf{a}$ represent the 4 information bits of the code.

The 8 coset representatives have the form:

$$\mathbf{r} = (\mathbf{a}^* G_{(2,3)/(1,3)}), (\mathbf{a}^* G_{(2,3)/(1,3)} + f(\mathbf{a}^*) G_{(1,3)/(0,3)}) \qquad (5)$$

where $\mathbf{a}^*$ is a vector containing the 3 information bits specifying the coset to be used.

Note that the second half of this vector contains the function $f(\mathbf{a}^*)$, therefore this is a twisted squaring construction.

It is the aim of our low complexity decoding technique to obtain an estimate of some of the information symbols before carrying out the full decoding so that we

23

may reduce the number of trellis paths that we must evaluate. Equation (5) shows how we may obtain such an estimate. Note that the second half of the codeword is equal to the first half plus a Reed Muller codeword encoded from a function of three information symbols. Since the function $f(\mathbf{a}^*)$ is a one to one map we may estimate the value of $\mathbf{a}^*$ by decoding the RM code and decode only the relevant trellis paths of the full NR code trellis.

4. Decoding.

In order to deduce the Reed Muller codeword which will provide us with the estimate of $\mathbf{a}^*$ we must take the binary sum of the first and second halves of the codeword. As the codeword is subject to error, our estimate will also be subject to error. The probability of bit error in the RM codeword is $2p(1-p)$ where p is the bit error probability in the original codeword. We can see from this expression that the probability of bit error in the RM codeword word is almost double that of the received codeword.The performance of the RM code is therefore degraded but we attempt to recover as much information as possible by performing a soft maximum likelihood decoding and obtaining a list of the most likely outcomes.

In order to combine soft symbol values (log likelihood ratios) we adopt a max-sum [9] approach. There are two outcomes of a binary addition (0 and 1) and there are two possible inputs for each (00 and 11 for an output of 0 and 01 and 10 for an output of 1). The output with the most likely input is selected (the one with the maximum sum of inputs) and the confidence of the output is assigned to be equal to the smallest of the input confidences.

In addition to $\mathbf{a}^*$ it is also possible to determine $a_1 + a_2$. If a_1 and a_2 are different then the result of the addition will be the inverse of the expected RM codeword. We are recovering the full 4 information bits from the (8,4,4) code which allows us to partition the trellis into 16 sets each containing 2 sub-trellises.

Once the likely values of $\mathbf{a}^*$ and $a_1 + a_2$ are determined it can be used to select the sub-trellises used in stage two of the decoding.

5. Complexity.

The complexity of a trellis is defined by both the number of vertexes and number of edges in the diagram. We shall compare the complexity of the NR decoder using various numbers of partitions with that of the (15,7,5) BCH code. The (15,7,5) BCH code is used as it is a linear code with good performance and a similar set of parameters to the NR code.

Each partition of the NR code contains 24 edges and 14 vertexes and the trellis of the (8,4,4) RM code used to select the sub trellis also contains 24 edges and 14 vertexes. Therefore, decoding a single partition consists of decoding the equivalent of 48 edges and 28 vertexes. The complexity of the RM stage increases when more partitions are decoded since the best two or more partitions must be identified. This increase in complexity is approximated by increasing the edges and vertexes of the trellis by 50% if two partitions are required and by 100% if three or more partitions are required. The BCH trellis is assumed to have 292 edges and 214 vertexes [10].

Figure 6 shows the number of edges and vertex equivalents required to decode 1, 2, 3 and 4 partitions of the NR trellis, the full trellis and the BCH code. The complexity of the four partition decoding is a little over a third of that of the full decoding and approximately half the complexity of the BCH trellis.

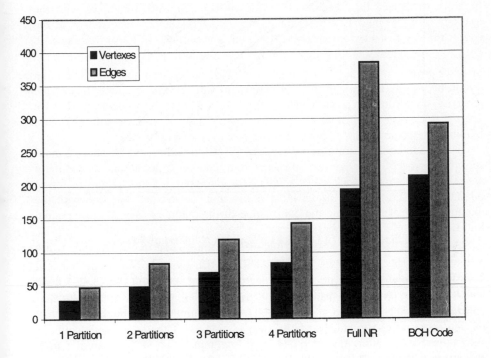

Figure 6 Trellis Edge and Vertex Comparison.

6. Performance.

Figure 7 shows the performance of the low complexity decoder for the same partitions and the BCH code. It can be seen from this figure that decoding 4 partitions gives similar performance to the (15,7,5) BCH code. Decoding 4 partitions (the best quarter of the full trellis) gives performance of only a small fraction of a dB worse than the full trellis but with a significant saving in terms of complexity.

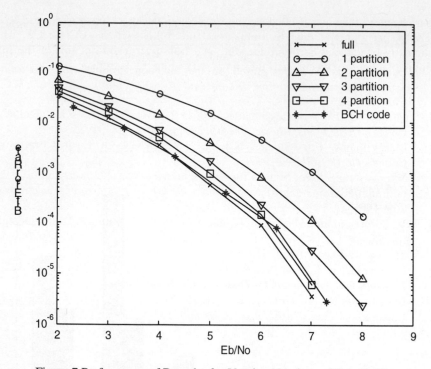

Figure 7 Performance of Decoder for Varying Numbers of Sub-Trellises.

7. Conclusions.

The squaring and twisted squaring constructions are powerful techniques for constructing codes and the trellises which represent them. Application of the twisted squaring construction leads to the partitioning of the set of codewords in such a way as to allow the decoding to be split into two stages resulting in a reduction in complexity with only a small performance penalty. In this paper the effects of applying the two stage decoding procedure to the Nordstrom Robinson code have been investigated showing that the new technique can achieve per-formance superior to that of the equivalent linear code with reduced complexity.

8. References.

[1]   A.W. Nordstrom, J.P. Robinson, "An Optimum Nonlinear Code", *Inform. Contr.*, **11**, pp. 613-616, 1967.

[2]   Honary B., Markarian G., Darnell M. "Low-complexity trellis decoding of linear block codes", *IEE Proceedings-Communications*, **142**-4, pp. 201-209, 1995.

[3]   Wu, J., Lin, S., Kasami, T., Fujiwara, T., Takata, T., "An Upper Bound On the Effective Error Coefficient of Two-Stage Decoding, and Good Two-

Level Decompositions of Some Reed-Muller Codes", *IEEE Trans Comms*, **42**, pp. 813-818, 1994.

[4]   B. Honary and G. Markarian and S. R. Marple, " Two-Stage Trellis Decoding of RS Codes Based on the Shannon Product", *International Symposium on Information Theory and Its Applications, Victoria, B.C., Canada*, 1996.

[5]   Forney, G. D., Jr, "Coset codes – Part II: Binary Lattices and Related Codes", *IEEE Trans. Inform. Theory*, **34**, pp. 1152-1187, 1988.

[6]   MacWilliams, F.J., Sloane, N.J.A., "The Theory Of Error Correcting Codes", *North Holland*, 1977.

[7]   Viterbi, A. J., "Error bounds for convolutional codes and an asymptotically optimum decoding algorithm." *IEEE Trans Inform. Theory*, **IT-13**, pp.260-269, 1967.

[8]   V. Sidorenko and Markarian, G. and Honary, B.," Minimal Trellis Design for Linear Codes based on the Shannon Product", *IEEE Trans Inform Theory*, **42-6**, pp.2048-2053, 1996.

[9]   Forney, G. D., Jr, "On Iterative Decoding And The Two-Way Algorithm", *International Symposium on Turbo Codes, Brest, France,* 1997.

[10]   Manoukian H. H., Honary, B., "BCJR Trellis Construction For Binary Linear Block Codes". *IEE Proc.-Commun,* **144**-6, 1997.

Bit Error Probability and Encoder Structure

Seán Coffey and Houshou Chen

Abstract. The problem of decoding a binary linear code used over a binary symmetric channel so as to minimize bit error probability, rather than codeword error probability, is studied. In general, there are substantial differences with the maximum likelihood case. The optimal decoding rule depends on the crossover probability of the channel, the bit error probability depends on the generator matrix used, and the optimal generator matrix itself depends on the crossover probability of the channel.

This paper demonstrates each of the above properties. In addition, an infinite class of codes whose optimal generator matrix is non-systematic when the channel crossover probability is small is demonstrated. A new demonstration of the following facts is presented: if the code has $d^\perp > 2$, then for a sufficiently noisy channel, the optimal generator matrix is (uniquely) a (wide-sense) systematic one, and the optimal decoding rule is to ignore the parity checks and to take the information bits as they are received. The infinite class mentioned above has $d^\perp > 2$, and thus has different optimal generator matrices at different channel crossover probabilities.

1. Introduction

This paper examines the problem of decoding a binary linear code used over a binary symmetric channel when the goal is to minimize the information bit error probability.

This topic, of obvious fundamental interest, has received new impetus from the success of turbocodes. Although turbocoding systems work very well experimentally, there are many problems in understanding why this is, and how to choose turbocode parameters optimally. One of the essential features of the turbo decoding algorithm is the use of bit error probability decoding rather than maximum likelihood, and the relationship with encoder structure.

Seán (aka John T.) Coffey is with the EECS Department, University of Michigan, Ann Arbor, Michigan 48109. e-mail: scoffey@eecs.umich.edu

Houshou Chen is with the Department of Electrical Engineering, National Chi-Nan University, Nantou, Taiwan 545. e-mail: houshou@ncnu.edu.tw

This work was supported in part by the U.S. Army Research Office under Grant DAAH04-96-1-0377.

We begin with an intuitive sketch of why the information bit decoding problem is relevant to turbocodes. The classical approach to achieving performance close to capacity was to fix the target probability of error, and to form a family of codes of increasing decoding complexity whose performance points on the plot of P_e versus E_b/N_0 moved (horizontally leftwards) towards capacity. Thus we could, for example, take $P_e = 10^{-5}$ and the class of rate $1/2$ convolutional codes. Then by increasing the constraint length, we get a set of performance points moving closer and closer to capacity. Unfortunately, beyond a certain point the decoding complexity becomes prohibitive in this approach.

Turbocodes instead can be thought of as approaching the eventual target point "vertically", i.e., by taking the E_b/N_0 to be fixed and, by repeated decoding, achieving a set of operating points that move downwards to the target error probability. Thus the early iterations for a turbocode operate in a region of very low signal to noise ratio, and very high error probability even for the decoded bits.

One issue arises immediately: the question of when the turbo decoding algorithm "fires up", i.e., the question of when the output decoded bits at the first iteration are even marginally more reliable than the received bits. For clearly, if this is not the case, we expect that the turbo decoding algorithm will yield the originally received bits as the decoded word.The critical channel quality at which there is even marginal improvement in reliability, and the relationship with the generator matrix, are of considerable interest.

Here we concentrate on the more tractable case of a binary symmetric channel. In Section 2, we review some of the main properties of the problem. (For an account of the history of contributions to the problem, we refer the reader to [3] and the references contained therein.) In Section 3, we present new demonstrations of results for general classes of codes. We construct an infinite class of codes that have non-systematic optimal generator matrices when the channel is very quiet, and present a new and simplified demonstration of the result that, if the code has dual distance greater than 2, then for sufficiently noisy channels the optimal generator matrix to use is systematic, and the optimal decoding rule is to take the information bits as they are.

2. Basic properties

The information bit decoding problem differs substantially from the maximum likelihood decoding problem. Suppose, for example, that we are presented with a list of all codewords of the linear code C, plus a received word r, and are told that the channel is binary symmetric, with crossover probability

$0 < p < 1/2$. Do we have enough information to make an optimal estimate of the codeword?

If our goal is to minimize the codeword error probability, then the answer is Yes: we find a coset leader for the coset containing r and declare that to be the error pattern. In particular, we do not need to know either the generator matrix that has been used, or the crossover probability of the channel.

If, however, our goal is to minimize the information bit error probability, then the answer is No: the decoded codeword depends on, i.e., varies with, both the generator matrix used and the crossover probability of the channel.

In fact, minimum bit error probability has the following properties, each of which will be demonstrated later:

I. **The optimal decoding rule depends on p.**

II. **The optimal decoding rule depends on the generator matrix.**

III. **The bit error probability depends on the generator matrix.**

IV. **The optimal generator matrix depends on p.**

By "decoding rule" here, we mean the rule for determining which codeword (which in turn determines which set of k information bits) will be chosen by the decoder given a particular received word.

Consider for illustrative purposes the $[5,3,2]$ code with generator matrix

$$G = \begin{pmatrix} 1 & 0 & 0 & 1 & 1 \\ 0 & 1 & 0 & 1 & 0 \\ 0 & 0 & 1 & 0 & 1 \end{pmatrix}.$$

The standard array is

00000	10011	**01010**	**00101**	11001	10110	**01111**	11100
00001	10010	**01011**	**00100**	11000	10111	**01110**	11101
00010	10001	**01000**	**00111**	11011	10100	**01101**	11110
10000	00011	**11010**	**10101**	01001	00110	**11111**	01100

Consider the problem of decoding the first information bit. We divide the code into codewords for which this bit is 0, i.e., $\{00000, 01010, 00101, 01111\}$, and codewords for which this bit is 1. We divide each of the cosets correspondingly, as in the standard array above.

Suppose we receive the word 10000; then the error pattern belongs to the last coset. If the error pattern is one of $\{10000, 11010, 10101, 11111\}$, i.e., one of those listed in bold face, the transmitted codeword has first information bit 0; if not, i.e., if the error pattern is one of $\{00011, 01001, 00110, 01100\}$, the first information bit is 1. To decide which is more probable, we compare the total probability of each of these sets of possible error patterns, choosing

31

the one that is more likely. In this case, the sets have probabilities $p(1 - p)^4 + 2p^3(1 - p)^2 + p^5$ (for the set of words in bold face) and $4p^2(1 - p)^3$ (for the words in regular font). The first set is more probable if $p \leq 0.228$, while the second is more probable if $p > 0.228$. This demonstrates property I above: *the optimal decoding rule depends on the value of p.* Note that for maximum likelihood decoding, one word in the coset rather than one set is chosen, and the word of weight 1 is optimum for all p; for minimum bit error probability decoding, however, the four words of weight 2 collectively outweigh the single word of weight 1 in probability when the channel is noisy enough.

In general, given a received word r, we estimate the jth information bit u_j as the bit that maximizes

$$\max_{\substack{u_j=0,1}} \sum_{\substack{u \in \mathcal{U} \\ u_j}} p^{|r+uG|}(1 - p)^{n-|r+uG|}, \tag{1}$$

choosing arbitrarily if the two are equal. The probability of receiving a word in a given coset and also making a decoding error for the jth information bit is the sum of the probabilities of the less probable set in that coset. (Note that the partition, and hence the probability, depends on the information bit being decoded. Also the estimate of the information bit depends on the received word r; however, the probability that this estimate is incorrect depends only on the coset.)

The overall probability of the jth information bit being in error is then obtained by summing over all cosets. Thus

$$p_{\text{inf}}^{(j,G)} = \sum_{q \in Q} \min \left(\sum_{\substack{u \in \mathcal{U} \\ u_j=1}} p^{|q+uG|}(1 - p)^{n-|q+uG|}, \sum_{\substack{u \in \mathcal{U} \\ u_j=0}} p^{|q+uG|}(1 - p)^{n-|q+uG|} \right), \tag{2}$$

where Q is a set of coset representatives, and $\mathcal{U}$ is the set of possible information sequences.

For this code, it may be verified that for each of the other cosets, and for each of the other information bits, the optimal information bit decision is to use a coset leader as estimate of the error pattern. The average information bit error probability, $\bar{p}_{\text{inf}}^{(G)} = \left(p_{\text{inf}}^{(1)} + p_{\text{inf}}^{(2)} + p_{\text{inf}}^{(3)} \right) / 3$, is then

$$\bar{p}_{\text{inf}}^{(G)} = \begin{cases} \frac{1}{3} \left(2p + 8p^2 - 20p^3 + 20p^4 - 8p^5 \right) & \text{for } p \leq 0.228 \\ p & \text{for } p > 0.228. \end{cases}$$

2.1 Generator matrices

It will emerge that it is important in this problem to define the term "systematic" carefully. Classically this means that the generator matrix is of the form $G = (I_k|P)$, i.e., that all the columns of the $k \times k$ identity matrix are present in the leftmost k positions of the generator matrix. We will refer to this as "narrow-sense systematic." A generator matrix will be said to be "wide-sense systematic" if the columns of the $k \times k$ identity matrix are each present somewhere in the generator matrix. This is sometimes referred to as a "separable" generator matrix.

Consider the non-systematic (in both senses) generator matrix for the same code

$$G_1 = \begin{pmatrix} 1 & 0 & 0 & 1 & 1 \\ 1 & 1 & 0 & 0 & 1 \\ 1 & 0 & 1 & 1 & 0 \end{pmatrix},$$

obtained by adding row 1 of G to rows 2 and 3. If we are interested in decoding the first information bit, we again compute the subcode for which this first information bit is zero, i.e., $\{00000, 11001, 10110, 01111\}$ and highlight the corresponding columns in the standard array:

00000	10011	01010	00101	11001	10110	01111	11100
00001	10010	01011	00100	11000	10111	01110	11101
00010	10001	01000	00111	11011	10100	01101	11110
10000	00011	11010	10101	01001	00110	11111	01100

Now if the word $r = 10000$ is received, we compare the probability of the highlighted subset within the corresponding coset, i.e., $\{10000, 01001, 00110, 11111\}$ to its complement, i.e., $\{00011, 11010, 10101, 01100\}$. In this case we have $p(1-p)^4 + 2p^2(1-p)^3 + p^5 > 2p^2(1-p)^3 + 2p^3(1-p)^2$ for all $p < 1/2$, so for all p we declare that the error pattern belongs to the highlighted set, and choose the first information bit as 0 accordingly. Thus, in particular, the received word $r = 10000$ is never decoded to the codeword 10011; on the other hand the results of Section 3.2 imply that for p sufficiently close to $1/2$ and a systematic generator matrix, $r = 10000$ must be decoded to 10011. This demonstrates property II: *the optimal decoding rule depends on the generator matrix.*

Repeating for the other cosets, and for the second and third information bits, we find that the average probability of information bit error with this

33

generator matrix is

$$\bar{p}_{\text{inf}}^{(G_1)} = \frac{1}{3}\left(4p - 2p^2\right).$$

Note that this is greater than p for $0 < p < 1/2$. Thus this generator matrix is substantially worse than the systematic one used earlier. More generally, we deduce property III above: *the bit error probability depends on the generator matrix used.*

3. General results

3.1 The quiet region

It is not always the case that a systematic generator matrix is best. In this section, we construct an infinite class of codes that have an optimal generator matrix that is non-narrow-sense-systematic when p is sufficiently small. From this we indicate how to construct an infinite class of codes that have optimal generator matrices that are not wide-sense-systematic when p is sufficiently small.

We will use a very useful result of Dunning [2]: given a linear code and a channel crossover probability, consider all possible generator matrices and the resulting bit error probabilities under optimal decoding. Arrange each set of k bit error probabilities in non-decreasing order $p_1^G \leq p_2^G \leq \cdots \leq p_k^G$. Then there exists a generator matrix with bit error probabilities achieving the minimum in each position of this ordered list simultaneously, i.e., $p_i^{G^*} \leq p_i^G$ for all i and G.

Consider codes with generator matrices of the following form:

$$G = \left[\begin{array}{c} 111111000\cdots00 \\ \hline G_1 \end{array}\right],$$

where G_1 generates a code with sufficiently large parameters, say $n \geq 1000$, $k \geq 100$, $d \geq 100$. The minimum distance of the code generated by G is 6, and thus the average bit error probability, even under optimal decoding, must be of the form $\bar{p}_{inf} = k \cdot p^3 + O(p^4)$ with $k > 0$. For sufficiently small p, we need to minimize the leading constant k. With any given generator matrix, the codeword of weight 6 is the sum of some subset of the rows of the generator matrix. The ith bit error probability under optimal decoding is of the form $p_i = k_i \cdot p^3 + O(p^4)$ with $k_i > 0$ if and only if the ith row of the generator matrix is involved in the sum that gives the codeword of weight 6. Otherwise the smallest weight codeword that gives an error in the ith information bit has weight at least 94, and so $p_i = O(p^{47})$ even with optimal decoding, i.e., far lower when p is very small.

34

It is possible to choose the codeword of weight 6 as a row of the generator matrix, as in G above. Then all information bits except one have error probability $O(p^{47})$. By Dunning's result, the optimal generator matrix will therefore have these probabilities, and hence the codeword of weight 6 must involve only one row of the generator matrix. Thus we must have a generator matrix of the form of G above when p is very small. This is non-narrow-sense-systematic.

We now sketch a construction of a code with an optimal generator matrix that is not systematic in the wide sense as $p \to 0$. We select G_1 to be some large-parameter $[n_1, k_1, d_1]$ code as above, but replace each 1 in the generator matrix by a randomly chosen binary string of length 6 and weight 3, and replace each 0 by a string of six zeros, to obtain a new generator matrix G_1' that generates a $[6n_1, k_1, \geq 3d_1]$ code. We form G by adjoining n_1 non-overlapping words of weight 6 to G_1': these words collectively cover every position.

Now any codeword involving a row from G_1' must have weight at least d_1, no matter how many of the rows of weight 6 are involved in the sum: this is the reason for the modification of G_1 to G_1'. Once again we can argue that all the weight 6 codewords must be included in the optimal generator matrix for all sufficiently small p. But then the additional k_1 rows cannot be chosen in a way that ensures that all the columns of the $k \times k$ identity matrix are present, i.e., the generator matrix cannot be wide-sense systematic.

3.2 The noisy region

We present a simplified demonstration of the following results, which were first found in a more general form by Kiely, Coffey, and Bell [3]. Delsarte [1] had previously noted, via direct computation of half-coset weight enumerators, that the 'ignore parity checks' decoding rule is optimum for many codes for sufficiently high p when the generator matrix is systematic.

THEOREM: *For any binary linear code with $d^\perp > 2$ transmitted over the binary symmetric channel, the optimal generator matrix to use for p sufficiently close to $1/2$ is wide-sense systematic, and the optimal decoding rule is to ignore the parity check bits and to accept the information bits as they are received.*

Here the "information" bits are those in the positions in which the columns of the identity matrix appear, and the "parity check" bits are the others.

(There is an unfortunate misstatement of the result in the abstract of Kiely *et al.* [3], in which it is stated that a wide-sense systematic generator matrix is optimal for binary symmetric channels for codes with $d^\perp > 2$, without the qualification that this is necessarily true only for sufficiently noisy channels. The result is stated correctly in the conclusions of the same paper.)

Proof: Writing $p = 1/2 - \varepsilon$ and substituting into (2), we find that

$$
P_{\text{inf}}^{(j,G)} = \frac{1}{2^n} \sum_{q \in Q} \min \left(\sum_{u \in \mathcal{U}:u_j=1} (1-2\varepsilon)^{|q+uG|}(1+2\varepsilon)^{n-|q+uG|}, \right.
$$

$$
\left. \sum_{u \in \mathcal{U}:u_j=0} (1-2\varepsilon)^{|q+uG|}(1+2\varepsilon)^{n-|q+uG|} \right)
$$

$$
= \frac{1}{2^n} \sum_{q \in Q} \min \left(\sum_{u \in \mathcal{U}:u_j=1} \left(1+2(n-2|q+uG|)\varepsilon + O\left(\varepsilon^2\right)\right), \right.
$$

$$
\left. \sum_{u \in \mathcal{U}:u_j=0} \left(1+2(n-2|q+uG|)\varepsilon + O\left(\varepsilon^2\right)\right) \right)
$$

$$
= \frac{1}{2} + n\varepsilon - \frac{4}{2^n} \sum_{q \in Q} \max \left(\sum_{\substack{u \in \mathcal{U} \\ u_j=1}} |q+uG|, \sum_{\substack{u \in \mathcal{U} \\ u_j=0}} |q+uG| \right) \varepsilon + O\left(\varepsilon^2\right)
$$

since for all sufficiently small ε, the minimum is achieved by minimizing the first order term.

The optimal estimate of u_j for small ε is then the complement of the choice that maximizes the sum of the weights in the half cosets given by the value of u_j, if there is not a tie, i.e., the optimal estimate of u_j barring a tie is the complement of

$$
\arg \max_{u_j=0,1} \sum_{\substack{u \in \mathcal{U} \\ u_j}} |r+uG|. \tag{3}
$$

The generator matrix G must at least achieve the maximum

$$
\text{argmax}_G \sum_{j=1}^{k} \max_{u_j=0,1} \sum_{q \in Q} \sum_{\substack{u \in \mathcal{U} \\ u_j}} |q+uG|. \tag{4}
$$

We fix q and to each of the terms $\sum_{u \in \mathcal{U}:u_j=0} |q+uG|$ and $\sum_{u \in \mathcal{U}:u_j=1} |q+uG|$ we add the sum

$$
\sum_{\substack{u \in \mathcal{U} \\ u_j=0}} |uG|. \tag{5}
$$

36

Now the first sum is

$$\sum_{\substack{u\in\mathcal{U}\\u_j=1}}|q+uG|+\sum_{\substack{u\in\mathcal{U}\\u_j=0}}|uG|=\sum_{u\in\mathcal{U}}|uG'| \tag{6}$$

where G' is the generator matrix obtained by changing the jth row of G from g_j to g_j+q. Similarly the second sum is

$$\sum_{\substack{u\in\mathcal{U}\\u_j=0}}|q+uG|+\sum_{\substack{u\in\mathcal{U}\\u_j=0}}|uG|=\sum_{u\in\mathcal{U}}|uG''| \tag{7}$$

where G'' is the generator matrix obtained by changing the jth row of G from g_j to q.

It is well known [4, p. 156] that every position in a binary linear code either assumes the values 0 and 1 equally often, or is always 0. The sum of the weights of the codewords of an $[n,k]$ binary linear code is then at most $n\cdot 2^{k-1}$, with equality if and only if none of the columns of the generator matrix is 0.

We note that the sum in Eq. (5) is the sum of codeword weights for an $[n,k-1]$ code, with generator matrix obtained by deleting the jth row of G. G has no columns consisting of all zeros (since $d^\perp > 1$) and at most one column consisting of a 1 in the jth row and zeros elsewhere (since $d^\perp > 2$). Thus the generator matrix obtained by deleting the jth row of G has at most one zero column; it has exactly one if and only if G contains the jth column of a $k\times k$ identity matrix. We have

$$\sum_{\substack{u\in\mathcal{U}\\u_j=0}}|uG|=\begin{cases}n\cdot 2^{k-2} & \text{if } G \text{ does not contain } e_j\\(n-1)\cdot 2^{k-2} & \text{if } G \text{ does contain } e_j.\end{cases} \tag{8}$$

This then shows that

$$\max\left(\sum_{\substack{u\in\mathcal{U}\\u_j=1}}|q+uG|,\sum_{\substack{u\in\mathcal{U}\\u_j=0}}|q+uG|\right)\le n\cdot 2^{k-1}-(n-1)2^{k-2}$$

if the code has $d^\perp > 2$, and substituting into the expansion obtained for $p_{\text{inf}}^{(j,G)}$ earlier we find

$$p_{\text{inf}}^{(j,G)}\ge\frac{1}{2}-\varepsilon+O\left(\varepsilon^2\right)$$

and we achieve this if and only if the column e_j is contained in G.

37

From this, the error probability in the noisy region differs from p by a factor that is at most $O(\varepsilon^2)$; the remaining question is the crucial one of whether the information bit error probability is greater than or less than p.

We take the received word r as coset representative. The optimal choice of u_j is the complement of the one that maximizes the sum in Eq. (3). If e_j is a column in G, this maximum contains a 1 in jth position in every word of the sum, i.e., is the sum in which $\bar{u}_j + r_j = 1$. Thus the optimal choice of u_j is just r_j, i.e., we take the jth information bit as it is. Then it is trivial that the error probability for this jth bit is exactly p in the very noisy region, i.e.,

$$p_{\text{inf}}^{(j,G)} = \frac{1}{2} - \varepsilon.$$

The same reasoning holds for each of the k information bits, and so overall we have, if the code has dual distance greater than 2,

$$\bar{p}_{\text{inf}}^{(G)} \geq p$$

in some region $p_{crit} \leq p < 1/2$, with equality if and only if the generator matrix is wide-sense systematic, i.e., contains all the columns of the $k \times k$ identity matrix.

3.3 Property IV

The general construction in Section 3.1 produces codes with $d^{\perp} > 2$ with high probability. Combining the results of Sections 3.1 and 3.2, we find that for such codes the optimal generator matrix cannot be wide-sense systematic when p is sufficiently small, and must be wide-sense systematic when p is sufficiently large. Thus we have demonstrated property IV: *the optimal generator matrix depends on p.*

REFERENCES

[1]   P. Delsarte, "Partial-optimal piecewise decoding of linear codes," *IEEE Trans. on Inform. Theory*, vol. IT-24, no. 1, pp. 70–75, Jan. 1978.

[2]   L. A. Dunning, "Encoding and decoding for the minimization of message symbol error rates in linear block codes," *IEEE Trans. on Inform. Theory*, vol. IT-33, no. 1, pp. 91–104, Jan. 1987.

[3]   A. B. Kiely, J. T. Coffey, and M. R. Bell, "Optimal information bit decoding of linear block codes," *IEEE Trans. on Inform. Theory*, vol. 41, no. 1, pp. 130–140, Jan. 1995.

[4]   R. J. McEliece, *The Theory of Information and Coding.* Reading, Mass.: Addison-Wesley, 1977.

Some Information-Theoretic Aspects
of Uniquely Decodable Codes

Valdemar C. da Rocha Jr.*
Communications Research Group - CODEC
Department of Electronics and Systems
Federal University of Pernambuco
PO Box 7800, Recife 50711-970 PE BRASIL

ABSTRACT

A source code C is considered containing K codewords with lengths w_i, $1 \leq i \leq K$, respectively, where K is a non negative integer. The capacity C of a source code is defined as the code maximum information rate in bits per code digit, and turns out to be a function only of the codeword lengths. Shannon's mathematical approach to compute the capacity of discrete noiseless channels is used to compute the capacity of a source code. The concept of matching between an information source and a source code is introduced as well as a new definition of code efficiency. A novel proof of the McMillan inequality is presented, i.e., that a D-ary code C is uniquely decodable if and only if the condition $\sum_{i=1}^{K} D^{-w_i} \leq 1$ is satisfied by its codeword lengths.

1 INTRODUCTION

Shannon [1, p.36] defined a discrete channel as a system whereby a sequence of choices from a finite set of elementary symbols x_1, $x_2,\ldots$, x_D can be transmitted from one point to another. Each of the symbols x_i was assumed to have a certain duration t_i seconds, not necessarily the same for different x_i. It was not required that all possible sequences of the x_i be capable of transmission on the system, i.e., certain sequences only may be allowed. These would be possible signals for the channel. We take the view that the setup described by Shannon remains fully applicable if we consider instead of symbols, the transmission or storage of blocks of symbols, i.e., codewords of a given source code. For our purposes it will suffice to consider that all letters x_i have the same duration. Henceforth whenever we refer to a code we will mean a uniquely decodable code,

---

*The author acknowledges partial support of this work by the Brazilian National Council for Scientific and Technological Development (CNPq) under the grant No.304214/77-9.

i.e., a code which allows *exact* reconstruction of the source output from its encoded representation. In *Section 2* we look at source codes in the framework of Shannon's discrete noiseless channels. In *Section 3* we introduce our definition of code capacity, i.e., a measure C of the ability of such a code to transmit or to store information. It turns out that C is a function only of the codeword lengths, i.e., of the number of letters in each codeword and not of the size D of the code alphabet. It is implied here that, for the given set of codeword lengths, the minimum value of D must satisfy the condition $C \leq \log D$, where here and hereafter all logarithms will be in base 2. We then present the definitions of *matching* and *code efficiency* in *Section 4* and follow that with a simple proof for the McMillan inequality in *Section 5*. In *Section 6* we illustrate the practical use of non integer codeword lengths by means of homophonic coding. In *Section 7* we present a few results relative to the codeword lengths of a uniquely decodable code and we close the paper in *Section 8* presenting some conclusions. We refer the interested reader to an expanded version in this book of reference [2], containing new results and rigorous and explicit proofs of some older but very relevant results presented by Shannon in [1], relative to the discrete noiseless channel.

2   DISCRETE NOISELESS CHANNELS

Let S denote a discrete memoryless source with K symbols $s_1, s_2, \ldots, s_K$, occurring with probabilities $p(s_1), p(s_2), \ldots, p(s_K)$, respectively. We consider a source encoder to be a one-to-one mapping of the K symbols of a given source S into the codewords z_i, $1 \leq i \leq K$, of a code C defined over an appropriate alphabet, whose lengths are denoted as $w_i, 1 \leq i \leq K$, respectively. For the purpose of transmission or storage the output of the source encoder will be the codeword z_i when the input is the symbol s_i, for $1 \leq i \leq K$. Following Shannon [1, p.36] we will consider a discrete channel whereby a sequence of choices from a finite set of symbols is made, however with the distinction that in our case blocks of symbols constituting codewords are selected from the (finite) set of codewords of C, according to the probability distribution of S. We will denote by $\overline{L}$ the average codeword length, i.e.,

$$\overline{L} = \sum_{i=1}^{K} p(s_i) w_i, \tag{1}$$

and will denote by $H(C)$ the ratio $H(S)/\overline{L}$ between the source entropy $H(S)$ and the average codeword length $\overline{L}$, i.e, the *uncertainty per code letter*. Let $p_1, p_2, \ldots, p_D$ denote the probability distribution of the D-ary letters in the codewords of code C, driven by the source S. Since there are constraints on the possible sequences of code letters, and constraints reduce uncertainty, it follows that

$$H(C) = H(S)/\overline{L} \le H(p_1, p_2, \ldots, p_D) = -\sum_{i=1}^{D} p_i \log p_i \le \log D, \qquad (2)$$

with equality in the first inequality if and only if the code letters are statistically independent, and with equality in the second inequality if and only if the sequence of code letters constitute a sequence of independent and uniformly distributed D-ary random variables. In a more general situation, e.g., when S is a Markov source [3, p.22], there can be constraints on the allowable sequences of codewords and for our purposes the following definition of capacity of a code will suffice.

3 CODE CAPACITY

Definition 1 *The capacity C of a code is defined as*

$$C = \lim_{L \to \infty} \frac{\log N(L)}{L} \qquad (3)$$

given the limit exists, and where $N(L)$ is the number of allowed sequences of length L formed by a concatenation of codewords.

As a consequence of the above definition it follows from (2) that

$$H(S)/\overline{L} \le C = \max_{p(s_i)} H(C) \le \max_{p(s_i)} H(p_1, p_2, \ldots, p_D) \le \log D. \qquad (4)$$

In [2], working with symbols, the authors call (3) the *combinatorial capacity*, and call $C = \max_{p(s_i)} H(C)$ the *statistical capacity*, and formally prove that they are equal. In our case, this result follows unchanged when we consider codewords, i.e., blocks of symbols, instead of symbols.

3.1 Computing Code Capacity

Suppose we allow all possible sequences formed by the K codewords of C and we want to determine the corresponding code capacity C. We consider the number $N(L)$ of distinct sequences of L letters formed by a concatenation of codewords of C as follows.

$$N(L) = N(L - w_1) + N(L - w_2) + \ldots + N(L - w_K),$$

i.e., the total number of distinct sequences of length L formed by a concatenation of codewords of C is equal to the sum of the corresponding number of sequences of length L terminated by codeword z_1, plus the corresponding number of sequences of length L terminated by codeword z_2, etc., plus the corresponding number of sequences of length L terminated by codeword z_K. Equivalently to

41

the statement in [1, p.37], $N(L)$ is the asymptotic to large L to AX_0^L, where A is a constant and X_0 is the largest real solution of the equation

$$X^{-w_1} + X^{-w_2} + \ldots + X^{-w_K} = 1, \tag{5}$$

or

$$\sum_{i=1}^{K} X^{-w_i} = 1, \tag{6}$$

and therefore the capacity $\mathcal{C}$ is given by

$$\mathcal{C} = \lim_{L \to \infty} \frac{\log AX_0^L}{L} = \log X_0. \tag{7}$$

3.2 THE CAPACITY ACHIEVING DISTRIBUTION

It follows from (4) that the capacity $\mathcal{C}$ of a code is the maximum (supremum) of its uncertainty per code letter $H(C)$ over all possible source probability distributions $p(s_i), 1 \leq i \leq K$. Therefore, equivalently, we can write (4) as

$$\mathcal{C} = \max_{p(s_i)} H(C) = \max_{p(s_i)} H(S)/\overline{L}$$

or

$$\mathcal{C} = \max_{p(s_i)} \frac{\sum_{i=1}^{K} -p(s_i) \log p(s_i)}{\sum_{i=1}^{K} p(s_i) w_i}.$$

By using simple calculus we find that

$$p(s_i) = 2^{-w_i \mathcal{C}}, 1 \leq i \leq K, \tag{8}$$

is the capacity achieving probability distribution for the source symbols.

4 MATCHING AND EFFICIENCY

We say that a source S with K symbols is *matched* to a given source code C with K codewords if the source symbol probability distribution is the capacity achieving distribution for C.

Definition 2 *We define the matching μ between a source S and a source code C as the ratio between $H(S)/\overline{L}$ and $\mathcal{C}$, i.e.,*

$$\mu = H(S)/\overline{L}\mathcal{C}. \tag{9}$$

Definition 3 *We define the code efficiency λ of a D-ary code C as the ratio between its capacity $\mathcal{C}$ and $\log D$, i.e.,*

$$\lambda = \mathcal{C}/\log D. \tag{10}$$

Definition 4 *We define the overall source coding efficiency η as the product between the matching (9) and the code efficiency (10), i.e.,*

$$\eta = \mu\lambda = \frac{H(S)}{C\overline{L}} \times \frac{C}{\log D} = H(S)/\overline{L}\log D. \tag{11}$$

The following two lemmas are immediate consequences of the above definitions.

Lemma 1 *The matching μ is bounded as follows*

$$0 \le \mu \le 1.$$

Proof: The proof follows by noticing that $\mu = 0$ if and only if $H(S) = 0$ and that $\mu = 1$ if and only if $H(S)/\overline{L}$ achieves its maximum value C. □

Lemma 2 *The code efficiency λ is bounded as follows*

$$0 \le \lambda \le 1.$$

Proof: The proof follows by noticing that $\lambda = 0$ if and only if $C = 0$, which occurs when the code has a single codeword, and that $\lambda = 1$ if and only if C achieves its maximum value $\log D$. □

We notice further that *Definition 2* will coincide with the usual definition of (overall) source coding efficiency if and only if $C = \log D$, i.e., if for the set of codeword lengths employed it is possible to achieve $\log D$ bits per code digit.

Example 1 *Let $w_1 = w_2 = 1$ and $w_3 = w_4 = 2$ be the codeword lengths of a ternary $(D = 3)$ code with four codewords, and let $p(s_1) = .4$, $p(s_2) = .3$, $p(s_3) = .2$ and $p(s_4) = .1$ be the source probability distribution. For the given codeword lengths we obtain $C = 1.45$ and for the probabilities given we compute $H(S) = 1.846$. It follows that $\overline{L} = 1.3$ which leads to $\mu = H(S)/C\overline{L} = .9796$, $\lambda = 1.45/\log 3 = .9148$ and $\eta = H(S)/\overline{L}\log 3 = .896$.*

Example 2 *As in the previous example, let $w_1 = w_2 = 1$ and $w_3 = w_4 = 2$ be the codeword lengths of a ternary $(D = 3)$ code with four codewords, which give $C = 1.45$. For the source probability distribution let $p(s_1) = p(s_2) = .3661$, $p(s_3) = p(s_4) = .1339$, which obey (8) and lead to $H(S) = 1.838$. It follows that $\overline{L} = 1.268$ and thus we obtain $\mu = H(S)/C\overline{L} = 1$, $\lambda = 1.45/\log 3 = .9148$ and $\eta = H(S)/\overline{L}\log 3 = .9148$.*

5 McMILLAN INEQUALITY

The McMillan inequality [3, p.59] specifies the necessary and sufficient condition to be satisfied by the codeword lengths of a uniquely decodable code. Specifically, a D-ary code C with K codewords with lengths w_1, w_2, $\ldots$, w_K, is uniquely decodable if and only if $\sum_{i=1}^{K} D^{-w_i} \leq 1$. Based on the concept of code capacity we present next a simple derivation of the McMillan inequality. Since X_0 is a root of (6) it follows that

$$\sum_{i=1}^{K} X_0^{-w_i} = 1. \tag{12}$$

From (4) and (7) it follows that $\mathcal{C} = \log X_0 \leq \log D$, and thus that $X_0 \leq D$, which we take into (12) to obtain

$$\sum_{i=1}^{K} D^{-w_i} \leq 1,$$

which is the well known McMillan inequality.

6   HOMOPHONIC CODING

Homophonic coding is a well known technique [4, 5, 6] applied in cryptography for source coding, whose aim is to hide the original source statistics. By using a D-ary code for homophonic coding, ideally the code digits appear as coming from a D-ary symmetric source. We use homophonic coding in this section to illustrate the practical use of codewords whose (effective) lengths are not integers. In Figure 1 whenever the source selects the symbol s_1 the code will select either the codeword v_1 with probability $P(v_1|s_1) = 1/3$ or will select codeword v_2 with probability $P(v_2|s_1) = 2/3$. We interpret this situation as the code associating to s_1 a codeword with average length $2 \times 1/3 + 1 \times 2/3 = 4/3$. It follows from (6) that for a code with two codewords whose lengths are $w_1 = 4/3$ and $w_2 = 2$, respectively, the capacity is $\mathcal{C} = .6085$. We compute $H(S) = .8113$ and $\overline{L} = 1.5$ and thus we obtain $\mu = .8888$ and since $D = 2$ we have $\lambda = .6085$. The overall coding efficiency is thus $\eta = \mu\lambda = .5408$. Notice that $P(V = v_1) = 1/4$, $P(V = v_2) = 1/2$ and $P(V = v_3) = 1/4$, and thus $H(V) = 1.5$ which leads to the ratio $H(V)/\overline{L} = 1$, i.e., the binary digits after homophonic coding appear as coming from a binary symmetric source.

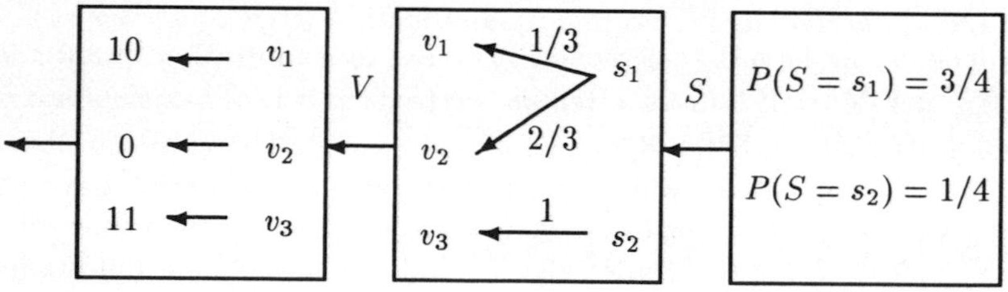

Figure 1: Homophonic coding.

7 PROPERTIES OF WORD LENGTHS

Proposition 1 *Let C be a uniquely decodable binary code with K codewords whose lengths are w_1, w_2, ..., w_K, respectively. The sum $\sum_{i=1}^{K} w_i$ of the codeword lengths of C satisfies the inequalities*

$$\sum_{i=1}^{K} w_i \geq i2^i + (K - 2^i)(i + 2) \geq \lceil K(\log K)/C \rceil,$$

where $2^i \leq K \leq 2^{i+1}$ and C is the code capacity.

Proof: We prove the first inequality in this proposition by induction. For $K = 2$ the obvious binary code has two codewords both of length one, which gives $\sum_{j=1}^{2} w_j = 2$, a minimum. For $K = 3$ we construct the uniquely decodable binary code with one codeword of length one and two codewords of length two, e.g., $0, 10, 11$, for which $\sum_{j=1}^{3} w_j = 5$, again a minimum. In this manner we can construct, from a given binary uniquely decodable code C whose sum of codeword lengths is a minimum, a new binary uniquely decodable code C_1 whose sum of codeword lengths is also a minimum, containing more codewords than the original code. We simply choose a codeword from C, say v, among those of shortest length, append a 0 to it, forming the concatenation $v|0$, and append a 1 to v forming the concatenation $v|1$, add to the codebook of C_1 the new codewords $v|0$ and $v|1$ and remove their "prefix" v. In this manner, each codeword of shortest length can be removed from the codebook after acting as a parent of two new codewords both one letter longer than its parent. We remark that in binary that is the best that we can do, i.e., from one codeword of length l generate two distinct codewords of length $l + 1$, in the sense that it is not possible to generate more than two distinct codewords and the increase in length can not be less than 1 letter per new codeword.

In order to prove the second inequality we notice that the minimisation of the sum $\sum_{i=1}^{K} w_i$ is equivalent to the maximization of the product $\prod_{i=1}^{K} X_0^{-w_i}$, since we can write

$$\prod_{i=1}^{K} X_0^{-w_i} = X_0^{-\sum_{i=1}^{K} w_i},$$

where X_0 denotes the largest real root of (6), i.e., a maximization under the constraint $\sum_{i=1}^{K} X_0^{-w_i} = 1$. This is a well known problem whose solution states that all the terms $X_0^{-w_i}$ in $\sum_{i=1}^{K} X_0^{-w_i} = 1$ must be equal. Therefore it follows that $K X_0^{-w_i} = 1$, $1 \leq i \leq K$, which by taking logarithms on both sides and simplifying gives $w_i \log X_0 = \log K$, or finally by summing for all values of i we obtain $\sum_{i=1}^{K} w_i = K \log K/C$, since $\log X_0 = C$. The proposition follows by noticing that $\sum_{i=1}^{K} w_i$ must be a non negative integer. $\square$

We observe that the proof of the second inequality in *Proposition 1* is valid for D-ary codes in general. The generalisation of the first inequality for the

D-ary case is straightforward and we shall not present its proof.

Proposition 2 *The sum $\sum_{j=1}^{K} w_j$ of the codeword lengths of a uniquely decodable D-ary code satisfies the inequalities*

$$\sum_{j=1}^{K} w_j \geq iD^i + (K - D^i)(i+1) + \lceil (K - D^i)/(D-1) \rceil \geq \lceil K(\log K)/\mathcal{C} \rceil,$$

where $D^i \leq K \leq D^{i+1}$ and $\mathcal{C}$ is the code capacity.

Definition 5 *[7] A D-ary tree is a rooted tree such that either D branches or no branches stem outward (i.e., away from the root) from each node.*

It is useful to show the digits in the codewords of some code as the labels on the branches of a rooted tree.

Proposition 3 *The only prefix-free codes that can achieve a capacity of $\log D$ bits per code digit are those whose digits in the codewords are the labels on the branches of a D-ary fully labelled tree.*

Proof: Let N_i, $1 \leq i \leq L$, denote the number of terminal nodes reached after traversing i branches in a D-ary tree. Let N denote the total number of terminal nodes, i.e., let $N = N_1 + N_2 + \ldots + N_L$. It is easy to check that for a D-ary tree the following relation holds

$$N_1 + N_2/D + \ldots + N_L/D^{L-1} = D, \tag{13}$$

or

$$N_1 D^{-1} + N_2 D^{-2} + \ldots + N_L D^{-L} = 1.$$

But this last expression can, equivalently, be written as

$$\sum_{i=1}^{L} N_i D^{-i} = \sum_{i=1}^{N} D^{-w_i} = 1,$$

which we recognise as equation (5) satisfied for $X = D$, i.e., D is a root of (5) and since the average uncertainty in a D-ary alphabet cannot exceed $\log D$ we conclude that the capacity of the code with N D-ary codewords is $\mathcal{C} = \log D$. On the other hand if the codewords of a prefix-free code are such that their digits are not sufficient to label the branches of a D-ary fully labelled tree then

$$N_1 + N_2/D + \ldots + N_L/D^{L-1} < D,$$

which implies

$$\sum_{i=1}^{N} D^{-w_i} < 1,$$

46

and by the above reasoning such a code will have a capacity $\mathcal{C}$ strictly less than $\log D$. □

By using expression (13), together with $N = N_1 + N_2 + \ldots + N_L$, we count the number of essentially distinct prefix-free codes having N codewords, which achieve the capacity value of $\log D$ bits per code digit.

8 CONCLUSION

In this paper we introduced the capacity of a source code. It became clear that the code properties depend only on the codeword lengths and not on the code alphabet nor on the probability distribution of the source driving the code. By using the concept of code capacity a simple proof for the McMillan inequality was derived. In *Section 6* we provided an alternative interpretation for homophonic coding as source coding with non integer codeword lengths. Finally, the relationship between D-ary trees and codes was exploited to prove *Proposition 3*.

References

[1] C.E. Shannon and W. Weaver, *The Mathematical Theory of Communication*, University of Illinois Press, 1972.

[2] A. Khandekar, R.J. McEliece and E. Rodemich, " The Discrete Noiseless Channel Revisited", 5th *International Symposium on Communication Theory and Applications*, Ambleside, England, 11-16 July 1999, pp.164-166.

[3] N. Abramson, *Information Theory and Coding*, McGraw-Hill Book Company, 1963.

[4] Ch.G. Günther, "A Universal Algorithm for Homophonic Coding", pp. 405-414 in *Advances in Cryptology- Eurocrypt'88*, Lecture Notes in Computer Science, No.330. Heidelberg and New York: Springer, 1988.

[5] H.N. Jendal, Y.J.B. Kuhn and J.L. Massey, "An Information-Theoretic Approach to Homophonic Substitution", pp. 382-394 in *Advances in Cryptology-Eurocrypt'89* (Eds. J.-J. Quisquater and J. Vandewalle), Lecture Notes in Computer Science, No.434. Heidelberg and New York: Springer, 1990.

[6] V.C. da Rocha Jr. and J.L. Massey, "On the Entropy Bound for Optimum Homophonic Substitution", *IEEE International Symposium on Information Theory*, Ulm, Germany, 1997.

Decoding of Reed-Muller codes on Pascal triangles

Ilya Dumer*

Abstract

New soft- and hard decision decoding algorithms are presented for general Reed-Muller codes $RM(r,m)$. We use conventional $(u, u + v)$ construction with subblocks $u \in RM(r, m-1)$ and $v \in RM(r-1, m-1)$. When repeated, such a partition maps arbitrary codes $RM(s, j)$ onto (j, s)-nodes of Pascal triangles. In decoding, we first try to find subblock v from the better protected code $RM(r-1, m-1)$ and then proceed with the block u. Thus, decoding is relegated to the two constituent codes. We repeat this recursion and execute decoding only at the nodes $(j, 1)$ and $(j, j - 1)$ of Pascal triangle. On all intermediate nodes we only recalculate the reliabilities of the received symbols in a way similar to belief propagation performed on the bipartite graphs. The overall complexity has low order of $n \min(r, m-r)$. We show that this decoding substantially outperforms other algorithms of polynomial complexity known for RM codes.

1   Introduction

Reed-Muller codes $RM(r, m)$ [8] have parameters:

$$n = 2^m, \ k = \sum_{i=0}^{r} \binom{m}{i}, \ d = 2^{m-r}.$$

Despite having relatively bad code distance, these codes have been considered in numerous publications thanks to efficient decoding procedures. First, *majority decoding* was considered in [11] followed later by many developments and generalizations (see [3], [5], [9], [10], [12], [15], and references therein). Such a decoding has complexity order at most nk and corrects all error patterns of weight $\lfloor (d - 1)/2 \rfloor$ or less.

It is also known [6] that majority decoding corrects many error patterns of higher weights. Namely, for fixed r and $m \to \infty$, we can correct most error

---

*The author is with the College of Engineering, University of California, Riverside, CA 92521. This research was supported by the NSF grant NCR-9703844.

vectors of Hamming weight $n(1 - h_m)/2$ with a vanishing residual term

$$h_m = (m/d)^{1/2^{r+1}}. \tag{1}$$

For RM codes of fixed rate R, majority decoding corrects most error vectors of Hamming weights up to $d \ln d/4$. This represents $(\ln d/4)$-times increase over the bounded distance decoding. Recently, majority decoding has been generalized for soft-decision channels [16]. It is proven that for long low-rate codes soft decision algorithm gains $10 \log_{10}(\pi/2) \approx 2$ dB over its conventional hard decision counterpart regardless of the output error rate α.

To decrease decoding complexity, *recursive algorithms* [4], [7] were developed on both hard and soft-decision channels. The algorithms provide for bounded distance decoding and have the lowest complexity order $n \min(r, m - r)$ known for RM codes to date. Simulation results presented in [14] also showed that recursive soft-decision algorithms can increase decoding domain of bounded distance decoding. Another efficient algorithm considered in [13] for codes $RM(2, m)$, gives a slightly higher complexity $O(n^2 m)$ while correcting most error patterns of a higher weight $n(1 - h)/2$, where h has a vanishing order of $(m/n)^{1/4}$ as $m \to \infty$. Finally, algorithm [1] reduces complexity of full maximum-likelihood (ML) decoding by designing an efficient trellis structure. Yet, this complexity is an exponent in n.

In this paper, we wish to further develop decoding algorithms for RM codes and improve their performance both on short and long lengths. Such an improvement is especially important for short and moderate lengths on which RM codes are on par with the best codes known to date. In particular, when compared with BCH codes, RM codes have similar parameters for the lengths up to $n \le 256$. In this regard, RM codes represent a good choice for moderate lengths when coupled with low-complexity decoding that operates well above the limit $\lfloor (d - 1)/2 \rfloor$ of bounded distance decoding. Note that optimum maximum likelihood decoding has huge complexity even on moderate lengths. On the other hand, iterative procedures applied to turbo codes and low-parity check codes achieve good performance on the lengths of a few thousands and above. Therefore our particular goal is to fill the gap between ML decoding and iterative procedures by designing new efficient algorithms for RM codes.

2 The idea of the algorithm

2.1 Code construction

For brevity, below we use notation $\left\{ \begin{smallmatrix} m \\ r \end{smallmatrix} \right\}$ for codes $RM(r, m)$. It is well known [8] that RM codes can be designed by repetitive employment of the Plotkin $(\mathbf{u}, \mathbf{u} + \mathbf{v})$ construction. Here the original block $(\mathbf{u}, \mathbf{u} + \mathbf{v}) \in \left\{ \begin{smallmatrix} m \\ r \end{smallmatrix} \right\}$ is represented by two subblocks $\mathbf{u} \in \left\{ \begin{smallmatrix} m-1 \\ r \end{smallmatrix} \right\}$ and $\mathbf{v} \in \left\{ \begin{smallmatrix} m-1 \\ r-1 \end{smallmatrix} \right\}$. Now we can specify

50

general $(\mathbf{u}, \mathbf{u} + \mathbf{v})$ construction as

$$\left\{ {m \atop r} \right\} = \left\{ {m-1 \atop r} \right\}, \left\{ {m-1 \atop r} \right\} + \left\{ {m-1 \atop r-1} \right\}, \tag{2}$$

with the same codeword $\mathbf{u} \in \left\{ {m-1 \atop r} \right\}$ taken on both halves. In turn, $\mathbf{u}$ can be split onto two halves taken from $\left\{ {m-2 \atop r} \right\}$ and $\left\{ {m-2 \atop r-1} \right\}$, while $\mathbf{v}$ is split onto vectors taken from $\left\{ {m-2 \atop r-1} \right\}$ and $\left\{ {m-2 \atop r-2} \right\}$. Hence, all codes $\left\{ {m \atop r} \right\}$ can be obtained successively.

On step m, we first take the repetition code $\left\{ {m \atop 0} \right\}$ and full code $\left\{ {m \atop m} \right\}$, while all other codes $\left\{ {m \atop r} \right\}$ are obtained by recursion (2) from the previous step. Thus, any code $\left\{ {m \atop r} \right\}$ can be mapped onto the (m, r)-node of the Pascal triangle. This is schematically shown in Fig. 1 for RM codes of the fourth order. Given any intermediate node (j, s), we move up and left to achieve the node $(j - 1, s - 1)$; or up and right to reach the node $(j - 1, s)$. Note also that we can end our recursion on any level. In the sequel, we terminate our splitting at the nodes $(j, 1)$ (corresponding to biorthogonal codes) or at the nodes $(j, j - 1)$ (corresponding to even-weight codes with $d = 2$).

Now let K_r^m denote the block of k information bits for any $(\mathbf{u}, \mathbf{u} + \mathbf{v}) \in \left\{ {m \atop r} \right\}$. It is also important that recursion (2) splits K_r^m into two subblocks K_r^{m-1} and K_{r-1}^{m-1} that correspond to vectors $\mathbf{u}$ and $\mathbf{v}$ respectively. In this way, the new information strings are split again until we arrive at the end nodes $(j, 1)$ or $(j, j - 1)$. Obviously, there exist a number of "eligible" ways connecting our initial node (m, r) to any end node $(j, 1)$ or $(j, j - 1)$. Thus, any specific codeword can be encoded from (multiple) information strings assigned to the end nodes.

More precise analysis shows that there exist $L_j = \binom{m-j-1}{r-2}$ ways that connect our starting point (m, r) with the left end $(j, 1)$ without entering any end node. Here $j \le m - r + 1$. Similarly, there exist $R_j = \binom{m-j-1}{r-j+1}$ ways that link (m, r) with the right end $(j, j - 1)$ for any $j \le r$. We note also that each way retrieves either $j + 1$ information bits when connected to the end $(j, 1)$ or 2^{j-1} information bits when connected to the end $(j, j - 1)$.

In the sequel, we will use the same recursion in decoding process. Given an output $\mathbf{y} = (\mathbf{y}', \mathbf{y}'')$ with halves $\mathbf{y}'$ and $\mathbf{y}''$, we wish to perform two steps:

1. *combine* $\mathbf{y}'$ and $\mathbf{y}''$ to find $\mathbf{v} \in \left\{ {m-1 \atop r-1} \right\}$.

2. *combine* $(\mathbf{y}', \mathbf{y}'')$ and $(\mathbf{0}, \mathbf{v})$ to find $\mathbf{u} \in \left\{ {m-1 \atop r} \right\}$.

In turn, shorter codes $\left\{ {m-1 \atop r-1} \right\}$ and $\left\{ {m-1 \atop r} \right\}$ will be split further, while actual decoding procedures will be relegated to the end nodes. In the following sections, this procedure is discussed in more detail.

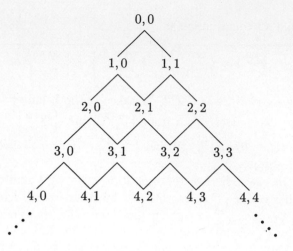

Figure 1: Mapping RM codes of length 16 onto Pascal Triangle

2.2   Channels

Consider now the channel with Gaussian noise $\mathcal{N}(0, \sigma^2)$ and probability density function

$$G(y) = (1/\sqrt{2\pi}\sigma)e^{-y^2/2\sigma^2}. \tag{3}$$

The two symbols 0 and 1 are transmitted as $+1$ and -1. These two take arbitrary real values y at the receiver end with probability densities $G(y + 1)$ and $G(y - 1)$, respectively. In hard decision reception, we arrive at the BSC with transition error probability $p = Q(1/\sigma)$, where

$$Q(x) = \int_x^\infty e^{-y^2/2}dy/\sqrt{2\pi}.$$

In brief, we call these two channels AWGN(σ^2) and BSC(p) respectively.

Below we use the code $\left\{ \begin{smallmatrix} m \\ r \end{smallmatrix} \right\}$ of length $n = 2^m$. Suppose that the codeword $\mathbf{z}$ is transmitted and $\mathbf{y} \in \mathcal{R}^n$ is received. Given any output signal $y \in \mathcal{R}$, we can find the posterior probabilities $p \stackrel{def}{=} p(1|y)$ and $q \stackrel{def}{=} p(0|y)$. By using the Bayes' rule we find that

$$p = e^{-g/2}/(e^{g/2} + e^{-g/2}), \quad q = e^{g/2}/(e^{g/2} + e^{-g/2}), \tag{4}$$

where

$$g = \log(q/p) = 2y/\sigma^2 \tag{5}$$

is the *likelihood* of symbol 0. Finally, we introduce the *spread* (which is the hyperbolic tangent of g)

$$h = q - p = (e^{g/2} - e^{-g/2})/(e^{g/2} + e^{-g/2}) = \tanh(g) \tag{6}$$

52

between the two probabilities q and p.

Given an output vector $\mathbf{y} = (y_1, ..., y_n)$, we can find the quantities q_j, p_j, h_j, and g_j for any position j. In decoding, we will use the original vector $\mathbf{y}$, as well as the corresponding vectors $\mathbf{h} = (h_1, ..., h_n)$ and $\mathbf{g} = (g_1, ..., g_n)$. Note that $\tanh(g)$ is a one-to-one mapping. Therefore the three vectors are interchangeable:

$$\mathbf{y} \Leftrightarrow \mathbf{g} \Leftrightarrow \mathbf{h}. \tag{7}$$

We denote such a decoding $\mathbf{z} = \Psi_r^m(\mathbf{y}) = \Psi_r^m(\mathbf{h}) = \Psi_r^m(\mathbf{g})$, where $\mathbf{z} \in \left\{ {m \atop r} \right\}$ is our decoding result.

In ML decoding, we can first consider the string of hard decision outputs

$$a_j = \begin{cases} 0, & \text{if } y_j \geq 0, \\ 1, & \text{if } y_j < 0, \end{cases} \tag{8}$$

and try to find the most reliable codeword

$$\mathbf{z}^*: \sum_{j:z_j^* \neq a_j} |g_j| \leq \sum_{j:z_j \neq a_j} |g_j|$$

among all codewords $\mathbf{z} \in \left\{ {m \atop r} \right\}$. In our decoding below we also wish to minimize $\sum_{j:z_j \neq a_j} |g_j|$. However, this will be done on the premise that $\mathbf{y}$ is not heavily corrupted by noise. The corresponding threshold levels will be defined for BSC(p) and AWGN(σ^2) in Theorems 4 and 5, respectively.

2.3 Recalculating the probabilities

Let $\mathbf{z}'$ and $\mathbf{z}''$ denote the left- and right halves of any vector $\mathbf{z} \in \left\{ {m \atop r} \right\}$. We also use odd positions $j = 2s - 1$ on the left half and their even counterparts $2s$ on the right one for any $s = 1, ..., n/2$. Similar notations are used for all other vectors, say $\mathbf{y}, \mathbf{h}$ and $\mathbf{g}$. Given any vector $\mathbf{z} = (\mathbf{u}, \mathbf{u} + \mathbf{v})$ at the transmitter end, we can find

$$\mathbf{v} = \mathbf{z}' + \mathbf{z}'' \pmod{2} = (z_1 + z_2, z_3 + z_4, ..., z_{n-1} + z_n).$$

By contrast, at the receiver end we know only the strings $\mathbf{p} = (p_1, ..., p_n)$, $\mathbf{g}$, and $\mathbf{h}$ (see (7)) that define the probability distribution on the transmitted symbols. Our first problem is to find the induced spread $\mathbf{h}_*$ on vectors $\mathbf{v} = \mathbf{z}' + \mathbf{z}''$ given the original spread $\mathbf{h} = (\mathbf{h}', \mathbf{h}'')$ on vectors $\mathbf{z} = (\mathbf{z}', \mathbf{z}'')$.

Lemma 1 *(addition* $\mod 2$*). Vectors* $\{\mathbf{z}' + \mathbf{z}''\}$ $(\mod 2)$ *have the spread*

$$\mathbf{h}_* = \mathbf{h}'\mathbf{h}'' = (h_1 h_2, ..., h_{n-1} h_n).$$

53

Proof. Note that $v_s = z_{2s-1} + z_{2s} \pmod 2$ is equal to 0 iff $z_{2s-1} = z_{2s}$. Therefore we can find $q(v_s) \overset{def}{=} p(v_s = 0 | y_{2s-1}, y_{2s})$. Namely, $q(v_s) = q_{2s-1} q_{2s} + p_{2s-1} p_{2s}$ and $p(v_s) = q_{2s-1} p_{2s} + p_{2s-1} q_{2s}$. Then direct recalculation shows that $q(v_s) - p(v_s) = h_{2s-1} h_{2s}$. □

Given an output $\mathbf{y}$, we now find the probability spreads $\mathbf{h}$ and $\mathbf{h}^*$ on vectors $\mathbf{z}$ and $\mathbf{z}' + \mathbf{z}''$. Then our decoding $\Psi_r^m(\mathbf{h}) = (\mathbf{u}, \mathbf{u} + \mathbf{v})$ can first try to find $\mathbf{v} = \Psi_{r-1}^{m-1}(\mathbf{h}^*)$. Once vector $\mathbf{v}$ is found, we wish to find the remaining block $(\mathbf{u}, \mathbf{u} + \mathbf{v}) + (\mathbf{0}, \mathbf{v}) = (\mathbf{u}, \mathbf{u})$ in the second step of our decoding. Here we need to change symbols z_{2s} on the right half whenever $v_s = 1$. Correspondingly, we need to change the spreads h_{2s} and likelihoods g_{2s} for such symbols. Obviously, symbols $z_{2s} + v_{2s}$ have likelihoods

$$\overline{g}_{2s} = \begin{cases} g_{2s}, & \text{if } v_s = 0, \\ -g_{2s}, & \text{if } v_s = 1. \end{cases}$$

In other words, we change the sign of g_{2s} whenever $v_{2s} = 1$. The result is the string $\overline{\mathbf{g}}(\mathbf{u}, \mathbf{u}) = (\overline{\mathbf{g}}', \overline{\mathbf{g}}'')$, where the left half $\overline{\mathbf{g}}'$ is taken from the original vector $\mathbf{g}$ and equals $\mathbf{g}'$. The string $\overline{\mathbf{g}}(\mathbf{u}, \mathbf{u})$ represents likelihoods for arbitrary vectors $(\mathbf{u}, \mathbf{u})$ with two equal parts. Then we find the likelihoods $\mathbf{g}_*(\mathbf{u})$ given the two estimates $\overline{\mathbf{g}}', \overline{\mathbf{g}}''$.

Lemma 2 *(repetition). A string of likelihoods $(\overline{\mathbf{g}}', \overline{\mathbf{g}}'')$ given on repeated vectors $(\mathbf{u}, \mathbf{u})$ gives the string of likelihoods*

$$\mathbf{g}_*(\mathbf{u}) = \overline{\mathbf{g}}' + \overline{\mathbf{g}}''.$$

for vectors $\mathbf{u}$.

Proof. Obvious. □

Once the likelihoods $\mathbf{g}_*$ are found, we execute decoding $\Psi_r^{m-1}(\mathbf{g}_*)$ that finds $\mathbf{u} \in \left\{ {m-1 \atop r} \right\}$ and $(\mathbf{u}, \mathbf{u} + \mathbf{v})$. We perform both decodings $\Psi_{r-1}^{m-1}(\mathbf{h}_*)$ and $\Psi_r^{m-1}(\mathbf{g}_*)$ in a recursive way. In particular, Ψ_r^{m-1} is split into decodings Ψ_{r-2}^{m-2} and Ψ_{r-1}^{m-2}. Similarly, Ψ_r^{m-1} is split into Ψ_{r-1}^{m-2} and Ψ_r^{m-2}. In this process, we only recalculate spreads $\mathbf{h}$ and likelihoods $\mathbf{g}$ while using new (shorter) codes. Our recursion moves along the edges of Pascal triangle until recalculated vectors $\mathbf{h}$ and $\mathbf{g}$ arrive at the end nodes $(j, 1)$ and $(j, j-1)$. At the end nodes, we perform ML decoding. Now we can describe algorithm Ψ_r^m in a general soft-decision setting.

54

2.4   Recursive decoding for codes $\left\{ {m \atop r} \right\}$

1. Receive vector $\mathbf{y} \in \mathcal{R}^n$. Calculate $\mathbf{g} = \mathbf{g}\,_r^m$ and $\mathbf{h} = \mathbf{h}\,_r^m$ according to (5) and (6). *Call procedure* $\Psi\,_r^m$. Output decoded vector $\mathbf{z}\,_r^m \in \left\{ {m \atop r} \right\}$ and its information set $K\,_r^m$.

2. *Procedure* Ψ_s^j. Input $\mathbf{h}_s^j$ and $\mathbf{g}_s^j$.

2.1. Find $\mathbf{h}_{s-1}^{j-1} = (\mathbf{h}_s^j)' \cdot (\mathbf{h}_s^j)''$. Go to 3 if $s = 2$ or *call* Ψ_{s-1}^{j-1} otherwise.

2.2. Find $\mathbf{g}\,_s^{j-1} = (\overline{\mathbf{g}}_s^j)' + (\overline{\mathbf{g}}_s^j)''$. Go to 4 if $s = j - 2$ or *call* $\Psi\,_s^{j-1}$ otherwise.

2.3. Find $K\,_s^j = K\,_{s-1}^{j-1} \cup K\,_s^{j-1}$ and vector $\mathbf{z}\,_s^j = (\mathbf{z}\,_s^{j-1}, \mathbf{z}\,_s^{j-1} + \mathbf{z}\,_{s-1}^{j-1})$. *Return* vector $\mathbf{z}\,_s^j \in \left\{ {j \atop s} \right\}$ and its information set $K\,_s^j$.

3. Execute ML decoding $\Psi\,_1^{j-1}$. *Return* $\mathbf{z}\,_1^{j-1}$ and $K\,_1^{j-1}$.

4. Execute ML decoding Ψ_{j-2}^{j-1}. *Return* $\mathbf{z}_j^j$ and K_j^j.

Qualitative analysis. Note that increasing the noise power σ^2 reduces the means of the spreads $\mathbf{h}$ and likelihoods $\mathbf{g}$. In particular, it can be shown (see [16]) that for large noise $\sigma \to \infty$, the first two moments Eh and Eh^2 of the random variable $h = \tanh(2y/\sigma^2)$ satisfy the relation

$$Eh \sim Eh^2 \sim \sigma^{-2}. \tag{9}$$

In decoding process, we replace our original decoding $\Psi\,_r^m$ by $\Psi\,_{r-1}^{m-1}$. The latter operates in a less reliable setting with the lower spread $\mathbf{h}_{r-1}^{m-1} = (\mathbf{h}_r^m)' \cdot (\mathbf{h}\,_r^m)''$ versus the original spread $\mathbf{h}\,_r^m$. Then the newly derived means $E(\mathbf{h}\,_{r-1}^{m-1})$ are the componentwise products of the corresponding means $E(\mathbf{h}\,_r^m)'$ and $E(\mathbf{h}\,_r^m)''$. According to (9), this multiplication is equivalent to replacing the original noise power σ^2 by the larger power σ^4. On the other hand, we also increase the relative distance d/n by using a better protected code $\left\{ {m-1 \atop r-1} \right\}$ instead of the original code $\left\{ {m \atop r} \right\}$. Our next decoding $\Psi\,_r^{m-1}$ is performed in a better channel. Here we change the original likelihoods $\mathbf{g}\,_r^m$ for $\mathbf{g}\,_r^{m-1} = (\overline{\mathbf{g}}\,_r^m)' + (\overline{\mathbf{g}}\,_r^m)''$. As a result, our average likelihoods are doubled. This is equivalent to the map $\sigma^2 \Rightarrow \sigma^2/2$. In other words, code $\left\{ {m-1 \atop r} \right\}$ operates on a channel whose noise power is reduced two times. However, we also reduce the relative distance by using a weaker code $\left\{ {m-1 \atop r} \right\}$ instead of $\left\{ {m \atop r} \right\}$. In the next section, we present the *quantative* results of decoding performance.

3   Summary of results

We first consider hard decision reception on the channel $BSC(p)$ with transition error probability $p = (1 - h)/2$.

Theorem 3 *Recursive decoding of codes $\left\{ \begin{smallmatrix} m \\ r \end{smallmatrix} \right\}$ used on a $BSC(p)$, gives the output bit error probability $\alpha \leq Q(\mu)$, where*

$$\mu = 2^{(m-r)/2} h^{2^{r-1}} / \sqrt{1 - h^{2^r}}, \quad p = (1 - h)/2. \tag{10}$$

We then consider the asymptotic capacity of recursive algorithms for long codes $\left\{ \begin{smallmatrix} m \\ r \end{smallmatrix} \right\}$ as $m \to \infty$. To obtain $\alpha \to 0$, we need to get $\mu \to \infty$, in which case $2^{(m-r)/2} h^{2^{r-1}} \to \infty$. In turn, this defines the decoding domain. We consider separately low-rate codes of fixed order r and those of fixed rate R. The latter implies that $r/m \to 0.5$. Let c be any constant exceeding $\ln 2$.

Theorem 4 *For $m \to \infty$, recursive decoding of codes $\left\{ \begin{smallmatrix} m \\ r \end{smallmatrix} \right\}$ corrects most error patterns of weight:*

$$t \leq \begin{cases} n(1 - (cm/d)^{1/2^r})/2, & \text{if } r = const, \\ d(\ln d - \ln 2m)/2, & \text{if } 0 < R < 1. \end{cases} \tag{11}$$

with decoding complexity order $n \min(r, m - r)$.

Note that for fixed code rate R, the latter estimate is almost twice the bound $d \ln d/4$ known for majority decoding. For low-rate codes of fixed order r we correct almost $n/2$ errors. Here we reduce the former residual term (1) $h_m = 1 - 2t/n$ of majority decoding to its square $h = (cm/d)^{1/2^r}$. For $r = 2$, this new term coincides with the one derived in [13]. We note also that this threshold h is now obtained for all orders r and is achieved with a lower complexity order $n \min(r, m - r)$ due to recursive decoding.

Our next goal is to show that this residual term h essentially limits the noise power σ^2 that can be sustained on the $BSC(p)$ with $p = Q(1/\sigma)$. We wish to find the maximum order σ^2 that gives the output error probability $\alpha \to 0$. In particular, $\sigma^2 \to \infty$ if $R \to 0$. In this case $p = Q(1/\sigma) \simeq (1 - \sqrt{2/\pi}/\sigma)/2$. Then correcting most error patterns of relative weight $p = (1 - h)/2$ allows us to successfully transmit up to the threshold $\sigma^2 = 2/(\pi h^2)$. Therefore our spread $h = (cm/d)^{1/2^r}$ obtained in Theorem 4 corresponds to the noise power $\sigma^2 = 2(d/cm)^{1/2^{r-1}}/\pi$. This is $(d/cm)^{1/2^r}$ times more than the noise acceptable by majority decoding.

On the negative side, ML decoding executed for the best codes of rate $R \to 0$ allows to obtain $\sigma^2 \to 1/(2R \ln 2)$ according to the Shannon theorem. For RM codes of low rate $R \sim (\log n)^r/n$, this best decoding raises σ^2 to the order of $n/(\log n)^r$, while our case yields a much smaller order of $(n/\log n)^{1/2^{r-1}}$ for any $r > 1$.

56

Our next issue is to consider the performance of recursive decoding on AWGN channels by using soft decision likelihoods **g**. Given any output bit error rate $\alpha < 1/2$, we compare the corresponding noise powers σ_s^2 and σ_h^2 that sustain this probability in soft and hard decision decoding. The corresponding transition error probabilities $p_s = Q(1/\sigma_s)$ and $p_h = Q(1/\sigma_h)$ are called α-*sustainable*.

Theorem 5 *Given any output bit error probability α, soft decision recursive decoding of long codes $\left\{ \begin{smallmatrix} m \\ r \end{smallmatrix} \right\}$ of fixed order r increases $\pi/2$ times α-sustainable noise power of hard decision decoding:*

$$\sigma_s^2/\sigma_h^2 \to \pi/2, \quad m \to \infty. \tag{12}$$

Soft decision decoding of long codes $\left\{ \begin{smallmatrix} m \\ r \end{smallmatrix} \right\}$ of fixed code rate R increases $4/\pi$ times α-sustainable transition error probability of hard decision decoding:

$$p_s/p_h \to 4/\pi, \quad m \to \infty. \tag{13}$$

The above theorem shows that for long low-rate RM codes we can gain $10 \log_{10}(\pi/2) \approx 2.0$ dB over hard decision decoding for any output error rate α. For fixed code rate R the situation is different. It turns out that $\sigma_s^2/\sigma_h^2 \to 1$ as $m \to \infty$. Practically, for medium and high rates, soft-decision decoding brings only a small gain over its hard decision counterpart. However, according to (13), even in this case, we increase $4/\pi$ times the maximum Hamming weight of correctable error patterns.

The following corollary concerns the Euclidean weights of error patterns correctable by our algorithm. We show that for fixed r we exceed the bounded distance decoding weight $\sqrt{d}$ more than $2^{r/2}$ times. For fixed code rate R, we have a similar increase and outperform bounded distance decoding $2^{r/2}/\sqrt{m \ln 2}$ times.

Corollary 6 *For $m \to \infty$, soft decision recursive decoding of codes $\left\{ \begin{smallmatrix} m \\ r \end{smallmatrix} \right\}$ corrects virtually all error patterns of Euclidean weight:*

$$\rho \leq \sqrt{n}(d/2m)^{1/2^r}, \qquad if \ r = const, \tag{14}$$

$$\rho \leq \sqrt{n/m \ln 2}, \qquad if \ 0 < R < 1. \tag{15}$$

4 Comparison and analysis

In Table 1 we compare the asymptotic performance of the newly developed algorithms with both the majority decoding and former recursive algorithms. This comparison is done for hard and soft decision decoding of low-rate codes of fixed order r and for codes of fixed rate R. Low-rate codes must correct almost $n/2$ errors to approach channel capacity of the BSC. Therefore we use the residual term $h = 1 - 2t/n$ in our comparisons for low-rate codes. We note that before it was only proved that recursive decoding does provide bounded distance capacity $d/2$. By contrast, now both terms h and h_m (known for recursive and majority decoding) tend to 0. More to the point, the newly derived h grows as the square of h_m. For soft decision decoding of low rate codes we use the squared Euclidean distance ρ^2. Again, the newly derived distance ρ^2 surpasses the one known for majority decoding.

Finally, for medium code rates R we use the threshold weight t, for which decoding still corrects most error patterns. In this case, we double decoding capacity of the former algorithms as seen from Table 1.

Table 1. Comparison of decoding algorithms for $\left\{ \begin{smallmatrix} m \\ r \end{smallmatrix} \right\}$ codes.

Decoding capacity	Majority Decoding	Former Recursive	New Recursive
Hard decision, h for fixed r	$(m/n)^{1/2^{r+1}}$	$d/2$	$h \sim (m/n)^{1/2^r}$
Soft decision, ρ^2 for fixed r	$(n/m)^{1/2^{r+1}}\sqrt{n}$	$\sqrt{d}$	$(n/m)^{1/2^r}\sqrt{n}$
Hard decision, t for fixed R	$d\ln d/4$	$d/2$	$d\ln d/2$

On the other hand, we wish to compare new algorithms with the ones known for other classes of codes. In this regard, bounded distance decoding of BCH codes or their duals $\text{BCH}^\perp$ is of particular interest. Below in Table 2 we first compare asymptotic code distances of RM codes versus BCH codes and their duals $\text{BCH}^\perp$ for low, medium, and high rates R. For RM codes we also list the corresponding orders r. This comparison shows that RM codes have much weaker asymptotic. As a result, correcting only $d/2$ errors in BCH codes still outperforms the capacity $d\ln d/2$ obtained for recursive decoding of RM codes. By contrast, for low rates recursive decoding of RM codes is superior. Even bounded-distance decoding of codes $\text{BCH}^\perp$ would[1] correct only about $n/4$ errors instead of almost $n/2$ errors corrected by RM codes.

Table 2. Asymptotic distances of RM and BCH codes.

Rate R	low R	medium R	high R
Order r	fixed r	$r = m/2$	fixed $m - r$
Distance d of $\left\{ \begin{smallmatrix} m \\ r \end{smallmatrix} \right\}$	$n/2^r$	$\sqrt{n}$	2^r
Distance d of BCH, $\text{BCH}^\perp$	$\frac{n}{2} - k\sqrt{n}/m$	$\sim n/\ln n$	$\sim m^{r-1}/r!$

[1] Such a decoding is not known yet for codes $\text{BCH}^\perp$.

From the practical standpoint, we develop an analytical technique that gives tight output bit error rates for our decoding. When these bounds were checked against simulation results for some codes, both turned out to be almost identical. Below in Tables 3 and 4, we compare bit error rates (BER) obtained by applying recursive and majority decoding to codes $\left\{\begin{smallmatrix} 9 \\ 4 \end{smallmatrix}\right\}$ and $\left\{\begin{smallmatrix} 9 \\ 3 \end{smallmatrix}\right\}$ of length 512. In Table 3 we also exhibit the results of computer simulation presented for code $\left\{\begin{smallmatrix} 9 \\ 4 \end{smallmatrix}\right\}$ in [14]. Here, however, block error probabilities were used in recursive decoding.

Finally, the last row in Tables 3 and 4 represents a refined version of recursive decoding. This improvement uses the fact that recursive decoding gives different error rates at different end nodes. In particular, the worst error rates are obtained on the leftmost node $(m - r + 1, 1)$, and the next worst results are obtained at the node $(m - r, 1)$. This asymmetrical performance can be justified by our qualitative analysis given above. We can see that the leftmost end node operates at the highest noise power σ^{2^r}.

The next important observation is to set the corresponding information bits as zeros. In this way we arrive at the subcodes of the original code $\left\{\begin{smallmatrix} m \\ r \end{smallmatrix}\right\}$ obtained by eliminating only a few least protected information bits. This gives a substantial improvement to recursive algorithms as seen from Tables 3 and 4. Also, it turned out that unlike iterative algorithms, such a recursion gives block error probabilities comparable with the corresponding BER. In particular, the algorithm refined for the code $\left\{\begin{smallmatrix} 9 \\ 4 \end{smallmatrix}\right\}$ gives block error probabilities 0.2, 0.02, and $2 \cdot 10^{-4}$ at 2, 3, and 4 dB, respectively. This part of the work is performed jointly with K. Shabunov and will be reported separately in more detail.

Table 3. Decoding performance for code $\left\{\begin{smallmatrix} 9 \\ 4 \end{smallmatrix}\right\}$.

SNR (dB)	2	3	4	5
Recursive [14]	0.9	0.5	0.2	0.015
Majority [16]	0.3	0.15	0.1	0.01
Recursive (new)	0.2	0.03	0.002	
BER for subcodes	0.05	0.003	$3 \cdot 10^{-5}$	

Table 4. Decoding performance for code $\left\{\begin{smallmatrix} 9 \\ 3 \end{smallmatrix}\right\}$.

SNR (dB)	2	3	4	5
Majority [16]	0.3	0.2	0.1	0.02
Recursive (new)	0.2	0.05	0.007	
BER for subcodes	0.02	0.0015	$5 \cdot 10^{-5}$	

5   Concluding remarks

It is interesting to compare the presented recursive algorithm with a few former variants considered in [4], [7], and [14]. Our algorithm is similar to these

59

especially to the one presented in [4]. As a result, we achieve the same complexity order of $n \min(r, m - r)$. However, there are three differences. Firstly, the former papers concerned bounded-distance decoding. We set a different problem and find the actual decoding domain and decoding capacity of recursive algorithms. Secondly, in this new setting we use probabilistic tools and explicitly recalculate posterior probabilities while moving along the edges of Pascal triangle. Due to a different setting, the former results used reliability approximations. Lastly, we use a different stopping rule and terminate any branch after reaching the codes $\left\{ \begin{smallmatrix} j \\ 1 \end{smallmatrix} \right\}$ of the first order. The algorithms considered before were terminated at codes $\left\{ \begin{smallmatrix} j \\ 0 \end{smallmatrix} \right\}$ of order zero. By using probabilistic tools described above, one can prove that using codes of order zero gives asymptotic performance similar to that of majority decoding. Therefore our increase in decoding capacity mostly results from a different stopping rule. It is also worth noting that decoding performance can be further improved by applying code constructions different from the Plotkin construction considered in this paper.

Acknowledgment. The author wishes to thank K. Shabunov for a substantial work performed on refining the algorithms presented in this paper.

References

[1] G.D. Forney, "Coset codes-part II: Binary lattices and related codes," *IEEE Trans. Info. Theory*, vol. 34, pp. 1152-1187, 1987.

[2] R.G. Gallager, *Low-density Parity Check Codes.* Cambridge, MA: M.I.T. Press, 1963.

[3] W.C. Gore, "The equivalence of L-step generalization and a Reed decoding procedure," *IEEE Trans. Info. Theory*, vol. IT-15, pp. 184–186, 1969.

[4] G.A. Kabatyanskii, "On decoding of Reed-Muller codes in semicontinuous channels," *Proc. 2nd Int. Workshop "Algebr. and Combin. Coding Theory"*, Leningrad, USSR, 1990, pp. 87-91 (in Russian).

[5] V.D. Kolesnik, "Probabilistic decoding of majority codes," Probl. Info.Transmission, vol. 7, no. 3, pp. 193-200, 1971.

[6] R.E. Krichevskiy, "On the Number of Reed-Muller Code Correctable Errors," *Dokl. Soviet Acad. Sciences*, vol. 191, pp. 541-547, 1970.

[7] S.N. Litsyn, "On decoding complexity of low-rate Reed-Muller codes," *Proc. 9th All-Union Conf. on Coding Theory and Info. Transmission*, Part 1, Odessa, USSR, pp. 202-204, 1988 (in Russian).

[8]   F.J. MacWilliams and N.J.A. Sloane, *The Theory of Error-Correcting Codes*, North Holland, Amsterdam, 1977.

[9]   J.L. Massey, *Threshold decoding.* Cambridge, MA: M.I.T. Press, 1963.

[10]   A.H. Murad and T.E. Fuja, "Distributed decoding of cyclic block codes using a generalization of majority-logic decoding," *IEEE Trans. Info. Theory*, vol. 39, pp. 1535-1545, 1993.

[11]   I.S. Reed, "A class of multiple error correcting codes and the decoding scheme," *IEEE Trans. Info. Theory*, vol. IT-4, pp.38-49, 1954.

[12]   L.D. Rudolph, "Threshold decoding of cyclic codes," *IEEE Trans. Info. Theory*, vol. IT-15, pp.590-592, 1969.

[13]   V. Sidel'nikov and A. Pershakov, "Decoding of Reed-Muller Codes with a Large Number of Errors," *Probl. Info. Transmission*, vol. 28, pp. 80-94, 1992.

[14]   G. Schnabl and M. Bossert, "Soft-Decision Decoding of Reed-Muller Codes as Generalized Multiple Concatenated Codes," *IEEE Trans. Info. Theory*, vol. 41, pp. 304-308, 1995.

[15]   H. Vater, "Binary coding by integration of polynomials," *IEEE Trans. Info. Theory*, vol. 40, pp. 1417-1424, 1994.

[16]   I. Dumer and R. Krichevskiy, "Soft decision majority decoding of Reed-Muller codes," to appear in *IEEE Trans. Info. Theory*.

Modified Generalized Weighted Sum Codes for Error Control

Peter Farkaš *, *Member IEEE* and John Baylis †

Abstract

In [1] a new family of error detection codes called Weighted Sum Codes was proposed. In [2] it was noted, that these codes are equivalent to lengthened Reed Solomon Codes, and shortened versions of lengthened Reed Solomon codes respectively over $GF(2^{(h/2)})$. It was also shown that it is possible to use these codes for correction of one error in each codeword over $GF(2^{(h/2)})$. In [3] a generalization of Weighted Sum Codes was done which allows the correction of more than two erasures in each codeword, and a large family of codes with relatively long codeword length and a simple decoding procedure were introduced, based on the Generalized Weighted Sum Codes. In the present paper we present a new family of error – correcting modified generalized weighted sum codes with higher code rates than ordinary Reed Solomon codes over the same finite fields.

1 Introduction

In most communication networks, data are organized in units of fixed length, so - called packets. Because of channel impairments a transmitted packet can be received in error or might be completely lost. For example, in ATM networks the second case is prevalent. Error control codes can be used to protect the transmitted information. Taking into account the explosive growth of Internet, and possible data services in next generations of mobile systems, it seems that not only reliable transport services, but also partially reliable transport services could be advantageous in such applications [6]. These are the main motivation factors for development of error control codes presented

---

*P. Farkaš is with the Department of Telecommunications, Faculty of Electrical Engineering and Information Technology, Slovak Technical University in Bratislava, Ilkovičova 3, 812 19 Bratislava, Slovakia, IEEE Log Number 3495181,e-mail:farkas@ktl.elf.stuba.sk

†J. Baylis is with the Department of Mathematics, Statistics & Operational Research, faculty of Science & Mathematics, The Nottingham Trent University, Burton Street, Nottingham NG1 4BU, e-mail:jbaylis@maths.ntu.ac.uk

in this paper. In Section II a brief review of Weighted Sum Codes is given. In Section III t - information error correcting codes are presented. In Section IV a class of single error correcting codes is introduced. In Section V a similar class of conditionally double error correcting codes is introduced. In Section VI some remarks on possible applications of the presented codes are given. In Section VII are some concluding remarks.

2 Weighted Sum Codes

A new family of codes that use polynomial arithmetic and process $h/2$ bit symbols was introduced in [1]. The next part is shortened description of these codes, called Weighted Sum Codes (WSC). We will use first the original formulations, terminology, and symbols from [1] (subindexed uppercase letters refer to symbols $h/2$ bits long).

After transmitting n symbols of data Q_i the sender transmits parity symbols, P_1 and P_0 (in that order). The sender chooses P_1 and P_0 to obey the equations:

$$P_1 = \sum_{i=0}^{n-1} W_i \otimes Q_i \, mod M \tag{1}$$

$$P_0 = P_1 \oplus \sum_{i=0}^{n-1} Q_i \tag{2}$$

where the multiplication ($\otimes$) and addition ($\oplus$) are of two $h/2$ bit polynomial M of degree $h/2$. The W_i always go through a maximal length sequence, including all possible $2^{(h/2)}$ symbols except for 0 and 1.

In [2] the same WSC codes were described using finite fields. Primitive polynomial M can be used for generation of all nonzero elements of $GF(2^{(h/2)})$ using (11) of [1]. In WSC-1 code with maximal length of code words:

$$W_0 = \alpha, \ W_1 = \alpha^2, \cdots, W_{n-1} = \alpha^{(2^{h/2-2})} \tag{3}$$

where α is the primitive element of $GF(2^{(h/2)})$.

The second variant WSC-2 uses in (1) and (2) of [1] weights W_i defined by

$$W_i = [i + 2] \, mod M \tag{4}$$

except 1 and 0, with $[j]$ being the polynomial representation of the integer j. Because W_i go through a maximal length sequence, we have again all nonzero elements of $GF(2^{(h/2)})$ except 1.

It is obvious that these codes are equivalent to lengthened Reed Solomon codes (RS codes) over $GF(2^{(h/2)})$ with a control matrix $\mathbf{H}$

$$\mathbf{H} = \begin{bmatrix} \alpha^{(2^{h/2-2})} & \alpha^{(2^{h/2-3})} & \cdots & \alpha & 1 & 0 \\ 1 & 1 & \cdots & 1 & 1 & 1 \end{bmatrix} \tag{5}$$

If the number of data symbols in the code word of the weighted sum code is less than k, then these codes are equivalent to shortened RS codes, and the $\mathbf{H}$ can be obtained by deleting the columns corresponding to the unused coordinates of code words over $GF(2^{(h/2)})$. Reordering of columns of $\mathbf{H}$ leads to equivalent code [4]. The receiver gets potentially corrupted versions P_i, Q_i, which we denote as $\hat{Q}_i, \hat{P}_i$. As far as combination of error detection capabilities and implementation complexity are concerned, in [1] it was concluded, that WSC codes outperform CRC codes, Fletcher checksum, Internet checksum and XTP-CXOR.

3 t - Information - Error Correcting Codes

One form of the Generalized Weighted Sum Codes constructed over finite fields $GF(q)$ in [3] possess the $\mathbf{H}$ matrix (6) where $\mathbf{I}$ is an identity submatrix and α is a primitive element of the finite field $GF(q)$.

$$\mathbf{H} = \begin{bmatrix} 1 & \cdots & 1 & 1 & 1 & 1 & 1 & 0 & 0 & \cdots & 0 \\ \alpha^{(q-2)} & \cdots & \alpha^3 & \alpha^2 & \alpha^1 & \alpha^0 & 0 & 1 & 0 & \cdots & 0 \\ \vdots & \vdots\ \vdots & \vdots & \vdots & \vdots & \vdots & \vdots & \vdots & \ddots & \vdots \\ \alpha^{(q-2)(2t-1)} & \cdots & \alpha^{3(2t-1)} & \alpha^{2(2t-1)} & \alpha^{2t-1} & \alpha^0 & 0 & 0 & \cdots & 0 & 1 \end{bmatrix} = [\mathbf{A}\,\mathbf{I}] \tag{6}$$

In general the matrix defined above will have sets of $2t$ dependent columns so the minimum distance of the linear code it defines is at most $2t$, and the code is therefore not t - error - correcting. However, it does have the slightly weaker property defined below:

Definition:

A code is called $t - information - error - correcting$ if it can correct all instances of up to t errors per received word, provided that no errors occur in the check symbols.

The code defined by (6) has this property. To see this, note that any $2t$ columns of $\mathbf{A}$ form a Vandermonde matrix [5], so these columns are independent. Now consider the set of all error patterns of weight at most t in which all the non-zero components are in the first $q - 1$ symbols (the information symbols). If any two of these error patterns have the same syndrome there are two distinct linear combinations of t columns of $\mathbf{A}$ which are the same, and hence a linear combination of $2t$ columns equal zero. This contradicts the Vandermonde property of $\mathbf{A}$.

Hence the error patterns described above may all be chosen as coset leaders, so that all received words with these errors are correctly decoded. The error correction may be done via a syndrome look-up table or by solving the set of syndrome equations. If Y_i denotes the magnitude of the ith error and X_i is its locator, these equations are:

$$S_0 = Y_1 + Y_2 + \cdots + Y_t$$

$$S_1 = \sum_{i=1}^{t} Y_i X_i \qquad (7)$$

$$S_{2t-1} = \sum_{i=1}^{t} Y_i X_i^{2t-1}$$

Here, error Y_i occurs in the position i corresponding to the entry α^i in row 2 of $\mathbf{H}$, so X_i is just the field element α^i.

The codes introduced in [3] for erasure correction can have $\mathbf{H}$ matrices of the following form:

$$\mathbf{H} = [\mathbf{A} \cdots \mathbf{A} \mathbf{I}] \qquad (8)$$

where the $\mathbf{A}$ submatrix can be repeated more than once. These codes cannot be used for error correction because the position of the errors cannot be evaluated exactly from similar control equations as (8). In next Section a modification is introduced which overcomes this disadvantage and a class of single error correcting codes is introduced.

4 Single Error Correcting Codes

A new family of codes which allow the correction of one error in each codeword can be described using the following $\mathbf{H}$ matrix:

$$\mathbf{H} = \left[\begin{array}{cccccc} \mathbf{A} & \mathbf{A} & \mathbf{A} & \cdots & \mathbf{A} & \cdots & \mathbf{A} \\ \bar{\mathbf{0}} & \bar{\mathbf{a}}_0 & \bar{\mathbf{a}}_1 & \cdots & \bar{\mathbf{a}}_j & \cdots & \bar{\mathbf{a}}_{q-2} \end{array} \ \ \mathbf{I} \right] = [\mathbf{B} \mathbf{I}] \qquad (9)$$

where the vectors: $\bar{\mathbf{0}} = (0,0,\cdots,0), \bar{\mathbf{a}}_0 = (1,1,\ldots,1), \bar{\mathbf{a}}_1 = (\alpha,\alpha,\ldots,\alpha), \bar{\mathbf{a}}_2 = (\alpha^2,\alpha^2,\ldots,\alpha^2),\ldots, \bar{\mathbf{a}}_{q-2} = (\alpha^{q-2},\alpha^{q-2},\ldots,\alpha^{q-2})$ all have $q-1$ coordinates and $\mathbf{A}$ is:

$$\mathbf{A} = \left[\begin{array}{cccccc} 1 & \cdots & 1 & 1 & 1 & 1 \\ \alpha^{q-2} & \cdots & \alpha^3 & \alpha^2 & \alpha^1 & \alpha^0 \end{array} \right] \qquad (10)$$

or the positions of the vectors $\bar{\mathbf{a}}_i$ may be permuted freely, so that, for example:

66

$$H = \begin{bmatrix} \mathbf{A} & \mathbf{A} & \cdots & \mathbf{A} & \cdots & \mathbf{A} & \mathbf{A} \\ & & & & & & & \mathbf{I} \\ \bar{\mathbf{a}}_{q-2} & \bar{\mathbf{a}}_{q-3} & \cdots & \bar{\mathbf{a}}_j & \cdots & \bar{\mathbf{a}}_0 & \bar{\mathbf{0}} \end{bmatrix} \tag{11}$$

or:

$$H = \begin{bmatrix} \mathbf{A} & \mathbf{A} & \cdots & \mathbf{A} & \cdots & \mathbf{A} & \mathbf{A} \\ & & & & & & & \mathbf{I} \\ \bar{\mathbf{a}}_1 & \bar{\mathbf{a}}_0 & \cdots & \bar{\mathbf{a}}_j & \cdots & \bar{\mathbf{a}}_{q-2} & \bar{\mathbf{0}} \end{bmatrix} \cdots \tag{12}$$

Theorem 1: The codes given by (9) are one error correcting.

Proof: If the error has occurred in an information position then the syndromes for the code defined by (9) are:

$$S_0 = Y_1 \tag{13}$$
$$S_1 = Y_1 \alpha^i \tag{14}$$
$$S_2 = Y_1 \alpha^j \tag{15}$$

It is obvious, that (13) gives the value of the error, (14) determines that the error has occurred in the position corresponding to the locator α^i in one of the submatrices $\mathbf{A}$ and j in (15) determines that the error position is one covered by the vector $\bar{\mathbf{a}}_j$ or if $S_2 = 0$, the error position is covered by vector $\bar{\mathbf{0}}$. Solving these equations we get the needed information about the position and the value of the error:

$$Y_1 = S_0 \tag{16}$$
$$\alpha^i = S_1/S_0 \tag{17}$$
$$\alpha^j = S_2/S_0 \tag{18}$$

If the error has occurred in a control position, then only one syndrome is different from zero and that syndrome determines the position of the error and also the value of the error.

Corollary: Any code matrix having an $\mathbf{H}$ matrix with "permuted" vectors $\bar{\mathbf{0}}, \bar{\mathbf{a}}_0, \bar{\mathbf{a}}_1, \bar{\mathbf{a}}_2$ e. g. (11) or (12) etc. is one error correcting.

Proof: is straightforward.

The "expansion" made in (9) can be continued further:

$$H = \begin{bmatrix} \mathbf{B} & \mathbf{B} & \mathbf{B} & \cdots & \mathbf{B} & \cdots & \mathbf{B} \\ & & & & & & & \mathbf{I} \\ \bar{\mathbf{0}} & \bar{\mathbf{b}}_0 & \bar{\mathbf{b}}_1 & \cdots & \bar{\mathbf{b}}_j & \cdots & \bar{\mathbf{b}}_{q-2} \end{bmatrix} = [\mathbf{CI}] \tag{19}$$

$$H = \begin{bmatrix} \mathbf{C} & \mathbf{C} & \mathbf{C} & \cdots & \mathbf{C} & \cdots & \mathbf{C} \\ & & & & & & & \mathbf{I} \\ \bar{\mathbf{0}} & \bar{\mathbf{c}}_0 & \bar{\mathbf{c}}_1 & \cdots & \bar{\mathbf{c}}_j & \cdots & \bar{\mathbf{c}}_{q-2} \end{bmatrix} = [\mathbf{DI}] \tag{20}$$

and where the vectors $\bar{\mathbf{b}}_i, \bar{\mathbf{c}}_i, \ldots$ etc. have all their components equal to α^i and the length of $\bar{\mathbf{b}}_i$ is $(q-1)q$, the length of the vectors $\bar{\mathbf{c}}_i$ is $(q-1)q^2$ etc.. We will call the codes defined by (9) *squared* or *of exponent 2*, the codes given by (19) *cubed* or *of exponent 3* and codes given by (20) *quadrupled* or *of exponent 4*, and of exponent e for the eth expansion. It is obvious, that such codes exist for any positive integer i, and all such codes can correct one symbol error in a codeword.

The code rate of the new single error correcting codes of exponent e is:

$$R = \frac{(q-1)q^{e-1}}{(q-1)q^{e-1} + e + 1} \tag{21}$$

The code rate is higher than the code rate of ordinary Reed Solomon codes correcting one error over the same field for any $e > 0$. For example in GF(8) the code rate of ordinary RS codes correcting one error is $6/7 \simeq 0.86$ and if $e = 5$, then from (21) $R \simeq 0.9998$. This improvement of code rate has a very small cost of slightly increased decoder complexity. Specifically, in the chosen example it means that the decoder, in order to get the location of the error, must evaluate 4 syndromes more plus 4 divisions in GF(8).

5 Conditionally Double Error Correcting Codes

A similar construction to that proposed in the previous section for one error correcting codes can also be made for double error correcting codes. But as we will see, such codes, in contrast to one error correcting codes, do not correct all combinations of double errors because the control equations set can in some cases fail to have a unique solution. This drawback is the same as in GWSC for multiple erasure correction in [3]. Let us start again with the simplest $\mathbf{H}$ matrix for double error correcting codes of exponent $e = 2$:

$$\mathbf{H} = \begin{bmatrix} \mathbf{A}' & \mathbf{A}' & \cdots & \mathbf{A}' & \cdots & \mathbf{A}' & \\ & & & & & & \mathbf{I} \\ \bar{\mathbf{a}}_0 & \bar{\mathbf{a}}_1 & \cdots & \bar{\mathbf{a}}_j & \cdots & \bar{\mathbf{a}}_{q-2} & \\ \bar{\mathbf{a}}'_0 & \bar{\mathbf{a}}'_1 & \cdots & \bar{\mathbf{a}}'_j & \cdots & \bar{\mathbf{a}}'_{q-2} & \end{bmatrix} = [\mathbf{B}'\mathbf{I}] \tag{22}$$

where $\bar{\mathbf{a}}_0 = (\alpha^0, \alpha^1, \ldots, \alpha^{q-2})$, $\bar{\mathbf{a}}_i$ is the ith left cyclic shift of $\bar{\mathbf{a}}_0$, $\bar{\mathbf{a}}'_i$ is the ith right cyclic shift of $\bar{\mathbf{a}}_0$ and:

$$\mathbf{A}' = \begin{bmatrix} 1 & \cdots & 1 & 1 & 1 & 1 \\ \alpha^{q-2} & \cdots & \alpha^3 & \alpha^2 & \alpha^1 & \alpha^0 \\ \alpha^{2(q-2)} & \cdots & \alpha^6 & \alpha^4 & \alpha^2 & \alpha^0 \\ \alpha^{3(q-2)} & \cdots & \alpha^9 & \alpha^6 & \alpha^3 & \alpha^0 \end{bmatrix} \qquad (23)$$

It can be shown, that the codes given by (22) if they are defined over finite fields with characteristic 2 can correct in most cases double errors in each codeword. If the two errors both occur in the information symbols of a received word, then the system of control equations will have the following form:

$$S_0 = Y_1 + Y_2 \qquad (24)$$

$$S_1 = Y_1\alpha^i + Y_2\alpha^j \qquad (25)$$

$$S_2 = Y_1(\alpha^i)^2 + Y_2(\alpha^j)^2 \qquad (26)$$

$$S_3 = Y_1(\alpha^i)^3 + Y_2(\alpha^j)^3 \qquad (27)$$

$$S_4 = Y_1\alpha^{i+k} + Y_2\alpha^{j+l} \qquad (28)$$

$$S_5 = Y_1\alpha^{i-k} + Y_2\alpha^{j-l} \qquad (29)$$

The solution can in most cases be found in two steps. In the first step determine, if possible, Y_1, Y_2, i and j from (24)-(29). In the second step use Y_1, Y_2, to find, k and l from (28) and (29).

The solutions could be found using the following expressions:

$$\alpha^k = \frac{S_4 + Y_2\alpha^j\alpha^l}{Y_1\alpha^i} \qquad (30)$$

$$\alpha^l = \frac{Y_2\alpha^j}{S_5 + Y_1\alpha^i\alpha^{-k}} \qquad (31)$$

We get the following quadratic equation for α^l:

$$S_5Y_2\alpha^j(\alpha^l)^2 + (S_5S_4 + Y_1{}^2\alpha^{2i} + Y_2{}^2\alpha^{2j})\alpha^l + S_4Y_2\alpha^j = 0 \qquad (32)$$

which can be solved by several standard methods. See for example [5].

Note: From the form of $\mathbf{H}$ in (22) we see that the information symbols are partitioned into $q - 1$ blocks, each of length $q - 1$. i determines the position of the first error within its block and k fixes in which block it is located. Together, i and k fix the exact location of the first error. Similarly j and l locate the second error precisely.

These equations need not have a unique solution, so extending the terminology introduced previously, this code is a *conditionally 2 - information - error - correcting*.

69

The code rate of the new conditionally - double - information - error - correcting code is:

$$R = \frac{(q-1)^2}{(q-1)^2 + 6} \tag{33}$$

Again like in the previous section the code rate is higher in comparison with ordinary RS codes over the same $GF(q)$. For example in $GF(8)$ code rate of RS code correcting 2 errors is $3/7 \simeq 0.43$ and from (33), $R \simeq 0.89$.

The decoding complexity increases only slightly in comparison with RS codes. The disadvantage in comparison with RS codes is that, in some cases the decoding procedure cannot be accomplished correctly.

It can be shown that the equations (24)-(29) only fail to have a unique solution with probability P, which is upper bounded for any q by:

$$P < \frac{1}{q-1} \tag{34}$$

In other words, the probability that step I cannot be completed is given by (34).

6 Possible Application Area of the New Codes

GWSC offer efficient software and hardware implementation as required in many networks. On the other hand in [6], it was shown that provision of reliable transport services in networks which experience loss of packets can be very costly and hence losses up to a certain level might be considered as an alternative approach. In that case, we call the transport service as being partially reliable. Generalized Weighted Sum Codes could find application in such partially reliable transport services. For example in [7] a hybrid ARQ scheme for partially reliable transport services was proposed. The scheme is based on Generalized Weighted Sum Codes (GWSC) which were introduced in [3] and are used for erasure correction. In the ARQ scheme each codeword symbol represents one transmitted packet. The basic idea of the ARQ scheme is, that in contrast to SRARQ only parity symbols P_i on the transmitting side are computed and stored. Corresponding symbols $\prod_i$ are computed and stored on the receiving side. If requested, then the parity symbols from the transmitting side are sent to the receiving side and they are protected in the information part of the next codeword (Fig1). If the parity symbols are received on the receiving side, then the syndromes are calculated using the following equations:

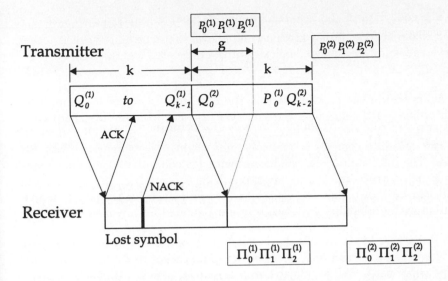

Figure 1: One new hybrid ARQ

$$S_0 = \prod_0 + \hat{P}_0 \tag{35}$$

$$S_1 = \prod_1 + \hat{P}_1 \tag{36}$$

$$S_2 = \prod_2 + \hat{P}_2 \tag{37}$$

The receiving side can from (35) - (37) calculate up to three lost packets (erasures).

The adaptation of that ARQ scheme when applying codes introduced in this paper is straightforward. In case that the positions of the lost packets (symbols) are not known, then the error correcting code could be used e.g. Reed Solomon code or the code presented in this paper.

7 Conclusion

We have proposed one error correcting codes defined over finite fields and shown that these codes can have codewords with lengths $n > (q-1)^e$ for any integer $e > 0$. One simple method for encoding such codes was also illustrated. Further, another large family of similar codes which are conditionally double-information- error-correcting was introduced. A method for decoding such codes, when defined over finite fields with characteristic 2, was described.

71

Both classes of codes exhibit higher code rates in comparison with ordinary Reed Solomon codes if they are constructed over the same finite field. Another advantage is low decoding complexity of the presented codes.

References

[1] A. J. McAuley, "Weighted sum codes for error detection and their comparison with existing codes," *IEEE/ACM Transaction on Networking*, vol. 2, no. 1, pp. 16-22, 1994.

[2] P. Farkaš, "Comments on "Weighted sum codes for error detection and their comparison with existing codes," *IEEE/ACM Transaction on Networking*, vol. 3, no. 2, pp. 222-223, 1995.

[3] P. Farkaš, M. Rakús, "Weight distribution of some weighted sum codes for erasure correction," accepted for publication in 22nd *International Conference - TSP'99*, Brno, Czech Republic, Sept 8 - 10, 1999.

[4] R. E. Blahut, "Theory and practise of error control codes," Reading, MA: Addison-Wesley, 1983.

[5] F. J. McWilliams, N. J. A. Sloane "The theory of error correcting codes", North-Holland, 1993.

[6] R. Marasali, P. D. Amer, P. T. Conrad, "Retransmission-based partially reliable transport service: An analytic model," In *Proc.*, pp. 5c.4.1-5c.4.9, 1996.

[7] P. Farkaš, I. Grellneth, "One new hybrid ARQ," submitted to *6th Symposium on DSP for Communications Systems – DSPCS'2000*, Bratislava, Slovakia, Sept, 2000.

Improved GPT Public Key Cryptosystems

Ernst M. Gabidulin, Alexei V. Ourivski
Moscow Institute of Physics and Technology, Russia

Abstract

A modification of the GPT PKC proposed that uses a rectangular scramble matrix. It was shown that such a modification allows one to keep the size of the public key relatively small (about 13 Kbit) while improving security against attacks on it (the most efficient attack requires 2^{100} operations in $GF(2^{32})$).

A modification of MRD codes, which we called rank-like codes, used for construction of a new PKC based on the GPT PKC. Thorough examination of generalizations of known attacks on the GPT PKC with respect to the new system has been given. We managed to show that high security can be obtained (breaking algorithm requires approximately 2^{80} operations in $GF(2^{29})$) while having the volume of the public key reasonably small (about 19 Kbit).

We also describe quite an efficient technique of increasing transmission rate for the McEliece type PKC based on any family of codes.

1 Introduction

The public key cryptosystem based on rank error correcting codes was proposed in [2, 3].

Let $\mathbf{x} = (x_1, x_2, \ldots, x_n)$ be any vector with coordinates in $GF(q^n)$. The *Rank* norm of $\mathbf{x}$ is defined as the *maximal* number of x_i, which are linearly independent over the base field $GF(q)$. The *Rank* distance between $\mathbf{x}$ and $\mathbf{y}$ is defined as the rank norm of the difference $\mathbf{x} - \mathbf{y}$. The theory of optimal MRD (Maximal Rank Distance) codes is given in [1]. A *generator* matrix G of a MRD code is defined by

$$\mathbf{G} = \begin{bmatrix} g_1 & g_2 & \cdots & g_n \\ g_1^{[1]} & g_2^{[1]} & \cdots & g_n^{[1]} \\ g_1^{[2]} & g_2^{[2]} & \cdots & g_n^{[2]} \\ \vdots & \vdots & \ddots & \vdots \\ g_1^{[k-1]} & g_2^{[k-1]} & \cdots & g_n^{[k-1]} \end{bmatrix}, \tag{1}$$

where $g_1, g_2, \ldots, g_n$ are any set of elements of the extended field $GF(q^n)$ which are linearly independent over the base field $GF(q)$ and $g^{[i]} := g^{q^i}$ means the ith Frobenius power of g.

The GPT cryptosystem is described as follows.

A **Plaintext** is any k-vector $\mathbf{m} = (m_1, m_2, \ldots, m_k)$, $m_s \in GF(q^n)$, $s = 1, 2, \ldots, k$.

73

The **Public key** is a $k \times n$ matrix

$$\mathbf{C_{cr}} = \mathbf{SG} + \mathbf{X}, \qquad (2)$$

where $\mathbf{G}$ is given by Eq. (1), $\mathbf{S}$ is a non singular scramble matrix $\mathbf{S}$ of order k, and $\mathbf{X}$ is a randomly chosen $k \times n$ distortion matrix such that for any plaintext $\mathbf{m}$ the vector $\mathbf{mX}$ has rank norm at most $t_1 < t = (d-1)/2 = (n-k)/2$, where t_1 is a *design* parameter.

The **Private keys** are matrices $\mathbf{S}, \mathbf{G}, \mathbf{X}$ and (explicitly) a fast decoding algorithm of an MRD code.

Encryption: Let $\mathbf{m} = (m_1, m_2, \ldots, m_k)$ be a plaintext. The ciphertext is given by

$$\mathbf{c} = \mathbf{mG_{cr}} + \mathbf{e} = \mathbf{mSG} + (\mathbf{mX} + \mathbf{e}), \qquad (3)$$

where $\mathbf{e}$ is an artificial vector of errors of the rank $t_2 = t - t_1$ or less, randomly chosen and added by the sending party. Note that for any plaintext $\mathbf{m}$ we have

$$\mathrm{Rank}\,(\mathbf{mX} + \mathbf{e}) \leq \mathrm{Rank}\,(\mathbf{mX}) + \mathrm{Rank}\,(\mathbf{e})) \leq t_1 + (t - t_1) = t.$$

Decryption: The legitimate receiver upon receiving $\mathbf{c}$ applies a Fast Decoding Algorithm to obtain $\mathbf{mS}$ and then multiplies it by $\mathbf{S}^{-1}$ to obtain the plaintext $\mathbf{m}$.

J.K. Gibson [4, 5] proposed two kind of attacks on the GPT cryptosystems described above which are efficient for practical values of parameters ($n \leq 30$).

In this paper, we propose two modifications of the GPT cryptosystems to prevent the Gibson attacks.

The paper is organised as follows. In Section 2, Gibson attacks are briefly described. In Section 3, a system using *a rectangular* scramble matrix is described and possible attacks are analysed. In Section 4, extended rank codes are considered and cryptosystems based on those codes are investigated.

2   Gibson Attacks

Linear codes that correct rank errors effectively withstand direct attacks, which try to get a plaintext from a ciphertext. However, matrices describing these codes (both generator and parity check) are highly structured. This seems to be the most weak point of rank codes (from cryptography point of view). J.K. Gibson presented two algorithms that recover a secret key from the public key [4, 5]. Here we give just a short description of them. For further details the reader is referred to papers [4, 5], [3].

2.1   First Gibson Attack

Suppose the distortion matrix $\mathbf{X}$ of the system has *row* rank $r(\mathbf{X}|q) = t_1$ over the base field $GF(q)$ and rank $r(\mathbf{X}|q^n) = s$ over the extended field $GF(q^n)$. Then it can be represented as a product $\mathbf{X} = \mathbf{AB}$, where $\mathbf{A}$ is a $k \times s$ matrix with entries in $GF(q^n)$ whose columns are linearly independent over the same field, and $\mathbf{B}$ is a $s \times n$

matrix with entries in $GF(q^n)$ as well. The j-th column of $\mathbf{X}$ is a linear combination of columns of $\mathbf{A}$ with coefficients from the j-th column of $\mathbf{B}$.

Partition $\mathbf{G}$ into two parts:

$$
\mathbf{G}_1 = \begin{bmatrix} g_1 & g_2 & \cdots & g_k \\ g_1^{[1]} & g_2^{[1]} & \cdots & g_k^{[1]} \\ \vdots & \vdots & \ddots & \vdots \\ g_1^{[k-1]} & g_2^{[k-1]} & \cdots & g_k^{[k-1]} \end{bmatrix}, \quad
\mathbf{G}_2 = \begin{bmatrix} g_{k+1} & g_{k+2} & \cdots & g_n \\ g_{k+1}^{[1]} & g_{k+2}^{[1]} & \cdots & g_n^{[1]} \\ \vdots & \vdots & \ddots & \vdots \\ g_{k+1}^{[k-1]} & g_{k+2}^{[k-1]} & \cdots & g_n^{[k-1]} \end{bmatrix}. \tag{4}
$$

Make the same partition in $\mathbf{X}$ and $\mathbf{B}$: $\mathbf{X} = [\mathbf{X}_1\ \mathbf{X}_2]$, $\mathbf{B} = [\mathbf{B}_1\ \mathbf{B}_2]$. Reduce the public key to the systematic form:

$$
\mathbf{G}_{syst} = (\mathbf{S}\mathbf{G}_1 + \mathbf{X}_1)^{-1}\mathbf{G}_{cr} = [\mathbf{I}_k\ \mathbf{R}], \tag{5}
$$

where $\mathbf{I}_k$ is the identity matrix of order k, $\mathbf{R} = [R_{i,j}]$, $i = 0, 1, \ldots, k-1$, $j = k+1, k+2, \ldots, n$.

Denote $\mathbf{C} = [c_{iv}] = \mathbf{S}^{-1}\mathbf{A}$, $\mathbf{D} = [d_{vj}] = \mathbf{B}_2 - \mathbf{B}_1\mathbf{R}$, $v = 1, 2, \ldots, s$. From (5) we have the matrix equation

$$
\mathbf{G}_1\mathbf{R} = \mathbf{G}_2 + \mathbf{C}\mathbf{D}. \tag{6}
$$

For any i, $0 \le i \le k-1$, raise the i-th row of this equation to the q^{n-i} power. Thus, we get the system of $k(n-k)$ algebraic equations

$$
g_1 R_{0j}^{[n-i]} + g_2 R_{1j}^{[n-i]} + \ldots + g_k R_{k-1,j}^{[n-i]} = g_j + \sum_{v=1}^{s} c_{iv}^{[n-i]} d_{vj}^{[n-i]}, \tag{7}
$$

$i = 0, 1, \ldots, k-1$, $j = k+1, k+2, \ldots, n$, where g_j, c_{iv}, d_{vj} are $(s+1)n$ unknowns.

Let $f_{ij} = c_{ij}^{[n-i]}$, $\mathbf{F}_v = (f_{0v}, f_{1v}, \ldots, f_{k-1,v})$, $\mathbf{D}_{vj} = \text{diag}[d_{vj}^{[n]}, d_{vj}^{[n-1]}, \ldots, d_{vj}^{[n-k+1]}]$. Then we obtain the following matrix system,

$$
\mathbf{g}_1\mathbf{R}_j = g_j\boldsymbol{\eta} + \sum_{v=1}^{s} \mathbf{F}_v\mathbf{D}_{v,j}, \tag{8}
$$

where

$$
\mathbf{R}_j = \begin{bmatrix} R_{0,j}^{[n]} & R_{0,j}^{[n-1]} & \cdots & R_{0,j}^{[n-k+1]} \\ R_{1,j}^{[n]} & R_{1,j}^{[n-1]} & \cdots & R_{1,j}^{[n-k+1]} \\ \vdots & \vdots & \ddots & \vdots \\ R_{k-1,j}^{[n]} & R_{k-1,j}^{[n-1]} & \cdots & R_{k-1,j}^{[n-k+1]} \end{bmatrix},
$$

$\mathbf{g}_1 = (g_1, g_2, \ldots, g_k)$, $\boldsymbol{\eta} = (1, 1, \ldots, 1)$ — k-vector of 1, $j = k+1, k+2, \ldots, n$.

Without loss of generality we can assume that $g_{k+3} = 1$ and $\mathbf{D}_{v,k+3} = \text{diag}[1, \ldots, 1]$, $v = 1, 2, \ldots, s$. Suppose that $s = 1$ (it is just the case of the original GPT system). Then $\mathbf{F}_v = \mathbf{F}_1 = \mathbf{f}$, $\mathbf{D}_{k+3} = \mathbf{I}_k$, $d_{vj} = d_j$. The first three equation of (8) are

$$
\mathbf{g}_1\mathbf{R}_{k+1} = g_{k+1}\boldsymbol{\eta} + \mathbf{f} : \mathbf{D}_{k+1}, \tag{9}
$$

$$
\mathbf{g}_1\mathbf{R}_{k+2} = g_{k+2}\boldsymbol{\eta} + \mathbf{f} : \mathbf{D}_{k+2}, \tag{10}
$$

$$
\mathbf{g}_1\mathbf{R}_{k+3} = g_{k+3}\boldsymbol{\eta} + \mathbf{f}, \tag{11}
$$

Guess a value of d_{k+2}, and $\mathbf{D}_{k+2}$ respectively. If d_{k+2} correctly guessed, then the other unknowns can be computed rather easily using the following calculations.

Equations (10),(11) together give

$$\mathbf{g}_1 = g_{k+2}\mathbf{z} + \mathbf{w}, \quad \mathbf{f} = g_{k+2}\mathbf{r} + \mathbf{s}, \tag{12}$$

where

$$\mathbf{z} = \boldsymbol{\eta}(\mathbf{R}_{k+2} - \mathbf{R}_{k+3}\mathbf{D}_{k+2})^{-1}, \quad \mathbf{w} = -\boldsymbol{\eta}\mathbf{D}_{k+2}(\mathbf{R}_{k+2} - \mathbf{R}_{k+3}\mathbf{D}_{k+2})^{-1},$$
$$\mathbf{r} = \mathbf{z}\mathbf{R}_{k+3}, \qquad\qquad \mathbf{s} = \mathbf{w}\mathbf{R}_{k+3} - \boldsymbol{\eta} -$$

are known vectors, as long as $\mathbf{R}_{k+2} - \mathbf{R}_{k+3}\mathbf{D}_{k+2}$ is non singular.

Combining (12) together with (9), we get

$$g_{k+2}(\mathbf{z}\mathbf{R}_{k+1} - \mathbf{r}\mathbf{D}_{k+1}) = g_{k+1}\boldsymbol{\eta} + \mathbf{s}\mathbf{D}_{k+1} - \mathbf{w}\mathbf{R}_{k+1}, \tag{13}$$

It is a system of k equations in the three unknowns g_{k+1}, g_{k+2}, d_{k+1}. This system is a linear one with respect to g_{k+1}, g_{k+2}, so it has a solution in the only case when three k-vectors $\boldsymbol{\eta}, \mathbf{z}\mathbf{R}_{k+1} - \mathbf{r}\mathbf{D}_{k+1} = \boldsymbol{\mu} - \mathbf{r}\mathbf{D}_{k+1}$, $\mathbf{s}\mathbf{D}_{k+1} - \mathbf{w}\mathbf{R}_{k+1} = \boldsymbol{\nu} + \mathbf{s}\mathbf{D}_{k+1}$ are *linear dependent*. This means that all 3-determinants obtained from corresponding successive coordinates of these vectors must be zero. First determinant is

$$\begin{vmatrix} 1 & 1 & 1 \\ \mu_1 - r_1 d_{k+1}^{[n]} & \mu_2 - r_2 d_{k+1}^{[n-1]} & \mu_3 - r_3 d_{k+1}^{[n-2]} \\ \nu_1 + s_1 d_{k+1}^{[n]} & \nu_2 + s_2 d_{k+1}^{[n-1]} & \nu_3 + s_3 d_{k+1}^{[n-2]} \end{vmatrix} = 0. \tag{14}$$

Denote $d_{k+1}^{[n-2]}$ by y, we obtain from (14) first algebraic equation of degree $q^2 + q$ in y. Similarly, the second determinant gives us a second equation of degree $q^2 + q$ in y. And so on. Hence, we get a system of $k - 2$ equations in the unknown y of degree $q^2 + q$. Solving this system, for example with Euclidean division algorithm, we obtain the unknown d_{k+1}, and from (13) — g_{k+1}, g_{k+2}.

Continuing in the same way, from the fourth equation of (8) we receive g_{k+4}, d_{k+4}, $\mathbf{g}_1$ and $\mathbf{f}$ already known. In a similar way, we obtain the remaining unknowns g_j, d_j, $j = k + 5, \ldots, n$. Gibson's algorithm requires *guessing* a value of d_{k+2}, solving linear equations and solving a system of polynomial equations of degree $q^2 + q$. Thus, the complexity of this algorithm is at least $W_{G1} = O(n^3 q^n)$ arithmetical operations in $GF(q^n)$.

In general case (when s is not 1), the cryptanalyst must guess s unknown quantities $d_{v,k+2}$ (or, what is the same, $\mathbf{D}_{v,k+2}$), $v = 1, \ldots, s$, from $GF(q^n)$ for solving (8). Then he must solve an algebraic system of equations in s unknowns $d_{v,k+1}^{[n-2]}$ of degree $q^{s+1} + q^s + \cdots + q$. Thus, in the binary case the complexity of algorithm is $W_{Gibson1} = O(n^3 2^{sn})$ operations in $GF(2^n)$ in the best for the cryptanalyst case.

The complexity of the first Gibson attack grows exponentially with length n. So it seems to be feasible for reasonable code lengths $n \sim 20 - 30$ and $s \geq 3$.

2.2 Second Gibson Attack

In [5], Gibson presented quite an efficient attack on the GPT system for general case of choosing a distortion matrix. Below we describe only the main points of this attack, so some details are missing.

Note: throughout in this subsection it is assumed that $q = 2$.

First we cite two lemmas stated by Gibson in [5] that are not specific to the GPT PKC, but are being used greatly in this attack, and are of independent interest. The proofs are omitted, only approach to them is outlined.

Let us introduce the following notation. If $\mathbf{M}$ is a matrix over $GF(2^n)$, then $\mathbf{M}^r$, $r > 0$, is formed from $\mathbf{M}$ elementwise. (Notation $\mathbf{M}^{-1}$ always means that it is the inverse of $\mathbf{M}$.)

Note. In the following two lemmas all notations are not related to those in this section elsewhere denoted by the same letters.

Lemma 1 (The rank 1 lemma) *Let* $\mathbf{G}$ *be a* $k \times k$ *matrix over* $GF(2^n)$ *of the form (1) with generating vector* $\mathbf{g}$. *Let* $\mathbf{H}$ *be a* $k \times s$ *matrix over* $GF(2^n)$ *of the same form but with generating vector* h. *Suppose that vector* $[\mathbf{g} \ \mathbf{h}]$ *has independent coordinates over* $GF(2)$. *Let* $\mathbf{X}$ *be a* $k \times s$ *matrix over* $GF(2^n)$ *with* $\mathbf{GX} = \mathbf{H}$. *Then* $\mathbf{X} + \mathbf{X}^2$ *has rank 1, and has no zero elements.*

Proof. The proof is based on the following fact. Suppose $\mathbf{L}$ is the $k - 1 \times k$ matrix of the form (1) with generating vector $\mathbf{g}^2$. Then $\mathbf{L}(\mathbf{X} + \mathbf{X}^2) = \mathbf{0}$. ∎

Note. Matrix $\mathbf{X} + \mathbf{X}^2$ will still have rank 1 under the relaxed constraint that $\mathbf{g}$, but not necessarily $[\mathbf{g} \ \mathbf{h}]$, has independent coordinates over $GF(2)$. In this case $\mathbf{X} + \mathbf{X}^2$ may have zero elements.

Lemma 2 (The matrix update lemma) *Let* $\mathbf{Q}$ *be a* $k \times k$ *non-singular matrix over* $GF(2^n)$, $\mathbf{P} = \mathbf{Q}^{-1}$, *and* $\mathbf{R} = \mathbf{P} + \mathbf{P}^2$. *Suppose* $\mathbf{Q}^*$ *is obtained from* $\mathbf{Q}$ *by adding an* $r + d \times k$ *binary matrix* $\mathbf{B}$ *to the first* $r + d$ *rows of* $\mathbf{Q}$, *and that* $\mathbf{Q}^*$ *is invertible. Let* $\mathbf{P}^* = (\mathbf{Q}^*)^{-1}$ *and* $\mathbf{R}^* = \mathbf{P}^* + \mathbf{P}^{*2}$. *Suppose the row-reduced echelon forms* $\mathbf{E}$ *and* $\mathbf{E}^*$ *of* $\mathbf{R}$ *and* $\mathbf{R}*$ *are given by*

$$\mathbf{E} = \begin{bmatrix} \mathbf{I}_r & \mathbf{X} \\ \mathbf{0} & \mathbf{0} \end{bmatrix} \begin{matrix} r \\ s \end{matrix} \ , \qquad \mathbf{E}^* = \begin{bmatrix} \mathbf{I}_r & \mathbf{X}^* \\ \mathbf{0} & \mathbf{0} \end{bmatrix} \begin{matrix} r \\ s \end{matrix} \ ,$$

where $s = k - r$.

Suppose futher that there is a sequence $\mathbf{Q}_0, \ldots, \mathbf{Q}_m$ *of invertible* $k \times k$ *matrices with* $\mathbf{Q}_0 = Q$ *and* $\mathbf{Q}_m = \mathbf{Q}^*$, *and such that for* $i = 1, \ldots, m$, $\mathbf{Q}_i - \mathbf{Q}_{i-1}$ *is a binary matrix with one non-zero element, and that if* $\mathbf{P}_i = \mathbf{Q}_i^{-1}$ *and* $\mathbf{R}_i = \mathbf{P}_i + \mathbf{P}_i^2$ *then the row-reduced echelon form of* $\mathbf{R}_i$ *is in systematic form with rank* r.

Let $\mathbf{P}_r$ *and* $\mathbf{P}_s$ *denote the first* r *and last* s *columns of* $\mathbf{P}$, *and* $\mathbf{U} = \mathbf{P}_r\mathbf{X} + \mathbf{P}_s$.

Let $\mathbf{B}'_r$ *and* $\mathbf{B}'_d$ *denote the first* r *and last* d *rows of* $\mathbf{B}$.

Let $\mathbf{U}_d$, $\mathbf{X}_d$, $\mathbf{X}_d^*$ *denote the first* d *columns of* $\mathbf{U}$, $\mathbf{X}$, *and* $\mathbf{X}^*$. *Then*

$$\mathbf{L} = \mathbf{I}_d + \mathbf{B}'_d\mathbf{U}_d \ \text{is invertible,}$$

and

$$\mathbf{X}^* = \mathbf{X} + [\mathbf{I}_r \ \mathbf{X}_d^*]\,\mathbf{BU},$$

where

$$\mathbf{X}_d^* = (\mathbf{B}'_r\mathbf{U}_d + \mathbf{X}_d)\,\mathbf{L}^{-1}.$$

77

Proof. The proof is based on the Sherman-Morrison formula for inversion of the sum of an invervtible matrix and matrix of rank 1. ∎

Suppose the public key of the system is in the form $\mathbf{Z} = \mathbf{S}(\mathbf{G} + \mathbf{X})$, where the distortion matrix $\mathbf{X}$ is such that $r(\mathbf{X}|q) = t_1$ and $r(\mathbf{X}|q^n) = s$. (In fact, for the crypt-analyst it doesn't matter in which form the open key is written: either $\mathbf{Z} = \mathbf{SG} + \mathbf{X}$ or $\mathbf{Z} = \mathbf{S}(\mathbf{G} + \mathbf{X})$ since the matrix $\mathbf{S}$ is non singular.) Then any such $\mathbf{X}$ can be represented as $\mathbf{X} = \mathbf{AB}$, where $\mathbf{A}$ is a $k \times t_1$ matrix over $GF(2^n)$ with $r(\mathbf{A}|q) = t_1$ and $r(\mathbf{A}|q^n) = s$, and $\mathbf{B}$, the *column distortion* matrix, is a binary $t_1 \times n$ matrix of full rank t_1. By writing $\mathbf{AB} = \mathbf{ATT}^{-1}\mathbf{B}$, where $\mathbf{T}$ is non-singular binary matrix, $\mathbf{B}$ can always be normalized so that it is in row-reduced echelon form.

The attack proceeds in three stages. We will describe them in reverse order.

Stage 3. Suppose that we do know the column distortion matrix $\mathbf{B}$. Denote $f = n - k - t_1$. Use column permutations to adjust $\mathbf{B}$ to be in the form

$$\mathbf{B} = [\mathbf{B}_k \ \mathbf{I}_{t_1} \ \mathbf{B}_f], \tag{15}$$

where suffices on matrix blocks till the end of this section denote the number of columns the blocks have, and $\mathbf{I_p}$ is the $p \times p$ identity matrix. Use the same permutations to adjust the public key $\mathbf{Z}$, the matrix $\mathbf{G}$ and its generating vector $\mathbf{g}$ according to $\mathbf{B}$.

$$\mathbf{Z} = [\mathbf{Z}_k \ \mathbf{Z}_{t_1} \ \mathbf{Z}_f], \qquad \mathbf{G} = [\mathbf{G}_k \ \mathbf{G}_{t_1} \ \mathbf{G}_f], \qquad \mathbf{g} = [\mathbf{g}_k \ \mathbf{g}_{t_1} \ \mathbf{g}_f].$$

Let $\mathbf{C}$ be an $n \times n - t_1$ binary matrix whose columns form a basis of null space of $\mathbf{B}$, i.e. $\mathbf{BC} = \mathbf{0}$. It is easily seen that

$$
\mathbf{C} = \begin{array}{c} \\ \left[\begin{array}{cc} \mathbf{I}_k & \mathbf{0} \\ \mathbf{B}_k & \mathbf{B}_f \\ \mathbf{0} & \mathbf{I}_f \end{array} \right] \end{array} \begin{array}{c} {\scriptstyle k \quad f} \\ \begin{array}{c} k \\ t_1 \\ f \end{array} \end{array} .
$$

Since $\mathbf{Z} = \mathbf{S}(\mathbf{G} + \mathbf{AB})$ we have

$$\mathbf{ZC} = \mathbf{SGC} = \mathbf{SH},$$

where $\mathbf{H}$ is a $k \times n - t_1$ matrix of the form (1) with generating vector $\mathbf{h}$. Since $\mathbf{C}$ is binary and its columns are independent over $GF(2)$ we obtain that vector $\mathbf{h}$ has linearly independent coordinates over $GF(2)$ (recall that vector $\mathbf{g}$ has rank n over $GF(2)$).

On the other hand

$$\mathbf{ZC} = [\mathbf{Z}_k + \mathbf{Z}_{t_1}\mathbf{B}_k \ \ \mathbf{Z}_{t_1}\mathbf{B}_f + \mathbf{Z}_f] = [\mathbf{Q} \ \ \mathbf{QX}],$$

where $\mathbf{X} = \mathbf{Q}^{-1}(\mathbf{Z}_{t_1}\mathbf{B}_f + \mathbf{Z}_f)$. Comparing the two formulae, it follows that

$$\mathbf{H}_f = \mathbf{H}_k\mathbf{X}, \tag{16}$$

$$\mathbf{Q} = \mathbf{SH}_k, \tag{17}$$

where $\mathbf{H} = [\mathbf{H}_k \ \mathbf{H}_f]$. Actually, equation (16) is simplified version of (6). Without loss of generality, one can assume the first coordinate of $\mathbf{h}_f$ ($\mathbf{h} = [\mathbf{h}_k \ \mathbf{h}_f]$) to be 1 (choose $\mathbf{S}$ appropriately, and adjust $\mathbf{g}$ and $\mathbf{A}$ accordingly). So this equation is solved very easily. From (17), we get $\mathbf{S}$. In fact, it is implicitly assumed that $\mathbf{Q}$ is always non-singular.

Since $\mathbf{h} = \mathbf{gC}$, we get

$$[\mathbf{g}_k\ \mathbf{g}_f] = [\mathbf{h}_k\ \mathbf{h}_f] + \mathbf{g}_{t_1}[\mathbf{B}_k\ \mathbf{B}_f]. \tag{18}$$

This equation does not determine $\mathbf{g}_{t_1}$, so the full vector $\mathbf{g}$ is obtained from it by repeatedly choosing $\mathbf{g}_{t_1}$ at random until $\mathbf{g}$ has all coordinates independent over $GF(2)$. It is suspected that only a few attempts will be needed to find $\mathbf{g}$.

Thus, it is rather easy to find a trapdoor to the system using the public key, provided the column distortion matrix $\mathbf{B}$ is known.

Stage 2. Suppose that we only know the *partial column distortion* matrix $\mathbf{P}$, which consists of the first $k + \tau + 2$ columns of $\mathbf{B}$, whose rank is τ, and τ is the largest possible. Suppose futher that $\tau = t_1$, with columns $k + 1, \ldots, k + t_1$ of $\mathbf{B}$ forming an identity matrix.

Let us remember that from Stage 3 we have $\mathbf{H}_f = \mathbf{H}_k\mathbf{X}$. Applying the rank 1 lemma, $\mathbf{X} + \mathbf{X}^2$ has rank 1 and has no zero coordinates.

Set

$$\mathbf{U} = \mathbf{Q}^{-1}[\mathbf{Z}_{t_1}\ \mathbf{Z}_f] = [\mathbf{U}_{t_1}\ \mathbf{U}_f], \quad \mathbf{V} = \mathbf{U} + \mathbf{U}^2, \quad \mathbf{Y} = \begin{bmatrix} \mathbf{B}_f \\ \mathbf{I}_f \end{bmatrix} \begin{matrix} t_1 \\ f \end{matrix} \quad \overset{f}{}.$$

Then $\mathbf{X} + \mathbf{X}^2 = \mathbf{VY}$ (see equations on Stage 3).

Lemma 3 (The stage 2 lemma) $\mathbf{VY}$ *has rank 1, and has no zero coordinates.*

Calculate $\mathbf{E}$ — the row-reduced echelon form of $\mathbf{V}$. Suppose it takes the form

$$\mathbf{E} = \begin{bmatrix} \mathbf{I}_r & \mathbf{E}_\xi \\ 0 & 0 \end{bmatrix} \begin{matrix} r \\ k - r \end{matrix} \quad ,$$

where $\xi = n - k - r = t_1 + f - r$.
Set

$$\mathbf{D} = \begin{bmatrix} I_{t_1} & \mathbf{B}_f \end{bmatrix} t_1, \qquad \mathbf{W} = \begin{bmatrix} \mathbf{E}_\xi \\ \mathbf{I}_\xi \end{bmatrix} \begin{matrix} r \\ \xi \end{matrix}$$

Set $d = t + 1 - r$.

Theorem 4 (The stage 2 theorem) *The rank of* $\mathbf{DW}$ *is* d.

Proof. The proof considers two cases.
Case 1: $r > t_1$. Let $p = r - t_1$. Let $\mathbf{B}_p$ and $\mathbf{B}_\xi$ denote the first p and last ξ columns of $\mathbf{B}_f$, let $\mathbf{E}'_{t_1}$ and $\mathbf{E}'_p$ denote the first t_1 and last $r - t_1$ rows of $\mathbf{E}_\xi$, and partition $\mathbf{D}$, $\mathbf{W}$, $\mathbf{E}$, $\mathbf{Y}$ as follows.

79

$$\mathbf{D} = \begin{array}{c} \begin{array}{ccc} t_1 & p & \xi \end{array} \\ \left[\begin{array}{ccc} \mathbf{I}_{t_1} & \mathbf{B}_p & \mathbf{B}_\xi \end{array}\right] \begin{array}{c} t_1 \end{array} \end{array} \qquad \mathbf{W} = \begin{array}{c} \;\; \xi \\ \left[\begin{array}{c} \mathbf{E}'_{t_1} \\ \mathbf{E}'_p \\ \mathbf{I}_\xi \end{array}\right] \begin{array}{c} t_1 \\ p \\ \xi \end{array} \end{array}$$

$$\mathbf{E} = \begin{array}{c} \begin{array}{ccc} t_1 & p & \xi \end{array} \\ \left[\begin{array}{ccc} \mathbf{I}_{t_1} & \mathbf{0} & \mathbf{E}'_{t_1} \\ \mathbf{0} & \mathbf{I}_p & \mathbf{E}'_p \\ \mathbf{0} & \mathbf{0} & \mathbf{0} \end{array}\right] \begin{array}{c} t_1 \\ p \\ k-r \end{array} \end{array} \qquad \mathbf{Y} = \begin{array}{c} \begin{array}{cc} p & \xi \end{array} \\ \left[\begin{array}{cc} \mathbf{B}_p & \mathbf{B}_\xi \\ \mathbf{I}_p & \mathbf{0} \\ \mathbf{0} & \mathbf{I}_\xi \end{array}\right] \begin{array}{c} t_1 \\ p \\ \xi \end{array} \end{array}$$

Then

$$\mathbf{EY} = \begin{array}{c} \begin{array}{cc} p & \xi \end{array} \\ \left[\begin{array}{cc} \mathbf{B}_p & \mathbf{B}_\xi + \mathbf{E}'_{t_1} \\ \mathbf{I}_p & \mathbf{E}'_p \\ \mathbf{0} & \mathbf{0} \end{array}\right] \begin{array}{c} t_1 \\ p \\ k-r \end{array} \end{array},$$

so $\mathbf{EY}$ has rank 1 if and only if $p = 1$, i.e. $r = t_1 + 1$, and $\mathbf{E}'_{t_1} + \mathbf{B}_p \mathbf{E}'_p + \mathbf{E}_\xi = \mathbf{0}$. Thus, $\mathbf{B}_p$ is a non-zero column t_1-vector, and $\mathbf{E}'_p$ is a row ξ-vector. Calculation of $\mathbf{DW}$ now shows that $\mathbf{DW} = \mathbf{0}$ as required.

Case 2: $r \le t_1$. Let $q = t_1 - r$. Let $\mathbf{B}'_r$ and $\mathbf{B}'_q$ denote the first r and last q rows of $\mathbf{B}_f$, let $\mathbf{E}_q$ and $\mathbf{E}_f$ denote the first q and last f columns of $\mathbf{E}_\xi$. Then

$$\mathbf{EY} = \left[\begin{array}{c} \mathbf{B}'_r + \mathbf{E}_q \mathbf{B}'_q + \mathbf{E}_f \\ \mathbf{0} \end{array}\right].$$

So $\mathbf{EY}$ has rank 1 if and only if $\mathbf{B}'_r + \mathbf{E}_q \mathbf{B}'_q + \mathbf{E}_f = \mathbf{x}^T \mathbf{y}$, where $\mathbf{x}$ is a non-zero r-vector, and $\mathbf{y}$ is an f-vector. Since $\mathbf{VY}$ has no zero elements, an additional piece of information is that $\mathbf{y}$ has no zero coordinates. Calculation of $\mathbf{DW}$ now gives

$$\mathbf{DW} = \begin{array}{c} \begin{array}{cc} q & f \end{array} \\ \left[\begin{array}{cc} \mathbf{E}_q & \mathbf{E}_q \mathbf{B}'_q + \mathbf{x}^T \mathbf{y} \\ \mathbf{I}_q & \mathbf{B}'_q \end{array}\right] \begin{array}{c} r \\ q \end{array} \end{array}$$

It follows that the rank of $\mathbf{DW}$ is $q + 1 = t_1 - r + 1 = d$. $\blacksquare$

A simple corollary of this theorem is used to determine the columns of $\mathbf{B}_f$ sequentially when the first column is given. Let $\mathbf{b}_j$, $j = 1, \ldots, f$, be the j-th column of $\mathbf{B}_f$, and let $\mathbf{w}_j$, $j = 2, \ldots, f$, be the $d+j-1$-th column of $\mathbf{E}_\xi$. Let $\mathbf{E}_d$ denote the first d columns of $\mathbf{E}_\xi$. Put

$$\mathbf{D}^{(j)} = \begin{array}{c} \begin{array}{ccc} t_1 & 1 & 1 \end{array} \\ \left[\begin{array}{ccc} \mathbf{I}_{t_1} & \mathbf{b}_1 & \mathbf{b}_j \end{array}\right] \begin{array}{c} t_1 \end{array} \end{array} \qquad \mathbf{W}^{(j)} = \begin{array}{c} \begin{array}{cc} d & 1 \end{array} \\ \left[\begin{array}{cc} \mathbf{E}_d & \mathbf{w}_j \\ \mathbf{I}_d & \mathbf{0} \\ \mathbf{0} & 1 \end{array}\right] \begin{array}{c} r \\ d \\ 1 \end{array} \end{array},$$

$j = 2, \ldots, f$.

Corollary 5 (The stage 2 corollary) *The rank of $\mathbf{D}^{(j)} \mathbf{E}^{(j)}$ is d, $j = 2, \ldots, f$.*

Proof. $\mathbf{D}^{(j)}\mathbf{E}^{(j)}$ consists of columns $1, \ldots, d$ and column $d+j-1$ of $\mathbf{DW}$. For $d = 0$ the result is obvious, and for $d > 0$ it follows on observing that the first d columns of $\mathbf{DW}$ are independent, and $\mathbf{DW}$ is of rank d. ∎

Thus, knowing the first $k + t_1 + 2$ columns of $\mathbf{B}$, the stage 2 allows the rest of the columns of $\mathbf{B}$ to be determined.

Stage 1. The input data to stage 1 is just the public key of the system. The aim of this stage is to find partial column distortion matrix $\mathbf{P}$, i.e. the first $k + t_1 + 2$ columns of $\mathbf{B}$. Suppose that $\mathbf{P}$ has rank t_1, and that its $k + 1, \ldots, k + t_1$ columns form an identity matrix.

Let $c = \min(k, n - k)$. The subsequent analysis shows that it is necessary that $c \geq t_1 + 2$. Denote $e = c - t_1$. Normalize $\mathbf{Z}$ with row transformations so that

$$\mathbf{Z} = [\mathbf{Q}_0 \ \mathbf{Z}_{t_1} \ \mathbf{Z}_e \ *], \tag{19}$$

where

$$
\mathbf{Q}_0 = \begin{array}{c} {\scriptstyle c \ \ k-c} \\ \left[\begin{array}{cc} * & \mathbf{0} \\ & \mathbf{I}_{k-c} \end{array} \right] \end{array}
\qquad
\mathbf{Z}_{t_1} = \left[\begin{array}{c} \mathbf{I}_{t_1} \\ \mathbf{0} \\ \mathbf{0} \end{array} \right] \begin{array}{c} t_1 \\ e \\ k-c \end{array}
\qquad
\mathbf{Z}_e = \left[\begin{array}{c} \mathbf{0} \\ \mathbf{I}_e \\ \mathbf{0} \end{array} \right] \begin{array}{c} t_1 \\ e \\ k-c \end{array} ,
$$

and stars denote matrix blocks whose value is immaterial.

Return to the equation of stage 3: $\mathbf{B} = [\mathbf{B}_k \ \mathbf{I}_{t_1} \ \mathbf{B}_e \ *]$. Then

$$
\mathbf{Q} = \mathbf{Z}_k + \mathbf{Z}_{t_1}\mathbf{B}_k = \mathbf{Q}_0 + \begin{array}{c} {\scriptstyle k} \\ \left[\begin{array}{c} \mathbf{B}_k \\ \mathbf{0} \end{array} \right] \begin{array}{c} t_1 \\ k - t_1 \end{array} \end{array} .
$$

This is the key relation which plays a very important role in stage 1.

Similarly to stage 2 make the following calculations:

$$
\mathbf{U} = \mathbf{Q}^{-1}[\mathbf{Z}_{t_1} \ \mathbf{Z}_e], \quad \mathbf{V} = \mathbf{U} + \mathbf{U}^2, \quad \mathbf{Y} = \left[\begin{array}{c} \mathbf{B}_e \\ \mathbf{I}_e \end{array} \right] \begin{array}{c} t_1 \\ e \end{array} , \quad \mathbf{X} = \mathbf{UY}
$$

Also $\mathbf{H} = [\mathbf{H}_k \ \mathbf{H}_e \ *]$. Then $\mathbf{H}_k\mathbf{X} = \mathbf{H}_e$, and $\mathbf{X} + \mathbf{X}^2 = \mathbf{VY}$, so by the rank 1 lemma $\mathbf{VY}$ has rank 1. On the other hand for $\mathbf{R} = \mathbf{Q}^{-1} + (\mathbf{Q}^{-1})^2$ it is easily seen that

$$
\mathbf{VY} = \mathbf{R} \begin{array}{c} {\scriptstyle e} \\ \left[\begin{array}{c} \mathbf{Y} \\ \mathbf{0} \end{array} \right] \begin{array}{c} c \\ k - c \end{array} \end{array} .
$$

Reducing $\mathbf{R}$ to canonical form

$$
\mathbf{E} = \begin{array}{c} {\scriptstyle r \ \ \ \sigma \ \ \ k-c} \\ \left[\begin{array}{ccc} \mathbf{I}_r & \mathbf{E}_\sigma & \mathbf{0} \\ \mathbf{0} & \mathbf{0} & \mathbf{0} \end{array} \right] \begin{array}{c} r \\ k-r \end{array} \end{array} ,
$$

81

we get that the rank of $\mathbf{FY}$ is 1, where $\mathbf{F} = [\mathbf{I}_r \ \mathbf{E}_\sigma]$.

Calculate the row-reduced echelon form $\mathbf{E}_0$ of $\mathbf{R}_0 = \mathbf{Q}_0^{-1} + (\mathbf{Q}_0^{-1})^2$, similarly to $\mathbf{E}$ from $\mathbf{Q}$. Make the following essential assumption that $\mathbf{E}_0$ has the format as $\mathbf{E}$, namely,

$$\mathbf{E}_0 = \begin{array}{c} \\ \end{array} \overset{\begin{array}{ccc} r & \sigma & k-c \end{array}}{\left[\begin{array}{ccc} \mathbf{I}_r & \mathbf{E}_{0\sigma} & \mathbf{0} \\ \mathbf{0} & \mathbf{0} & \mathbf{0} \end{array} \right]} \begin{array}{c} r \\ k-r \end{array} .$$

Assume also that all the conditions of the matrix update lemma hold, so that the matrix $\mathbf{L}$ of the lemma is invertible.

Let $\mathbf{P}_{0r}$ and $\mathbf{P}_{0\sigma}$ denote the first r and the next σ columns of $\mathbf{Q}_0^{-1}$.

Set

$$\mathbf{D}_0 = \overset{\begin{array}{ccc} k & t_1 & e \end{array}}{\left[\begin{array}{ccc} \mathbf{B}_k & \mathbf{I}_{t_1} & \mathbf{B}_e \end{array} \right]} \begin{array}{c} t_1 \end{array} \qquad \mathbf{W}_0 = \overset{\begin{array}{c} \sigma \end{array}}{\left[\begin{array}{c} \mathbf{P}_{0r}\mathbf{E}_{0\sigma} + \mathbf{P}_{0\sigma} \\ \mathbf{E}_{0\sigma} \\ \mathbf{I}_\sigma \end{array} \right]} \begin{array}{c} k \\ r \\ \sigma \end{array} .$$

Theorem 6 (The stage 1 theorem) *The rank of $\mathbf{D}_0\mathbf{W}_0$ is $d = t_1 - r + 1$.*

Proof. The proof is conducted in a similar manner to that of the stage 2 theorem but uses the result of the matrix update lemma. First case considers $r > t_1$, when it shows that $\mathbf{D}_0\mathbf{W}_0 = 0$ and $d = 0$. Case $r \leq t_1$ gives that the rank of $\mathbf{D}_0\mathbf{W}_0$ is d, and that the first d columns of $\mathbf{D}_0\mathbf{W}_0$ are independent. ∎

This theorem was derived on the assumption that columns $k+1, \ldots, k+t_1$ of $\mathbf{B}$ form an identity matrix. Suppose now that $\mathbf{D}_0$ is *any* $t_1 \times k + t_1 + e$ binary matrix of rank t_1 for which the rank of $\mathbf{D}_0\mathbf{W}_0$ is d. Any such $\mathbf{D}_0$ is only determined up to the systematic form, so suppose $\mathbf{D}_0$ is in this form. Then there is a permutation π such that columns $k+1, \ldots, k+t_1$ of $\mathbf{D}_0\pi$ do form an identity matrix. So, if the analysis of stage 1 were conducted using $\mathbf{Z}\pi$ instead of $\mathbf{Z}$, then $\mathbf{D}_0\pi$ would be obtained as the first $k+t_1+e$ columns of $\mathbf{B}\pi$. Hence, $\mathbf{D}_0$ must be the first $k+t_1+e$ columns of $\mathbf{B}$.

In order for the analysis of stage 1 to be valid, it is necessary that $\sigma \geq 1$. Then $c \geq r+1$, so $c = \min(k, n-k) \geq t_1 + 2$ as stated at the beginning of stage 1, and $\sigma \geq d+1$.

To reduce the work to determine the first $k+t_1+2$ columns of $\mathbf{B}$, especially in case $\sigma > d+1$, a simple corollary of stage 1 theorem can be used.

Corollary 7 *Let $\mathbf{P}$ be the partial column distortion matrix, i.e the first $k+t_1+2$ columns of $\mathbf{B}$. Let $\mathbf{W}_{d+1}$ denote the first $d+1$ columns of $\mathbf{W}_0$. Then the rank of $\mathbf{P}\mathbf{W}_{d+1}$ is d.*

Proof. For $d = 0$ the statement is obvious. For $d > 0$ it follows on observing that the first d columns of $\mathbf{D}_0\mathbf{W}_0$ are independent, and that $\mathbf{D}_0\mathbf{W}_0$ has rank d. ∎

Now we describe how these results are applied to breaking the system.

Step 1.

Put $c = \min(k, n - k)$, it is required $c \geq t_1 + 2$.

Choose some non-singular $k \times k$ matrix $\mathbf{T}_1$ and some permutation matrix π_1 so that $\mathbf{T}_1 \mathbf{Z} \pi_1 = [\mathbf{Q}_0 \; \mathbf{Z}_c \; \mathbf{Z}_{n-k-c}]$ (see eq. (19)). It is necessary to record π_1 since the trapdoor found will be that for the system with the public key $\mathbf{Z} \pi_1$.

Calculate the systematic form $\mathbf{E}_0$ of $\mathbf{R}_0 = \mathbf{Q}_0^{-1} + (\mathbf{Q}_0^{-1})^2$. Specifically, write $\mathbf{E}_0 = \pi_2 \mathbf{T}_2 \mathbf{R}_0 \pi_3$, where π_2 and π_3 are some permutations, and $\mathbf{T}_2$ row transformations that do not include permutations. Matrices π_2 and π_3 must be recorded (for the same reasons as for π_1).

The matrix $\mathbf{E}_0$ takes the form

$$
\mathbf{E}_0 = \begin{array}{ccc} \rho & \sigma & k-c \\ \left[\begin{array}{ccc} \mathbf{I}_\rho & \mathbf{E}_{0\sigma} & 0 \\ 0 & 0 & 0 \end{array} \right] & \begin{array}{c} \rho \\ k-\rho \end{array} \end{array} ,
$$

where $1 \leq \rho \leq t_1 + 1$ (if it is not so, then $\mathbf{Z}$ is not the public key of any GPT system complying with restrictions on t_1).

Let $\mathbf{P}_{0\rho}$ and $\mathbf{P}_{0\sigma}$ be the first ρ and the next σ columns of $\mathbf{Q}_0^{-1}$. Set

$$
\mathbf{W}_0 = \begin{array}{c} \sigma \\ \left[\begin{array}{c} \mathbf{P}_{0\rho}\mathbf{E}_{0\sigma} + \mathbf{P}_{0\sigma} \\ \mathbf{E}_{0\sigma} \\ \mathbf{I}_\sigma \end{array} \right] \begin{array}{c} k \\ \rho \\ \sigma \end{array} \end{array} .
$$

Let $\mathbf{P}$ be a partial column distortion matrix, which consists of the first $k + \tau + 2$ columns of $\mathbf{B}$, whose rank is τ, and $\dot{\tau}$ is the largest possible. Of course, knowledge of $\mathbf{Z}$, t_1, and s does not imply knowledge of τ.

Put $\delta = \tau + 1 - \rho$.

Let $\mathbf{W}_{\delta+1}$ denote the first $\delta + 1$ columns of $\mathbf{W}_0$. Then according to results of stage 1 the rank of $\mathbf{P}\mathbf{W}_{\delta+1}$ is δ.

Since $\delta \leq \sigma - 1$ we can calculate τ and $\mathbf{P}$ as follows. For i from 1 to $\sigma - 1$ do until success:

– set $\delta = i$ and $\tau = \rho - 1 + \delta$;

– find a binary $\tau \times k + \tau + 2$ matrix $\mathbf{P}$ of rank τ for which the rank of $\mathbf{P}\mathbf{W}_{\delta+1}$ is δ.

For $\delta = 0$ this problem can be solved with $O((k+t_1+2)^2)$ additions over $GF(2^n)$.

For $\delta > 0$ this is a search problem, and one useful result is deployed: it can be proved that if $\mathbf{P}_\delta'$ is the first δ rows of $\mathbf{P}$, and $\mathbf{V}_\delta$ is the first δ columns of $\mathbf{W}_{\delta+1}$, then the $\delta \times \delta$ matrix $\mathbf{P}_\delta'\mathbf{V}_\delta$ is non-singular. So the search can be carried out over the first δ rows and last $k + 2$ columns of $\mathbf{P}$. The resulting complexity is at most $O((k+t_1+2)\delta + \delta^3)2^{\delta(k+2)})$ multiplications and $O((k+t_1+2)^2 2^{\delta(k+2)})$ additions over $GF(2^n)$.

On successful exit, $\mathbf{P}$ is the candidate for the partial distortion matrix and τ may be the largest possible. But for $\delta > 0$ they may not be correct.

Step 2.

Normalize $\mathbf{P}$ from step 1 so that columns $k+1, \ldots, k+\tau$ form an identity matrix, recording any column permutation needed to do so.

Thus

$$\begin{array}{ccc} k & \tau & \eta \end{array}$$
$$\mathbf{B} = \left[\begin{array}{ccc} \mathbf{B}_k & \mathbf{I}_\tau & \mathbf{B}_\eta \\ \mathbf{0} & \mathbf{0} & \mathbf{C}_\eta \end{array} \right] \begin{array}{c} \tau \\ t_1 - \tau \end{array} \quad .$$

The method is to start by assuming $t_1 = \tau$, when it turns out that the columns of $\mathbf{B}_\eta$ can be calculated one by one in accordamce with the result of stage 2. The first column of $\mathbf{B}_\eta$ for which the method fails can be taken as the $\tau + 1$-th unit vector (the $\tau + 1$-th coordinate in 1, the others are zero). This column then can be inserted as the $k + \tau + 1$-th column of $\mathbf{B}$. The method can then be restarted, with τ increased by 1, and η decreased by 1. The total cost of step 2 is at most $O(k^3) + O(t_1(n-k)2^d)$ multiplications over $GF(2^n)$, where $d = \delta$ when $\tau = t_1$. .

Step 3.

The step 3 is fully coincides with calculations of stage 3, so its complexity is $O(k^3)$ multiplications over $GF(2^n)$.

Thus the total cost of the breaking algorithm is $O(k^3 + (k + t_1 + 2)d2^{d(k+2)})$ multiplications over $GF(2^n)$. The quantity d was defined earlier. In all cases $d \leq t_1$. In his work, Gibson claims that if matrices $\mathbf{A}$ and $\mathbf{B}$ were chosen at random, then in almost all cases *in practice* $d = max(0, t_1 - 2s)$, though no theoretical evidence was presented. Besides, the legal user can calculate d easily when creating a public key since he knows $\mathbf{B}$ (using step 1, he computes ρ when $\tau = t_1$, and $d = \tau + 1 - \rho$). So the question arsises: does for any $\mathbf{G}$, $\mathbf{S}$, and $\mathbf{A}$ a set of matrices $\mathbf{B}$ large enough exist such that $d \geq d_0$, d_0 fixed, for the public key $\mathbf{Z} = \mathbf{S}(\mathbf{G} + \mathbf{AB}_i)$,where $\mathbf{B}_i$ is any element from the set.

3 Rectangular scramble matrix in the GPT system

Taking into account that Gibson's attacks are applicable for practical lengths of codes $(n \sim 20 - 30)$, it is a natural aspiration to increase the length of the code to improve security. But this leads to a very large volume of the public key (it is proportional to the 3-d power of n) and this is not always acceptable. That is why it is desirable to construct a public key cryptosystem which uses codes in rank metric and withstands attacks on the public key effectively. Two methods of building such a system are described below.

Let us consider the following public key cryptosystem. The open key is a matrix

$$\mathbf{G}_{open} = \mathbf{SG} + \mathbf{X},$$

where $\mathbf{G}$ is a $k \times n$ generator matrix (n, k) of Maximum Rank Distance (MRD) code in the form (1); $\mathbf{S}$ is a $(k-p) \times k$ scramble matrix with entries in $GF(q^n)$ of full rank $k - p$; p is a *design* parameter; $\mathbf{X}$ is a distortion matrix such that $r(\mathbf{X}|q) = t_1$ and $r(\mathbf{X}|q^n) = s$.

Encryption is analogous to that in the GPT system. Let $\mathbf{m}$ be a $(k-p)$-plaintext vector with coordinates from $GF(q^n)$. The ciphertext is

$$\mathbf{c} = \mathbf{m}\mathbf{G}_{open} + \mathbf{e}.$$

Here $\mathbf{e}$ is a vector of rank t_2, with $t = t_1 + t_2$ not exceeding the rank-error correcting capacity of the code with generator matrix $\mathbf{SG}$.

Decryption is as follows. Let $\mathbf{c}$ be a received ciphertext, so $\mathbf{c} = \mathbf{mSG} + \mathbf{mX} + \mathbf{e}$, where $\mathbf{mX} + \mathbf{e}$ can be regarded as an error vector for the code with generator matrix $\mathbf{SG}$. Then, since $r(\mathbf{X}|q) = t_1$, $r(\mathbf{mX} + \mathbf{e}) \leq t_1 + t_2 = t$ this is a correctable error, using one of the fast decoding algorithms for MRD codes, the legal user gets $\hat{\mathbf{m}} = \mathbf{mS}$. Solving the equation $\hat{\mathbf{m}} = \mathbf{mS}$ in $\mathbf{m}$, $\mathbf{S}$ being known, he finds the plaintext $\mathbf{m}$. This equation has a unique solution since $r(\mathbf{S}|q^n) = k - p$ and it is exactly the number of unknown coordinates of $\mathbf{m}$. So decryption is unambiguous.

3.0.1 Possible attacks

One can easily see that a rectangular scramble matrix selects some subcode from an MRD code. If this subcode has a generator matrix and parity check matrix that cannot be represented in the form of those matrices of full MRD code, then it will be difficult to apply both Gibson's attacks to it for they efficiently use structure of MRD codes.

Lemma 8. *Suppose that in the GPT PKC a rectangular scramble matrix is used. Also suppose that a* design *parameter p can be chosen. Then there exist such subcodes of MRD codes, given by scramble matrices, and such values of parameter p that the GPT PKC cannot be broken by Gibson's attacks at least from the practical point of view.*

The rest of this section is devoted to proving this lemma.

It seems that it might also be proven that the fraction of subcodes for which the GPT system is unbreakable, parameter p being fixed, is essentially greater than zero, and this fraction tends to 1, p growing.

Let us examine the simplified case when the distortion matrix is missed, that is the public key takes the form $\tilde{\mathbf{G}}_{open} = \mathbf{SG}$.

Attacks on generator matrix. Let the cryptanalyst somehow, for example using the Gibson attack, try   to find a solution of the equation $\tilde{\mathbf{G}}_{open} = \mathbf{S}_1 \mathbf{G}_1$, where $\mathbf{S}_1$ is a $(k-p) \times (k-p)$ non-singular matrix, and $\mathbf{G}_1$ is a generator matrix of some $(n, k-p)$ MRD code:

$$\mathbf{G}_1 = \begin{bmatrix} f_1 & f_2 & \cdots & f_n \\ f_1^{[1]} & f_2^{[1]} & \cdots & f_n^{[1]} \\ \vdots & \vdots & \ddots & \vdots \\ f_1^{[k-p-1]} & f_2^{[k-p-1]} & \cdots & f_n^{[k-p-1]} \end{bmatrix}.$$

Generally, choosing $\mathbf{S}$ randomly, the rank distance d of the code with generator matrix $\tilde{\mathbf{G}}_{open}$ is equal to $d = n - k + 1$, but the rank distance of the code with generator matrix $\mathbf{S}_1 \mathbf{G}_1$ strictly equals $d_1 = n - k + p + 1$. Hence, this equation has no solution. From this it follows that the legal user should choose $\mathbf{S}$ such that $d < n - k + p + 1$ in order to avoid this kind of attack. In particular, those matrices are not suitable that have a non-singular matrix in $(k - p)$ successive columns, the other columns being zero-columns.

85

In what follows, the code with generator matrix $\mathbf{SG}$ will be considered to have the rank distance $d = n - k + 1$.

$\tilde{\mathbf{G}}_{open}$ can be represented in the following form

$$\tilde{\mathbf{G}}_{open} = \mathbf{SG} = \mathbf{S}_2\mathbf{G}_2 + \mathbf{X}_2, \tag{20}$$

where $\mathbf{S}_2$ and $\mathbf{G}_2$ possess the same properties as $\mathbf{S}_1$ and $\mathbf{G}_1$ respectively, and $\mathbf{X}_2$ such that $r(\mathbf{X}_2|q) = \tilde{t} \leq (n - k + p)/2$. Choose a $(k - p)$-vector $\mathbf{m}$ such that the vector $\mathbf{m}\tilde{\mathbf{G}}_{open}$ has the rank weight d. Then rank of the vector $\mathbf{m}\mathbf{S}_2\mathbf{G}_2$ is at least $d + p$. As long as rank weight is a norm, so from the equality $\mathbf{m}\tilde{\mathbf{G}}_{open} = \mathbf{m}(\mathbf{S}_2\mathbf{G}_2 + \mathbf{X}_2)$ it follows that $r(\mathbf{m}\mathbf{X}_2|q) \geq p$. This means that $r(\mathbf{X}_2|q) = \tilde{t} \geq p$.

During encryption an artificial error vector $\mathbf{e}$ with $r(\mathbf{e}|q) = \lfloor \frac{d-1}{2} \rfloor$ must be added to the vector $\mathbf{m}\tilde{\mathbf{G}}_{open}$, where $\mathbf{m}$ is a plaintext vector. At the same time if (20) is true, then for unambiguous decryption using $\mathbf{S}_2\mathbf{G}_2$, it is necessary that the rank of $\mathbf{e}$ should not exceed $\lfloor \frac{d+p-1}{2} \rfloor - p$. Since $\lfloor \frac{d-1}{2} \rfloor > \lfloor \frac{d+p-1}{2} \rfloor - p$ for any $p \geq 2$, representation (20) leads to wrong decoding, and therefore to wrong decryption. Thus, even if a solution of the form (20) exists, the cryptanalyst cannot decrypt all intercepted ciphertexts.

Let us try to use the technique Gibson used in his attack on the original GPT system (see eq. (6)).

Partition $\mathbf{G}$ into two parts: $\mathbf{G} = [\mathbf{G}_1\ \mathbf{G}_2]$, where

$$\mathbf{G}_1 = \begin{bmatrix} g_1 & g_2 & \cdots & g_{k-p} \\ g_1^{[1]} & g_2^{[1]} & \cdots & g_{k-p}^{[1]} \\ \vdots & \vdots & \ddots & \vdots \\ g_1^{[k-1]} & g_2^{[k-1]} & \cdots & g_{k-p}^{[k-1]} \end{bmatrix}, \mathbf{G}_2 = \begin{bmatrix} g_{k-p+1} & g_{k-p+2} & \cdots & g_n \\ g_{k-p+1}^{[1]} & g_{k-p+2}^{[1]} & \cdots & g_n^{[1]} \\ \vdots & \vdots & \ddots & \vdots \\ g_{k-p+1}^{[k-1]} & g_{k-p+2}^{[k-1]} & \cdots & g_n^{[k-1]} \end{bmatrix}, \tag{21}$$

Make the same partition in the public key: $\tilde{\mathbf{G}}_{open} = [\tilde{\mathbf{G}}_1\ \tilde{\mathbf{G}}_2]$, where $\tilde{\mathbf{G}}_1 = \mathbf{SG}_1$ is the first $k - p$ columns of $\tilde{\mathbf{G}}_{open}$, and $\tilde{\mathbf{G}}_2 = \mathbf{SG}_2$ is the remaining part of $\tilde{\mathbf{G}}_{open}$. Reduce the open key $\tilde{\mathbf{G}}_{open}$ to the row-reduced echelon form

$$\tilde{\mathbf{G}}_{open}^{syst} = [\mathbf{I}_{k-p}\ \tilde{\mathbf{R}}], \tag{22}$$

where $\mathbf{I}_{k-p}$ is the identity matrix of order $k - p$,

$$\tilde{\mathbf{R}} = [\tilde{R}_{ij}],$$

$$i = 0, 1, \ldots, k - p - 1;\ j = k - p + 1, \ldots, n.$$

Reducing to the row-reduced echelon form is equivalent to multiplying $\tilde{\mathbf{G}}_{open}$ by $\tilde{\mathbf{G}}_1^{-1}$ to the left: $\mathbf{SG}_1\tilde{\mathbf{R}} = \mathbf{SG}_2$. Thus, we get an equation in the unknown matrices $\mathbf{S}, \mathbf{G}_1, \mathbf{G}_2$:

$$\mathbf{S}(\mathbf{G}_1\tilde{\mathbf{R}} - \mathbf{G}_2) = \mathbf{0}. \tag{23}$$

Matrix $\mathbf{S}$ has rank $k - p$, and consequently, in general, $\mathbf{X}_3$

$$\mathbf{X}_3 = \mathbf{G}_1\tilde{\mathbf{R}} - \mathbf{G}_2 \tag{24}$$

has rank $r(\mathbf{X}_3|q^n) = p$.

Partition $\mathbf{X}_3$: $\dot{\mathbf{X}}_3$ is the upper $k-p$ rows of $\mathbf{X}_3$, and $\ddot{\mathbf{X}}_3$ is the rest of $\mathbf{X}_3$. Partition $\mathbf{G}_1$ and $\mathbf{G}_2$ similarly. If $k - p \geq p$, then in general $\dot{\mathbf{X}}_3$ has rank p, that is equal to the rank of $\mathbf{X}_3$.

Let us examine the following equation

$$\dot{\mathbf{X}}_3 = \dot{\mathbf{G}}_1 \tilde{\mathbf{R}} - \dot{\mathbf{G}}_2. \tag{25}$$

One can use the technique that Gibson used for solving (6) (extended algorithm for breaking the original GPT PKC) in the unknowns $\dot{\mathbf{X}}_3$, $\dot{\mathbf{G}}_1$, $\dot{\mathbf{G}}_2$. The rest of the equations of the system (24) should be used for checking a solution, if any.

In section 2, it was shown that complexity of solving equation (25) for $q = 2$ is estimated as $O(n^3 2^{pn})$ multiplications in $GF(2^n)$. So, for $p = 3$ and $n = 20$ solving this equation is infeasible.

Attacks on parity check matrix. Denote $r = n - k$. Hereafter let us suppose that the following conjecture holds.

Conjecture 9. *Let the matrix*

$$\mathbf{G}_{op} = \mathbf{G}_1 + \mathbf{X}_1$$

be given, where $\mathbf{G}_1$ is the $k \times n$ generator matrix of an MRD code C_1, $\mathbf{X}_1$ is such that

$$r(\mathbf{X}_1|q) = t_1 < \left\lfloor \frac{n - k}{2} \right\rfloor. \tag{26}$$

Then the equality

$$\mathbf{G}_{op} = \mathbf{G}_1 + \mathbf{X}_1 = \mathbf{S}\mathbf{G}_2 + \mathbf{X}_2, \tag{27}$$

where $\mathbf{G}_2$ is a generator matrix of an MRD code C_2 (the code C_2 has the same parameters as the code C_1, but they are not necessarily the same codes), $\mathbf{S}$ is a square non-singular matrix of order k, and $\mathbf{X}_2$ is such that

$$r(\mathbf{X}_2|q) = t_2 < t_1, \tag{28}$$

is impossible.

Now we show how to construct different matrices $\mathbf{X}_1$ for any fixed $\mathbf{G}_1$, for which (27) under conditions (26), (28) is certainly to be impossible.

Choose a vector $\mathbf{m}$ such that $r(\mathbf{m}\mathbf{G}_1 = \mathbf{g}|q) = d$. The number of vectors of that kind is $A_d(n, d) \sim q^{n+n-d}$, $d = n-k+1$. Find $\mathbf{x}$ such that $r(\mathbf{x}|q) = t_1$ and $r(\mathbf{g} + \mathbf{x}|q) = d - t_1$. Solve the equation $\mathbf{m}\mathbf{X}_1 = \mathbf{x}$ in the unknown $\mathbf{X}_1$. Choose from received solutions those for which (26) holds. For the chosen $\mathbf{m}$ we have $r(\mathbf{m}\mathbf{G}_1 + \mathbf{m}\mathbf{X}_1|q) = r(\mathbf{g} + \mathbf{x}|q) = d - t_1$. Since $r(\mathbf{m}\mathbf{S}\mathbf{G}_2|q) \geq d$ and the rank distance is a norm, we see that (26) is impossible for any $\mathbf{S}$, $\mathbf{G}_2$, $\mathbf{X}_2$.

Turn back to our system. The matrix $\tilde{\mathbf{G}}_{open}$ is a generator matrix of some MRD code C. Compute the matrix $\tilde{\mathbf{H}}$ of size $(n - k + p) \times n$ orthogonal to $\tilde{\mathbf{G}}_{open}$. $\tilde{\mathbf{H}}$ is a parity check matrix of C. It can be represented as

$$\tilde{\mathbf{H}} = \mathbf{S}^* \begin{bmatrix} \mathbf{H} \\ \mathbf{C} \end{bmatrix} = \mathbf{S}^* \begin{bmatrix} h_1 & h_2 & \cdots & h_n \\ h_1^{[1]} & h_2^{[1]} & \cdots & h_n^{[1]} \\ \vdots & \vdots & \ddots & \vdots \\ h_1^{[r-1]} & h_2^{[r-1]} & \cdots & h_n^{[r-1]} \\ c_{11} & c_{12} & \cdots & c_{1n} \\ c_{21} & c_{22} & \cdots & c_{2n} \\ \vdots & \vdots & \ddots & \vdots \\ c_{p1} & c_{p2} & \cdots & c_{pn} \end{bmatrix}, \tag{29}$$

where $\mathbf{S}^*$ is a non-singular matrix of order $r + p$, $\mathbf{H}$ is a parity check matrix of the code with generator matrix $\mathbf{G}$, and $\mathbf{C}$ is some matrix of size $p \times n$ that selects some subcode from it.

Rewrite $\tilde{\mathbf{H}}$ in a different form.

$$\tilde{\mathbf{H}} = \mathbf{S}^*(\mathbf{H}^* + \mathbf{C}^*) =$$

$$\mathbf{S}^* \left(\begin{bmatrix} h_1 & \cdots & h_n \\ \vdots & \ddots & \vdots \\ h_1^{[r-1]} & \cdots & h_n^{[r-1]} \\ h_1^{[r]} & \cdots & h_n^{[r]} \\ \vdots & \ddots & \vdots \\ h_1^{[r+p-1]} & \cdots & h_n^{[r+p-1]} \end{bmatrix} + \begin{bmatrix} 0 & \cdots & 0 \\ \vdots & \ddots & \vdots \\ 0 & \cdots & 0 \\ c_{11} - h_1^{[r]} & \cdots & c_{1n} - h_n^{[r]} \\ \vdots & \ddots & \vdots \\ c_{p1} - h_1^{[r+p-1]} & \cdots & c_{pn} - h_n^{[r+p-1]} \end{bmatrix} \right). \tag{30}$$

The cryptanalyst can try to apply Gibson's attacks to $\tilde{\mathbf{H}}$ since $\mathbf{H}^*$ can be regarded as a generator matrix of some $(n, n - k + p)$ MRD code, and $\mathbf{C}^*$ as a distortion matrix (see section 2). Having computed the generating vector $\mathbf{h} = (h_1, h_2, \ldots, h_n)$, the cryptanalyst can then calculate the generating vector $\mathbf{g} = (g_1, g_2, \ldots, g_n)$. This would completely break the system.

Let us show how one can choose the values of the quantities n, k, p so as to make difficult the application of Gibson's attacks.

If one chooses $r(\mathbf{C}^*|q^n) = s > 2$, then the complexity of the extended version of the Gibson attack on the original GPT PKC will be at least $O(n^3 q^{3n})$ arithmetical operations, and just for $n \sim 20$ it is infeasible from practical point of view.

To avoid the second Gibson attack, it is necessary that the inequality $r(\mathbf{C}^*|q) > \min(r + p, \ n - r - p) - 2$ holds. Usually $r \sim n - r$, so it is sufficient to have $r(\mathbf{C}^*|q) > n - r - p - 2$. For example, $\mathbf{C}^*$ might be built as follows. Let the rank of $(c_{11} - h_1^{[r]}, c_{12} - h_2^{[r]}, \ldots, c_{1n} - h_n^{[r]})$ be $n - r - p - 1$. It is easy to see that the rank of $\mathbf{C}^*$ over $GF(q)$ is not less than $n - r - p - 1$, so the inequality is met, and the second Gibson attack cannot be applied. Instead of the first row of $\mathbf{C}^*$ one can use any non-zero row of it.

Another requirement can be imposed on choosing $\mathbf{C}$ (and consequently on choosing $\mathbf{C}^*$). Require some $r + 1$ columns of $\tilde{\mathbf{H}}$ to be linear independent. This will result in minimum rank distance of the code with generator matrix $\tilde{\mathbf{G}}_{open}$ to be strictly equal to $d = r + 1 = n - k + 1$, as it was required to ensure high security against attacks on $\tilde{\mathbf{G}}_{open}$.

88

Studying the simplified case shows that even if a distortion matrix equals zero one can choose the parameters for the system to be secure.

General case. Let us analyze the system in general case, that is when a distortion matrix is not omitted:

$$\mathbf{G}_{open} = \mathbf{S}\mathbf{G} + \mathbf{X},$$

$r(\mathbf{X}|q) = t_1$ and $r(\mathbf{X}|q^n) = s$. Suppose that the cryptanalyst was able to represent the open key in the form $\mathbf{G}_{open} = \mathbf{S}_4\mathbf{G}_4 + \mathbf{X}_4$, where $\mathbf{G}_4$ is a generator matrix of an $(n, k - p)$ MRD code, $\mathbf{S}_4$ is some scramble matrix of size $k - p \times k - p$, $\mathbf{X}_4$ is some distortion matrix. As it was done above it is easy to verify that in general case the rank of $\mathbf{X}_4$ over $GF(q)$ must satisfy the inequality $r(\mathbf{X}_4|q) \geq p + t_1$. If it is the case, then the cryptanalyst *can not decrypt all ciphertexts*. Hence, the matrices $\mathbf{G}_4$, $\mathbf{S}_4$ and $\mathbf{X}_4$ are of little value for the cryptanalyst.

Now suppose that the cryptanalyst is going to make use of the technique Gibson used in the attack on the original GPT PKC, viz. he reduces the open key to the row-reduced echelon form:

$$\mathbf{G}_{open}^{syst} = [\mathbf{I}_{k-p}\ \mathbf{R}],$$

where $\mathbf{I}_{k-p}$ is the identity matrix of order $k - p$,

$$\mathbf{R} = [R_{ij}],$$

$$i = 0, 1, \ldots, k - p - 1;\ j = k - p + 1, \ldots, n.$$

He obtains the following matrix equation in the unknown components of the secret key:

$$\mathbf{S}(\mathbf{G}_1\mathbf{R} - \mathbf{G}_2) = \mathbf{X}'' - \mathbf{X}'\mathbf{R}, \tag{31}$$

where $\mathbf{X}'$ is the first $k - p$ columns of $\mathbf{X}$, $\mathbf{X}''$ is the rest of $\mathbf{X}$.   Only $\mathbf{R}$ is known here. How to solve this equation in $\mathbf{S}$, $\mathbf{G}$, $\mathbf{X}$ in appropriate time is unknown.

Consider what piece of information the cryptanalyst can get analyzing a matrix orthogonal to the matrix of the open key. Examine the simplified case when $r(\mathbf{X}|q^n) = 1$. Such a distortion matrix can be represented in the form $\mathbf{X} = \mathbf{a}^T\mathbf{b}$, where $\mathbf{a}$, $\mathbf{b}$ are vectors of suitable dimensions. One can easily show that the row-reduced echelon form of the public key takes the form:

$$\mathbf{G}_{open}^{syst} = [\mathbf{I}_{k-p}\ \ \tilde{\mathbf{R}} + \tilde{\mathbf{a}}^T\mathbf{b}_2],$$

where $\tilde{\mathbf{R}}$ is as defined earlier (see eqn (22)); $\tilde{\mathbf{a}}$ is a vector $(\tilde{a}_1, \ldots, \tilde{a}_{k-p})$ depending on $\mathbf{a}$, $\mathbf{b}$, and $\mathbf{G}$; $\mathbf{b}_2 = (b_{k-p+1}, \ldots, b_n)$ (subvector of $\mathbf{b}$). Then orthogonal to $\mathbf{G}_{open}$ takes the form

$$\tilde{\mathbf{H}} = \mathbf{S}^*(\mathbf{H}^* + \mathbf{C}^* + \mathbf{\Delta}).$$

Here $\mathbf{H}^*$, $\mathbf{C}^*$ are defined in (30). Matrix $\mathbf{\Delta}$ has rank 1 and

$$\mathbf{\Delta} = \hat{\mathbf{S}}\mathbf{b}_2^T(\tilde{a}_1, \ldots, \tilde{a}_{k-p}, 0, \ldots, 0), \tag{32}$$

where last $n - k + p$ components of $(\tilde{a}_1, \ldots, \tilde{a}_{k-p}, 0, \ldots, 0)$ are zeros, and $\hat{\mathbf{S}}$ is the known non-singular matrix (depending on $\tilde{\mathbf{G}}_{open}$). Everything that has been said about choosing $\mathbf{C}^*$ and its parameters for ensuring security for the system is evidently extended to $\mathbf{C}^* + \Delta$.

Thus, usage of a distortion matrix doesn't impair the security of the system but improves it since attacks become harder, and the cryptanalyst has more flexibility in choosing system parameters.

3.1 Rank-like codes

3.1.1 New code construction

Consider a code with the following generator matrix:

$$
\mathbf{G}_{new} = [\mathbf{I}_k \ \mathbf{G}] = \begin{bmatrix} 1 & 0 & \dots & 0 & 0 & g_1 & g_2 & \dots & g_{n-1} & g_n \\ 0 & 1 & \dots & 0 & 0 & g_1^{[1]} & g_2^{[1]} & \dots & g_{n-1}^{[1]} & g_n^{[1]} \\ \vdots & \vdots & \ddots & \vdots & \vdots & \vdots & & \ddots & \vdots & \vdots \\ 0 & 0 & \dots & 1 & 0 & g_1^{[k-2]} & g_2^{[k-2]} & \dots & g_{n-1}^{[k-2]} & g_n^{[k-2]} \\ 0 & 0 & \dots & 0 & 1 & g_1^{[k-1]} & g_2^{[k-1]} & \dots & g_{n-1}^{[k-1]} & g_n^{[k-1]} \end{bmatrix}. \tag{33}
$$

The left part of $\mathbf{G}_{new}$ is the identity matrix of order k, the right part of $\mathbf{G}_{new}$ is a generator matrix of some (n, k) MRD code with generating vector $g_{gener} = (g_1, g_2, \dots, g_n)$. The dimension of this code is k, and the length is $n + k$.

3.1.2 Distances and error correction

Evidently, the minimum rank distance of the new code is greater than or equal to that of the code with $\mathbf{G}$ as a generator matrix, viz. $d_r > n - k + 1$. It can easily be shown that the minimum Hamming distance of the code is at least $d_H \geq n - k + 4$, provided n is a prime number. In what follows, the rank distance of the code is assumed to be $d_r = n - k + 1$ and the Hamming distance $d_H = n - k + 4 = d_r + 3$. Since new codes are not optimal versus their parent codes (MRD codes), we call new codes "Rank-like codes".

The new code can correct any error vector, in which the subvector with components $k+1, k+2, \dots, k+n$ has rank not greater than $t_r \leq \lfloor (d_r - 1)/2 \rfloor = \lfloor (n-k)/2 \rfloor$ and any Hamming weight as well as all error vectors with Hamming weight not greater than $t_H \leq \lfloor (d_H - 1)/2 \rfloor = \lfloor (n - k + 3)/2 \rfloor$.

Rank errors are corrected as follows. From a received vector extract the subvector with components $k + 1, \dots, n + k$, that is the vector whose components correspond to the location of the matrix $\mathbf{G}$ in $\mathbf{G}_{new}$. Applying any fast decoding algorithm for MRD codes to this subvector, one gets an information vector (plaintext).

In case $d_r = 2m$, there exists a very simple decoding algorithm for errors with Hamming weight up to $t_r + 1 = m$, although details are not described here. Fast decoding algorithm for any decodable Hamming's error is not known.

3.1.3 New PKC description

Let us use $\mathbf{G}_{new} = [\mathbf{I}_k \ \mathbf{G}]$ (see (33)) to construct a new PKC on the basis of GPT PKC in order to improve security of the system.

The public key is a matrix

$$\mathbf{G}_{open} = \mathbf{S}(\mathbf{G}_{new} + \mathbf{X})\mathbf{P}, \qquad (34)$$

where $\mathbf{S}$ is a square non-singular matrix of order k; $\mathbf{X}$ — a $k \times (n+k)$ matrix such that its $k \times n$ submatrix $\mathbf{X}_2$ consisting of columns $k+1, k+2, \ldots, n+k-1, n+k$ has given column rank $r(\mathbf{X}_2|q) = t_1$ over $GF(q)$; $\mathbf{P}$ — a $(k+n) \times (k+n)$ column permutation matrix. Conditions imposed on the submatrix $\mathbf{X}_1$ consisting of the first k columns of $\mathbf{X}$ will be discussed later.

The private keys of the system are matrices $\mathbf{G}_{new}$, $\mathbf{S}$ and $\mathbf{P}$ separately. Since $\mathbf{X}$ is not used during decryption and encryption, and only knowledge of its column rank is needed, so it is not a part of the secret key. But it should be kept in secret, since if $\mathbf{X}$ is known, the cryptanalyst might get extra piece of information about the secret key, so it can be destroyed after building of the open key.

Encryption. Let $\mathbf{m}$ be an information k-vector (plaintext). A ciphertext is given by

$$\mathbf{c} = \mathbf{m}\mathbf{G}_{open} + \mathbf{e} = \mathbf{m}\mathbf{S}(\mathbf{G}_{new} + \mathbf{X})\mathbf{P} + \mathbf{e}, \qquad (35)$$

where $\mathbf{e}$ is an artificial vector of errors of rank $t_2 = t_r - t_1 = \lfloor (n-k)/2 \rfloor - t_1$ or less.

Decryption. On receiving the ciphertext $\mathbf{c}$, the legitimate user calculates

$$\mathbf{c}' = (c_1', c_2', \ldots, c_{n+k}') = \mathbf{c}\mathbf{P}^{-1} = \mathbf{m}\mathbf{S}(\mathbf{G}_{new} + \mathbf{X}) + \mathbf{e}\mathbf{P}^{-1}.$$

Then from $\mathbf{c}'$ he extracts the subvector

$$\mathbf{c}'' = (c_{k+1}', c_{k+2}', \ldots, c_{n+k}') = \mathbf{m}\mathbf{S}\mathbf{G} + \mathbf{m}\mathbf{X}_2 + \mathbf{e}'',$$

where $\mathbf{e}''$ is the subvector of $\mathbf{e}\mathbf{P}^{-1}$, and consequently $r(\mathbf{e}''|q) \leq t_2$. Taking into account that $r(\mathbf{m}\mathbf{X}|q) \leq t_1$, it follows that $r(\mathbf{m}\mathbf{X}_2 + \mathbf{e}''|q) \leq t_1 + t_2 = t$. Applying a fast decoding algorithm to $\mathbf{c}''$, the legitimate user obtains $\mathbf{m}\mathbf{S}$, and therefore $\mathbf{m}$, $\mathbf{S}$ given.

3.1.4 Possible attacks on the system

It is readily seen that like GPT PKC this modified version resists direct attacks on ciphertexts effectively. So we focus our attention on attacks on the open key.

To break the system, the cryptanalyst must *guess* the exact positions of columns of $\mathbf{G}$ in the whole matrix $\mathbf{G}_{new}$, and then apply one of the Gibson attacks to them. Apparently, in this case, complexity of breaking this PKC can be estimated as

$$W_{new} = O\left(\binom{n+k}{n} W_{Gibson} \right), \qquad (36)$$

where $\binom{n+k}{k}$ is a binomial coefficient — the number of ways of selecting n columns of $\mathbf{G}_{open}$ from $n+k$ columns, W_{Gibson} is the work function of corresponding Gibson's attack.

Example 1. *Let* $q = 2$, $n = 24$, $k = 12$, $t_1 = 4$, *and let* $\mathbf{X}_2$ *be a matrix of rank 1 over* $GF(q^n)$. *Then* $W_{Gibson} = O(n^3 2^n)$, *and the total complexity is* $W_{new} = 2^{68}$ *arithmetical operations over* $GF(q^n)$.

91

It follows from (36) that the main difficulty is to find specified n columns from $n+k$ columns quickly. Thus, any attack on this PKC will be useful if it doesn't make an exhaustive search through all columns of $\mathbf{G}_{open}$.

Hereafter we assume that $t_1 < k$.

Let the cryptanalyst have chosen some n columns of $\mathbf{G}_{open}$. They constitute a matrix $\mathbf{G}_n$. Then the cryptanalyst tries to resolve this matrix into two components:

$$\mathbf{G}_n = \tilde{\mathbf{S}}(\tilde{\mathbf{G}} + \tilde{\mathbf{X}}), \qquad (37)$$

where $\tilde{\mathbf{G}}$ is a generator matrix of some MRD code in the form (1), $\tilde{\mathbf{S}}$ — some square scramble matrix, $\tilde{\mathbf{X}}$ — some distortion matrix. If the rank of $\tilde{\mathbf{X}}$ over $GF(q)$ is not greater than t_1, which is not greater than the rank of $\mathbf{X}_2$ over the same field, then matrices $\tilde{\mathbf{S}}, \tilde{\mathbf{G}}$ and $\tilde{\mathbf{X}}$ will obviously allow the cryptanalyst to decrypt intercepted ciphertexts, and complexity of such an attack will be W_{Gibson}. Examine opportunity of getting representation (37) thoroughly.

First let us introduce some notation. Denote columns of the identity matrix by $\mathbf{e}_j$, $j = 1, 2, \ldots, k$, namely, $\mathbf{e}_j$ is the column with 1 in the j-th row and the other elements are zeros. Columns of $\mathbf{X}$ will be denoted by $\mathbf{x}_j$, $j = 1, 2, \ldots, n+k$, with columns $1, 2, \ldots, k$ relating to $\mathbf{X}_1$. Columns of $\mathbf{G}$ will be denoted by $\mathbf{g}_j$, $j = k+1, k+2, \ldots, k+n$, where $\mathbf{g}_{k+i}$ is the i-th column of the matrix $\mathbf{G}$. Any column of the form $(f_j, f_j^{[1]}, \ldots, f_j^{[k-1]})^T$, except columns of $\mathbf{G}$, will be denoted as $\mathbf{f}_j$, where $f_j \in GF(q^n)$. The range of j's is defined by all different f_j.

Let the cryptanalyst have selected some n columns from $\mathbf{G}_{open}$: m columns from the part corresponding to $\mathbf{I}_k + \mathbf{X}_1$ and $n - m$ columns from the part corresponding to $\mathbf{G} + \mathbf{X}_2$. Then $\mathbf{G}_n$ takes the form

$$\mathbf{G}_n = \mathbf{S}\left[\ \mathbf{e}_{j_1} + \mathbf{x}_{j_1}\ \cdots\ \mathbf{e}_{j_m} + \mathbf{x}_{j_m}\ \mathbf{g}_{j_{m+1}} + \mathbf{x}_{j_{m+1}}\ \cdots\ \mathbf{g}_{j_n} + \mathbf{x}_{j_n}\ \right]\tilde{\mathbf{P}}, \qquad (38)$$

$$1 \le j_1 < j_2 < \ldots < j_m \le k, \quad k + 1 \le j_{m+1} < j_{m+2} < \ldots < j_n \le n + k,$$

where $\tilde{\mathbf{P}}$ is some fixed permutation matrix, $\mathbf{S}$ is the same scramble matrix that was used for the public key construction.

Represent $\mathbf{G}_n$ in the form

$$\mathbf{G}_n = \mathbf{S}(\tilde{\mathbf{G}} + \tilde{\mathbf{X}})\tilde{\mathbf{P}}, \qquad (39)$$

where

$$\tilde{\mathbf{G}} = \left[\ \mathbf{f}_{j_1}\ \mathbf{f}_{j_2}\ \cdots\ \mathbf{f}_{j_m}\ \mathbf{g}_{j_{m+1}}\ \mathbf{g}_{j_{m+2}}\ \cdots\ \mathbf{g}_{j_n}\ \right] \qquad (40)$$

is a generator matrix of an MRD code, if the elements $\mathbf{f}_{j_1}, \mathbf{f}_{j_2} \ldots, \mathbf{f}_{j_m}$ are chosen properly (they must be linear independent over $GF(q)$),

$$\tilde{\mathbf{X}} = \left[\ \mathbf{e}_{j_1} + \mathbf{x}_{j_1} - \mathbf{f}_{j_1}\ \cdots\ \mathbf{e}_{j_m} + \mathbf{x}_{j_m} - \mathbf{f}_{j_m}\ \mathbf{x}_{j_{m+1}}\ \cdots\ \mathbf{x}_{j_n}\ \right] \qquad (41)$$

is a distortion matrix.

For the sake of convenience, partition $\tilde{\mathbf{X}}$:

$$\tilde{\mathbf{X}} = [\mathbf{Y}_1\ \ \mathbf{Y}_2], \qquad (42)$$

$$\mathbf{Y}_1 = [\mathbf{e}_{j_1} + \mathbf{x}_{j_1} - \mathbf{f}_{j_1}\ \ \mathbf{e}_{j_2} + \mathbf{x}_{j_2} - \mathbf{f}_{j_2}\ \ \cdots\ \ \mathbf{e}_{j_m} + \mathbf{x}_{j_m} - \mathbf{f}_{j_m}] \qquad (43)$$

92

is a $k \times m$ matrix,

$$\mathbf{Y}_2 = \begin{bmatrix} \mathbf{x}_{j_{m+1}} & \mathbf{x}_{j_{m+2}} & \cdots & \mathbf{x}_{j_n} \end{bmatrix} \qquad (44)$$

is a $k \times (n - m)$ matrix,

$$1 \leq j_1 < j_2 < \ldots < j_m \leq k, \quad k + 1 \leq j_{m+1} < j_{m+2} < \ldots < j_n \leq n + k.$$

Selecting any m columns of $\mathbf{I}_k + \mathbf{X}_1$ and adding columns $(f_j, f_j^{[1]}, \ldots, f_j^{[k-1]})^T$ to each of them, with f_j being linear independent over $GF(q)$, the cryptanalyst obtains all different $\mathbf{Y}_1$ with m columns. Varying the value of m from 1 to k, he gets all possible $\mathbf{Y}_1$. All possible matrices $\mathbf{Y}_2$ will be obtained if any m columns are deleted from $\mathbf{X}_2$, m being from 1 to k. However, the total number of columns in the pair $\mathbf{Y}_1$, $\mathbf{Y}_2$ must be n.

Since any permutation within the components of a vector doesn't change its rank, we have representations (37) and (39) are equivalent for the correct decryption. If $\tilde{\mathbf{X}}$ has rank over $GF(q)$ strictly greater than t_1, then such a representation will be of little value to the cryptanalyst since it *doesn't allow him to decrypt all intercepted ciphertexts*. Hence, the aim of the cryptographer is to choose matrices $\mathbf{X}_1\mathbf{X}_2$ such that in any selection $\mathbf{G}_n$ in (39), except the case when $\tilde{\mathbf{G}} = \mathbf{G}$ (and also $\tilde{\mathbf{X}} = \mathbf{X}_2$), the rank of $\tilde{\mathbf{X}}$ over $GF(q)$ would be strictly greater than t_1.

We will say that a matrix $\tilde{\mathbf{X}}$ is *"weak"*, if $r(\tilde{\mathbf{X}}|q) \leq t_1$. Otherwise we will say that this matrix is *"strong"*. A matrix $\mathbf{Y}_2$ may have any rank over $GF(q)$ in the range from 0 to t_1 if $m \geq t_1$, and from 1 to t_1 if $m < t_1$ (all possible $\mathbf{Y}_2$ are some fixed $n - m$ columns of $\mathbf{X}_2$). A matrix $\mathbf{Y}_1$ may have any rank over $GF(q)$ from 0 to m. The exact value of its rank depends on the choice of $\mathbf{X}_1$. Suppose $m > t_1$; then $r(\mathbf{Y}_1|q) = m > t_1$ if all the columns of $\mathbf{Y}_1$ are linear independent over $GF(q)$. In this case $r(\tilde{\mathbf{X}}|q) > t_1$, so $\tilde{\mathbf{X}}$ is *"strong"*.

From this we see that if we choose $\mathbf{X}_1$ such that the rank of *any* $\mathbf{Y}_1$ over $GF(q)$ is equal to the number of its columns, then $\tilde{\mathbf{X}}$ will be *"weak"* in the only case $m \leq t_1$. Conversely $\tilde{\mathbf{X}}$ will be *"strong"*.

Now we are going to describe one method of choosing $\mathbf{X}_1$ satisfying to the above condition.

Let $\mathcal{T}$ be a matrix transformation such that for any matrix $\mathbf{W} = [w_{ij}]$, $i = 1, \ldots, k$, it sets into correspondence a matrix $\mathbf{W}_{\mathcal{T}} = [w_{\mathcal{T}_{ij}}]$, $i = 1, \ldots, k - 1$ by the rule

$$w_{\mathcal{T}_{ij}} = w_{ij}^{[1]} - w_{i+1,j}$$

Lemma 10 *In order that for any $m \leq k$ the rank of a matrix $\mathbf{Y}_1$ over $GF(q)$ to be equal to the number of columns of $\mathbf{Y}_1$ it is sufficient that $r((\mathbf{X}_1 + \mathbf{I}_k)_{\mathcal{T}}|q) = k$, where $(\mathbf{X}_1 + \mathbf{I}_k)_{\mathcal{T}}$ is the matrix obtained from $\mathbf{X}_1 + \mathbf{I}_k$ by the transformation $\mathcal{T}$.*

Proof. Let $\mathbf{F}$ be a $k \times k$ matrix of the form

$$\mathbf{F} = [\mathbf{f}_1, \mathbf{f}_2, \ldots, \mathbf{f}_k] = \begin{bmatrix} f_1 & f_2 & \cdots & f_k \\ f_1^{[1]} & f_2^{[1]} & \cdots & f_k^{[1]} \\ \vdots & \vdots & \ddots & \vdots \\ f_1^{[k-1]} & f_2^{[k-1]} & \cdots & f_k^{[k-1]} \end{bmatrix}, \qquad (45)$$

where $\mathbf{f}_i$ is the i-th column of $\mathbf{F}$, $f_i \in GF(q^n)\backslash\{0\}$ and all the f_i are linear independent over $GF(q)$, $i = 1, \ldots, k$.

Write $\mathbf{X}_1 + \mathbf{I}_k$ as

$$\mathbf{X}_1 + \mathbf{I}_k = [\mathbf{x}_1, \mathbf{x}_2, \ldots, \mathbf{x}_k],$$

where $\mathbf{x}_i$ is the i-th column of $\mathbf{X}_1 + \mathbf{I}_k$, $i = 1, \ldots, k$. Evidently, any $\mathbf{Y}_1$ with m columns is some m columns of $\mathbf{X}_1 + \mathbf{I}_k - \mathbf{F}$. So if we prove that the matrix $\mathbf{X}_1 + \mathbf{I}_k - \mathbf{F}$ has column rank k over $GF(q)$ then we prove the Lemma.

The proof is by reductio ad absurdum. Let the columns of

$$\mathbf{Y} = \mathbf{X}_1 + \mathbf{I}_k - \mathbf{F} = [\mathbf{y}_1, \mathbf{y}_2, \ldots, \mathbf{y}_k]$$

are linear dependent over $GF(q)$. Then there are some $a_i \in GF(q)$, $i = 1, \ldots, k$, not all equal zero at the same time, such that

$$a_1\mathbf{y}_1 + a_2\mathbf{y}_2 + \ldots + a_k\mathbf{y}_k = \mathbf{0}.$$

From here we see that

$$a_1\mathbf{x}_1 + a_2\mathbf{x}_2 + \ldots + a_k\mathbf{x}_k = a_1\mathbf{f}_1 + a_2\mathbf{f}_2 + \ldots + a_k\mathbf{f}_k. \tag{46}$$

It is readily seen that the vector

$$\tilde{\mathbf{f}} = a_1\mathbf{f}_1 + a_2\mathbf{f}_2 + \ldots + a_k\mathbf{f}_k$$

is not equal to zero and is of the form

$$\tilde{\mathbf{f}} = (\tilde{f}_1, \tilde{f}_2, \ldots, \tilde{f}_k) = (\tilde{f}, \tilde{f}^{[1]}, \ldots, \tilde{f}^{[k-1]})^T \tag{47}$$

for some $\tilde{f} \in GF(q^n)\backslash\{0\}$.

Apply to $\tilde{\mathbf{f}}$ the transformation $\mathcal{T}$ to get the vector $\tilde{\mathbf{f}}_{\mathcal{T}}$ of size $k - 1$.

By construction, any $\tilde{\mathbf{f}}_{\mathcal{T}}$ that was built from $\tilde{\mathbf{f}}$ of the form (47) by the transformation T must be zero. In the inverse direction, if $\tilde{\mathbf{f}}_{\mathcal{T}}$ has a zero component, then it cannot be obtained by applying T to some $\tilde{\mathbf{f}}$ of the form (47).

Applying $\mathcal{T}$ to equation (46), we have:

$$a_1\mathbf{x}_{\mathcal{T}_1} + a_2\mathbf{x}_{\mathcal{T}_2} + \ldots + a_k\mathbf{x}_{\mathcal{T}_k} = \mathbf{0} \tag{48}$$

for some $a_i \in GF(q)$ not all equal zero at the same time, $i = 1, \ldots, k$. The columns $\mathbf{x}_{\mathcal{T}_i}$ are the result of application T to the columns $\mathbf{x}_i$.

Form a matrix $\mathbf{X}_{\mathcal{T}}$ of size $(k - 1) \times k$ from the columns $\mathbf{x}_{\mathcal{T}_i}$. From (48) it follows that the columns of $\mathbf{X}_{\mathcal{T}}$ are linear dependent over $GF(q)$.

In the case all the columns of $\mathbf{X}_{\mathcal{T}}$ are linear independent over $GF(q)$, that is

$$r(\mathbf{X}_{\mathcal{T}}|q) = k \tag{49}$$

equation (48) doesn't hold for any a_i (except when all a_i are zeros), and $\mathbf{X}_1 + \mathbf{I}_k$ doesn't possess the required property. This concludes the proof. ∎

Thus, to construct a matrix $\mathbf{X}_1 + \mathbf{I}_k$ having the property that for any $\mathbf{F}$ of the form (45) all columns of $\mathbf{X}_1 + \mathbf{I}_k - \mathbf{F}$ are linear independent over $GF(q)$, the following steps should be taken.

94

1. Choose a row $\mathbf{u} = (u_1, u_2, \ldots, u_m)$ such that all its components are linear independent over $GF(q)$.

2. Resolve $\mathbf{u}$ as $\mathbf{u} = \mathbf{v}_1 - \mathbf{v}_2$, where $\mathbf{v}_1^{[-1]}$ and $\mathbf{v}_2$ must be linear independent over $GF(q^n)$ (for $\mathbf{X}_1 + \mathbf{I}_k$ to be of full rank).

3. Taking $\mathbf{v}_1^{[-1]}$ to be the first row of $\mathbf{X}_1 + \mathbf{I}_k$, and $\mathbf{v}_2$ to be second one, and choosing other entries of $\mathbf{X}$ so as $\mathbf{X}$ to be of full rank over $GF(q^n)$, we get a matrix with the property just specified above.

There is another approach. Choose $\mathbf{X}_1 + \mathbf{I}_k$ randomly and apply $\mathcal{T}$ to every column of $\mathbf{X}_1 + \mathbf{I}_k$. If $r((\mathbf{X}_1 + \mathbf{I}_k)_{\mathcal{T}}|q) = k$, then $\mathbf{X}_1 + \mathbf{I}_k$ possesses the required property. If it is not the case, then return to the beginning and choose another $\mathbf{X}_1 + \mathbf{I}_k$. Do until success.

There also exists a different method for constructing the sum $\mathbf{X}_1 + \mathbf{I}_k$ possessing the specified property.

Lemma 11 Let $(0, \ldots, 0, \alpha, 0, \ldots, 0)$ be the i_1-th row of the sum $\mathbf{I}_k + \mathbf{X}_1$, and $(\beta_1, \beta_2, \ldots, \beta_k)$ be the i_2-th row of $\mathbf{I}_k + \mathbf{X}_1$, $1 \leq i_1, i_2 \leq k$, $i_1 \neq i_2$. Also suppose that $\beta_j \in GF(q)$ for any j, $j = 1, \ldots, k$, and $\alpha^{[i_2 - i_1]} \in GF(q^n) \backslash GF(q)$. Then all columns of $\mathbf{X}_1 + \mathbf{I}_k - \mathbf{F}$ are linear independent over $GF(q)$, where F defined by (45).

Proof. The proof is trivial. ∎

For any selection of $\mathbf{G}_n$ all m columns of $\mathbf{Y}_1$ are linear independent over $GF(q)$, so they form a basis of some vector subspace over $GF(q)$. For the same reason $(r(\mathbf{X}_2|q) = t_1)$ some t_1 columns of $\mathbf{X}_2$ form a basis of some vector subspace over $GF(q)$ (these two subspaces might be different from each other). From this it follows that $r(\mathbf{Y}_2|q) \geq t_1 - m$. Depending on the relation between these two subspaces, the column rank of $\tilde{\mathbf{X}}$ over $GF(q)$ can vary from 0 to $m + t_1$.

Lemma 12 Let vector subspaces of columns of $\mathbf{Y}_1$ and $\mathbf{X}_2$ over $GF(q)$ not intersect. Then for $\tilde{\mathbf{X}}$ to be "weak" (that is $r(\tilde{\mathbf{X}}|q) \leq t_1$), it is necessary and sufficient to have $r(\mathbf{Y}_2|q) = t_1 - m$.

Proof. Vector subspaces of columns of $\mathbf{X}_2$ и $\mathbf{Y}_1$ do not intersect. Neither do vector subspaces of $\mathbf{Y}_1$ and $\mathbf{Y}_2$. Since $r(\mathbf{Y}_2|q) \geq t_1 - m$ and $r(\mathbf{Y}_1|q) = m$, we have $r(\tilde{\mathbf{X}}|q) \geq t_1$. Therefore, $\tilde{\mathbf{X}}$ is "weak" if and only if $r(\tilde{\mathbf{X}}|q) = t_1$

Let $\tilde{\mathbf{X}}$ be a "weak" matrix. This means that $r(\tilde{\mathbf{X}}|q) = t_1$. Then from the facts that vector subspaces of columns of $\mathbf{Y}_2$ and $\mathbf{Y}_1$ over $GF(q)$ do not intersect, and $r(\mathbf{Y}_1|q) = m$, it follows that $r(\mathbf{Y}_2|q) = t_1 - m$.

The proof in the reverse direction is trivial. ∎

Estimate now the number of matrices $\mathbf{X}_2$ such that vector subspaces of their columns over $GF(q)$ do not intersect with vector subspaces of *all possible* $\mathbf{Y}_1$. Denote this number by M_X. We will consider the case $m = t_1$. The case $m < t_1$ is included in the previous one. In case $m > t_1$ $\tilde{\mathbf{X}}$ is always "strong".

First we will find a set $\mathcal{S}_Y$ of all vectors, which are included in all possible vector subspaces of columns of all admissible matrices $\mathbf{Y}_1$. Denote by M_Y the cardinality of the set $\mathcal{S}_Y$.

95

Recall that $\mathbf{Y}_1$ is in the form

$$\mathbf{Y}_1 = \begin{bmatrix} \mathbf{e}_{j_1} + \mathbf{x}_{j_1} - \mathbf{f}_{j_1} & \mathbf{e}_{j_2} + \mathbf{x}_{j_2} - \mathbf{f}_{j_2} & \dots & \mathbf{e}_{j_{t_1}} + \mathbf{x}_{j_{t_1}} - \mathbf{f}_{j_{t_1}} \end{bmatrix}, \tag{50}$$

$$1 \le j_1 < j_2 < \dots < j_{t_1} \le k,$$

where $\mathbf{e}_{j_i}$ are columns of the identity matrix; $\mathbf{x}_{j_i}$ are columns of $\mathbf{X}_1$; $\mathbf{f}_{j_i}$ are some columns of the form $(f_{j_i}, f_{j_i}^{[1]}, \dots, f_{j_i}^{[k-1]})^T$, where $f_{j_i} \in GF(q^n)$, all f_{j_i} being linear independent over $GF(q)$, $1 \le i \le t_1$. There exist q^n columns of the form $\mathbf{f}_j$ (it is the number of different elements of the field $GF(q^n)$). Some of those columns cannot be used, because they form matrix $\mathbf{G}$. But we are going to establish the upper bound for M_Y, so we will not take it into account.

Partition all columns $\mathbf{f}_j$ into batches of q columns: a batch contains some fixed column and all its multiples with coefficients from $GF(q)$. Trivially there are q^{N-1} batches. To choose some t_1 columns forming a basis over $GF(q)$, fix any t_1 distinct numbers of batches and select one column from every batch. Hence, there exist

$$q^{t_1} \binom{q^{n-1}}{t_1}$$

ways of choosing the set of vectors $\mathbf{f}_{j_1}, \dots, \mathbf{f}_{j_{t_1}}$.

The matrix $\mathbf{X}_1$ is fixed for it has been chosen by a cryptographer. The number of ways of choosing t_1 columns from $\mathbf{I}_k + \mathbf{X}_1$ is the number of all the permutations of k columns of $\mathbf{I}_k + \mathbf{X}_1$ taking t_1 at a time. In other notation, it is $\binom{k}{t_1} t_1!$. This yields that there are not greater than

$$q^{t_1} \binom{q^{n-1}}{t_1} \binom{k}{t_1} t_1!$$

matrices $\mathbf{Y}_2$. The columns of each matrix is a basis of vector subspace over $GF(q)$ of dimension t_1. Hence, all such subspaces contain

$$M_Y \le t_1! \binom{q^{n-1}}{t_1} \binom{k}{t_1} q^{t_1 + t_1} < \binom{k}{t_1} q^{(n+1)t_1} \tag{51}$$

vectors.

Further, if we choose a basis of vector subspace of columns of $\mathbf{X}_2$ from vectors of the set $X^k \backslash_Y$ (X^k is the set of all k-columns with coordinates from $GF(q^N)$), then vector subspaces of columns of $\mathbf{Y}_1\mathbf{X}_2$ over $GF(q)$ will not intersect. There are $q^{nk} - M_Y$ ways of choosing the first column of the basis, $q^{nk} - M_Y - q$ ways of choosing the second column. Continuing in the same way, the t_1-th column of the basis can be chosen by $q^{nk} - M_Y - q^{t_1-1}$ ways. This means that there are not greater than

$$N_{base} = (q^{nk} - M_Y)(q^{nk} - M_Y - q) \dots (q^{nk} - M_Y - q^{t_1-1}) \tag{52}$$

bases of spaces of columns of $\mathbf{X}_2$. Every

$$N_{same} = (q^{t_1} - 1)(q^{t_1} - q) \dots (q^{t_1} - q^{t_1-1}) \tag{53}$$

bases produce the same space.

Take t_1 base columns to form a matrix $\mathbf{X}_2^{base}$ of size $k \times t_1$. To build a matrix $\mathbf{X}_2$ from $\mathbf{X}_2^{base}$, multiply $\mathbf{X}_2^{base}$ to the right by a matrix $\mathbf{B}_x$ of size $t_1 \times n$ of full rank t_1 with entries in $GF(q)$: $\mathbf{X}_2 = \mathbf{X}_2^{base}\mathbf{B}_x$. Different matrices $\mathbf{B}_x$ yield different $\mathbf{X}_2$ since columns of $\mathbf{X}_2^{base}$ form a basis over $GF(q)$. So in this way we can build all possible $\mathbf{X}_2$. The number of distinct $\mathbf{B}_x$ is

$$(q^n - 1)(q^n - q)\ldots(q^n - q^{t_1-1}).$$

Thus, the full number of distinct matrices $\mathbf{X}_2$ such that vector subspaces of their columns do not intersect with space of columns of $\mathbf{Y}_1$ over $GF(q)$ and that $r(\mathbf{X}_2|q) = t_1$ is

$$M_X \geq \frac{N_{base}(q^n - 1)(q^n - q)\ldots(q^n - q^{t_1-1})}{N_{same}} = \tag{54}$$

$$\frac{(q^{nk} - M_Y)(q^{nk} - M_Y - q)\ldots(q^{nk} - M_Y - q^{t_1-1})(q^n - 1)(q^n - q)\ldots(q^n - q^{t_1-1})}{(q^{t_1} - 1)(q^{t_1} - q)\ldots(q^{t_1} - q^{t_1-1})}.$$

Denote by γ_x the proportion of matrices $\mathbf{X}_2$ among all $k \times n$ matrices with entries in $GF(q^n)$ and of rank t_1 over $GF(q)$. The value of γ_x satisfies the inequality

$$\gamma_x \geq \frac{(q^{nk} - M_Y)(q^{nk} - M_Y - q)\ldots(q^{nk} - M_Y - q^{t_1-1})}{(q^{nk} - 1)(q^{nk} - q)\ldots(q^{nk} - q^{t_1-1})}. \tag{55}$$

Taking into account that $M_Y >> q^{t_1}$, $q^{nk} >> q^{t_1}$, some straightforward manipulations give

$$\gamma_x \geq 1 - \frac{t_1 M_Y}{q^{Nk}} > 1 - \frac{t_1\binom{k}{t_1}}{q^{n(k-t_1)-t_1}}. \tag{56}$$

Example 2 *Let $k = n/2$. Then $\max t_1 < n/4$. From (56) it follows that*

$$\gamma_x \approx 1 - \frac{n(n/2)!}{4((n/4)!)^2\, q^{(n^2-n)/4}}.$$

Applying Stirling's formula $n! \simeq \sqrt{2\pi n}(n/e)^n$, we have

$$\gamma_x \approx 1 - \frac{\sqrt{n/\pi}\, 2^{n/2}}{2\, q^{(n^2-n)/4}} \tag{57}$$

From this estimation it is easily seen that γ_x quickly approaches 1, n increasing. In particular, for $q = 2$

$$\gamma_x > 1 - \frac{\sqrt{n/\pi}}{2^{1+(n^2-3n)/4}},$$

and even for $n = 20$ this gives $\gamma_x > 1 - 1/2^{84}$.

In other words, if some matrix $\mathbf{X}_2$ has been randomly and uniformly chosen from the set of all $k \times n$ matrices of rank t_1 over $GF(q)$, then with probability just

$$\Pr_f \leq \frac{t_1\binom{k}{t_1}}{q^{n(k-t_1)-t_1}} \tag{58}$$

it will be the matrix whose columns form vector subspace over $GF(q)$ that intersects with space of columns of some $\mathbf{Y}_1$ over the same field. This probability also determines the probability of "improper" choice of a basis of $\mathbf{X}_2$ (in the sense just discussed above).

In what follows, we assume that the cryptographer can choose basis columns for $\mathbf{X}_2$ such that vector subspaces of columns of $\mathbf{Y}_1$ and $\mathbf{X}_2$ over $GF(q)$ *do not* intersect. Now we represent a technique of building a matrix $\mathbf{X}_2$ with the property that if we delete any m columns ($m \leq t_1$) from it, then the remaining matrix (any $n - m$ columns) will have column rank over $GF(q)$ strictly greater than $t_1 - m$.

Choose some t_1 basis columns $\mathbf{z}_1, \mathbf{z}_2, \ldots, \mathbf{z}_{t_1}$. Form the matrix

$$\mathbf{Z} = [\mathbf{z}_1 \quad \mathbf{z}_2 \quad \ldots \quad \mathbf{z}_{t_1}]. \tag{59}$$

Choose some square non-singular matrix $\mathbf{W} = [w_{ij}]$ of dimension t_1 with entries in the base field $GF(q)$. Multiply $\mathbf{Z}$ to the right by $\mathbf{W}$. We get the matrix $\mathbf{Z}_w = \mathbf{ZW}$. Obviously, $r(\mathbf{Z}_w|q) = t_1$.

Construct the matrix $\mathbf{X}_2$:

$$\mathbf{X}_2 = [\mathbf{Z} \ \mathbf{Z}_w \ \mathbf{Z}_{aux}], \tag{60}$$

where $\mathbf{Z}_{aux}$ is any matrix with entries in $GF(q^n)$ of size $k \times (n - 2t_1)$. Since always $n \geq 2t_1$, such a construction always can be conducted.

Lemma 13 *Suppose $\mathbf{X}_2$ has been constructed as described above. Then it has the property that any $k \times (n - m)$ submatrix has a column rank over $GF(q)$ at least $t_1 - \lfloor m/2 \rfloor$ for any $m \leq 2t_1$.*

Proof. First consider the case when all deleted columns are the columns of $\mathbf{Z}$ and $\mathbf{Z}_w$ only.

Delete only one column, that is $m = 1$. If this column is a column of $\mathbf{Z}$, then $\mathbf{Z}_w$ has t_1 basis columns. The same situation we have when a column of $\mathbf{Z}_w$ has been deleted. Hence, $t_1 = t_1 - \lfloor m/2 \rfloor$.

Delete any $m = 2$ columns. If both columns are from $\mathbf{Z}$, then $\mathbf{Z}_w$ has t_1 basis columns. If both columns are from $\mathbf{Z}_w$, then t_1 are now in $\mathbf{Z}$. If one column is from $\mathbf{Z}_w$ and the other from $\mathbf{Z}$, then both $\mathbf{Z}$ and $\mathbf{Z}_w$ have at least $t_1 - 1$ basis columns each. Hence, the column rank over $GF(q)$ of the remaining matrix is greater than or equal to $t_1 - 1 = t_1 - \lfloor m/2 \rfloor$.

Consider general case when exactly m columns have been deleted. If $\lfloor m/2 \rfloor$ or less columns are from $\mathbf{Z}$ and the others from $\mathbf{Z}_w$, then $\mathbf{Z}_w$ has at least $t_1 - \lfloor m/2 \rfloor$ basis columns. The same takes place if we change $\mathbf{Z}_w$ to $\mathbf{Z}$. Thus, again the column rank over $GF(q)$ of the remaining matrix is at least $t_1 - \lfloor m/2 \rfloor$.

Suppose now that among m deleted columns i columns are from $\mathbf{Z}_{aux}$. Then from $\mathbf{Z}_w$ and $\mathbf{Z}$ together only $m - i$ columns have been deleted. Returning to the previous case, again we see that Lemma holds. ∎

Corollary 14 *Suppose $\mathbf{X}_2$, $r(\mathbf{X}_2|q) = t_1$, is constructed as*

$$\mathbf{X}_2 = [\mathbf{Z} \quad \mathbf{Z}_{w1} \quad \mathbf{Z}_{w2} \ldots \mathbf{Z}_{wr} \quad \mathbf{Z}_{aux}],$$

where $\mathbf{Z}$ is a $k \times t_1$ matrix with entries in $GF(q^n)$ and $r(\mathbf{Z}|q) = t_1$, $\mathbf{Z}_{wi} = \mathbf{Z}\mathbf{W}_i$, $\mathbf{W}_i$ is any q-ary square non-singular matrix of order t_1, $i = 1, 2, \ldots, r$. Then the column rank over $GF(q)$ of any $k \times (n-m)$ its submatrix is greater than or equal to

$$ t_1 - \left\lfloor \frac{m}{(r+1)} \right\rfloor $$

for any $m \le (r+1)t_1$.

If we use all admissible bases $\mathbf{Z}$ (the probability of choosing an admissible basis is γ_x, see (56)), all square q-ary non-singular matrices $\mathbf{W}$, any matrices $\mathbf{Z}_{aux}$, and multiply $[\mathbf{Z} \quad \mathbf{Z}\mathbf{W} \quad \mathbf{Z}_{aux}]$ to the right by any column permutation matrix of order n, then we construct all matrices $\mathbf{X}_2$. It is clear that the number of $\mathbf{X}_2$ constructed in the way described above is not less than $N_{base} \sim q^{knt_1}$.

Construction of the parts $\mathbf{X}_1, \mathbf{X}_2$ of a distortion matrix $\mathbf{X}$ proceeds in three stages.

1. Using Lemma 10 or Lemma 11, construct $\mathbf{X}_1$.

2. Choose basis $\mathbf{Z}$ for $\mathbf{X}_2$. $\mathbf{X}_2$ satisfies the conditions of Lemma 12 with probability γ_x that differs by a negligible small quantity from 1.

3. Using Lemma 13, construct $\mathbf{X}_2$.

This algorithm for constructing $\mathbf{X}_1$ and $\mathbf{X}_2$ always gives a "strong" $\tilde{\mathbf{X}}$.

Thus, we have proved that the representation (37) with $\tilde{\mathbf{X}}$ such that $r(\tilde{\mathbf{X}}|q) \le t_1$ can be obtained in the only case when the chosen n columns are the columns corresponding to the location of the matrix $\mathbf{G}$ in $\mathbf{G}_{new}$. Hence, this proves that the estimation of the complexity of the most efficient attack on the new PKC is given by formula (36).

3.2 Practical recommendations and numerical examples

As shown above to ensure security of GPT PKC with a rectangular scramble matrix, it is only necessary to have $p \ge 3$ for reasonable code length $n \sim 30$. It is also desirable to have the value of p as small as possible, since transmission rate decreases, with p increasing. Detailed recommendations on the choice of a scramble matrix and a distortion matrix have been given in section 3.0.1. Artificial errors of maximum admissible Hamming weight and rank over $GF(q)$ adding to a code vector should be used.

Example 3 *Let the following parameters have been chosen: $q = 2$, $n = 32$, $k = 16$, $p = 3$, $d = 17$, $t = 8$, $t_1 = 4$. Then the system performance is as follows. Transmission rate*

$$ R = \frac{k-p}{n} = \frac{13}{32} > 0.4. $$

Volume of the public key

$$ V_{key} = (k-p)n^2 = 13 * 2^{10} = 13Kbit. $$

99

Number of messages (plaintexts)

$$N_{message} = q^{n(k-p)} = 2^{416}.$$

Complexity of direct attacks

$$W_{direct} > q^{(n+k-p-t_1)t_1} = 2^{164}$$

arithmetical operations in $GF(2^{32})$.
Complexity of attacks on the public key

$$W_{key} = O(n^3 q^{pn}) \sim 2^{111}$$

multiplications in $GF(2^{32})$.
Number of artificial errors

$$N_{error} > q^{(2n+t_1-t)(t-t_1)} = 2^{240}.$$

Recommendations on choosing artificial errors for the PKC based on rank-like codes are the same: it is desirable to choose errors with maximum admissible Hamming weight and rank over $GF(q)$. While choosing values of n, k, it is necessary to keep balance between transmission rate and complexity of attacks on the public key from one hand, and correcting capacity of the code from the other hand. The first two quantities increase, k growing, but it precisely when the code should be easier to break with direct attacks. The algorithm of choosing distortion matrices is described in the course of the analysis of the system. The condition $k > t_1$ stated in section 3.1.4 is not crucial from practical point of view, since if it doesn't hold, the transmission rate falls below 0.25.

Example 4 *Let the following parameters have been chosen: $q = 2$, $N = 29$, $n = 29$, $k = 15$, $s = 1$, $d = 15$, $t = 7$, $t_1 = 4$. Then the system performance is as follows.*
Transmission rate

$$R = \frac{k}{k+n} = \frac{15}{44} > 0.34.$$

Value of the public key

$$V_{key} = k(k+n)n = 19140 \ bit.$$

Number of messages (plaintexts)

$$N_{message} = q^{nk} = 2^{435}.$$

Complexity of direct attacks

$$W_{direct} > q^{(n+k-t_1)t_1} = 2^{160}$$

multiplications in $GF(2^{29})$.

Complexity of attacks on the public key

$$W_{key} = O\left(C_{n+k}^k n^3 q^n\right) \sim 2^{81}$$

multiplications in $GF(2^{29})$.

Number of artificial errors

$$N_{error} > q^{(2n+k+t_1-t)(t-t_1)} = 2^{210}.$$

Compare performances of the GPT PKC and the new PKC based on rank-like codes. Suppose the transmission rate and the volume of the public key are the same in both systems, viz. $R = 0.34$ and $V_{key} \sim 20$ Kbit. Then for GPT PKC the length of the code is $N = 39$, and for a distortion matrix of rank 1 the complexity of Gibson's attack is $O(n^3 2^n) \sim 2^{55}$ operations in $GF(2^{39})$.

Making use of rank-like codes and a rectangular scramble matrix in a PKC simultaneously might significantly decrease the value of the transmission rate, so this seems to be not advantageous. However, we propose a new very simple technique of increasing the transmission rate. Let us consider *an artificial error* vector, which sending party adds to a code vector *as a part of a message*. In other words, a message now consists of two parts: an information vector (plaintext) and a vector of errors. If the cryptanalyst can determine or find the error vector, then he can calculate the information vector (plaintext). But it is just what was the case when the artificial error was not considered as a part of the message. So complexity of direct attacks remains the same. The only changes are that the secret key must contain the distortion matrix as a part of it, because it is needed for a complete decryption of the new (two-parted) message.

By way of example let us consider the system with the following parameters: $q = 2$, $k = n/3$, $d = 2k + 1$, $t = k$, $t_1 = k/2 = n/6$. The transmission rate without regard for artificial error as a part of a message is $R = k/(k + n) = 0.25$, and the number of information vectors is $N_{message} = q^{nk} = 2^{nk} = 2^{n^2/3}$. Assume that the sending party uses only artificial errors of maximum admissible rank $t - t_1 = t_1 = n/6$. The number of errors of that kind is $N_{er} \simeq q^{(2n+k+t_1-t)(t-t_1)} = q^{13n^2/36} = 2^{13n^2/36}$. The total transmission rate, artificial errors considered, becomes

$$R_{tot} = \frac{nk + log_2 2^{13n^2/36}}{(n+k)n} = \frac{n^2/3 + 13n^2/36}{4n^2/3} > 1/2.$$

This means that the transmission rate became   twice as large, but the volume of the public key remained the same. Similarly, in Examples 3,4 the transmission rates increase approximately by 50%.

This technique of increasing transmission rate can be applied to any McEliece PKC based on any family of error-correcting codes.

References

[1] E.M. Gabidulin, "Theory of Codes with Maximum Rank Distance," *Probl. Inform. Transm.*, vol. 21, No. 1, pp. 1–12, July, 1985.

[2] E.M. Gabidulin, A.V. Paramonov, O.V. Tretjakov, "Ideals over a Non-commutative Ring and Their Application in Cryptology", in: *Advances in Cryptology — Eurocrypt '91*, Editor: D.W. Davies, Lecture Notes in Computer Science, No 547, pp. 482–489, Berlin and Heidelberg: Springer-Verlag, 1991.

[3] E.M. Gabidulin, "Public-Key Cryptosystems Based on Linear Codes over Large Alphabets: Efficiency and Weakness," in: *Codes and Ciphers*, Editor: P.G. Farrell, pp. 17–32, Essex: Formara Limited, 1995.

[4] J.K. Gibson, "Severely Denting the Gabidulin Version of the McEliece Public Key Cryptosystem," in: *Designs, Codes and Cryptography*, 1993.

[5] J.K. Gibson, "Algebraic Coded Cryptosystems", *Ph.D. Thesis*, University of London, Royal Holloway and Bedford New College, 1995.

[6] R.J. McEliece, "A Public Key Cryptosystem Based on Algebraic Coding Theory," *JPL DSN Progress Report 42-44*, Pasadena, CA, pp. 114–116, 1978.

Suboptimum Decoding Based on the Recursive Maximum Likelihood Decoding Algorithm

Yuichi Kaji[†]   Eiji Kasai[†]   Toru Fujiwara[‡]   Tadao Kasami[⋆]

† Grad. School of Information Science, Nara Institute of Science & Technology
  8916-5 Takayama, Ikoma, Nara 630-0101, Japan
‡ Graduate School of Engineering Science, Osaka University
  1-3 Machikaneyama, Toyonaka, Osaka 560-8531, Japan
⋆ Faculty of Information Science, Hiroshima City University
  3-4-1 Ozuka-Higashi, Numata, Asa-Minami, Hiroshima 731-3194, Japan

Abstract: A suboptimum decoding algorithm is presented. The algorithm is derived by approximating some computations in the *recursive maximum likelihood decoding* (*RMLD*) algorithm. In the RMLD algorithm, the most likely code vector is computed by constructing tables of most likely local vectors in a divide-and-conquer manner. In the proposed suboptimum algorithm, vectors in the tables are pruned according to   certain criteria. The relation between the criteria of pruning, error performance and the decoding complexity is discussed.

1   Introduction

An efficient decoding algorithm of error correcting codes plays an essential role for realizing high speed and reliable communication. The decoding scheme that maximizes the reliability (i.e. minimizes the decoding failure and error rate) is the *maximum likelihood decoding* (*MLD*). However, the conventional MLD algorithm, known as the *Viterbi algorithm*[5] has quite a large decoding complexity since it requires an implementation of a whole *trellis diagram* of the code. This problem is especially serious for linear block codes since block codes usually have more complicated and larger trellis diagrams than convolutional codes.

Recently, another MLD algorithm, the *recursive maximum likelihood decoding* (*RMLD*) algorithm has been proposed[2]. The RMLD algorithm uses structural properties of linear codes, and succeeds in reducing the decoding complexity of MLD significantly. Another direction for reducing the decoding complexity is the realization of *suboptimum decoding* algorithms. Suboptimum algorithms do not give as good error performance as ML decoders, but suboptimum algorithms usually have quite smaller decoding complexity than ML decoders and good for implementing high speed communication systems.

A new suboptimum decoding algorithm is proposed in this paper. The algorithm is obtained by approximating some computation in the RMLD al-

103

gorithm. In the RMLD algorithm, the computation of the most likely code vector is carried out as a kind of table construction procedure. By pruning insignificant values from the table, the decoding complexity which is measured by the number of addition equivalent operations of metrics can be reduced significantly compared to the RMLD algorithm. The relation among the criteria for the pruning, the error correcting performance and the decoding complexity of the obtained suboptimum decoder is discussed. A preliminary result for the third order Reed-Muller code of length 64 shows that we can realize a suboptimum decoder which achieves almost the same error performance as an ML decoder and costs only one-fourth decoding complexity compared to the RMLD algorithm. The proposed algorithm inherits many implementation advantages of the RMLD algorithm. For example, the algorithm computes the most likely code vector by the divide-and-conquer strategy. This structure of the algorithm enables us to implement a decoder with the parallel and pipeline techniques[2].

2   Structure of Codes and the RMLD Algorithm

The proposed algorithm is based on the RMLD algorithm[2], and the RMLD algorithm uses structural properties of linear block codes. Notations and concepts necessary for describing the proposed algorithm are briefly reviewed in this section (see [1] and [2] for details). Assume that an (n, k) binary linear block code C is used for error control over an AWGN channel with BPSK signaling. On receiving a signal sequence, the *bit metric* $m_i(b)$ of a symbol $b \in \{0, 1\}$ at the bit position i with $1 \leq i \leq n$ is defined according to the channel statistics. Intuitively, larger metric $m_i(b)$ means larger probability that the symbol b has been sent as the i-th bit symbol. The metric of a code vector $v = (v_1, \ldots, v_n)$ is defined to be the sum of bit metrics; $m(v) = \sum_{i=1}^{n} m_i(v_i)$. The code vector which maximizes the metric among all code vectors is called the *most likely (ML) code vector*, denoted c_{opt}. If a decoder of the code C always find the most likely code vector, then the decoder is called a *maximum likelihood decoder*. Otherwise, it is called a *suboptimum decoder*. It is common to measure the complexity of decoders (or decoding algorithms) by the number of addition equivalent operations (addition, subtraction, comparison and so on) of metrics, since the number is considered to affect the number of full-adders and the chip size of an IC-implemented decoder.

The RMLD algorithm is a more efficient way for finding the most likely code vector than the conventional Viterbi algorithm. The RMLD algorithm computes the most likely code vector in the divide-and-conquer manner. The division is made according to the code structure of C. For a binary vector $v = (v_1, v_2, \ldots, v_n)$ of length n, and integers x and y such that $0 \leq x < y \leq n$, define $p_{xy}(v) \triangleq (v_{x+1}, \ldots, v_y)$ and define $p_{xy}(C) \triangleq \{p_{xy}(v) : v \in C\}$. Also define

104

C_{xy} as the set of code vectors in C whose first x and the last $n-y$ symbols are all zero, that is, $\hat{C}_{xy} \triangleq \{(0,\ldots,0,v_{x+1},\ldots,v_y,0,\ldots,0) \in C\}$. Since $p_{xy}(C_{xy})$ is a linear subcode of $p_{xy}(C)$, $p_{xy}(C)$ can be partitioned to cosets of $p_{xy}(C_{xy})$. Let L_{xy} be the set of cosets of $p_{xy}(C_{xy})$ in $p_{xy}(C)$. For a coset $D_{xy} \in L_{xy}$, let $v(D_{xy})$ denote the vector in D_{xy} which has the maximum metric among all vectors in D_{xy}. The vector $v(D_{xy})$ is called the *most likely local vector in* D_{xy}, and the metric of $v(D_{xy})$ is denoted by $m(D_{xy})$. The following simple lemma holds.

Lemma 2.1: For an ML code vector c_{opt}, there is a coset $D_{xy} \in L_{xy}$ such that $v(D_{xy}) = p(c_{\text{opt}})$. □

For two vectors $u = (u_1, u_2, \ldots, u_i)$ and $v = (v_1, v_2, \ldots, v_j)$, we write $u \circ v$ for the concatenated vector $(u_1, u_2, \ldots, u_i, v_1, v_2, \ldots, v_j)$. Similarly, for sets of vectors A and B, define $A \circ B \triangleq \{u \circ v : u \in A, v \in B\}$. Let z be an integer such that $x < z < y$. Since $p_{xz}(C_{xz}) \circ p_{zy}(C_{zy})$ is a linear subcode of $p_{xy}(C_{xy})$, each coset $D_{xy} \in L_{xy}$ can be partitioned to a set of cosets of $p_{xz}(C_{xz}) \circ p_{zy}(C_{zy})$ in $p_{xy}(C)$ in such a way that

$$D_{xy} = \bigcup_{i=1}^{s} D_{xz}^i \circ D_{zy}^i \tag{1}$$

where $s = |p_{xy}(C)|/(|p_{xz}(C_{xz})| \cdot |p_{zy}(C_{zy})|)$, $D_{xz}^i \in L_{xz}$ and $D_{zy}^i \in L_{zy}$ for $1 \leq i \leq s$. It follows from (1) that

$$m(D_{xy}) = \max_{1 \leq i \leq s} \{m(D_{xz}^i) + m(D_{zy}^i)\} \tag{2}$$

and

$$v(D_{xy}) = v(D_{xz}^i) \circ v(D_{zy}^i) \tag{3}$$

where i is the integer which maximizes $m(D_{xz}^i) + m(D_{zy}^i)$.

Let CBT(x,y) be a table which records $v(D_{xy})$ and $m(D_{xy})$ for every coset $D_{xy} \in L_{xy}$. We recall that $L_{0,n} = \{C\}$ and hence CBT$(0,n)$ contains the most likely code vector and its metric. The equations (2) and (3) imply that CBT(x,y) is easily computed if CBT(x,z) and CBT(z,y) have been already computed. Based on this idea, the following algorithm RMLD constructs CBT(x,y) for given section boundaries x and y with $0 \leq x < y \leq n$.

Algorithm 2.1 RMLD(x,y): A positive integer a with $1 < a < n$ is properly chosen. If $1 \leq y - x < a$, then execute the following **makeCBT(x,y)** procedure. If $y - x \geq a$, then choose an integer z with $x < z < y$ and execute the following **combCBT$(x,y;z)$** procedure.

makeCBT(x,y): Compute metrics of all vectors in $p_{xy}(C)$, and, for every coset $D_{xy} \in L_{xy}$, find the vector with the maximum metric among all vectors in D_{xy}.

combCBT$(x, y; z)$: First, execute RMLD(x, z) and RMLD(z, y) to construct tables CBT(x, z) and CBT(z, y), respectively. Then, use (2) and (3) to construct CBT(x, y). $\qquad\square$

We remark that the decoding complexity of the RMLD algorithm depends on the selection of the integer a and the choice of the integer z in the recursive step. The optimum choices (sectionalization) which minimize the decoding complexity can be made by using a dynamic programming method[2]. A sectionalization where $a = 2^h$ for $h > 0$ and $z = (x + y)/2$ at the recursive steps of the RMLD algorithm is called a binary sectionalization. If the binary sectionalization is adopted for a code of length 2^m, then the RMLD procedure is executed with section boundaries $x = i2^j$ and $y = (i+1)2^j$ for $0 \leq i < 2^{m-j}$ at the recursion level $m - j$ with $h \leq j < m$. (The procedure call RMLD$(0, 2^m)$ is regarded to be a recursion level 0).

3   Suboptimum Decoding Algorithm

A suboptimum realization of the RMLD is considered in this section. The key idea is to approximate the equations (2) and (3). There are many different ways for the approximation. In this paper, we show an approximation method for a class of transitive invariant binary block codes[3]. Reed-Muller codes and extended BCH codes belong to the class. For a code C of length 2^m in this class, it is known in [3] that, for $1 \leq j \leq m$ and $0 \leq i \leq 2^{m-j}$, $p_{i2^j,(i+1)2^j}(C) = p_{0,2^j}(C)$, $C_{i2^j,(i+1)2^j} = C_{0,2^j}$ and therefore

$$L_{i2^j,(i+1)2^j} = L_{0,2^j}.$$

It is also shown that the binary sectionalization provides the minimum or near minimum number of addition-equivalent operations of metrics for most Reed-Muller codes of length 128 or less, and extended BCH codes of length 128 or less and rate less that 0.4[3]. Equation (3) reduces the number of parameters to be considered for approximation considerably. Throughout this section, the third order Reed-Muller (64,42,8) code, denoted RM$_{3,6}$, is used as a running example. For this code, a binary sectionalization is almost optimum sectionalization for the RMLD algorithm.

A simple way for the approximation is to prune some cosets with relatively small metrics from the table CBT(x, y). For example, consider that there are M cosets in L_{xy}, and we are going to keep only θ best metrics in the table CBT(x, y) where $1 \leq \theta \leq M$. The remaining $M - \theta$ cosets which have smaller metrics than the θ-th best coset are pruned. If a coset $D_{xy} \in L_{xy}$ is pruned, then the metric $m(D_{xy})$ is regarded to be "negligible small", and will not be used for the computation in the upper recursion level. To minimize the degradation of the error performance of the suboptimum decoding algorithm, the threshold θ for the pruning must be chosen appropriately.

106

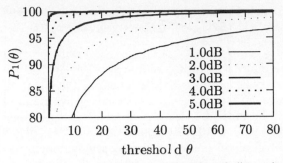

Figure 1: The distribution of $P_1(\theta)$ for CBT(0,32) ($|L_{0,32}| = 1024$).

To give a criterion for determining the threshold θ, the statistical behavior of the metrics of received sequences is observed by computer simulation. For simplicity, the binary sectionalization is adopted for the decoding. That is, the table CBT(0,64) is constructed from CBT(0,32) and CBT(32,64), CBT(0,32) is constructed from CBT(0,16) and CBT(16,32), CBT(0,16) is constructed from CBT(0,8) and CBT(8,16), and so on. Tables CBT($8i, 8(i + 1)$) with $0 \leq i < 8$ are constructed directly by the **makeCBT** procedure because the direct construction is more efficient than the recursive construction for these tables. Without loss of generality, we assume that the zero vector $\mathbf{0} = (0, 0, \ldots, 0)$ is transmitted over an AWGN channel. For received sequences $\mathbf{r} = (r_1, r_2, \ldots, r_n)$'s which are correctly decoded to the zero vector by an ML decoder, we take the ordered statistics of the metric of the coset which contains the zero vector. Let x and y be integers such that $0 \leq x < y \leq n$. Since $(0, 0, \ldots, 0) \in p_{xy}(C)$, there is a coset $D_{xy}^0 \in L_{xy}$ such that $(0, 0, \ldots, 0) \in D_{xy}^0$. It follows from Lemma 2.1 that if $\mathbf{r}$ is decoded to the zero vector by an ML decoder, then $v(D_{xy}^0) = (0, 0, \ldots, 0)$ and $m(D_{xy}^0)$ is the metric of the local zero vector. For $1 \leq l < m$, let $P_l(\theta)$ denote the probability that coset $D_{0,2^{m-l}}^0$ has one of the largest θ metrics in $L_{0,2^{m-l}}$ (i.e. $D_{0,2^{m-l}}^0$ is not pruned in CBT($0, 2^{m-l}$)) under the condition for the zero vector to be the ML code vector. Figs. 1 to 3 show the distributions of the probability $P_l(\theta)$ with $1 \leq l \leq 3$ (with respect to the tables CBT(0,32), CBT(0,16) and CBT(0,8), respectively). We remark that the result for the table CBT(32,64) is the same as that for CBT(0,32), since $L_{0,32} = L_{32,64}$ from (3), and the channel is memoryless. Similarly, CBT($16i, 16(i + 1)$) with $0 \leq i < 4$ and CBT($8i, 8(i + 1)$) with $0 \leq i < 8$ have the same distribution as CBT(0,16) and CBT(0,8), respectively.

These figures show the relation between the threshold θ and, for $1 \leq l \leq 3$, the probability $P_l(\theta)$ that the coset $D_{i2^{m-l},(i+1)2^{m-l}}^0$ with $(0, 0, \ldots, 0) \in D_{i2^{m-l},(i+1)2^{m-l}}^0$ remains in a CBT table. For example, consider to use $\theta = 20$ as the threshold for pruning cosets in CBT(0,32). Fig. 1 shows that the coset

107

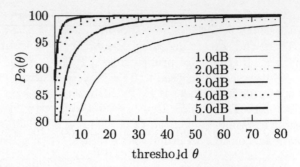

Figure 2: The distribution of $P_2(\theta)$ for CBT(0,16) ($|L_{0,16}| = 1024$).

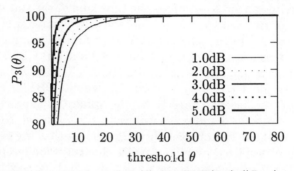

Figure 3: The distribution of $P_3(\theta)$ for CBT(0,8) ($|L_{0,8}| = 128$).

$D_{0,32}^0$ remains in CBT(0,32) with probability about 0.88 at $E_b/N_0 = 1.0$dB, and is pruned with probability about 0.12. If $D_{0,32}^0$ is pruned, then the suboptimum decoding fails to output the correct code vector. Remark that the figure shows the distribution under the condition that the received sequence is correctly decoded to the zero vector by an ML decoder. Under this condition, the suboptimum decoding gives the correct code vector if and only if both of $D_{0,32}^0$ and $D_{32,64}^0$ survive in CBT(0,32) and CBT(32,64), respectively. Actually, even if $D_{0,32}^0$ (resp. $D_{32,64}^0$) does not have the largest metric in CBT(0,32) or CBT(32,64), $m(D_{0,32}^0) + m(D_{32,64}^0)$ has the largest metric among all code vectors. To realize good error performance, we must choose the threshold so that $D_{0,32}^0$ and $D_{32,64}^0$ remain in CBT tables as frequently as possible. For a chosen threshold θ, since $P_1(\theta)$ is the probability that $D_{0,32}^0$ remains in CBT(0,32) and the channel is memoryless, the probability that both of $D_{0,32}^0$ and $D_{32,64}^0$ survive in each CBT table is $P_1(\theta)^2$. Consequently, the correct decoding probability of the suboptimum decoder is $P_1(\theta)^2 p_M$ where p_M is the correct decoding probability of an ML decoder. Similar discussion holds for the case that cosets are pruned from smaller CBT tables. For example, consider to prune cosets from $\text{CBT}(2^{6-2}i, 2^{6-2}(i+1))$ with $o \le i < 4$. For a chosen threshold θ, $P_2(\theta)$ denote the probability that $D_{0,16}^0$ remains in $\text{CBT}(0,16)$. Then, the correct decoding probability of the suboptimum decoder is $P_2(\theta)^4 p_M$. If cosets are pruned from $\text{CBT}(2^{6-3}i, 2^{6-3}(i+1))$ with $0 \le i < 8$ and the threshold is chosen to be θ, then the correct decoding probability of the suboptimum decoder is $P_3(\theta)^8 p_M$ where $P_3(\theta)$ is the probability that $D_{0,8}^0$ remains in $\text{CBT}(0,8)$ for the threshold θ.

It is possible to prune cosets from CBT tables of some different recursion levels. For example, consider to prune cosets from $\text{CBT}(x,y)$ with $y - x = 16$ by using a threshold θ_2, and from $\text{CBT}(x,y)$ with $y - x = 8$ by using a threshold θ_3. In this case, the correct coset $D_{0,16}^0$ remains in $\text{CBT}(0,16)$ if and only if $D_{0,8}^0$ and $D_{8,16}^0$ remain in $\text{CBT}(0,8)$ and $\text{CBT}(8,16)$, respectively, and $D_{0,16}^0$ is not pruned. Thus the probability that $D_{0,16}^0$ remains in $\text{CBT}(0,16)$ is given as $P_2(\theta_2, \theta_3) = P_3(\theta_3)^2 P_2(\theta_2|\theta_3)$ where $P_2(\theta_2|\theta_3)$ is the conditional probability that $D_{0,16}^0$ remains in $\text{CBT}(0,16)$ under the condition that cosets are pruned from $\text{CBT}(0,8)$ and $\text{CBT}(8,16)$ by using the threshold θ_3. Since $P_2(\theta_2|\theta_3) \ge P_2(\theta_2)$, hence $P_2(\theta_2, \theta_3) \ge P_3(\theta_3)^2 P_2(\theta_2)$. For this case, the correct decoding probability $P_2(\theta_2, \theta_3)^4 p_M$ can be lower-bounded by

$$P_3(\theta_3)^8 P_2(\theta_2)^4 p_M.$$

Similarly, if we prune cosets from $\text{CBT}(x,y)$ with $y - x = 32$ using a threshold θ_1 in addition to $y - x = 16$ and 8, then the correct decoding probability can be lower-bounded by

$$P_3(\theta_3)^8 P_2(\theta_2)^4 P_1(\theta_1)^2 p_M.$$

Summarizing the above discussion, we can determine appropriate thresholds by using Figs. 1 to 3 to achieve a specified error performance.

Example 3.1: Assume that we are going to design a decoder whose correct decoding probability is about 90% of that of an ML decoder at $E_b/N_0 = 3.0\text{dB}$. Thresholds θ_1, θ_2 and θ_3 are chosen so that

$$P_3(\theta_3)^8 P_2(\theta_2)^4 P_1(\theta_1)^2 \approx 0.90.$$

There are many solutions for choosing the thresholds which satisfy this equation. As a simple example, we can choose $\theta_1 = 7$, $\theta_2 = 1024$ and $\theta_3 = 128$. Since $L_{0,32} = 1024$, $L_{0,16} = 1024$ and $L_{0,8} = 128$, this means that cosets are not pruned at the recursion levels 2 and 3. This choice of thresholds makes $P_1(\theta_1) = 0.954$, $P_2(\theta_2) = P_3(\theta_3) = 1.000$ and hence the correct decoding probability is about 91% of that of an ML decoder. We can also choose $\theta_1 = 1024$, $\theta_2 = 20$ and $\theta_3 = 128$ (no pruning at the recursion levels 1 and 3) which makes $P_2(\theta_2) = 0.977$, $P_1(\theta_1) = P_3(\theta_3) = 1.000$ and realizes the error performance similar to the former choice. Among many choices of thresholds, we should choose one which minimizes the decoding complexity. □

109

4 Complexity of the Suboptimum Algorithm

Pruning cosets from CBT tables reduces the decoding complexity, which is measured by the number of addition equivalent operations of metrics. In this section, the relation between the threshold and the decoding complexity is considered. To prune cosets from CBT tables, we need some additional operations for finding θ best cosets which have larger metrics than the other cosets. Assume that we use a knock-out tournament selection algorithm[4] to find θ best cosets in a table $CBT(x,y)$ (which contains $|L_{xy}|$ cosets). The best coset is found with $|L_{xy} - 1|$ comparisons by constructing a tournament tree, and the second and later cosets are found with at most $\log_2 |L_{xy}|$ comparisons for each by using the constructed tournament tree. Hence the number of comparisons necessary for the selection is upper bounded by $|L_{xy} - 1| + (\theta - 1) \log_2 |L_{xy}|$. This is the overhead necessary for pruning.

On the other hand, pruned cosets can be ignored in the construction of CBT tables of the upper recursion levels, which reduces the decoding complexity. For example, if a part of cosets in $CBT(0,16)$ and $CBT(16,32)$ have been pruned, then the number of addition equivalent operations for constructing $CBT(0,32)$ will be smaller than the original RMLD algorithm in which no cosets are pruned. Unfortunately, it is difficult to analyze the relation between the threshold and the reduction of the decoding complexity in a theoretical way. Structural properties of weight distributions of cosets will be necessary for the analysis. Instead, the relation can be observed by computer simulation.

The total changes of the decoding complexity are shown in Figs. 4 to 6. For example, Fig. 4 shows that if we prune cosets from $CBT(0,32)$ and $CBT(32,64)$ with a threshold $\theta = 20$, then the number of operations necessary for constructing $CBT(0,64)$ can be reduced by 842 at $E_b/N_0 = 3.0$dB. If θ is chosen over 100, then the overhead is larger than the reduction made by the pruning, and the total cost will be increased. If no cosets are pruned from CBT tables, then the constructions of $CBT(x,y)$ with $y - x = 64$, $y - x = 32$, $y - x = 16$ and $y - x = 8$ require 2048, 131072, 16384 and 512 operations, respectively. Since we need two $CBT(x,y)$ tables with $y - x = 32$, four $CBT(x,y)$ tables with $y - x = 16$ and eight $CBT(x,y)$ tables with $y - x = 8$ for decoding, the total number of addition equivalent operations for a decoding is $2048 + 2 \times 131072 + 4 \times 16384 + 8 \times 512 = 334592$. If cosets are pruned from $CBT(0,32)$ and $CBT(32,64)$ with a threshold $\theta_1 = 7$, then we can save 961 operations at $E_b/N_0 = 3.0$dB (Fig. 4) for constructing $CBT(0,64)$. The total number of addition equivalent operations is thus $334592 - 961 = 333631$. On the other hand, if cosets are pruned from $CBT(x,y)$ with $y - x = 16$ using a threshold $\theta_2 = 20$, then we can save 129821 operations for constructing a CBT table with $y - x = 32$ (Fig. 5). Since there are two CBT tables with $y - x = 32$, the total number of addition equivalent operations necessary for decoding is $334592 - 2 \times 129821 = 74950$, which is less than one-fourth of the original RMLD algorithm. Remark that the choices $(\theta_1, \theta_2) = (7, 1024)$

110

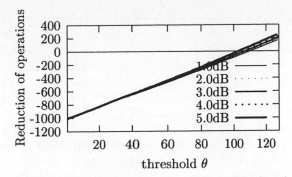

Figure 4: Complexity reduction for constructing CBT(0,64) by pruning CBT(0,32) and CBT(32,64).

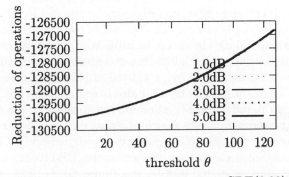

Figure 5: Complexity reduction for constructing CBT(0,32) by pruning CBT(0,16) and CBT(16,32).

and $(\theta_1, \theta_2) = (1024, 20)$ give similar error performance, as we have seen in Example 3.1. Therefore, in this case, choosing $(\theta_1, \theta_2) = (1024, 20)$ is much better.

Consider another example. Thresholds are chosen so that $\theta_1 = 1024$, $\theta_2 = 50$ and $\theta_3 = 128$ (no pruning at the recursion levels 1 and 3). Since $P_2(\theta_2) = 0.995$, the total correct decoding probability will be $0.995^4 p_M = 0.98 p_M$ where p_M is the correct decoding probability of an ML decoder. From Fig. 5, 129285 operations can be saved for constructing a CBT table with $y - x = 32$. Thus the total decoding complexity is $334592 - 2 \times 129285 = 76022$. The obtained suboptimum decoder can achieve 98% performance of an ML decoder with only one-fourth decoding complexity.

111

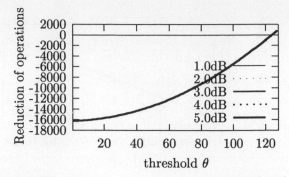

Figure 6: Complexity reduction for constructing CBT(0,16) by pruning CBT(0,8) and CBT(8,16).

5   Concluding Remark

A suboptimum decoding algorithm is proposed. The algorithm is based on the RMLD algorithm, and inherits many implementation advantages. The constructions of tables CBT(0,16), CBT(16,32), CBT(32,48) and CBT(48,64) can be carried out independently and simultaneously. Hence if we construct these tables in a parallel manner, then we can speed-up the decoding. On the other hand, the computation between different recursion levels can be done in a pipeline manner. For example, during the construction of CBT(0,64) of the first received signal sequence, we can construct CBT(0,32) and CBT(32,64) of the second received signal sequence. Tables CBT(0,32) and CBT(32,64) are immediately sent to the upper recursion level when the processing of CBT(0,64) of the first received sequence is finished. Such pipeline processing mechanism helps realizing a high speed decoder.

As a future research plan, a systematic way for determining the thresholds for pruning is under study. To realize a specified error performance, there are many solutions for choosing thresholds. From such solutions, we should choose one which minimizes the decoding complexity. The thresholds given in this paper are chosen heuristically based on the result of computer simulation. Near optimum choice of thresholds may be possible if we can model the relation between the threshold and the decoding complexity. Thresholds in terms of percentage of the maximum metrics may be more effective than those in terms of ordinal numbers. In this paper, RMLD algorithm based on add-compare-select procedure for solving (1) has been considered. Some improvement may be possible by approximating sort-add-compare-select procedure[2] for solving (1).

References

[1] G.D. Forney Jr.: "Dimension/length profiles and trellis complexity of linear block codes," IEEE Trans. Inf. Theory, **IT-40**, 6, pp.1741–1752 (1994).

[2] T. Fujiwara et al.: "A trellis-based recursive maximum likelihood decoding algorithm for linear codes," IEEE Trans. IT., **IT-44**, 3, pp.714–729 (1998).

[3] T. Kasami et al.: "A recursive maximum likelihood decoding algorithm for some transitive invariant binary block codes," IEICE Trans. Fundamentals, **E81-A**, 9, pp.1916–1924 (1998).

[4] D.E. Knuth: *The Art of Computer Programming, Volume 3, Sorting and Searching*, Addison-Wesley (1973).

[5] A.J. Viterbi: "Error bounds for convolutional codes and an asymptotically optimum decoding algorithm," IEEE Trans. IT., **IT-13**, pp.260–269 (1967).

The Discrete Noiseless Channel Revisited.[*]

Aamod Khandekar, Robert McEliece, and Eugene Rodemich

California Institute of Technology
Pasadena, California, USA

Abstract: *In this paper, we will discuss two of the lesser-known gems, viz., Theorems 1 and 8, from Shannon's 1948 classic paper, A Mathematical Theory of Communication [9], both dealing with the capacity of what he called the discrete noiseless channel. Although our paper is largely tutorial, it contains a few new ideas and results, including: a careful treatment of the case of symbols of different durations, including non-integer durations, the introduction of a new proof technique, which we call the "partition function" technique, and a theorem on the maximum entropy of a Markov chain defined on a digraph, subject to a constraint on the average edge duration.*

1. Introduction.

This paper deals with the *discrete noiseless channel*, which was the first topic treated in Shannon's classic 1948 paper [9, Section 1]. To paraphrase Shannon, a discrete noiseless channel is a channel which allows the noiseless transmission of a sequence of symbols chosen from a finite alphabet A, each symbol having a certain duration in time, possibly different for different symbols. Furthermore, there may be restrictions on the allowed sequences of symbols from A. The question is, what is the capacity of such a channel to transmit information?

To be more precise, we suppose A is a q-letter alphabet, and that associated with each letter $a \in A$ is a positive number $\tau(a)$ called the *duration* of a. Here are two examples: (1) the *standard q-ary alphabet*, with $A = \{0, 1, \ldots, q-1\}$, and $\tau(0) = \tau(1) = \cdots \tau(q-1) = 1$; and (2) *Shannon's telegraphy alphabet*, with $A = \{d, D, s, S\}$ and durations given in the following table: [1]

a	$\tau(a)$
d	2
D	4
s	3
S	6

(1.1)

A *word of length* k over A is a finite string of k letters from A. If $\alpha = a_1 a_2 \cdots a_k$ is such a word, its duration is defined to be $\tau(\alpha) = \tau(a_1) + \cdots + \tau(a_k)$. For example, 010110 is a word of length 6 and duration 6 over the

---

[*] This work was partially supported by NSF grant no. CCR-9804793, and grants from Sony and Qualcomm.
[1] In Shannon's terminology, d is "dot", D is "dash", s is "letter space", and S is "word space".

standard binary alphabet, 01221022 is a word of length 8 and duration 8 over the standard 3-ary alphabet, and

$$dddsddddsdDsDdsDdsDDDsDdS$$

is a word of length 25 and duration 74 over Shannon's telegraphy alphabet.

A *language* $\mathcal{L}$ over A is a collection of words over A. The discrete noiseless channel associated with $\mathcal{L}$, the $\mathcal{L}$-channel for short, is the channel which is only allowed to transmit sequences from $\mathcal{L}$, although it transmits them without error. We ask, what is the capacity of the $\mathcal{L}$-channel?

For a general language $\mathcal{L}$, not much can be said, and so we must restrict the class of languages, as did Shannon. In this paper we will consider only *Shannon* languages. Roughly, a Shannon language is defined by a directed graph whose edges are labelled with letters from the alphabet A. The corresponding language $\mathcal{L}$ is then defined to be the set of words that result by reading off the edge labels on paths of the graph. (We will give a more precise definition in Section 4.)

For example, if the graph consists of a single vertex v and q self-loops at v, each labelled with a different element of A, the resulting language consists of all possible sequences over A. We will call this the *free language* over A. As an example of a more resrictive type, consider the directed graph of Figure 1, in which each of the edges is labelled with an element from Shannon's telegraphy alphabet. The resulting language consists of all sequences of d's, D's, s's and S's, except that no word containing two consecutive spaces is permitted.

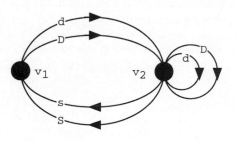

Figure 1. A directed graph with the branches labelled
by symbols from Shannon's telegraphy alphabet.

Shannon gave, in effect, two different definitions for the capacity of a noiseless channel corresponding to a Shannon language $\mathcal{L}$, and then showed that the two definitions gave the same value. This common value was thereby established unambiguously as the as the maximum rate, in bits[2] per second,

---

[2] Assuming the implied logarithms are base-2. In this paper, however, we

that information can be transmitted over the channel. We shall call these two definitions the *combinatorial* capacity and the *probabilistic* capacity.

If $\mathcal{L}$ is a Shannon language, we denote the total number of words in $\mathcal{L}$ of duration t by $N(t)$. The combinatorial capacity of the $\mathcal{L}$-channel is defined as[3]

$$(1.2) \qquad C_{\text{comb}} \overset{\Delta}{=} \limsup_{t \to \infty} \frac{1}{t} \log N(t).$$

Similarly, let (X_n) be a stationary discrete Markov chain defined on the labelled graph defining $\mathcal{L}$. If the entropy of (X_n) is H and the average branch duration is T, then the *information rate* of (X_n), in bits per second, is H/T. The probabilistic capacity of the $\mathcal{L}$-language is defined to be the maximum of this rate, over all possible Markov chains:

$$(1.3) \qquad C_{\text{prob}} \overset{\Delta}{=} \sup_{(X_n)} \frac{H}{T}.$$

As a very simple example, for the free language over the standard q-ary alphabet,

$$N(t) = \begin{cases} q^t & \text{if } t \text{ is an integer} \\ 0 & \text{if } t \text{ is not an integer,} \end{cases}$$

and so by (1.2), $C_{\text{comb}} = \log_2 q$. Similarly, it is easy to see in this case that the maximum-rate Markov chain is a sequence of i.i.d. uniform random variables, for which $H = \log q$ and $T = 1$, so $C_{\text{prob}} = \log q$ as well.

In his original paper, Shannon gave a simple algebraic method for computing C_{comb} (Theorem 1), and showed that the same value held for C_{prob} (Theorem 8). His proofs, however, were brief and in places quite cryptic. In this paper, we will give complete, and we hope clear, proofs of both of these important results. We will first treat the important special case of the free languages. The proofs in this case are quite simple, but they serve to introduce the more difficult ideas needed in the general case. Here is a guide to our paper:

• Shannon's Theorem 1 (C_{comb}): For free languages, Section 2; for general Shannon languages, Section 4.
• Shannon's Theorem 8 (C_{prob}): For free languages, Section 3; for general Shannon languages, Section 5.

In Section 6, we briefly sketch a kind of generalization of Shannon's Theorem 8 which we hope will be of interest, and then in Section 7 we give some concluding remarks.

---

will mostly use natural logarithms, and so information will be measured in nats.

[3] Actually, Shannon used "lim" instead of "lim sup," but in order to be fully rigorous, we will need the more precise term.

2. The Combinatorial Capacity of Free Languages.

The *free language* A^* over the alphabet A is simply the set of all possible strings of all lengths over A. To find the combinatorial capacity of the A^*-channel, we first define the *partition function*[4] for A as follows:

$$P(s) = \sum_{a \in A} e^{-s\tau(a)}, \quad \text{for } s \geq 0.$$

For example, for the standard q-ary alphabet, we have $P(s) = e^{-s} + e^{-s} + \cdots + e^{-s} = qe^{-s}$; and for Shannon's telegraphy alphabet (1.1), we have

$$(2.1) \qquad P(s) = e^{-2s} + e^{-3s} + e^{-4s} + e^{-6s}.$$

Here is the main result about the combinatorial capacity of free languages.

2.1 Theorem. *The combinatorial capacity of the free language A^* is given by*

$$C_{\text{comb}} = s_0 \text{ nats},$$

where s_0 is the unique solution of the equation $P(s) = 1$.

To prove Theorem 2.1, we study the convergence of the series

$$(2.2) \qquad Q(s) = \sum_{k \geq 0} P(s)^k$$

in two ways. On the one hand, it is clear that $Q(s)$ converges if and only if $P(s) < 1$. Thus, since $P(s)$ is strictly decreasing from $P(0) = q \geq 1$ to $P(\infty) = 0$, it follows that $Q(s)$ converges for $s > s_0$ and diverges for $s < s_0$. In short, s_0 is the *abscissa of convergence* for $Q(s)$.

The second approach to studying the convergence of $Q(s)$ involves an alternative expression for $Q(s)$, which appears as a corollary to the following proposition.

2.2 Proposition. *If k is a positive integer, then*

$$(2.3) \qquad P(s)^k = \sum_{t \in T} N_k(t) e^{-st},$$

where $N_k(t)$ denotes the number of words from A^* of length k and duration t, and T is the set of possible durations for words from A^*.

---

[4] A term borrowed from statistical mechanics, where a partition function is of the form $Z = \sum_r e^{-\beta E_r}$, with E_r being the energy associated with state r, and β is inversely proportional to the temperature [11].

Proof: We have

$$P(s)^k = P(s) \cdot P(s) \cdots P(s)$$

$$= \sum_{a_1 \in A} e^{-s\tau(a_1)} \cdot \sum_{a_2 \in A} e^{-s\tau(a_2)} \cdots \sum_{a_k \in A} e^{-s\tau(a_k)}$$

$$= \sum_{a_1 a_2 \cdots a_k} e^{-s(\tau(a_1)+\tau(a_2)+\cdots+\tau(a_k))}$$

$$= \sum_{a_1 a_2 \cdots a_k} e^{-s\tau(a_1 a_2 \cdots a_k)}$$

$$= \sum_{t \in T} N_k(t) e^{-st},$$

as asserted. ∎

2.3 Corollary. *If $Q(s)$ is as defined in (2.2), then*

$$(2.4) \qquad\qquad Q(s) = \sum_{t \in T} N(t) e^{-st},$$

where $N(t)$ is the number words from A^* of duration t.

Proof: Summing both sides of (2.3) for $k \geq 0$, we obtain

$$Q(s) = \sum_{k \geq 0} P(s)^k = \sum_{k \geq 0} \sum_{t \in T} N_k(t) e^{-st}$$

$$= \sum_{t \in T} e^{-st} \sum_{k \geq 0} N_k(t)$$

$$= \sum_{t \in T} N(t) e^{-st}. \quad \blacksquare$$

Equation (2.4) expresses $Q(s)$ as a discrete Laplace transform, or DLT. It follows from the convergence properties of DLTs (see Appendix A, Theorem A.2) that the abscissa of convergence of $Q(s)$ is

$$s_0 = \limsup_{t \in T} \frac{1}{t} \log N(t),$$

which by (1.2) is the combinatorial capacity of the A^*-channel. This completes the proof of Theorem 2.1. ∎

2.4 Example. Let's use Theorem 2.1 to find the combinatorial capacity of the free language over Shannon's telegraphy alphabet. As noted in (2.1), we have $P(s) = e^{-2s} + e^{-3s} + e^{-4s} + e^{-6s}$, and *Mathematica* tells us that the unique solution of the equation $P(s) = 1$ is $s_0 = 0.414012$, and so by Theorem 2.1, the capacity is 0.414012 nats (= 0.597294 bits) per second. ∎

2.5 Example. ([5], [8]) Suppose $S = \{\sigma_1, \sigma_2, \ldots\}$ is a uniquely decodable code over a q-letter alphabet, and that the length of σ_i is n_i. Think of S as the

119

alphabet for a discrete noiseless channel. By Theorem 2.1, the combinatorial capacity C (in nats per second) of the free language over S satisfies

$$\sum_i e^{-Cn_i} = 1.$$

On the other hand, since the underlying channel uses the standard q-ary alphabet, $C \leq \log q$, so that

$$\sum_i e^{-(\log q)n_i} \leq 1,$$

i.e.,

$$\sum_i q^{-n_i} \leq 1,$$

which is McMillan's inequality (see e.g. [2], sec. 5.5.) ∎

3. The Probabilistic Capacity of Free Languages.

Suppose we attach a probability $p(a)$ to each letter $a \in A$, and then let X be a random variable with $\Pr\{X = a\} = p(a)$. The average amount of information provided by one observation of X is the entropy $H(X) = -\sum_{a \in A} p(a) \log p(a)$, and the average duration of X is $T(X) = \sum_{a \in A} p(a)\tau(a)$, so that the average information per unit time is $H' = H(X)/T(X)$. The probabilistic capacity of the A^*-channel is defined to be the maximum of this quantity over all choices of the probability density $p(a)$:

$$C_{\text{prob}} \overset{\Delta}{=} \max_{p(a)} \frac{H(X)}{T(X)}.$$

It is satisfying that the probabilistic capacity is the same as the combinatorial capacity.

3.1 Theorem. *If A^* is the free language over the alphabet A, then*

$$C_{\text{prob}} = C_{\text{comb}},$$

i.e., $C_{\text{prob}} = s_0$, where s_0 is the unique solution to the equation $P(s) = 1$.

Proof: Since $P(s_0) = \sum_{a \in A} e^{-s_0 \tau(a)} = 1$, it is natural to define the probability density

$$p^*(a) \overset{\Delta}{=} e^{-s_0 \tau(a)}.$$

Then if $p(a)$ is an arbitrary probability density on A, by Jensen's inequality

$$\sum_a p(a) \log \frac{p^*(a)}{p(a)} \leq \log \sum_a p^*(a) = \log 1 = 0,$$

with equality if and only if $p(a) = p^*(a)$ for all $a \in A$. Thus

$$H(X) = \sum_a p(a) \log \frac{1}{p(a)} \leq \sum_a p(a) \log \frac{1}{p^*(a)} = \sum_a p(a)s_0\tau(a) = s_0 T(X),$$

with equality if and only if $p(a) = p^*(a)$ for all $a \in A$. This completes the proof of Theorem 3.1, and also identifies $p(a)^*$ as the optimizing probability density on A. ∎

120

3.2 Example. We saw in Example 2.4 that for the free language over Shannon's telegraph alphabet, $s_0 = 0.414012$. Thus the optimizing probabilities $p^*(a)$ for achieving the probabilistic capacity are

$$p^*(d) = e^{-2s_0} = 0.43691$$
$$p^*(D) = e^{-4s_0} = 0.19089$$
$$p^*(s) = e^{-3s_0} = 0.28880$$
$$p^*(S) = e^{-6s_0} = 0.08340. \quad \blacksquare$$

4. The Combinatorial Capacity of Shannon Languages.

In this section, we will define the full class of languages to which Shannon's theorems on discrete noiseless channels apply, and we will give Shannon's characterization of the combinatorial capacity. Shannon languages are defined by labelled, directed graphs.

A *directed graph* (or digraph) G has vertex set $V = \{v_1, \ldots, v_M\}$ and branch set $B = \{b_1, \ldots, b_N\}$. Each branch $b \in B$ has an *initial vertex* init$(b) \in V$ and a *final vertex* fin$(b) \in V$. The set of branches with initial vertex v and final vertex w is denoted by $B_{v,w}$:

(4.1) $$B_{v,w} \triangleq \{b \in B : \text{init}(b) = v, \text{fin}(b) = w.\}$$

Similarly, we define

(4.2) $$B_{v*} \triangleq \{b \in B : \text{init}(b) = v\}$$

(4.3) $$B_{*w} \triangleq \{b \in B : \text{fin}(b) = w\}.$$

For example, Figure 2 shows a digraph with $V = \{v_1, v_2\}$, and $B = \{b_1, \ldots, b_6\}$ described in Table 1 (ignore the entries marked $\lambda(b)$ and $\tau(b)$ for now):

e	init(b)	fin(b)	$\lambda(b)$	$\tau(b)$
b_1	v_1	v_2	d	2
b_2	v_1	v_2	D	4
b_3	v_2	v_2	d	2
b_4	v_2	v_2	D	4
b_5	v_2	v_1	s	3
b_6	v_2	v_1	S	6

Table 1. Tabular description of the digraph in Figures 1 and 2.

121

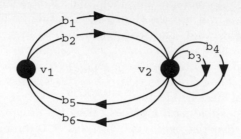

Figure 2. A digraph with two vertices and six branches.

The sets $B_{v,w}$ are as follows:

$$B_{1,1} = \emptyset$$
$$B_{1,2} = \{b_1, b_2\}$$
$$B_{2,1} = \{b_5, b_6\}$$
$$B_{2,2} = \{b_3, b_4\}.$$

A *path* P of length k from v to w in G is a sequence of k branches $P = b_1 b_2 \cdots b_k$ with $\mathrm{init}(b_1) = v$, $\mathrm{fin}(b_1) = \mathrm{init}(b_2)$, ..., $\mathrm{fin}(b_{k-1}) = \mathrm{init}(b_k)$, $\mathrm{fin}(b_k) = w$. We write $\mathrm{len}(P) = k$, $\mathrm{init}(P) = v$, and $\mathrm{fin}(P) = w$. For future reference, we denote the set of paths of length k from v to w by $B_{v,w}^k$:

$$B_{v,w}^k \triangleq \{P : \mathrm{len}(P) = k, \mathrm{init}(P) = v, \mathrm{fin}(P) = w\}.$$

The set of *all* paths from v to w will be denoted by $B_{v,w}^*$:

(4.4) $$B_{v,w}^* \triangleq \bigcup_{k \geq 0} B_{v,w}^k.$$

Given a digraph G and an alphabet A, we can generate a language by labelling each branch of G with an element of A. Let $\lambda : B \to A$ be such a labelling. We will assume that this labelling is *right-resolving*, i.e., for each vertex v, the labels on all branches with $\mathrm{init}(b) = v$ are distinct [4, Section 3.3]. For example, Figure 1 shows a right-resolving labelling of the digraph from Figure 2, where the labels come from Shannon's telegraphy alphabet—see Table 1.[5]

The label of a path $P = b_1 b_2 \cdots b_k$ is defined to be the concatenation of its branch labels:

$$\lambda(P) = \lambda(b_1)\lambda(b_2) \cdots \lambda(b_k).$$

---

[5] Our Figure 1 is essentially the same as Shannon's Figure 2.

122

For each path P, the corresponding label $\lambda(P)$ is therefore a word over A. In what follows, we will use the term *path duration* to mean the duration of the corresponding word, and write $\tau(P)$ instead of $\tau(\lambda(P))$. Note that different paths can have the same label. For example, in Figure 2, the paths $P_1 = b_3 b_3 b_4$ and $P = b_1 b_3 b_4$ both have the label ddD. However, the "right-resolving" assumption guarantees that two paths *with the same initial vertex and the same label* must be identical.

The set of all possible path labels is called *the (Shannon) language generated by* G, and denoted by $\mathcal{L}_{G,\lambda}$. Our goal is to find the combinatorial capacity of $\mathcal{L}_{G,\lambda}$. To do this, we must suitably generalize the notion of partition function introduced in Section 2.

Let s be nonnegative real number, and for each pair of vertices (v, w), define the *branch duration partition function* as follows:

$$(4.5) \qquad P_{v,w}(s) = \sum_{b \in B_{v,w}} e^{-s\tau(b)}.$$

The functions $P_{v,w}(s)$ can be thought of as entries in a $M \times M$ matrix $P(s)$. For example, for the labelled graph in Figure 1, the corresponding matrix is

$$P(s) = \begin{pmatrix} 0 & e^{-2s} + e^{-4s} \\ e^{-3s} + e^{-6s} & e^{-2s} + e^{-4s} \end{pmatrix}.$$

We denote the spectral radius (the magnitude of the largest eigenvalue) of the matrix $P(s)$ by $\rho(s)$. We call $\rho(s)$ the *partition function* for the language $\mathcal{L}_{G,\lambda}$. The function $\rho(s)$ has many interesting properties. For example, $\rho(s)$ is strictly decreasing, convex $\cup$, with $\lim_{s \to -\infty} \rho(s) = +\infty$, $\lim_{s \to +\infty} \rho(s) = 0$, with $\rho(0)$ bounded between the maximum and minimum out degree of any vertex of G. Furthermore, $\rho(s)$ is "log-convex," i.e., $\log \rho(s)$ is convex $\cup$. However, the only one of these properties we shall need in our proof is the fact that $\rho(s)$ is strictly decreasing. A proof of this appears in Appendix B, as Theorem B.5.

Here is the complete version of Shannon's Theorem 1 (Cf. Theorem 2.1).

4.1 Theorem (Shannon's Theorem 1). *The combinatorial capacity of the* $\mathcal{L}_{G,\lambda}$*-language is given by*

$$C_{\text{comb}} = s_0 \text{ nats,}$$

where s_0 *is the unique solution to the equation* $\rho(s) = 1$*. Alternatively,* C_{comb} *is the greatest positive solution of the equation* $q(s) = \det(I - P(s)) = 0$*.*

Proof: Our proof of Theorem 4.1 depends on a calculation of the abscissa of convergence of the matrix series

$$(4.6) \qquad Q(s) = \sum_{k \geq 0} P(s)^k$$

123

in two different ways.[6]

The first method for computing the a.o.c. of $Q(s)$ relies on certain known theorems in matrix theory (see Appendix B). By Theorem B.2, $Q(s)$ converges if and only if $\rho(s) < 1$. Next, by Theorem B.5, $\rho(s)$ is a strictly decreasing function of s. Thus if s_0 is the unique solution to the equation $\rho(s) = 1$, it follows that $\rho(s) < 1$ for all $s > s_0$, and $\rho(s) > 1$ for all $s < s_0$, so that s_0 is the r.o.c. for $Q(s)$. Finally, since by Theorem B.1, $\rho(s)$ is an eigenvalue of $P(s)$, we know that s_0 is the largest value of s for which $P(s)$ has 1 as an eigenvalue, i.e.,

$$s_0 = \sup\{s : \det(I - P(s)) = 0\}.$$

The second method for computing the a.o.c. for $Q(s)$ depends on an alternative expression for $Q(s)$ which appears as a corollary to the following theorem.

4.2 Theorem. *The (v, w)th entry in the matrix $P(s)^k$ is the DLT for durations of paths of length k from v to w, i.e.,*

$$(4.7) \qquad [P(s)^k]_{v,w} = \sum_{t \in T} N_{v,w}^{(k)}(t) e^{-st},$$

where $N_{v,w}^{(k)}(t)$ is the number of paths from v to w of length k and duration t, and T denotes the set of all possible path durations.

Proof: If we define the *weight* of a branch b by $W(b) = e^{-s\tau(b)}$, this follows immediately from Theorem C.1, Appendix C. ∎

4.3 Corollary. *If $Q(s)$ is defined as in (4.6), then*

$$(4.8) \qquad [Q(s)]_{v,w} = \sum_{t \in T} N_{v,w}(t) e^{-st},$$

where $N_{v,w}(t)$ denotes the number of paths from v to w of duration t.

Proof: The proof is virtually identical to that of Corollary 2.3. ∎

Equation (4.8) expresses $[Q(s)]_{v,w}$ as a discrete Laplace transform. It follows from the convergence properties of DLTs (see Appendix A) that the abscissa of convergence of $[Q(s)]_{v,w}$ is

$$C_{v,w} \overset{\Delta}{=} \limsup_{t \in T} \frac{1}{t} \log N_{v,w}(t),$$

so that the a.o.c. of $Q(s)$ itself is

$$s_0 = \max_{v,w} C_{v,w}.$$

---

[6] The a.o.c. of a matrix $A(s)$ is defined to be the infimum of the values of s for which each $A_{v,w}(s)$ converges.

124

Our proof of Theorem 4.1 will be complete if we can show that C as defined in eq. (1.2) equals $\max_{v,w} C_{v,w}$, i.e.,

$$\limsup_{t\in T}\frac{1}{t}\log N(t) = \max_{v,w}\left(\limsup_{t\in T}\frac{1}{t}\log N_{v,w}(t)\right),$$

where $N(t)$ denotes the total number of words in $\mathcal{L}_{G,\lambda}$ (= distinct path labels) of duration t. To accomplish this, we note that for all $t \geq 0$, we have

$$(4.9) \qquad \max_{v,w} N_{v,w}(t) \leq N(t) \leq \sum_{v,w} N_{v,w}(t).$$

The left-hand inequality in (4.9) follows from the fact that the labelling λ is right-resolving, so that for any pair (v, w) the paths from v to w have distinct labels. The right-hand inequality in (4.9) follows from the fact that every word in $\mathcal{L}_{G,\lambda}$ corresponds to at least one path in G. Since there are M vertices in G, we can upperbound $\sum_{v,w} N_{v,w}(t)$ with $M^2 \cdot \max_{v,w} N_{v,w}(t)$, obtaining

$$(4.10) \qquad \max_{v,w} N_{v,w}(t) \leq N(t) \leq M^2 \cdot \max_{v,w} N_{v,w}(t).$$

Taking logarithm of these inequalities, dividing by t, and passing to the "lim sup," we obtain

$$\max_{v,w}\left(\limsup_{t\in T}\frac{\log N_{v,w}(t)}{t}\right) \leq \limsup_{t\in T}\frac{\log N(t)}{t} \leq \max_{v,w}\left(\limsup_{t\in T}\frac{\log M^2 + \log N_{v,w}(t)}{t}\right)$$
$$= \max_{v,w}\left(\limsup_{t\in T}\frac{\log N_{v,w}(t)}{t}\right).$$

Thus $C = \max_{v,w} C_{v,w}$, as required. ∎

4.4 Example. For the telegraphy language defined by Figure 1, the matrix $I_2 - P(s)$ is

$$I_2 - P(s) = \begin{pmatrix} 1 & -e^{-2s} - e^{-4s} \\ -e^{-3s} - e^{-6s} & 1 - e^{-2s} - e^{-4s} \end{pmatrix},$$

whose determinant is $q(s) = 1 - e^{-2s} - e^{-4s} - e^{-5s} - e^{-7s} - e^{-8s} - e^{-10s}$. The greatest positive root of $q(s) = 0$ (in fact, the only root) is $s_0 = 0.373562$, so that the capacity is $C = 0.373562$ nats $= 0.538936$ bits per second. This value should be compared to the capacity of the *free* language over the telegraphy alphabet, which as we saw above was 0.597294 bits per second. The structure imposed by Figure 1 has reduced the capacity by 0.058 bits per second, or about 10%, relative to the free language over the same alphabet. ∎

5. The Probabilistic Capacity of Shannon Languages.

Suppose we have a labelled digraph[7] (G, λ) as in Section 4, and we assign to each branch $b \in B$ a positive probability p_b, such that

$$(5.1) \qquad \sum_{b \in B_{v*}} p_b = 1,$$

for all vertices $v \in V$. (The set B_{v*} is defined in (4.2).) Then the p_b's describe a finite ergodic Markov chain, so there exists a unique stationary probability density on the vertices, $\{\pi_v : v \in V\}$, which satisfies

$$(5.2) \qquad \sum_{b \in B_{*w}} \pi_{\text{init}(b)} p_b = \pi_w,$$

for all $w \in V$. (The set B_{*w} is defined in (4.3).) The average amount of information provided by one observation of this Markov chain is the entropy

$$H = -\sum_{v \in V} \pi_v \sum_{b \in B_{v*}} p_b \log p_b$$
$$= -\sum_{b \in B} \pi_{\text{init}(b)} p_b \log p_b,$$

and the average duration of an observation is

$$T = \sum_{v \in V} \pi_v \sum_{b \in B_{v*}} p_b \tau(b)$$
$$= \sum_{b \in B} \pi_{\text{init}(b)} p_b \tau(b).$$

Thus the average information per unit time is $H' = H/T$. The probabilistic capacity of the language $\mathcal{L}_{G,\lambda}$ is defined to be maximum of this quantity, over all choices of the branch probabilities p_b:

$$C_{\text{prob}} \stackrel{\Delta}{=} \max_{(p_b)} \frac{H}{T}.$$

As was the case for free languages, the probabilistic capacity is the same as the combinatorial capacity.

---

[7] In this section we will assume that G is strongly connected, i.e., there is at least one directed path between any two vertices. This will ensure that the resulting partition matrices are primitive and the Markov chains are ergodic.

5.1 Theorem (Shannon's Theorem 8). *The combinatorial and probabilistic capacites of the $\mathcal{L}_{G,\lambda}$-language are the same, i.e.,*

$$C_{\text{prob}} = C_{\text{comb}} = s_0,$$

where s_0 is the unique solution to the equation $\rho(s) = 1$.

Proof: Since $\rho(s_0) = 1$, by the Perron-Frobenius theorem [4, Sec. 4.2] the primitive matrix $P(s_0)$ has positive left and right "Perron" eigenvectors $\boldsymbol{\xi}$ and $\boldsymbol{\eta}$ associated with the eigenvalue 1 such that

(5.3) $$\boldsymbol{\xi} P(s_0) = \boldsymbol{\xi}$$

(5.4) $$P(s_0)\boldsymbol{\eta} = \boldsymbol{\eta}$$

(5.5) $$\boldsymbol{\xi} \cdot \boldsymbol{\eta} = 1.$$

Let us define branch probabilities by the formula

(5.6) $$p_b^* = \frac{\eta_{\text{fin}(b)}}{\eta_{\text{init}(b)}} e^{-s_0 \tau(b)}.$$

The stationary probability distribution for these branch probabilities turns out to be

(5.7) $$\pi_v^* = \xi_v \eta_v, \ v \in V.$$

We pause to prove that indeed the p_b^*'s satisfy (5.1), and the π_v^*'s satisfy (5.2).

5.2 Lemma. $\sum_{b \in B_{v*}} p_b^* = 1$, *for all $v \in V$.*

Proof: We have

$$\sum_{b \in B_{v*}} p_b^* = \sum_{b \in B_{v*}} \frac{\eta_{\text{fin}(b)}}{\eta_{\text{init}(b)}} e^{-s_0 \tau(b)} \qquad \text{(by (5.6))}$$

$$= \frac{1}{\eta_v} \sum_{b \in B_{v*}} \eta_{\text{fin}(b)} e^{-s_0 \tau(b)}$$

$$= \frac{1}{\eta_v} \sum_{w \in V} \eta_w \sum_{b \in B_{v,w}} e^{-s_0 \tau(b)}$$

$$= \frac{1}{\eta_v} \sum_w \eta_w P_{v,w}(s_0) \qquad \text{(by (4.5))}$$

$$= \frac{1}{\eta_v} \cdot \eta_v \qquad \text{(by (5.4))}$$

$$= 1. \qquad \blacksquare$$

5.3 Lemma. $\sum_{b\in B_{*w}} \pi^*_{\text{init}(b)} p^*_b = \pi^*_w$, for all $w \in V$.

Proof: We have

$$\sum_{b\in B_{*w}} \pi^*_{\text{init}(b)} p^*_b = \sum_{b\in B_{*w}} \xi_{\text{init}(b)} \eta_{\text{init}(b)} \frac{\eta_{\text{fin}(b)}}{\eta_{\text{init}(b)}} e^{-s_0\tau(b)} \qquad \text{(by (5.6) and (5.7))}$$

$$= \eta_w \sum_{b\in B_{*w}} \xi_{\text{init}(b)} e^{-s_0\tau(b)}$$

$$= \eta_w \sum_v \xi_v \sum_{b\in B_{v,w}} e^{-s_0\tau(b)}$$

$$= \eta_w \sum_v \xi_v P_{v,w}(s_0) \qquad \text{(by (4.5))}$$

$$= \eta_w \xi_w \qquad \text{(by (5.3))}$$

$$= \pi^*_w. \qquad \blacksquare$$

Now let (p_b) be an arbitrary set of branch probabilities and let (π_v) be the corresponding stationary vertex probabilities. Then by Jensen's inequality,

$$(5.8) \qquad \sum_{v\in V} \pi_v \sum_{b\in B_{v*}} p_b \log \frac{p^*_b}{p_b} \le 0,$$

with equality if and only if $p_b = p^*_b$ for all $b \in B$. If we expand (5.8), we get

$$H = \sum_{v\in V} \pi_v \sum_{b\in B_{v*}} p_b \log \frac{1}{p_b} \le \sum_{v\in V} \pi_v \sum_{b\in B_{v*}} p_b \log \frac{1}{p^*_b}$$

$$= \sum_{v\in V} \pi_v \sum_{b\in B_{v*}} p_b \left\{ s_0\tau(b) + \log \eta_{\text{init}(b)} - \log \eta_{\text{fin}(b)} \right\}$$

$$= s_0 T + \sum_v \pi_v \sum_{b\in B_{v*}} p_b \log \eta_{\text{init}(b)} - \sum_v \pi_v \sum_{b\in B_{v*}} p_b \log \eta_{\text{fin}(b)}$$

$$(5.9) \qquad = s_0 T + S_1 - S_2.$$

It is easy to see that S_1 and S_2 are equal. For on the one hand

$$S_1 = \sum_v \pi_v \sum_{b\in B_{v*}} p_b \log \eta_{\text{init}(b)}$$

$$= \sum_v \pi_v \log \eta_v \sum_{b\in B_{v*}} p_b$$

$$= \sum_v \pi_v \log \eta_v \qquad \text{(by (5.1))},$$

while on the other hand

$$S_2 = \sum_v \pi_v \sum_{b \in B_{v*}} p_b \log \eta_{\text{fin}(b)}$$

$$= \sum_{b \in B} \pi_{\text{init}(b)} p_b \log \eta_{\text{fin}(b)}$$

$$= \sum_w \log \eta_w \sum_{b \in B_{*w}} \pi_{\text{init}(b)} p_b$$

$$= \sum_w \log \eta_w \, \pi_w \qquad \text{(by (5.2)).}$$

Thus (5.9) becomes

$$H \leq s_0 T,$$

with equality if and only if $p_b = p_b^*$, for all $b \in B$. This completes the proof of Theorem 5.1, and furthermore identifies the branch probabilities (p_b^*) defined in (5.6) as the optimal ones. ∎

5.4 Example. We consider the application of Theorem 5.1 to Shannon's telegraphy language. We know from Example 4.4 that the capacity (combinatorial or probabilistic) is $s_0 = 0.373562$. A short calculation then shows that

$$P(s_0) = \begin{pmatrix} 0 & 0.698144 \\ 0.432369 & 0.698144 \end{pmatrix}.$$

The left and right Perron eigenvectors corresponding to the eigenvalue $\rho(s_0) = 1$ are then calculated to be (cf. (5.3)—(5.5))[8]

$$\boldsymbol{\xi} = (0.405048, 0.936811)$$
$$\boldsymbol{\eta} = (0.572441, 0.819946).$$

From these values, we can compute the optimal branch probabilities p_b^* as defined in (5.6), thus "completing" Table 1:

e	init(b)	fin(b)	$\lambda(b)$	$\tau(b)$	p_b^*
b_1	v_1	v_2	d	2	0.67856
b_2	v_1	v_2	D	4	0.32145
b_3	v_2	v_2	d	2	0.47373
b_4	v_2	v_2	D	4	0.22442
b_5	v_2	v_1	s	3	0.22764
b_6	v_2	v_1	S	6	0.07422

Table 2. The optimal branch probabilities
for the labelled digraph of Figure 1.

---

[8] Of course $\boldsymbol{\xi}$ and $\boldsymbol{\eta}$ are only determined up to a multiplicative constant.

Finally, we note that from (5.7), we have the stationary probabilities

$$\pi_1^* = 0.23187, \qquad \pi_2^* = 0.76813. \qquad \blacksquare$$

6. Maximum Entropy Markov Chains on Digraphs.

In this section we briefly sketch a kind of generalization of Shannon's Theorem 8. (The corresponding result for free languages is stated as Problem 1.8 in [6].)

The setup being the same as in Section 5, we ask the following question: for a given value of $T > 0$, what is the maximum possible entropy $H_{\max}(T)$ among all Markov chains whose average branch duration is T? The answer to a similar question was given by McEliece and Rodemich [7]. Here we summarize, and slightly extend, their answer.

If we define the branch duration matrix $P(s)$ as in (4.5), with corresponding spectral radius $\rho(s)$, then as the real variable s runs from $-\infty$ to $+\infty$, the $(H_{\max}(T), T)$ pairs are given parametrically by the equations

(6.1)
$$H(s) = \log \rho(s) - s \frac{\rho'(s)}{\rho(s)}$$

$$T(s) = -\frac{\rho'(s)}{\rho(s)}.$$

In (6.1), as s runs from $-\infty$ to $+\infty$, T decreases monotonically from its maximum possible value $T_{\max}$ to its minimum possible value $T_{\min}$; $T_{\max}$ and $T_{\min}$ are the maximum and minimum average branch durations, respectively, among the cycles in G.

Furthermore, since $P(s)$ is primitve, $P(s)$ has positive left and right Perron eigenvectors $\boldsymbol{\xi}(s)$ and $\boldsymbol{\eta}(s)$ such that (cf. (5.3)–(5.5))

$$\boldsymbol{\xi}(s)P(s) = \rho(s)\boldsymbol{\xi}(s)$$
$$P(s)\boldsymbol{\eta}(s) = \rho(s)\boldsymbol{\eta}(s)$$
$$\boldsymbol{\xi}(s) \cdot \boldsymbol{\eta}(s) = 1.$$

The optimal branch probabilities and the corresponding stationary vertex probabilities are then given by the formulas

$$p_b(s)^* = \frac{1}{\rho(s)} \frac{\eta_{\mathrm{fin}(b)}(s)}{\eta_{\mathrm{init}(b)}(s)} e^{-s\tau(b)}$$

$$\pi_v^*(s) = \xi_v(s)\eta_v(s).$$

As an application of this result, we can give a quick calculation of the probabilistic capacity, which is simply the maximum of the function $h(s) \stackrel{\Delta}{=} H(s)/T(s)$. According to (6.1), we have

(6.2)
$$h(s) = s - \log \rho(s) \frac{\rho(s)}{\rho'(s)},$$

130

so that

(6.3)
$$h'(s) = \log \rho(s) \left[\frac{\rho(s)\rho''(s) - \rho'(s)^2}{\rho'(s)^2} \right]$$

Since $\rho(s)$ is log-convex (proof omitted), the quantity $\rho(s)\rho''(s) - \rho'(s)^2$ is either identically zero (in which case $\tau(b)$ is the same for all branches), or strictly positive for all s. In the former case, $h(s)$ is independent of s, and the maximization problem is trivial. In the latter case, we have

$$\rho(s) > 1 \Longrightarrow h'(s) > 0$$
$$\rho(s) = 1 \Longrightarrow h'(s) = 0$$
$$\rho(s) < 1 \Longrightarrow h'(s) < 0.$$

Thus if s_0 is defined as the unique solution to the equation $\rho(s) = 1$, then by (6.2), we know that

$$h(s) = \frac{H(s)}{T(s)} \leq s_0,$$

with equality if and only if $s = s_0$. This gives an alternative proof of Theorem 5.1.

Finally we note that the maximum of $H(s)$ itself occurs at $s = 0$, and is $H_{\max} = \log \rho(0)$. This is because

$$H'(s) = -s \frac{\rho(s)\rho''(s) - \rho'(s)^2}{\rho(s)^2},$$

which is either identically 0, or is zero only at $s = 0$. If G is regular of degree r, $H_{\max} = \log r$. In the general case, $\rho(0)$ lies between the smallest and largest out-degree of any vertex.

6.1 Example. We briefly illustrate these results for the labelled digraph of Figure 1. In Figure 3, we have plotted the function $\rho(s)$, and in Figure 4 we have plotted $H(s)$ and $T(s)$. By eye we can estimate that the solution to $\rho(s) = 1$, i.e. the common value of C_{comb} and C_{prob}, is about 0.4 nats/sec; as we have seen (Example 4.4), the exact value is $s_0 = 0.373562$. In Figure 5, we have plotted the function $H_{\max}(T)$ vs. T using (6.1), and in Figure 6, we have plotted $H(s)/T(s)$. We see that $H_{\max}(T)$ is a convex $\cap$ function of T in the range $T \in [T_{\min}, T_{\max}] = [2.0, 5.0]$. (The self-loop b_2 has average branch duration $T_{\min} = 2$, and the loop (b_2, b_6) has average branch duration $T_{\max} = 5$.) The maximum of H occurs at $s = 0$, $T(0) = 3.4146$, and is $\log \rho(0) = \log(1 + \sqrt{5}) = 1.1744$. The maximum of $H(s)/T(s)$ occurs at $s = s_0$ and its value is also s_0. This example is entirely typical of the general case. ∎

131

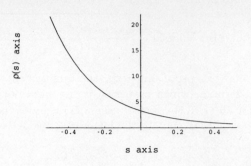

Figure 3. The function $\rho(s)$ for the labelled digraph of Figure 2.

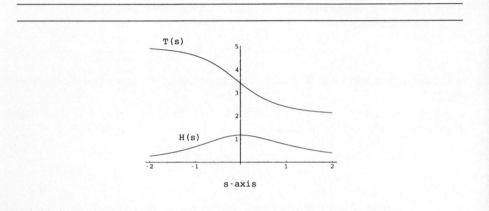

Figure 4. The functions $H(s)$ and $T(s)$.

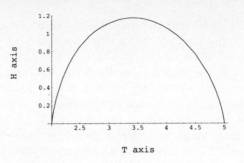

Figure 5. The function $H_{\max}(T)$.

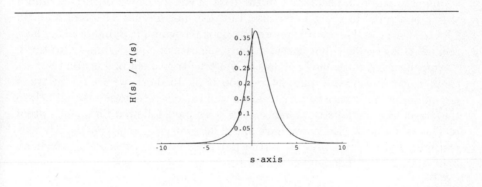

Figure 6. The function $H(s)/T(s)$.

133

7. Concluding Remarks.

Since (apart from Section 6) this paper contains no new results, the reader may wonder why the authors wrote this paper at all. In this section, we attempt to answer this reasonable question.

In the first place, we wished to reaffirm the continuing importance, after more than 50 years, of a relatively unsung part of Shannon's classic paper. (There is, for example, no mention of the discrete noiseless channel in the current standard information theory textbook [2].)

Second, and more important, we wished to provide clear and complete proofs of Shannon's Theorems 1 and 8. Shannon's own proof of Theorem 1, for example, seems not to apply to the case where the symbol durations are not all integers. His proof of Theorem 8, which appears in Appendix 4 in [9], is very brief and (for us) difficult to follow. The only information theory text that treats the discrete noiseless channel at all is [1, Chapter 2] which gives a complete proof of Theorem 1 in the case of equal symbol durations, and a sketch of a proof in the general case, but does not discuss Theorem 8 at all. The treatment of Theorem 1 in a recent book on symbolic dynamics [4, Theorem 4.3.3] is excellent, but considers only the case of equal symbol durations. Disappointingly, the same book has only a brief treatment of Theorem 8 in its chapter on "Advanced Topics" [4, Section 13.3]. In short, we are not aware of any published fully satisfactory treatment of the discrete noiseless channel, so this paper may be a first. Moreover, while we have followed Shannon's proof of Theorem 8 quite closely, we have found necessary to devise an entirely new method of proof for Theorem 1 (the partition function method), which we believe may be of independent interest.

Appendix A: Discrete Laplace Transforms.

Let $T = \{0 \leq t_0 < t_1 < \cdots\}$ be an increasing, countable sequence of positive real numbers which is not too dense, in the sense that for any integer $n \geq 0$,

$$(A.1) \qquad |\{t \in T : t < n\}| = O(n^K)$$

for some constant $K \geq 0$. For example, if $\tau_1, \ldots, \tau_q$ is a set of q positive real numbers, then the set of numbers of the form

$$t = n_1 \tau_1 + \cdots + n_q \tau_q,$$

where $n_1, \ldots, n_q$ are arbitrary nonnegative integers, satisfies (A.1), with $K = q$.

A.1 Lemma. *If T satisfies (A.1), and if $0 \leq \rho < 1$, then the series $\sum_{t \in T} \rho^t$ converges.*

Proof: If $0 \le \rho < 1$, we have

$$\sum_{t \in T} \rho^t \le \sum_{t \in T} \rho^{\lfloor t \rfloor}$$

$$= \sum_{n \ge 0} \rho^n \cdot |\{t \in T : n \le t < n+1\}|$$

$$\le \sum_{n \ge 0} \rho^n \cdot |\{t \in T : t < n+1\}|$$

$$= O\left(\sum_{n \ge 0} \rho^n (n+1)^K\right)$$

$$< \infty. \quad \blacksquare$$

If for each $t \in T$, $N(t)$ is a nonnegative real number, we define the *discrete Laplace transform* of $N(t)$ to be the series

$$(A.2) \qquad f(s) = \sum_{t \in T} N(t) e^{-st},$$

where $s \ge 0$ is a real number. The following theorem identifies the "abscissa of convergence" of $f(s)$.

A.2 Theorem. *Let*

$$s_0 = \limsup_{t \to \infty} \frac{1}{t} \log N(t).$$

Then $f(s)$ diverges for all $s < s_0$, and converges for all $s > s_0$.

Proof: We begin by rewriting the sum defining $f(s)$ as follows.

$$(A.3) \qquad f(s) = \sum_{t \in T} e^{-t(s - \log N(t)/t)}.$$

If $s < s_0$, then by the definition of $\limsup$, $\log N(t)/t > s$ infinitely often. But if $\log N(t)/t > s$, the corresponding term in (A.3) is ≥ 1, so $f(s)$ cannot converge.

On the other hand, if $s > s_0$, there exists $\epsilon > 0$ so that $s - \epsilon > s_0$. Then, again by the definition of $\limsup$, we know that $\log N(t)/t < s - \epsilon$ for all but a finite number of t's. But if $\log N(t)/t < s - \epsilon$, the corresponding term in (A.3) is $\le e^{-t\epsilon} = \rho^t$, where $\rho = e^{-\epsilon} < 1$. Thus $f(s)$ converges, by Lemma A.1. $\blacksquare$

Appendix B: Theorems on Matrices.

In this appendix we state for reference several theorems from matrix theory that are needed in the body of the paper. All these theorems deal with the *spectral radius*, i.e., the largest eigenvalue of, a matrix. If A is a square matrix, its spectral radius is denoted by $\rho(s)$.

B.1 Theorem. [3, Thm. 5.6.]. *If $A \geq 0$, then $\rho(A)$ is an eigenvalue of A; in short, the largest eigenvalue of a nonegative matrix is real and nonnegative.*

B.2 Theorem. [3, Section 5.6.]. *If A is a square matrix, the geometric series*

$$\sum_{k \geq 0} A^k$$

converges if and only if $\rho(A) < 1$. ∎

B.3 Theorem. [3, Corollary 8.1.19] *Let A and B be square matrices. If $0 \leq A \leq B$, then $\rho(A) \leq \rho(B)$.*

B.4 Theorem. [3, Theorem 6.3.12] *If $\rho(s)$ denotes the spectral radius of a primitive matrix function $A(s)$, and if $\boldsymbol{\xi}(s)$ and $\boldsymbol{\eta}(s)$ are the corresponding left and right Perron eigenvectors, then*

$$(B.1) \qquad \rho'(s) = \frac{\boldsymbol{\xi}(s) A'(s) \boldsymbol{\eta}(s)}{\boldsymbol{\xi}(s) \cdot \boldsymbol{\eta}(s)}.$$

B.5 Theorem. *The partition function $\rho(s)$ is strictly decreasing.*

Proof: The entries of the partition matrix $P(s)$ are either zero or of the form $\sum_i e^{-st_i}$, so that the derivatives of these entries are all nonpositive. On the other hand, the components of the Perron vectors $\boldsymbol{\xi}(s)$ and $\boldsymbol{\eta}(s)$ are strictly positive, so that by (B.1), $\rho'(s) < 0$. ∎

Appendix C: Path Weights in Digraphs.

In this appendix, we will prove a simple theorem of surprisingly wide applicability. We have quoted [10, Section 4.7], almost verbatim.

Let $G = (V, B)$ be a digraph, and let $W : B \to R$ be a *weight function* defined on the branches of G, taking values in some commutative ring R. (For most purposes, R will be the ring of real numbers or the ring of polynomials over the reals.) If $P = b_1 b_2 \cdots b_n$ is a path of length n, the weight of P is defined to be $W(P) = W(b_1) W(b_2) \cdots W(b_n)$. Now define

$$A_{v,w}(n) \triangleq \sum_{P \in B_{v,w}^n} W(P),$$

i.e., $A_{v,w}(n)$ is the sum of the weights of all paths of length n from v to w. The problem here is to find an efficient way to calculate the numbers $A_{v,w}(n)$. The key to the solution is to define the *branch weight matrix* $A = (A_{v,w})$ by

$$A_{v,w} \triangleq \sum_{b \in B_{v,w}} W(b).$$

136

C.1 Theorem. *Let n be a positive integer. Then the (v,w)th entry of A^n is $A_{v,w}(n)$.*

Proof: By a straightforward induction argument, the (v,w)th entry of the nth power of A is given by the formula

$$[A^n]_{v,w} = \sum A_{v,v_1} A_{v_1,v_2} \cdots A_{v_{n-1},w},$$

where the sum is over all possible sequences of vertices $(v_1, v_2, \ldots, v_{n-1})$. The summand is zero unless there is a path $b_1 b_2 \cdots b_n$ from v to w, with $\text{init}(b_1) = v$, $\text{fin}(b_1) = v_1$, $\text{init}(b_2) = v_1$, $\text{fin}(b_2) = v_2$, $\ldots$, $\text{init}(b_n) = v_{n-1}$, $\text{fin}(b_n) = w$. If one or more such paths exist, then the summand is the sum of the weights of all such paths. ∎

References.

1. Richard E. Blahut, *Principles and Practice of Information Theory*. Reading, Mass.: Addison-Wesley, 1987.

2. Thomas M. Cover and Joy A. Thomas, *Elements of Information Theory*. New York: John Wiley & Sons, 1991.

3. Roger A. Horn and Charles R. Johnson, *Matrix Analysis*. Cambridge: Cambridge University Press, 1985.

4. Douglas Lind and Brian Marcus, *Symbolic Dynamics and Coding*. Cambridge: Cambridge University Press, 1995.

5. D. J. C. MacKay, personal communication.

6. Robert J. McEliece, *The Theory of Information and Coding*. Reading, Mass.: Addison-Wesley, 1977.

7. Robert J. McEliece and Eugene R. Rodemich, "A maximum entropy Markov chain," *Proc. 17th Conf. Inform. Sciences and Systems* (Johns Hopkins University, March 1983), pp. 245–248.

8. V. C. da Rocha Jr., "Some information-theoretic aspects of uniquely decodable codes," this volume.

9. C. E. Shannon, *The Mathematical Theory of Communication*. Urbana, Illinois: University of Illinois Press, 1963.

10. Richard P. Stanley, *Enumerative Combinatorics, vol. I*. Monterey, Calif.: Wadsworth & Brooks/Cole, 1986.

11. J. M. Yeomans, *Statistical Mechanics of Phase Transitions*. Oxford: Oxford University Press, 1992.

Gallager Codes — Recent Results

David J. C. MacKay (mackay@mrao.cam.ac.uk)
Cavendish Laboratory, Cambridge, CB3 0HE, United Kingdom.

Abstract

In 1948, Claude Shannon posed and solved one of the fundamental problems of information theory. The question was whether it is possible to communicate reliably over noisy channels, and, if so, at what rate. He defined a theoretical limit, now known as the Shannon limit, up to which communication is possible, and beyond which communication is not possible. Since 1948, coding theorists have attempted to design error-correcting codes capable of getting close to the Shannon limit.

In the last decade remarkable progress has been made using codes that are defined in terms of sparse random graphs, and which are decoded by a simple probability–based message–passing algorithm.

This paper reviews low–density parity–check codes (Gallager codes), repeat–accumulate codes, and turbo codes, emphasising recent advances. Some previously unpublished results are then presented, describing (a) experiments on Gallager codes with small blocklengths; (b) a stopping rule for decoding of repeat–accumulate codes, which saves computer time and allows block decoding errors to be detected and flagged; and (c) the empirical power–laws obeyed by decoding times of sparse graph codes.

1   Introduction

The central problem of communication theory is to construct an encoding and a decoding system that make it possible to communicate reliably over a noisy channel. The encoding system uses the source data to select a codeword from a set of codewords. The decoding algorithm ideally infers, given the output of the channel, which codeword in the code is the most likely to have been transmitted; for an appropriate definition of distance, this is the 'closest' codeword to the received signal. A good code is one in which the codewords are well spaced apart, so that codewords are unlikely to be confused.

Designing a good and practical error correcting code is difficult because (a) it is hard to find an explicit set of well–spaced codewords; and (b) for a generic code, decoding, *i.e.*, finding the closest codeword to a received signal, is intractable.

However, a simple method for designing codes, first pioneered by Gallager (1962), has recently been rediscovered and generalized. The codes are defined in terms of sparse random graphs. Because the graphs are constructed randomly, the codes are likely to have well–spaced codewords. And because the codes' constraints are defined by a sparse graph, the decoding problem can be solved — almost optimally — by message–passing on the graph. The practical performance of Gallager's codes and their modern cousins is vastly better than the performance of the codes with which textbooks have been filled in the intervening years.

2   Sparse Graph Codes

In a **sparse graph code**, the nodes in the graph represent the transmitted bits and the constraints they satisfy. For a linear code with a codeword length N and rate $R = K/N$, the number of constraints is of order $M = N - K$. [There could be more constraints, if they happen to be redundant.] Any linear code can be described by a graph, but what makes a sparse graph code special is that each constraint involves only a small number of variables in the graph: the number of edges in the graph scales roughly linearly with N, rather than as N^2.

The graph defining a **low–density parity–check code**, or Gallager code (Gallager 1962; Gallager 1963; MacKay 1999), contains two types of node: codeword bits, and parity constraints. In a regular (j, k) Gallager code (figure 1a), each codeword bit is connected to j parity constraints and each constraint is connected to k bits. The connections in the graph are made at random.

Repeat–accumulate codes (Divsalar *et al.* 1998) can be represented by a graph with four types of node (figure 1b): equality constraints $\boxed{=}$, intermediate binary variables (black circles), parity constraints $\boxed{+}$, and the transmitted bits (white circles). The encoder sets each group of intermediate bits to values read from the source. These bits are put through a fixed random permutation. The transmitted stream is the accumulated sum (modulo 2) of the permuted intermediate bits.

In a **turbo code** (Berrou and Glavieux 1996), the K source bits drive two linear feedback shift registers, which emit parity bits (figure 1c).

All these codes can be decoded by a local message–passing algorithm on the graph, the sum–product algorithm (MacKay and Neal 1996; McEliece *et al.* 1998), and, while this algorithm is not the optimal decoder, the empirical results are record–breaking. Figure 2 shows the performance of various sparse graph codes on a Gaussian channel. In figure 2(a) turbo codes with rate 1/4 are compared with regular and irregular Gallager codes over GF(2), GF(8) and GF(16). In figure 2(b) the performance of repeat–accumulate codes of various blocklengths and rate 1/3 is shown.

THE BEST SPARSE GRAPH CODES

Which of the three types of sparse graph code is 'best' depends on the chosen rate and blocklength, the permitted encoding and decoding complexity, and

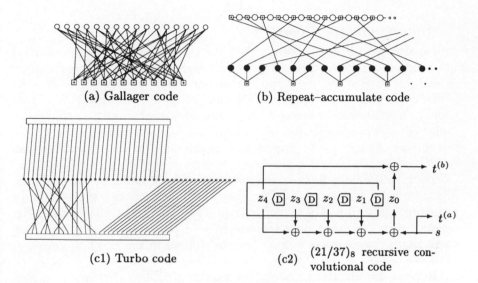

(a) Gallager code   (b) Repeat–accumulate code

(c1) Turbo code   (c2) $(21/37)_8$ recursive convolutional code

Figure 1. Graphs of three sparse graph codes.

    (a) A rate 1/4 low–density parity–check code (Gallager code) with blocklength $N = 16$, and $M = 12$ constraints. Each white circle represents a transmitted bit. Each bit participates in $j = 3$ constraints, represented by ⊞ squares. Each ⊞ constraint forces the sum of the $k = 4$ bits to which it is connected to be even.

    (b) A repeat–accumulate code with rate 1/3. Each white circle represents a transmitted bit. Each black circle represents an intermediate binary variable. Each ⊟ constraint forces the variables to which it is connected to be equal.

    (c) A turbo code with rate 1/3. (c1) The circles represent the codeword bits. The two rectangles represent rate 1/2 convolutional codes (c2), with the systematic bits $\{t^{(a)}\}$ occupying the left half of the rectangle and the parity bits $\{t^{(b)}\}$ occupying the right half.

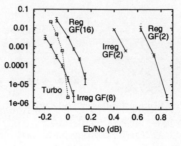

(a)

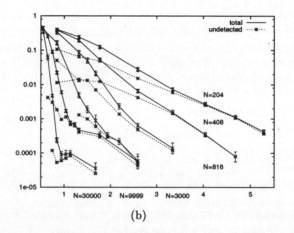

(b)

Figure 2. (a) Bit error probabilities for communication over a Gaussian channel at rate 1/4: left–right : Irregular LDPC, $GF(8)$, transmitted blocklength 24000 bits; JPL turbo, $N = 65536$ bits (dotted line); Regular LDPC, $GF(16)$, $N = 24448$ bits; Irregular LDPC, $GF(2)$, $N = 64000$ bits; Regular LDPC, $GF(2)$, $N = 40000$ bits. [From Davey and MacKay (1998).]

(b) Block error probability of repeat–accumulate codes with rate 1/3 and various blocklengths, versus E_b/N_0. The dotted lines show the frequency of undetected errors.

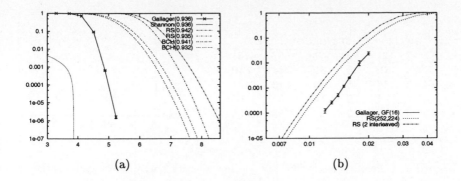

Figure 3. (a) A regular binary Gallager code with column weight $j = 4$, rate $R = 0.936$ and blocklength $N = 4376$ ($K = 4094$), compared with BCH codes and interleaved Reed–Solomon codes with similar rates, on a Gaussian channel. Hard–input bounded–distance decoding is assumed for the BCH and RS codes. Vertical axis: block error probability. Horizontal axis: E_b/N_0 [Curves that are further to the left are best.] (b) A Gallager code over GF(16), rate 8/9, blocklength $N = 3996$ bits, applied to a 16–ary symmetric channel, and compared with interleaved RS codes with similar rates. Vertical axis: block error probability. Horizontal axis: channel symbol error probability. [Curves that are further to the right are best.] From MacKay and Davey (1998).

the question of whether occasional undetected errors are acceptable (turbo codes and repeat–accumulate codes both typically make occasional undetected errors, even at high signal–to–noise ratios, because they have a small number of low weight codewords; Gallager codes do not typically show such an error floor).

Gallager codes are the most versatile; it's easy to make a competitive Gallager code with almost any rate and blocklength, as is illustrated in figure 3. Figure 3(a) shows the performance of a high–rate regular binary Gallager code; it outperforms BCH codes and Reed–Solomon codes on this channel. And figure 3(b) shows the performance of a high rate Gallager code over GF(16) on a 16–ary symmetric channel: even though this channel is the sort of channel for which Reed–Solomon codes are intended, the Gallager code still manages to perform a little better than the RS code.

The best binary Gallager codes found so far are *irregular* codes whose parity check matrices have nonuniform weight per column (Luby *et al.* 1998; Urbanke *et al.* 1999). The carefully constructed codes of Urbanke, Richardson and Shokrollahi outperform turbo codes at blocklengths longer than 10^4 bits, with especially impressive results at 10^6 bits, where a rate $1/2$ irregular Gallager code has a bit error probability of 10^{-6} at just 0.13 dB from capacity, beating comparable turbo codes by more than 0.3 dB. Turbo codes can

DIFFERENCE–SET CYCLIC CODES					
N	7	21	73	273	1057	4161
M	4	10	28	82	244	730
K	3	11	45	191	813	3431
d	4	6	10	18	34	66
k	3	5	9	17	33	65

Figure 4. Difference–set cyclic codes — low–density parity–check codes satisfying many redundant constraints — outperform equivalent Gallager codes. The table shows the N, M, K, distance d, and row weight k of some difference–set cyclic codes, highlighting the codes that have large d/N, small k, and large N/M. All DSC codes satisfy N constraints of weight k. In the comparison the Gallager code had $(j, k) = (4, 13)$, and rate identical to the DSC code. Vertical axis: block error probability; horizontal axis: E_b/N_0/dB. Data on DSC code performance provided by R. Lucas and M. Fossorier.

also be beaten by irregular Gallager codes defined over finite fields $GF(q)$ (Davey and MacKay 1998). However, these successes for Gallager codes have only been obtained by careful work, and it is notable how easily simple turbo codes and repeat–accumulate codes achieve almost as good results. The good performance of simple turbo codes and repeat–accumulate codes compared with simple Gallager codes can presumably be attributed to the use of state variables. It seems plausible therefore that the best codes will make use of state variables. Probably what is holding up the development of even better turbo codes is the need for a theory, comparable to the theory of irregular Gallager code design (Urbanke *et al.* 1999), for the construction of irregular graphs with state variables.

CODES WITH REDUNDANT CONSTRAINTS — 'THE TANNER CHALLENGE'

The performance of Gallager codes can be enhanced by making a non–random code with **redundant sparse constraints** (Tanner 1981; Lucas *et al.* 1999). There is a difference–set cyclic code, for example, that has $N = 273$, and $K = 191$, but the code satisfies not $M = 82$ but N, *i.e.*, *273*, low-weight constraints (figure 4). It is impossible to make random Gallager codes that have anywhere near this much redundancy among their checks. The redundant checks allow the sum–product algorithm to work substantially better, as shown in figure 4, in which a DSC code outperforms a comparable regular binary Gallager code by about 0.7 dB. The (73,45) DSC code has been implemented on a chip by Karplus and Krit (1991) following a design of Tanner (1981). Product codes are another family of codes with redundant constraints.

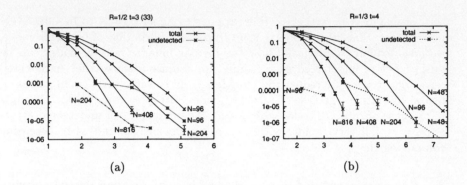

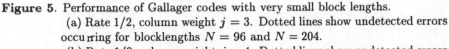

Figure 5. Performance of Gallager codes with very small block lengths.
(a) Rate 1/2, column weight $j = 3$. Dotted lines show undetected errors occurring for blocklengths $N = 96$ and $N = 204$.
(b) Rate 1/3, column weight $j = 4$. Dotted lines show undetected errors occurring for blocklengths $N = 48$ and $N = 96$ only. Vertical axis: block error probability; horizontal axis: E_b/N_0/dB.

For example, the product with itself of a $(n, k) = (64, 57)$ Hamming code satisfying $m = 7$ constraints is a $(N, K) = (n^2, k^2) = (4096, 3249)$ code. The number of independent constraints is $M = 847$, but the sum–product decoder can make use of $2nm = 896$ equivalent constraints. Such codes have recently been named 'turbo product codes', but I think they should be called 'Tanner product codes', since they were first investigated by Tanner (1981). Product codes have the disadvantage, however, that their distance does not scale well with blocklength; the distance of a product code with blocklength n^2, built from two codes with distance d, is only d^2, so the ratio of distance to blocklength falls.

An open problem is to discover codes sharing the remarkable properties of the difference–set cyclic codes but with larger blocklengths and arbitrary rates. I call this task **the Tanner challenge**, in honour of Michael Tanner, who recognised the importance of such codes twenty years ago.

3   Do Gallager codes ever make undetected errors?

I use the term 'undetected error' to denote a decoding which returns a valid codeword not actually equal to the transmitted codeword. In our empirical experience with Gallager codes of many shapes and sizes, Gallager codes do not make undetected errors; their only failure mode is a 'detected error', that is, a decoding that fails to converge to a valid codeword, so that the recipient is aware that the block has been mis–received (MacKay and Neal 1996). Of course, we are decoding Gallager codes at noise levels well above half the minimum distance of the code, so, logically, undetected errors must have non–

zero probability; nevertheless, they appear to be so rare as to be effectively nonexistent. Since this property is an important advantage of Gallager codes, we have explored empirically how far regular binary Gallager codes can be pushed before undetected errors show up. Figure 5 shows that undetected errors occur when we reduce the blocklength N to sufficiently small values — below 200 bits in the case of rate 1/3 codes with $j = 4$, and below 400 bits in the case of rate 1/2 codes with $j = 3$. The frequency of undetected errors appears to fall very rapidly with increasing blocklength and with increasing column weight j.

4 Stopping rules for the decoding of sparse graph codes

When we decode Gallager codes, we test the bit–by–bit best guess at each iteration to see if it is a valid codeword. If it is, then our decoder halts. Otherwise, the decoder continues, declaring a failure (a detected error) if some maximum number of iterations (*e.g.*, 200 or 1000) occurs without successful decoding.

In the turbo code and repeat–accumulate code community, a different decoding procedure is widely used. The decoding algorithm is run for a *fixed* number of iterations (irrespective of whether the decoder has actually settled in a consistent state at some earlier time), and performance curves are displayed as a function of the number of iterations. This practice is wasteful of computer time, and it blurs the distinction between undetected and detected errors. Undetected errors are of scientific interest because they reveal distance properties of a code. And in engineering practice, it would seem preferable for the detected errors to be labelled as erasures if practically possible — undetected errors are a great nuisance in many communication contexts.

I therefore demonstrate here that it is possible to detect convergence of the sum–product decoder of a repeat–accumulate code, just as in the case of turbo codes (Frey 1998). This assertion may be found confusing if the role of the decoder is viewed as 'finding the most probable state of the source bits'. Surely any hypothesis about the K source bits is a valid hypothesis, so how can we detect that the decoder has finished decoding? The answer is that decoding should be viewed as finding the most probable state of all the variables in the graph, not just the source bits. Early on in the decoding, there will be inconsistencies among the most probable states of internal variables in the graph. Only when a sensible decoding has been found will there be a state of harmony in the network. [Note that detecting convergence doesn't imply that we get rid of undetected errors; undetected errors will still occur if the decoder converges to an incorrect codeword.]

I used the following method to decide when to stop the decoding of a repeat–accumulate code.

1. While running the sum–product algorithm up and down the accumulator trellis, note the most probable state at each time. This state sequence — if you unaccumulate it — defines a sequence of guesses for the source bits, with each source bit being guessed q times, where q is the number of repetitions in the RA code.

2. When reading out the likelihoods from the trellis, and combining the q likelihoods for each of the source bits, compute the most probable state of each source bit. This is the state that maximizes the product of the likelihoods.

3. If *all* the guesses in (1) agree with the most probable state of the source bit found in (2) then the decoder has reached a valid state, so HALT. Otherwise continue.

The cost of these extra operations is small compared to the cost of decoding. Using this procedure, we can distinguish between undetected errors and detected errors in a repeat–accumulate code, as shown in the results of figure 2(b).

We can also evaluate how many iterations it takes to decode these codes, and quantify the potential savings from applying the above stopping rule. If, for example, the old–fashioned method runs all decodings for 20 iterations, the histogram in figure 6(b) shows that there would, for a particular code at 0.75 dB, be a block error probability of about 0.8 — roughly 80% of the decodings took more than 20 iterations. Since a small but substantial number took more than 40 iterations, you could run the old–fashioned decoder for twice as long, and the block error probability would fall by a factor of ten or so. However, using the stop–when–it's–done decoder, you can use roughly the same amount of computer time and get the error probability down by a factor of about one hundred.

Nothing is lost, because (if you log the stopping time in a file) you can always recover the old–fashioned graphs if anyone still wants them.

5 Empirical distribution of decoding times

We have investigated the number of iterations τ of the sum–product algorithm required to decode Gallager codes and repeat–accumulate codes. Given one code and a set of channel conditions the decoding time varies randomly from trial to trial. We find that the histogram of decoding times follows a power law, $P(\tau) \propto \tau^{-p}$, for large τ. The power p depends on the signal to noise ratio and becomes smaller (so that the distribution is more heavy–tailed) as the signal to noise ratio decreases.

147

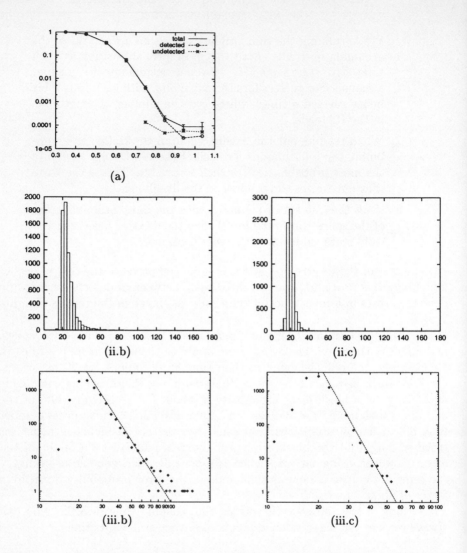

Figure 6. Histograms of number of iterations to find a valid decoding for a repeat–accumulate code with source block length $K = 10000$ and transmitted block length $N = 30000$. (a) Block error probability versus signal to noise ratio for the RA code. (ii.b) $x/\sigma = 0.89$, $E_b/N_0 = 0.749$ dB. (ii.c) $x/\sigma = 0.90$, $E_b/N_0 = 0.846$ dB. (iii.b, iii.c): Fits of power laws to (ii.b) $(1/\tau^6)$ and (ii.c) $(1/\tau^9)$.

148

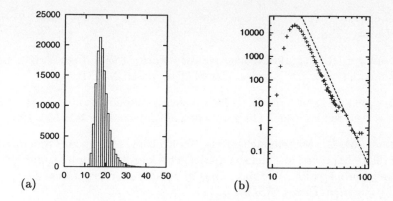

(a)

(b)

Figure 7. (a) Histogram of number of iterations for an irregular binary Gallager code, rate 1/2, blocklength $N = 9972$, at $E_b/N_0 = 1.4\,\text{dB}$. (b) Log/log plot of iterations histogram showing that the tail of the distribution is well approximated by a power law. The straight line has slope -8.5. From MacKay *et al.* (1999).

We have observed power laws in repeat–accumulate codes and in irregular and regular Gallager codes. Figures 6(ii) and (iii) show the distribution of decoding times of a repeat–accumulate code at two different signal–to–noise ratios. The power laws extend over several orders of magnitude. Figure 7 shows the distribution of decoding times for an irregular Gallager code. The tail is well approximated by the power law $P(\tau) \sim \tau^{-8.5}$.

It would be interesting to understand the reason for these power laws.

References

Berrou, C., and Glavieux, A. (1996) Near optimum error correcting coding and decoding: Turbo-codes. *IEEE Transactions on Communications* **44**: 1261–1271.

Davey, M. C., and MacKay, D. J. C. (1998) Low density parity check codes over GF(q). In *Proceedings of the 1998 IEEE Information Theory Workshop*. IEEE.

Divsalar, D., Jin, H., and McEliece, R. J. (1998) Coding theorems for 'turbo–like' codes. In *Proceedings of the 36th Allerton Conference on Communication, Control, and Computing, Sept. 1998*, pp. 201–210, Monticello, Illinois. Allerton House.

Frey, B. J. (1998) *Graphical Models for Machine Learning and Digital Communication*. Cambridge MA.: MIT Press.

Gallager, R. G. (1962) Low density parity check codes. *IRE Trans. Info. Theory* **IT-8**: 21–28.

Gallager, R. G. (1963) *Low Density Parity Check Codes*. Number 21 in Research monograph series. Cambridge, Mass.: MIT Press.

Karplus, K., and Krit, H. (1991) A semi–systolic decoder for the PDSC–73 error–correcting code. *Discrete Applied Mathematics* **33**: 109–128.

Luby, M. G., Mitzenmacher, M., Shokrollahi, M. A., and Spielman, D. A. (1998) Improved low–density parity–check codes using irregular graphs and belief propagation. In *Proceedings of the IEEE International Symposium on Information Theory (ISIT)*, p. 117.

Lucas, R., Fossorier, M., Kou, Y., and Lin, S., (1999) Iterative decoding of one-step majority logic decodable codes based on belief propagation. Submitted.

MacKay, D. J. C. (1999) Good error correcting codes based on very sparse matrices. *IEEE Transactions on Information Theory* **45** (2): 399–431.

MacKay, D. J. C., and Davey, M. C., (1998) Evaluation of Gallager codes for short block length and high rate applications. Available from `wol.ra.phy.cam.ac.uk/mackay/`.

MacKay, D. J. C., and Neal, R. M. (1996) Near Shannon limit performance of low density parity check codes. *Electronics Letters* **32** (18): 1645–1646. Reprinted *Electronics Letters*, **33**(6):457–458, March 1997.

MacKay, D. J. C., Wilson, S. T., and Davey, M. C. (1999) Comparison of constructions of irregular Gallager codes. *IEEE Transactions on Communications*. In press.

McEliece, R. J., MacKay, D. J. C., and Cheng, J.-F. (1998) Turbo decoding as an instance of Pearl's 'belief propagation' algorithm. *IEEE Journal on Selected Areas in Communications* **16** (2): 140–152.

Tanner, R. M. (1981) A recursive approach to low complexity codes. *IEEE Transactions on Information Theory* **27** (5): 533–547.

Urbanke, R., Richardson, T., and Shokrollahi, A., (1999) Design of provably good low density parity check codes. Submitted.

New Applications for McEliece's Cryptosystems

M.C. Rodríguez-Palánquex
Sección Departamental de Matemática Aplicada, Escuela Universitaria de Estadística,
Universidad Complutense de Madrid, Avda. Puerta de Hierro s/n, 28040 Madrid (Spain),
E-mail: mcrodri@eucmax.sim.ucm.es

L.J. García-Villalba, F. Montoya-Vitini
Departamento de Tratamiento de la Información y Codificación, Instituto de Física
Aplicada, Consejo Superior de Investigaciones Científicas (C.S.I.C.), Serrano 144,
28006 Madrid (Spain), E-mail: {luisj, fausto}@iec.csic.es

1. INTRODUCTION

A systematic study of properties of a new class of curves (the so-called *Quasihermitian* curves) and of Goppa codes obtained from them .is presented. Applications to McEliece's public-key cryptosystems are shown.

Let K be a finite field of characteristic 2, $K = F_q$ where $q = 2^j$.

Quasihermitian curve defined over K is given by the affine equation

$$y^a + \beta_1 y + \beta_2 x^{a+b} = 0$$

$$\forall\, a, b \in Z, \; a \geq 2, \; b > -a, \; \beta_1, \beta_2 \in K - \{0\}$$

Curves with many rational points are interesting in Coding Theory. In particular, Goppa geometric codes obtained from Hermitian curves have been extensively studied [5] [6] [7]. If $j = 2 j_0$ Quasihermitian curves include

- Hermitian curves, which have by homogeneous equation

$$Y^{2^{j_0}} Z + Y Z^{2^{j_0}} + X^{2^{j_0}+1} = 0$$

- The maximal curves [2] obtained from the affine equation

$$y^{2^{j_0}} + y = x^m$$

where m is a divisor of

$$(2^{j_0} + 1)$$

- And many new maximal curves [3], i.e., for the non-singular models of these curves, the number of F_q-rational points attains the Hasse-Weil upper bound

$$q+1+2g\sqrt{q}$$

The special arithmetic properties for the F_q-rational points of Quasihermitian curves have allowed to calculate the true minimum distance of such codes.

2. PREVIOUS RESULTS FOR QUASIHERMITIAN CURVES
There are the following results about Quasihermitian curves

Theorem 1 [4] $\forall\, a, b \in Z,\ a \geq 2,\ b > -a,\ a+b = 2^n b_0$, *if C is the curve*

$$Y^a Z^b + Y Z^{a+b-1} + X^{a+b} = 0 \quad \text{if } b \geq 0$$

$$Y^a + Y Z^{a-1} + X^{a+b} Z^{-a} = 0 \quad \text{if } b < 0$$

then its genus is

$$g(C) = \frac{s_0(b_0 - 1)}{2} - \alpha_0$$

where

$$a+b = 2^n b_0 \quad \text{with } n \geq 0 \text{ and } b_0 \geq 1 \text{ odd}$$

$$a-1 = 2^s s_0 \quad \text{with } s \geq 0 \text{ and } s_0 \geq 1 \text{ odd}$$

$$\alpha = gcd\,(a, b_0), \quad \alpha = 2\alpha_0 + 1$$

Theorem 2 [3] *Let g be the genus of a curve C defined over* F_2. *If* $\forall j \leq g$

$$N(C(F_{2^j})) = 2^j + 1$$

then C is maximal over $F_{2^{2g}}$

Theorem 3 [3] *If* $C_{2, 2g-1}$ *is a hyperelliptic curve over* F_2 *whose genus is* $g \geq 2$, *defined by the equation*

$$Y^2 Z^{2g-1} + Y Z^{2g} + X^{2g+1} = 0,$$

such that

$$gcd\,(2g+1, 2^j +1) = 1 \quad \forall\, j \leq g$$

152

Then $C_{2,2g+1}$ is maximal over $F_{2^{2g}}$.

3. APPLICATIONS TO CRYPTOSYSTEMS

From these results we have examples of McEliece's public-key cryptosystems from Quasihermitian curves.

In general, optimal codes for these cryptosystems are when $n \geq 1000$ and $k \geq 500$. According to the Work factor T required to attack McEliece's cryptosystem presented by Adams-Meijer [1], for Quasihermitian curves when

$$n = 1024$$
$$k = 654$$
$$t = \left[\frac{d-1}{2}\right] = 184$$

is

$$T \approx 10^{110.1}$$

This is the case for the following maximal Quasihermitian curves

$$Y^3 Z^2 + Y Z^4 + X^5 = 0$$

$$Y^2 Z^9 + Y Z^{10} + X^{11} = 0$$

The first curve is maximal on F_{2^4} and $F_{2^{12}}$, it has genus 2 with 4353 rational points on $F_{2^{12}}$. We can consider the next Goppa code obtained from the following divisors

$$D = Q_0 + Q_1 + \sum_{i=1}^{1022} P_i \quad with \quad Q_0 = (0,0,1) \quad Q_1 = (0,1,1)$$

$$G = 654 \, P_\infty \quad with \quad P_\infty = (0,1,0)$$

We have that

$$div\left(\prod_{\beta \in A}\left(\beta + \frac{x}{z}\right)\right) = \sum_{\beta \in A}\left(P_{\beta_1} + P_{\beta_2} + P_{\beta_3}\right) - 3\,(\# A)\, P_\infty$$

It is possible to get that $\# A = 218$ and therefore the rational function

153

$$\prod_{\beta \in A} \left(\beta + \frac{x}{z} \right)$$

has 654 different simple zeros, then it verifies that

$$\begin{cases} n = 1024 \\ k = 653 \\ d = 1024 - 654 = 370 \\ t = \left[\dfrac{369}{2} \right] = 184 \end{cases}$$

The second curve has genus 5 and it has 1345 rational points on $F_{2^{10}}$. We have that

$$\frac{x}{z} \in L(2P_\infty) - L(P_\infty) \quad P_\infty = (0,1,0)$$

$$\frac{y}{z} \in L(11P_\infty) - L(10P_\infty)$$

Moreover

$$WS(P_\infty) = <2,11>$$

We define the corresponding Goppa code from the divisors

$$D = Q_0 + Q_1 + \sum_{i=1}^{1022} P_i \quad with \quad Q_0 = (0,0,1), \quad Q_1 = (0,1,1)$$

$$G = m_0 \, P_\infty \quad with \quad 0 < m_0 < 1023$$

There are the next rational functions

$$\prod_{\beta \in A} \left(\beta + \frac{x}{z} \right) \prod_{\delta \in B} \left(\delta + \frac{y}{z} \right)$$

with $m_0 = 2(\# A) + 11(\# B)$ different simple zeros. For McEliece's cryptosystem, we can consider among a lot of possibilities, $m_0 = 658$ and therefore we have that

154

$$\begin{cases} n = 1024 \\ k = 654 \\ d = 1024 - 658 = 366 \\ t = \left[\dfrac{365}{2} \right] = 182 \end{cases}$$

4. CONCLUSIONS

If we use the following notation

$$If \quad m \geq a, \quad C_{a,m} := Y^a Z^{m-a} + YZ^{m-1} + X^m = 0$$

$$If \quad m < a, \quad D_{a,m} := Y^a + YZ^{a-1} + X^m Z^{a-m} = 0$$

$$\forall a \geq 2, \quad b \geq 0, \quad a + b = 2^n b_0 \quad with \ n \geq 0, \ b_0 \geq 1 \ and \ b_0 \ odd$$

We have, for every one of these Quasihermitian curves, many new maximal curves, considering that there is a purely inseparable rational map ϕ between the curves $C_{a,a+b}$ and $C_{a,c}$ with $c = 2^h b_0 \geq a$ and between the curves $C_{a,a+b}$ and $D_{a,c}$ with $c = 2^{h'} b_0 < a$. So, we can give other maximal curves from each one of the studied Quasihermitian curves. Therefore, we have a lot of new possibilities of McEliece's cryptosystems or another different cryptosystems. For example, other Quasihermian curves with identical values of parameters than $C_{3,5}$ are $C_{3,10}, C_{3,20}, C_{3,40}$. In the case of $C_{2,11}$ we have that the Quasihermitian curves $C_{2,22}, C_{2,44}, C_{2,88}$ have also identical values of parameters.

ACKNOWLEDGEMENTS

This work was supported by Fundación Ramón Areces, by Comisión Interministerial de Ciencia y Tecnología (CICYT) under grant TEL98-1020 and by Comunidad Autónoma de Madrid (CAM) under grant 07T-0044-1998.

REFERENCES

[1] C. M. Adams, H. Meijer. *Security-related comments regarding McEliece's public-key cryptosystem.* Advances in Cryptology-Proceedings of CRYPTO'87. LNCS 293, pp. 224-228, Springer-Verlag, Berlin, 1989.
[2] A. Cossidente, J. W. P. Hirschfeld, G. Korchmáros, F. Torres. *On plane maximal curves.* Math AG/9802113, 1998.

[3]   M. C. Rodríguez-Palánquex. Aritmética de curvas cuasihermíticas. Aplicaciones a Códigos Geométricos de Goppa. Ph. D. Dissertation. Universidad Complutense de Madrid, 1996.

[4]   M. C. Rodríguez-Palánquex, L. J. García-Villalba, F. Montoya-Vitini. *Genus of Quasihermitian curves*. Communications in Algebra. Preprint 1999.

[5]   H. Stichtenoth. *A note on Hermitian codes over GF(q^2)*. IEEE Trans. Inf. Theory, vol. 34(5), pp. 1345-1347, 1988.

[6]   H. Tiersma. *Remarks on codes from Hermitian curves*. IEEE Trans. Inf. Theory, vol. 33(4), 1987.

[7]   K. Yang, P. V. Kumar. *On the true minimum distance of Hermitian codes*. Univ. of Southern California, Los Angeles, 1991.

End-to-end Encryption
Synchronisation for Mobile Systems

M.I. Samarakoon[1], B.Honary[1] and M.Rayne[2]

ABSTRACT

Cryptographic techniques are used to provide security to digital mobile communication systems. This paper discusses synchronisation issues of end-to-end encrypted data transmission over mobile communication systems. The problems involved with the present end-to-end encryption synchronisation mechanism of TETRA (TErrestrial Trunked RAdio) standard [1][2][[3] are highlighted and an alternative encryption synchronisation technique known as frame insertion is introduced. This technique overcomes some of the drawbacks of the frame stealing technique used in TETRA standard in video and data transmission. A technique known as fly-wheeling, which overcomes synchronisation problems that arise from dropped data packets, is also presented. Finally practical implementation of the proposed techniques is described.

1. INTRODUCTION

There is now an increasing need for transmission of multimedia data over different types of communications networks with high level of security. This is a particular requirement of the military, commercial and public safety users of radio and PSTN networks. For these users it is important to secure the entire communications path from one mobile station (MS) to another, in addition to the security provided by the air

---

[1] Communications Research Centre, Lancaster University, Lancaster, LA1 4YR.

[2] SIMOCO International Ltd., PO Box 24, St. Andrews Road, Cambridge, CB4 1DP.

interface encryption system [5][6]. The method of providing end-to-end security in mobile systems is known as end-to-end encryption [7].

Communications over time-varying channels results in errors in the received data and, consequently, loss of synchronisation of the receiver to the incoming data stream. Loss of synchronisation in a stream of encrypted data will result in an erroneously deciphered data stream. Therefore, some means of providing synchronisation is required at the receiver. End-to-end encryption synchronisation is achieved by sending synchronisation information (synchronisation frames) to the receiver.

The TETRA system uses the technique of frame stealing [7] to periodically send synchronisation information from transmitter to the receiver. This technique is not appropriate for certain data types such as video because of the loss of data due to the stealing process. In this paper we propose a technique termed frame-insertion which overcomes the drawbacks of frame stealing technique and is more appropriate for video transmission. We also introduce the technique of fly-wheeling which can be used to avoid loss of synchronisation due to dropped data packets.

This paper is organised in the following manner. Important encryption synchronisation issues are discussed in section 2. The frame stealing technique is described in section 3. In section 4 the proposed frame insertion technique is presented. In section 5 the fly-wheeling technique is discussed. A method of securing the synchronisation frame is described in section 6. In section 7 an implementation of the proposed techniques is presented, and in section 8 some conclusions are derived.

2. SYNCHRONISATION ISSUES

In end-to-end encryption there are two synchronisation cases to consider. The first is the initial synchronisation, where the receiver is initially synchronised to an incoming encrypted data stream. Since the encrypted data is transmitted over a noisy mobile channel, robust initial synchronisation is required such that the probability of synchronising correctly is considerably higher than that of receiving the actual data correctly. The annoyance of missing the start of a call is great enough to make the investment of a time delay to ensure the receiver gets synchronised properly. This can be achieved by initially sending the synchronisation information several times so that the receiver has a better chance of achieving synchronisation. For example, if four successive synchronisation frames are sent over channel with a message error rate of 0.08, the probability of missing all four frames is about 0.00004, which is considerably less than the probability of receiving data correctly.

The second case is re-synchronisation, where the receiver maintains synchronisation to the incoming encrypted data stream after initial synchronisation. One way to maintain synchronisation would be to assume that the data stream is transmitted over the air at a constant rate. This allows the receiver to use an accurate timer to maintain synchronisation when portions of data are lost. However it does not work if the data rate is variable, or encrypted data streams from more than one application are multiplexed over a single data link, so that the data rate of each application is variable.

Therefore, re-synchronisation is achieved by periodically sending synchronisation information to the receiver. This is particularly required by continuous media such as speech and video. The re-synchronisation process provides the means to facilitate late entry, where a user is allowed to join a group call [3] that is already in progress.

The table below shows the late entry requirements of the different data types.

Media Type	Late Entry	
	Point to multi-point	**Point to point**
Video	Yes	No
Audio	Yes	No
Image	No	No
Text data	No	No
GPS position data	No	No

Several important factors should be considered when designing end-to-end encryption synchronisation schemes, i.e. type of media, mode of encryption, position of encryption, and synchronisation technique.

The synchronisation requirements vary with the media type. For continuous data types such as audio and video, intermittent transmission of synchronisation information is essential for the receiver to maintain synchronisation. Non continuous data such as image and text files can be transmitted using ARQ schemes. Therefore, image files and text file can be transmitted as encrypted files by encrypting them before transmisson. Therefore, end-to-end encryption synchronisation is not required for these types of data.

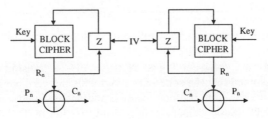

Figure 1: Block Cipher in OFB Mode

159

It is important to minimise the propagation of errors inherent in mobile radio channels and the mode of encryption is one of the contributing factors. The Output Feed Back (OFB) mode [8] shown in Figure 1 is not susceptible to error propagation since the plaintext is XORed with the encrypted initialisation vector (IV). This is the preferred mode of encryption for mobile applications where block encryption techniques are used.

The positioning of the encryption and decryption apparatus is also an important issue for encryption synchronisation. Position refers to the layer in which encryption is carried out. Figure 2 shows a basic block diagram of how multimedia applications are supported over a mobile communications system (for example TETRA).

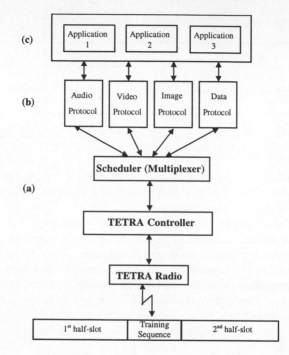

Figure 2: Multimedia Applications Supported over TETRA

The applications use different types of protocols to transmit different types of media. Here it is assumed that the scheduler fragments the variable length data packets passed down from the different protocol stacks, and passes fixed length packets, to the TETRA controller. The basic transmission transmit packet of TETRA is a half slot as shown in Figure 2, and the two half slots are separated by a training sequence. Depending on the status of the received pair of slots, the TETRA receiver reports to the

160

data terminal that the contents of the current pair of slots is GOOD, BAD (contents are corrupted), or NULL (training sequence is corrupted) [3]. If the header of a particular scheduler packet is corrupted the packet is dropped as the scheduler can not reliably determine which protocol stack it should assign the data of the corrupted packet.

There are three main positions where encryption can be performrd, as indicated by (a), (b), and (c) of Figure 2. The first is to perform encryption between the scheduler and the TETRA controller, i.e. position (a). In this case if one of the fixed length scheduler-packets was corrupted or stolen by the TETRA radio for signalling purposes, the number of missing bits is known, and the lost slot or half slot could be padded out to the requisite length. The IV of the decryption apparatus can be correctly updated as the size of the scheduler packet is known. Another benefit is that decryption is performed before the data is passed to the various protocol stacks. This avoids the synchronisation problems arising from the scheduler's inability to determine to which protocol stack it should assign a half slot of data carrying the header of a protocol data unit (PDU) marked as BAD or NULL. The disadvantage with this approach is that only a single encryption algorithm can be used to encrypt all the media types.

In the second position, encryption is done in the protocol layer, i.e. position (b). The advantage of this is that the various media types can be encrypted with separate algorithms. However, this poses a serious problem with regards to end-to-end synchronisation. In particular, the scheduler can not reliably determine to which protocol stack it should assign the half slot of data if it carries the header of a PDU marked as BAD or NULL. Loss of an unknown amount of data to a decryption unit will result in loss of encryption synchronisation, and failure to decrypt correctly. In other words the IV will not be updated at the necessary time for correct decoding of the data.

For the third position, encryption is done in the application layer, i.e. position (c). The advantage of this is that the encryption mechanism is easily interchangeable and can be controlled directly by the application. The problem of dropped packets can be avoided by implementing a sequence numbering system, allowing the receiving entity to count the packets as they arrive. If a packet is received out of sequence the IV can be updated as described in section 5 to maintain synchronisation.

The technique used for synchronisation is also a very important factor to consider. Two such encryption techniques are described in this paper. They are the frame stealing technique of TETRA standard and the new frame insertion technique. The various media types and the preferred method of synchronisation are summarised in the following table.

Media type	Synchronisation method
Video	Insertion
Audio	Stealing
Image	Not required
Text data	Not required
GPS	Insertion

The synchronisation techniques are discussed in greater detail in the following sections.

3. FRAME STEALING TECHNIQUE

This technique is used in TETRA for end-to-end encryption synchronisation. The frame stealing process periodically replaces the contents of a half slot of data with synchronisation information from time to time [7]. Because of this stealing process the replaced portions of data are lost. The TETRA speech codec is capable of tolerating some loss of data, and therefore frame stealing can be used for synchronisation of end-to-end encrypted speech. Also, speech is coded in the TETRA radio and the speech frames are directly mapped on to the transmission time slots of the radio. Therefore, the frame stealing strategy can be efficiently adopted for synchronisation of end-to-end encrypted speech.

However, this strategy is not suitable for certain data types because of the loss of data. For example, stealing portions of video frames is unlikely to have a harmless effect as in the case of speech. This is because majority of the video frames are differentially encoded and contain information about the difference between consecutive frames. Losing part of such a frame will therefore result in incorrectly interpreting the succeeding frames.

Unlike speech, video is coded in the host computer at the application layer. Therefore, there is no direct mapping of video frames to the transmission time slots of the radio. This makes it difficult to determine the timing for stealing half slots to send synchronisation frames. Additionally, as stealing is done in the data-link layer it is difficult to directly control the synchronisation scheme from the user application, which is another disadvantage of this mechanism.

4. FRAME INSERTION TECHNIQUE

This technique was specifically designed to overcome the drawbacks of the frame stealing technique in video transmission over TETRA. Here, synchronisation frames are inserted to the transmitted video stream between successive video frames. Unlike in frame stealing there is no loss of data. To permit insertion the application has to reduce the data rate to maintain the same overall transmission rate.

In this design it is assumed that the continuous media data is encrypted by a stream cipher system. Preferably the stream cipher is created by a block cipher operating in the output feedback (OFB) mode. In OFB mode the previous output of the encryption process is fed back as the input to the encryption process through a register (Z) and the plaintext is XORed with the output of encryption process to obtain the ciphertext as shown in Figure 1. The content of register Z is known as the initialisation vector (IV), and can be externally loaded if required. This IV value is used to resynchronise the receiver to the incoming encrypted data stream.

The following important fields identified in Figure 3 are included in the synchronisation frame.

1. A frame marker that identifies the beginning of the synchronisation frame, which may be an 8 bit frame-marker such as '01111110' or a PN sequence such as 1110000101001101 chosen for its impulsive autocorrelation properties. If required, its uniqueness may be ensured by the use of bit or byte stuffing in the data within the synchronisation frame. However, in a preferred implementation, the frame marker is validated by the use of a known length and a check-sum calculated over the entire synchronisation frame.
2. A key number that corresponds to the current session key in use to facilitate late entry in to a group call that is currently in progress
3. An algorithm number, if multiple encryption algorithms are in use, which also facilitates late entry into a group call that is currently in progress
4. Current IV to update the IV of receiver to keep the receiver key stream synchronised to the incoming encrypted data stream
5. A check sum (CRC-16) for error detection.

Frame Marker	Key Number	Algorithm Number	Encrypted IV	Check Sum (CRC)

Figure 3: Synchronisation Frame

Figure 4 illustrates the frame insertion mechanism at the transmitting end. The block encryption unit receives the continuous data frames, e.g. video frames, as its input.

163

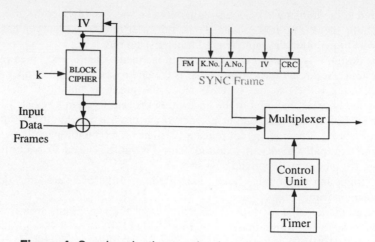

Figure 4: Synchronisation mechanism at the Transmitter

The encrypted data frames and the synchronisation frames are multiplexed according to the signals from the control unit. The control unit issues control signals to the multiplexer to select the synchronisation frame at times determined by the timer. Preferably the multiplexer waits for the current encrypted data frame to finish routing before it routes a synchronisation frame.

In the case of video, a synchronisation frame is inserted before every I-frame as these frames contain absolute information unlike the B and P-frames, which contain only differential information.

Before sending the frame marker, current key number, algorithm number and the current IV are included in the synchronisation frame. A check sum is also derived from the other four fields of the synchronisation frame and included in the synchronisation frame.

After encrypting each data packet the IV is updated in a particular manner in order to keep the decryption unit of the receiver synchronised to the incoming data stream when corrupted packets are dropped. This process is described in detail in section 5.

Figure 5 illustrates the synchronisation mechanism at the receiver. When a frame is received, the encryption synchronisation unit checks whether the received frame is a synchronisation frame. This is done by checking whether the received frame size is equal to the synchronisation frame size and, if so, checking whether the first byte of the received frame is equal to the synchronisation frame marker and, if so, checking whether the check sum (CRC) is valid.

164

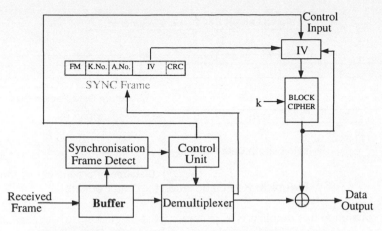

Figure 5: Synchronisation mechanism at the Receiver

After detecting a synchronisation frame at the receiver, the following operations are carried out. The current key is changed according to the key number; the algorithm is changed according to the algorithm number; and the IV of the receiver decryption unit is updated according to the received IV.

The decryption unit will decrypt the data frames received with the proper sequence numbers. After decrypting each data packet, the IV is updated as described in Figure 6 to avoid losing synchronisation due to dropped packets. If a particular packet is received out of sequence due to dropped packets, the IV of the decryption mechanism is updated as described in Figure 7 before decrypting it.

5. FLY-WHEELING MECHANISM

As described earlier, the packets received with corrupted headers will be dropped. It is very important to keep the receiver key stream synchronised to the incoming encrypted data stream at all times, i.e. even when corrupted packets are dropped. The main problem here is that when the packet size is not fixed (i.e. variable length packets), there is no way of determining the size of a dropped packet at the receiver. This is required to correctly synchronise the IV of the decryption unit to the incoming encrypted data stream to correctly decrypt the subsequent packets, which arrive after the dropped packet.

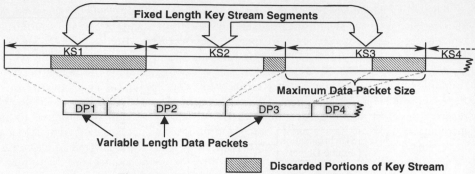

Figure 6: Key Generation for Data Packets

The solution to this problem is to generate fixed length key stream segments (KS1, KS2,...) to encrypt the variable length data packets (DP1, DP2,...) as shown in Figure 6. The length of each of these key stream segments is independent of the data packet sizes and should be equal to an allowable or expected maximum data packet size. After encrypting each data packet whose size is less than the expected maximum, the excess portion of the key stream segment is discarded.

In a practical implementation this can be achieved in the following manner. After each data packet is encrypted, the IV is updated 'n' times. In a block cipher based system, n is equal to the difference between a predetermined maximum data packet size and the current data packet size in terms of the block size of the cipher. Basically, n is the number of rounds that block cipher should operate. Here one round of encryption is equivalent to running the block cipher once.

For example, if the maximum packet size is 20000 bytes and the block size of the cipher is 8 bytes and the current data packet size is 16000 bytes, then;

n = (max packet size – current packet size)/ block size.
= $(20000 - 16000)/8$
= 500

In a stream cipher based system which produces one bit of key stream per round of operation of the cipher, n is equal to the difference between a predetermined maximum data packet size and the current data packet size in terms of bits per packet. Here one round is equivalent to the operation involved in producing one bit of key stream from the key stream generator. Basically one round equals one bit.

For example, if the maximum packet length is 25000 bits and the current data packet size is 15000 bits, then;

n = max packet size – current packet size
= $25000 - 15000$
= 10000

These two processes effectively derive constant length key stream segments to encrypt each variable length data packet. The length of each key stream segment is equal to the maximum allowable or expected data packet size. In this case, the starting IV value of encryption unit, to encrypt a particular data packet, is independent of the size of the previous data packet. Therefore, at the receiving end the starting IV value of decryption unit, to decrypt each received encrypted data packet, can be predetermined.

A sequence number is assigned to each encrypted data packet to facilitate the receiver to detect loss of packets in order to keep the key stream synchronised to the incoming encrypted data stream. The sequence number counter is started from zero and incremented by one for each data packet transmitted up to a predetermined maximum value. At the transmitter, and receiver, the sequence number counters are reset to zero when they reach the maximum value.

A data packet, which is received out of sequence, indicates an occurrence of a dropped packet. Therefore, if the packet $N+1$ is received immediately after the packet $N-1$ (i.e. packet N is dropped), the key stream segment KS_N, which is used to encrypt the packet N will be discarded as shown in Figure 7. Similarly, if the packet $N+2$ is received immediately after the packet $N-1$ (i.e. packets N and $N+1$ are dropped), then the key stream segments KS_N and KS_{N+1} should be discarded.

Basically, if an encrypted data packet is received out of sequence, the IV of the decryption unit should be updated accordingly before decrypting the particular packet. For example, consider a scenario where a block cipher with block size equal to 8 bytes is used in a system with a maximum data packet size of 20000 bytes. If the packet $N+1$ is received immediately after the packet $N-1$, then the IV should be updated 2500 $\{=20000/8\}$ times before decrypting the packet $N+1$. Similarly, if the packet $N+2$ is received immediately after the packet $N-1$, then IV should be updated 5000 $\{=(2\times20000)/8\}$ times before decrypting the packet $N+2$.

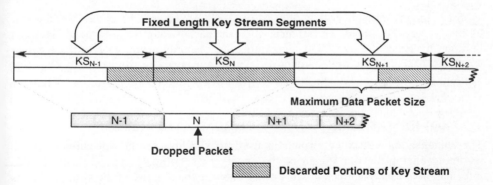

Figure 7: Re-synchronising after loss of data packets at the receiver

If this fly-wheeling mechanism is combined with the sequence numbering scheme it is possible for the receiver to compute the starting IV of a particular packet from the sequence number of the received packet. This means that the starting IV of each received packet is known to the receiver. Therefore, the transmitter does not have to send the IV to the receiver in order to resynchronise, as the sequence numbering scheme can compensate for dropped packets. Therefore, if there is initial synchronisation, then end-to-end encryption synchronisation can be achieved without insertion or stealing.

Initially a random IV (IV_R) can be negotiated between the transmitter and the receiver. This can be either done by securely sending the IV_R to the receiver by encrypting it, or computing a IV_R by combining a random seed with the session key (for example by hashing).

The initially negotiated IV_R will be the starting IV for the first packet. After that we can fly-wheel a predetermined number of times to obtain the starting IV of the subsequent received packets. Therefore, this method can be used to synchronise encrypted real time data, which does not need late entry.

This scheme can be implemented using a block cipher operating in counter mode. The counter can be incremented predetermined (M) times for each packet. Here also the starting IV for the first packet will be IV_R. The staring IV for the subsequent packets can be calculated by multiplying the packet number N by M and adding it to IV_R. Therefore, the starting IV of packet N denoted by IV_{NS} in the series of packets 0,1,2,3,…..,N-1,N,N+1,…

$$IV_{SN} = IV_R + N \times M$$

The value IV_{SN} can be calculated separately and can be loaded to the counter, so that it does not have to operate M times for each packet, thus saving some processing. Also, the packet numbers do   not have to be sequential. They can vary randomly, and a random number generator can be used to assign numbers to the packets. In this case N will be the random number assigned to the packet. Still the above equations for IV_{SN} will be valid.

Since the packet number field (e.g. 16 bits) will not be as large as the IV field (e.g. 64 bits), a new IV_R should be assigned when the packet count wraps around. This can be done by either the transmitter generating and sending a new IV_R to the receiver when the packet count wraps around or deriving a new IV_R from the old IV_R, (for example by hashing the old IV_R to obtain a new IV_R).

6.   PROVIDING SECURITY TO SYNCHRONISATION FRAME

The initialisation vector IV, which is used to synchronise the key stream to the incoming encrypted data stream at the receiver, is normally sent in clear. If this information is encrypted then it will further enhance the security of the system. This is particularly useful for stream cipher systems, in which the starting state of the key generator (i.e. the starting IV) is used as cipher key instead of an actual cipher key. This section describes a method for securing the synchronisation frame.

In a block cipher based system where OFB mode is used to encrypt the data, the current IV value of the block encryption apparatus can be encrypted in the ECB mode to secure the IV within the synchronisation frame as shown in Figure 8. Here Key 1 and Key 2 should be different if the two block ciphers are the same. It is possible to derive Key 2 from Key 1, for example by hashing, i.e. Key 2 = Hash(Key 1). The two ciphers can also be two different block cipher schemes. It is also possible for block cipher 2 to be the same as block cipher 1, except that it operates in decrypt mode, so that to obtain IV, the receiver has to operate in encrypt mode.

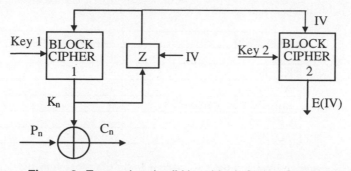

Figure 8: Encrypting the IV in a block Cipher System

In a key based stream cipher system the key and the IV will determine the ciphertext for a given plaintext. Unlike the block ciphers the stream ciphers do not have a mode equivalent to the ECB mode where an IV is not used. Therefore, a block cipher can be used here as well to encrypt the current IV as shown in Figure 9. Key 2 can be derived from Key 1 by hashing.

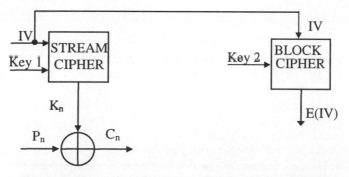

Figure 9: Encrypting the IV in a Stream Cipher System

For stream cipher systems where the starting state of the key generator (i.e. the starting IV denoted by IV_0) is used as the key, the current IV value can be encrypted by a block cipher in ECB mode with IV_0 or hashed IV_0 as the session key.

169

In obtaining Key 2 from Key 1 or IV_0 some padding of bits or exclusion of bits may be required to get the required key length for the block cipher. This method of securing the current IV value is not essential, but has the benefit of providing increased security.

7. IMPLEMENTATION OF FRAME INSERTION MECHANISM

The frame insertion and fly-wheeling mechanisms described earlier have been integrated with a H263 video coder [9] to transmit video over TETRA. The lengths of the different fields in the synchronisation frame are as follows;

Data Field	Length (bytes)
Flag	1
Key No	2
Algorithm No	1
Initialisation Value (IV)	8
CRC-16	2
TOTAL	*14*

The Flag is a unique byte and the CRC depends on the other four data-fields of the synchronisation frame. Therefore, out of the 14 bytes (112 bits) within the synchronisation frame, only the 11 bytes (88 bits) allocated for the key number, the algorithm number and the initialisation vector are variable.

Therefore, the probability (P) of a 14-byte data packet being mistaken for a synchronisation frame is very low, i.e. it is equal to

$$P = \frac{2^{88}}{2^{112}} = \frac{1}{2^{24}} = 5.96 \times 10^{-8}$$

Since the lengths of the H.263 video frames vary over a large range, the overall probability of a data packet being mistaken for a synchronisation packet becomes even lower.

At the transmitter the encryption unit receives variable size video frames as the input. These video frames are encrypted and passed to the multiplexer for transmission. A software timer is used to determine timing for insertion. The multiplexer is designed to insert synchronisation frames according to the timing indicated by the timer. It also inserts synchronisation frames before certain types of data packets (for example I-frames of video) are transmitted. Therefore, the video compression unit passes the frame type to the encryption unit along with the frame size.

The synchronisation frames are not transmitted within video frames. Therefore, if the timer signals to insert a synchronisation frame while a video frame is being encrypted, the multiplexer waits for the current frame to be encrypted and transmitted before inserting a synchronisation frame.

The video frames are encrypted using SAFER algorithm [10] in the OFB mode. A single byte sequence number is assigned to each encrypted video packet before transmission in order to detect dropped packets. The process described in section 5 is used to maintain synchronisation in situations where corrupted packets are dropped. A maximum video frame size of 20000 bytes is allowed in this implementation. Since the block size of SAFER is 8 bytes, if a packet is dropped the IV is updated 2500 (=20000/8) times before decrypting the succeeding packet.

8. CONCLUSIONS

A detailed description of end-to-end encryption synchronisation was presented. A novel encryption synchronisation mechanism for continuous media was introduced. This frame insertion technique has the advantage over the conventional frame stealing technique of not losing any data, and is very useful for video transmission over mobile communications systems. The fly-wheeling mechanism introduced offers a method of recovering synchronisation from dropped packets. Also, the frame insertion technique enables the synchronisation mechanism to be implemented in the application layer, which the application has more control over.

REFERENCES

[1]   B. Lovett, "TETRA: Setting New Standards For Digital PMR", TELECOMMUNICATIONS (International Edition), Vol 29, pp.5590-5595, Aug. 1995.

[2]   R. Pinter, Philips Telecom-Private Mobile Radio, "TETRA Approaches Fruition", Mobile Communications International 21, pp.38-43, April 1995.

[3]   ETSI Work Programme DE/RES-06001-2, Subtechnical Committee (STC) RES 06, "Radio Equipment and Systems (RES); Trans-European Trunked Radio (TETRA); Voice plus Data (V+D); Part 2: Air Interface, Draft Standard prETS 300 392-2, August 1995.

[4]   J. E. Wilkes, "Privacy and Authentication Needs of PCS", IEEE Personal Communications, August 1995.

[5]   D. Brown, "Techniques for Privacy and Authentication in Personal Communication Systems", IEEE Personal Communications, August 1995.

[6]   J. C. Cooke and R.L. Brewster, "Cryptographic security Techniques for Digital Mobile Telephones", Proceedings of the IEEE International Conference on selected Topics in Wireless Communications, Vancouver, B. C., Canada 1992.

[7]   ETSI Work Programme DE/RES-06001-7, Subtechnical Committee (STC) RES 06, "Radio Equipment and Systems (RES); Trans-European Trunked Radio (TETRA); Voice plus Data (V+D); Part 7: Security, Draft Standard prETS 300 392-7, March 1996.

[8]   B. Schneier, "APPLIED CRYPTOGRAPHY ", Published by John Wiley & Sons, Inc.

[9]   ITU-T Recommendation H.263, "Video codec for low bitrate communications", May 1996.

[10]   J. L. Massey, "SAFER K-64: A Bite-Oriented Block Cipher Algorithm", Lecture notes in Computer Science No. 809, Fast Software Encryption, (Ed. R. Anderson), New York, Spriger- Verlag, pp 1-17, 1994.

[11]   M. I. Samarakoon, B. Honary, M. Rayne, M. Darnell, "Data Encryption and Transmission", UK Patent No. 9915997.2, 9 July 1999.

Two Iterative Algorithms for Decoding Linear Codes Based on Their Tail Biting Trellises *

Rose Y. Shao, Shu Lin and Marc Fossorier
Department of Electrical Engineering
University of Hawaii at Manoa
Honolulu, Hawaii 96822, U.S.A.

Abstract

For convolutional codes, tail biting technique is used to terminate a code trellis without loss of code rate. This termination results in a trellis with multiple starting and ending states. Such a trellis is called a tail biting trellis. For block codes, tail biting trellis representation of a code significantly reduces the overall trellis state and branch complexities. In a tail biting trellis, each starting state has a unique corresponding ending state and they are the same state. A path in a tail biting trellis is a valid codeword if and only if it starts from a state and ends at the same state. Therefore, any tail biting trellis-based decoding algorithm must have a mechanism to estimate the starting state for each transmission of a codeword. Several Viterbi-type suboptimal algorithms for decoding codes based on their tail biting trellises have been proposed. All these decoding algorithms perform unidirectional iterative decoding process. In this paper, two new iterative algorithms for decoding codes based on their tail biting trellises are presented, one is unidirectional and the other is bidirectional. Both algorithms are computationally efficient and achieve virtually optimum error performance with a small number of decoding iterations. They outperform all the previous suboptimal decoding algorithms. The bidirectional algorithm also reduces decoding delay.

---

*This research was supported by NSF under Grants NCR 94-15374, CCR 97-32959, CCR 98-14054 and NASA under Grant NAG 5-8414.

1. Introduction

There are two types of trellis representation of codes, conventional trellis representation and tail biting trellis representation. In conventional trellis representation of a code [1-3], the code trellis has one starting state and one ending state, and the starting state and the ending state are the same state. The paths connecting the starting state and the ending state give all the codewords (or code sequences) of the code. In tail biting trellis representation of a code, the code trellis has multiple starting states and multiple ending states [4-6]. Each starting state has a unique corresponding ending state, and they are the same state. A path in a tail biting trellis is a valid codeword if and only if it starts from a state and ends at the same state. Such a path is called a **tail biting path**.

Tail biting trellis representation was first proposed by Solomon and van Tilborg [4] in 1979 for terminating the code trellis of a convolutional code without code rate loss. This tail biting trellis representation of a convolutional code was later generalized by Ma and Wolf [5] in 1986. Tail biting of a convolutional code results in a block code. Figure 1 depicts an 8-section tail biting trellis with 4 starting states and 4 ending states for a rate-1/2 convolutional code of memory 2 with generator sequences, $g_1 = (1,0,1)$ and $g_2 = (1,1,1)$ [1]. This tail biting convolutional code is a (16,8) linear block code. In [4], a link between quasi-cyclic codes and tail biting convolutional codes was also established. This link led to the most recent generalization of tail biting trellis representations of linear block codes by Calderbank, Forney and Vardy [6].

Tail biting trellis representation of a linear block code can significantly reduce the overall state and branch complexities of its conventional trellis representation, especially for long codes. Figures 2 and 3 depict a minimal 8-section conventional trellis and a minimal 8-section tail biting trellis for the (8,4,4) Reed-Muller (RM) code, respectively. The conventional trellis for this code has a total of 34 states and a total of 44 branches. The maximum state complexity(maximum number of states) is 8 which occurs at section boundary locations 3 and 5. The tail biting trellis for this code has two starting states, two ending states, a total of 30 states and a total of 40 branches. The maximum state complexity is 4. For this short code, the reduction in trellis state and branch complexities is small. Consider the (24,12,8) Golay code. This code has a minimal 12-section conventional trellis with a total number of 1,066 states and a total number of 1,960 2-bit branches. The maximum state complexity is 256 [7, 8]. However, this code has a 12-section regular tail biting trellis with 16 starting states and 16 ending states [6]. The number of states at each section boundary location is 16. Figure 4 shows the first 4 sections of the tail biting trellis for the code. It has a total of 208 states and a total of 384 2-bit branches. The maximum state complexity is 16. We see that tail biting trellis representation of the (24,12,8) Golay code results in a significant reduction in both state and branch complexities compared with the conventional trellis representation. The reduction in state and branch complexities of a code trellis results in a reduction of decoding complexity of a trellis-based decoding algorithm. General structure and construction of tail biting trellises for linear block codes have been further investigated lately [9-12]. In [12], tail biting trellises for RM codes have been analyzed, it shows that tail biting representations of these codes result in a significant reduction in both state and branch complexities.

As pointed out earlier, a path in a tail biting trellis is a valid codeword if and only if its starting and ending states are the same. Since there are multiple starting states, a transmitted codeword can start from any of its starting states which is unknown to the receiver. Therefore, any tail biting trellis-based decoding algorithm must have a mechanism to estimate the starting state for each transmission of a codeword. A simple minded maximum likelihood decoding (MLD) algorithm is to treat a tail biting trellis with M starting states and M ending states as a union of M subtrellises, each subtrellis consists of the paths that connect a starting state and its corresponding ending state [4]. Each subtrellis is then a conventional trellis. Process each subtrellis with the conventional Viterbi algorithm and determine its survivor. This results in M survivors, one for each subtrellis. Then compare these M survivors. The one with the best metric (the largest correlation metric or the smallest Euclidean distance metric) is then the most likely (ML) codeword and the decoded codeword. This simple minded MLD algorithm requires to process M subtrellises independently and then compares M survivors to make a decoding decision. If M is large, the computational complexity can be very large. If a single decoder is used, it also results in long decoding delay. If M decoders are used to process the M subtrellises in parallel, this reduces

175

the decoding delay but increases the hardware complexity. To reduce the decoding complexity, several suboptimal iterative Viterbi-type algorithms for decoding codes based on their tail biting trellises have been proposed [5,13-18].

In this paper, two new iterative algorithms for decoding codes based on their tail biting trellises are presented, one is an unidirectional wrap-around algorithm and the other is a bidirectional wrap-around algorithm. In these algorithms, both cumulative state metric and path metric are used to determine surviving paths and the final survivor. During the decoding iteration process, the decoder continues updating the best surviving path until certain termination condition is met. Both algorithms are computationally efficient and achieve virtually optimum error performance with a small number of iterations, say 2 to 4, for almost the entire range of signal-to-noise ratios (SNR) for many codes being simulated. They outperform all the previous suboptimal decoding algorithms. The bidirectional algorithm also reduces decoding delay.

2. Preliminary and Review

This section first provides some needed background information regarding tail biting trellises for linear codes and then gives a brief review of existing algorithms for decoding codes based on their tail biting trellises.

Let T be an L-section tail biting trellis for a binary linear code C with section boundary locations indexed by $0, 1, 2, \cdots, L$. These boundary locations also serve as time indices. For $0 \leq t \leq L$, let

$$\Sigma_t(C) = \{s_{t,1}, s_{t,2}, \cdots, s_{t,q_t}\} \tag{1}$$

denote the state space of the tail biting trellis T at boundary location-t (or time-t), where $q_t = |\Sigma_t(C)|$. Then $\Sigma_0(C)$ and $\Sigma_L(C)$ are the starting and ending (or final) state spaces of T, respectively, and

$$\Sigma_0(C) = \Sigma_L(C), \tag{2}$$

i.e., $\Sigma_0(C)$ and $\Sigma_L(C)$ consist of the same set of states. Hence, $q_0 = q_L$. For $1 \leq i \leq q_0$ (or q_L), $s_{0,i}$ and $s_{L,i}$ are the same state. A tail biting trellis for a convolutional code is time-invariant and the state spaces at all the boundary locations are the same, i.e.,

$$\Sigma_0(C) = \Sigma_1(C) = \cdots = \Sigma_L(C). \tag{3}$$

176

Figure 1 displays the time-invariant property of a tail biting trellis for a 4-state convolutional code. However, a tail biting trellis for a linear block code is in general time-varying, i.e., for $0 \leq i, j \leq L$ and $i \neq j$, $\Sigma_i(C)$ and $\Sigma_j(C)$ may not be the same. For example, the minimal 8-section tail biting trellis for the (8,4,4) RM code shown in Figure 3 is a time-varying tail biting trellis.

A path in the tail biting trellis T that connects a starting state in $\Sigma_0(C)$ and an ending state in $\Sigma_L(C)$ is a valid codeword (or code sequence) if and only if the starting state and the ending state are the same state. Such a path is called a **tail biting path**. The tail biting trellis T may be viewed as a union of q_0 subtrellises [4, 12]. Each subtrellis consists of those tail biting paths in T that connect a state $s_{0,i}$ at boundary location-0 to the same state $s_{L,i}$ at boundary location-L, i.e., the starting and ending states of each subtrellis are the same. For example, the tail biting trellis shown in Figure 1 consists of 4 subtrellises, and the tail biting trellis for the (8,4,4) RM code shown in Figure 3 consists of two subtrellises. The tail biting paths of the subtrellis T_0 of T which contains the all-zero path actually form a linear subcode C_0 of C [11, 12]. As a result, the other subtrellises of T are the trellises for the cosets of C_0 in C. Therefore, the q_0 subtrellises of T are structurally identical (or isomorphic). All these subtrellises share a common part from certain boundary location-t_1 to certain boundary location-t_2 with $t_1 \leq t_2$ [12]. For example, the 4 subtrellises of the tail biting trellis shown in Figure 1 share a common part from boundary location-2 to boundary location-6, i.e., they share 4 common trellis sections. The two subtrellises of the tail biting trellis for the (8,4,4) RM code shown in Figure 3 share 4 common trellis sections from boundary location-2 to boundary location-6.

Representing a linear code C by a tail biting trellis T with q_0 starting states and q_L ending states with $q_0 = q_L$, a transmitted codeword may start from any of the q_0 starting states. If a tail biting trellis based algorithm is used for decoding C, the decoding algorithm must first estimate the starting and ending states of the transmitted codeword and then determine the most likely codeword that connects the estimated starting and ending states. The simple minded tail biting trellis based MLD described in Section 1 requires to process q_0 subtrellises with the Viterbi algorithm independently. For simplicity, we call this Viterbi-type tail biting trellis based MLD the VTMLD algorithm. Define the Viterbi processing of a trellis of L section as a **Viterbi trial** (VT) and the processing of one trellis section (including all the addition, comparison and selection operations) as a **Viterbi update** (VU) [16]. Then the VTMLD algorithm requires a total of q_0 VT's and a total of $q_0 L$ VU's to make a decoding decision. For large q_0 and L, the VTMLD algorithm results in a large computational complexity.

To overcome the computational complexity problem of the VTMLD algorithm, several Viterbi-type suboptimal decoding algorithms have been proposed [13-18]. All these decoding algorithms are iterative in nature and they process the tail biting trellis T of a code with the conventional Viterbi algorithm repeatedly until certain stopping conditions are met or a preset maximum number of decoding iterations is reached. The differences between these suboptimal decoding algorithms are their starting conditions, termination conditions, methods for estimating the starting state, and methods for selecting the decoded codeword (or sequences). All these suboptimal decoding algorithms require much less VU's (or VT's) than the VTMLD algorithm at the expense of some performance degradation.

The first and the simplest suboptimal algorithm for decoding a code based on its tail biting trellis T is the Bar-David algorithm [5] which estimates the starting state based on a probabilistic approach. It consists of the following steps:

1) Choose an arbitrary starting state from $\Sigma_0(C)$.
2) Process the tail biting trellis T with the Viterbi algorithm to find all the survivors originated from the selected starting state to all the ending states in $\Sigma_L(C)$.
3) Select the survivor with the best metric among all the survivors as the **winning path**.
4) Check if the winning path is a tail biting path. If so, stop the decoding process and output the winning path as the decoded codeword. Otherwise, go to the next step.
5) Use the ending state of the winning path as a new starting state.
6) Check if this starting state has been used before. If so, go to Step 1), otherwise, go to step 2).

The above process continues until a winning tail biting path is found or the number of iterations reaches q_0. For the later case, the decoder simply outputs the best winning path at that time. If the winning path is not a tail biting path, it is not a valid codeword. The Bar-David algorithm is indeed very simple but has a significant performance degradation compared to the VTMLD algorithm, especially for low to medium SNR's. Even though, for large SNR, the average number of decoding iterations (or VT's) required is small. However, for small SNR, the number of decoding iterations required approaches q_0, which results in a large number of computations.

An improvement of Bar-David algorithm is the two-step algorithm devised by Ma and Wolf [5]. The first step of this algorithm is to obtain an ordered list of the q_0 starting states using an algebraic method called "continued fractions." The second step of this algorithm is to perform Viterbi trials using each entry in the list as the starting state. At the end of each Viterbi trial, check whether the winning path is a tail biting path. If so, stop the decoding process and output the winning path as the decoded codeword; otherwise, continue the iteration process with the next state on the list as the starting state. This two-step algorithm provides some improvement in performance and decoding complexity over the Bar-David algorithm, but it still requires a large number of Viterbi trials for small SNR.

To further improve the performance of Bar-David and Ma-Wolf's two-step algorithms and reduce their decoding complexities, Wang and Bhargava [13] proposed another iterative decoding algorithm. This algorithm starts processing the tail biting trellis T with the Viterbi algorithm from all the states in $\Sigma_0(C)$ with the same initial state metrics. Every state in $\Sigma_0(C)$ is equally likely regarded as the starting state of the transmitted codeword. When the processing reaches the end of the tail biting trellis T, tests are performed. Based on the results of these tests, the decoder either terminates the decoding process and outputs the best tail biting path that has been found or reduces the starting state space by eliminating those unlikely starting states and updates the candidate tail biting path (the candidate for the decoded codeword) that is stored in a buffer. For the latter case, the decoder processes the tail biting trellis T again with the states in the reduced starting state space as the starting states with the same state metrics. This iterative process continues until either the most likely tail biting path is found or the reduced starting state space is empty. Wang-Bhargava algorithm is asymptotically optimal, which improves the error performance of Bar-David and Ma-Wolf algorithms with reduced decoding complexity. However, this algorithm is quite complex with a number of test conditions and a variable workload. Even though, it is asymptotically optimum for high channel SNR, however, it performs relatively poorly compared to the VTMLD algorithm for low to medium SNR's. One reason for its poor performance for low to medium SNR's is that the algorithm does not transfer all available soft information from trial to trial (or from one iteration to the next iteration). For example, at each decoding iteration, all the starting states are assigned the same starting metrics. However, the metrics of the states in the reduced starting state space computed at the end of the previous Viterbi trial can be used as the starting state metrics for the current trial. This would allow the real starting state to gain momentum faster than the other states in the reduced state space. As a result, the iteration decoding process may converge faster.

To improve the performance of the Wang-Bhargava algorithm, several algorithms were devised based on continuous Viterbi processing of a trellis which is a multifold repetition (or concatenation) of the tail biting trellis T [14-16]. All the available soft information is transferred from one Viterbi trial to the next Viterbi trial. The state metrics at the end of one trial are used as the starting state metrics for the next trial. Among these algorithms, the most efficient one is the circular Viterbi (CV) algorithm devised by Cox and Sundberg[16]. Let $T^* = T \circ T \circ \cdots$ denote the multifold repetition of T where $\circ$ denotes the concatenation operation. The CV algorithm simply processes the extended trellis continuously with the Viterbi algorithm. Let t and t_0 be two nonnegative integers such that $0 \leq t_0 \leq L$ and $t = t_0 \ (modulo \ L)$. Then

$$\Sigma_t(C) = \Sigma_{t_0}(C). \tag{4}$$

At boundary location-t of T^*, let $M(t, i)$ denote the metric of state $s_{t,i}$ (this is simply the cumulative metric of the survivor that terminates at state $s_{t,i}$). The CV algorithm consists of the following steps:

1) Start from all the states in $\Sigma_0(C)$ with the same initial state metrics.

2) Apply the Viterbi algorithm continuously to process T^* section by section. At level-t (or boundary location-t), record the metric of the surviving path entering each state in $\Sigma_t(C)$ and save the information labeling bits of the surviving branches in a word, called the decision word for section-t.

3) After processing the first L sections of T^*, the decoder starts making decoding decision.

4) For some chosen small ϵ and some constant α, if

$$|M(t,i) - M(t-L,i) - \alpha| < \epsilon \qquad (5)$$

for $1 \leq i \leq q_t$, stop the decoding process and output the winning path between level-$(t-L)$ and level-t (a reordering of the decoded information bits may be needed). Otherwise, go to Step 2).

5) Repeat Steps 2 and 4 until the stopping condition of (5) is met or a maximum number of iterations I_{max} is reached.

With this algorithm, a large storage is required to store all the state metrics over a span of $L + 1$ sections. To simplify this algorithm, the following stopping rule was suggested [16]:

4*) Check the decision words separated by L sections. If m consecutive decision words are the same as their predecessors, the decoding process stops. Otherwise, go to Step 2).

Simulation results show that the two CV algorithms with stopping conditions 4 and 4*, respectively, perform almost equally well in terms of error performance and computational complexity. Simulation results also show that the CV algorithm performs better than the Wang-Bhargava algorithm for small to medium SNR's with significant reduction in decoding computational complexity. However, for large SNR, the Wang-Bhargava algorithm outperforms the CV algorithm. Both algorithms still have a significant performance degradation compared to the VTMLD algorithm.

The other two continuous Viterbi decoding algorithms[14, 15] based on processing T^* have similar features to the CV algorithm.

3. A Wrap-Around Viterbi Algorithm

This section presents a new iterative algorithm for decoding linear codes based on their tail biting trellises. This algorithm is also devised based on processing a tail biting trellis T repeatedly in a continuous manner with the Viterbi algorithm. Each Viterbi processing (or Viterbi trial) of T is called an iteration. The algorithm consists of a sequence of decoding iterations. The available soft information is transferred from one iteration to the next iteration. The algorithm starts the decoding process from all the states in $\Sigma_0(C)$ with the same initial state metrics at the first iteration. At the end of each iteration, if no decoding decision is made, the metrics of the ending states in $\Sigma_L(C)$ are used as the starting state metrics of the next iteration. This is called **wrap-around**. The wrap-around process results in a continuous Viterbi decoding over the tail biting trellis T. The wrap-around processing of T continues until certain stopping conditions are met. The algorithm uses cumulative path metric during the continuous wrap-around process to select the survivor into each state. However, at the end of each iteration, it uses the metric difference between a starting state in $\Sigma_0(C)$ and an ending state in $\Sigma_L(C)$ (if they are connected by a survivor) to determine the L-branch winning path for decoding decision. The decoding process stops if the winning path is a tail biting path in T (a codeword in C) or a maximum number of iterations is reached. Decoding decision is made at the end of each iteration. If no decoding decision in made at the end of an iteration, a candidate for the final decoded codeword is updated and stored. For simplicity, this iterative decoding algorithm is referred to as a **wrap-around Viterbi** (WA-V) algorithm.

3.1 The algorithm

Assume that the correlation metric is used as the decoding metric. Again let T be an L-section tail biting trellis for a linear code C with starting state space $\Sigma_0(C)$, ending state space $\Sigma_L(C)$ and $\Sigma_0(C) = \Sigma_L(C)$. For $0 \leq t \leq L$, let $\Sigma_t(C) = (s_{t,1}, s_{t,2}, \cdots, s_{t,q_t})$ denote state space of T at section boundary location-t. Since the WA-V algorithm processes T repeatedly with the Viterbi algorithm in a continuous manner, the metric of a state in T is updated during each iteration. A survivor terminated at a state in T at boundary location-t during the i-th decoding iteration is a surviving path originated from a starting state in $\Sigma_0(C)$ at the beginning of the first decoding iteration. For $i \geq 1$, $0 \leq t \leq L$ and $1 \leq k \leq q_t$, let $C_{t,k}^{(i)}$ denote the metric of state $s_{t,k}$ at the i-th decoding iteration which is defined as the cumulative path metric of the survivor of the i-th iteration terminated at state $s_{t,k}$. At the end of the i-th iteration, let $\mathbf{p}^{(i)}$ denote an L-branch surviving path that connects the starting state $s_{0,h}$ in $\Sigma_0(C)$ and the ending state $s_{L,j}$ in $\Sigma_L(C)$. The path metric of $\mathbf{p}^{(i)}$ denoted $\Delta_{\mathbf{p}^{(i)}}$, is defined as the following difference between the metric $C_{L,j}^{(i)}$ of state $s_{L,j}$ and the metric $C_{0,h}^{(i)}$ of state $s_{0,h}$:

$$\Delta_{\mathbf{p}^{(i)}} \triangleq C_{L,j}^{(i)} - C_{0,h}^{(i)}. \tag{6}$$

The L-branch path with the largest path metric among all the $q_L(=q_0)$ surviving L-branch paths in T at the end of the i-th decoding iteration is called the **best path**, denoted $\mathbf{p}_{best}^{(i)}$. Note that the best surviving path is not necessarily a tail biting path in T (or a codeword in C). If $\mathbf{p}_{best}^{(i)}$ is a tail biting path, decoding stops and the decoder outputs $\mathbf{p}_{best}^{(i)}$ as the decoded codeword. If $\mathbf{p}_{best}^{(i)}$ is not a tail biting path, the decoder finds the best surviving tail biting path, denoted $\mathbf{p}_{T,best}^{(i)}$, among all the surviving tail biting paths (if any) at the end of the i-th iteration. Use $\mathbf{p}_{best}^{(i)}$ and $\mathbf{p}_{T,best}^{(i)}$ to update the currently stored best path $\mathbf{p}_{best}$ and best tail biting path $\mathbf{p}_{T,best}$. Whenever $\mathbf{p}_{T,best}^{(i)} = \mathbf{p}_{best}^{(i)}$, decoding stops. When a maximum number of decoding iterations is reached, the decoder outputs $\mathbf{p}_{T,best}$ if it exists, otherwise, the decoder outputs $\mathbf{p}_{best}$. Let Δ_{best} and $\Delta_{T,best}$ denote the metrics of $\mathbf{p}_{best}$ and $\mathbf{p}_{T,best}$, respectively. Then the decoder needs to update and store $(\mathbf{p}_{best}, \Delta_{best})$ and $(\mathbf{p}_{T,best}, \Delta_{T,best})$ from iteration to iteration.

At the end of the i-th decoding iteration, if no decoding decision is made, the state metric vector

$$\mathbf{C}_L^{(i)} \triangleq (C_{L,1}^{(i)}, C_{L,2}^{(i)}, \cdots, C_{L,q_L}^{(i)}) \tag{7}$$

is used as the initial state metric vector for the $(i+1)$-th iteration, i.e., $\mathbf{C}_0^{(i+1)} = \mathbf{C}_L^{(i)}$. The WA-V algorithm can be formulated as follows:

1) Initialization - start from all the states in $\Sigma_0(C)$ with the same initial state metric.
2) For $1 \leq i \leq I_{max}$, execute the i-th decoding iteration with $\mathbf{C}_0^{(i)} = \mathbf{C}_L^{(i-1)}$ ($\mathbf{C}_L^{(0)}$ is the intial state metric vector). At section boundary location-L of T, compare the metrics of all the L-branch surviving paths that terminate at the ending states in $\Sigma_L(C)$. Select the best path $\mathbf{p}_{best}^{(i)}$ as the winning path of the i-th iteration. If $\mathbf{p}_{best}^{(i)}$ is a tail biting path, go to Step 4). Otherwise, update $(\mathbf{p}_{best}, \Delta_{\mathbf{p}_{best}})$ and go to Step 3).
3) Find the best surviving tail biting path $\mathbf{p}_{T,best}^{(i)}$ (if any). Compare the metrics of $\mathbf{p}_{T,best}^{(i)}$ and $\mathbf{p}_{T,best}$ and update $(\mathbf{p}_{T,best}, \Delta_{\mathbf{p}_{T,best}})$. Check whether $i < I_{max}$. If so, set $i = i+1$ and go to Step 2). Otherwise, go to Step 5).
4) Output $\mathbf{p}_{best}^{(i)}$ as the decoded codeword.
5) Output $\mathbf{p}_{T,best}$ as the decoded codeword if it exists. Otherwise, output $\mathbf{p}_{best}$ as the decoded word.

183

Figure 5 depicts the flowchart of the above WA-V algorithm.

At the beginning of the WA-V decoding, each initial state is treated equally with the same starting metric due to our ignorance of the real starting state of the transmitted codeword. After several iterations, different initial states may have different state metrics. A path stemming from an initial state with larger metric has a better chance to become the winning path than the ones stemming from the initial states with smaller metrics. The larger metric an initial state has, the more likely it is the real starting state of the transmitted codeword.

3.2 Analysis

Let C_s denote the set of all paths in T that connect the states in $\Sigma_0(C)$ and the states in $\Sigma_L(C)$ (i.e., from any state in $\Sigma_0(C)$ to any state in $\Sigma_L(C)$). Then C_s is a super code of C. The WA-V algorithm is characterized by a number of theorems given below.

Theorem 3.1 *If all the starting states in $\Sigma_0(C)$ at the beginning of the i-th iteration of the WA-V algorithm have the same initial state metrics, then the best L-branch surviving path $\mathbf{p}_{best}^{(i)}$ at the end of the i-th iteration has the largest metric among all the codewords in C_s for a given received sequence $\mathbf{r}$. If $\mathbf{p}_{best}^{(i)}$ is a tail biting path in T, $\mathbf{p}_{best}^{(i)}$ is the most likely codeword in C with respect to $\mathbf{r}$.*

Proof: First we note that at the end of the i-th iteration, each survivor terminated at a state in $\Sigma_L(C)$ has a larger cumulative path metric than its competitors at any state boundary location-t of T for $0 \leq t \leq L$. If all the states in $\Sigma_0(C)$ have the same initial state metric at the beginning of the i-th iteration, it follows from the definition of path metric of an L-branch path $\mathbf{p}^{(i)}$ given by (6) that the best L-branch surviving path $\mathbf{p}_{best}^{(i)}$ must have the largest metric among all the paths in T (or all the codewords in C_s) with respect to the received sequence $\mathbf{r}$. If $\mathbf{p}_{best}^{(i)}$ is a tail biting path, it is a codeword in C and hence the most likely codeword in C for the given received sequence $\mathbf{r}$. This proves the theorem. $\Delta\Delta$.

Since all the states in $\Sigma_0(C)$ have the same initial state metrics at the beginning of the first iteration, a direct consequence of Theorem 3.1 is Corollary 3.1.

Corollary 3.1 *At the first iteration of the WA-V algorithm, the best*

L-branch surviving path $\mathbf{p}_{best}^{(1)}$ *is the most likely codeword in* C_s. *If* $\mathbf{p}_{best}^{(1)}$ *is a tail biting path, it is the most likely codeword in* C.

From Corollary 3.1, we see that if decoding is done at the end of the first iteration of the WA-V algorithm, the decoder output is the most likely codeword in C.

Theorem 3.2 *For* $i > 1$, *if the states in* $\Sigma_0(C)$ *do not have the same initial metrics at the beginning of the* i-th *iteration, the best surviving* *L-branch path* $\mathbf{p}_{best}^{(i)}$ *may not be the most likely codeword in* C_s *and hence it may not be the most likely codeword in* C *even if it is a tail biting path in* T.

Proof: Recall that the selection of the survivor at a state is based on the cumulative path metric up to that state. From (6), we have

$$C_{L,j}^{(i)} = C_{0,h}^{(i)} + \Delta_{\mathbf{p}^{(i)}}. \tag{8}$$

It follows from (8) that for $i > 1$, a path with a larger path metric $\Delta_{\mathbf{p}^{(i)}}$ can be discarded by the WA-V algorithm in favor of a competitor which originates from a state in $\Sigma_0(C)$ with a larger state metric, if the difference between their path metrics is not enough to compensate for the difference between their initial state metrics. In this case, the best surviving L-branch path $\mathbf{p}_{best}^{(i)}$ is not the most likely codeword in C_s and hence it may not be the most likely codeword in C even if it is a tail biting path. $\triangle\triangle$.

Theorem 3.2 says that for $i > 1$, if the decoding is made at the end of the i-th iteration, the decoder output may not be the most likely codeword in C. This implies that the WA-V algorithm is not an optimal MLD algorithm. However, simulation results show that this algorithm achieves near optimum error performance with only 2 to 4 iterations for many codes (block or convolutional). It outperforms all the existing iterative algorithms described in Section 2 with smaller computational complexity.

3.3 Performance and Complexity
The WA-V algorithm has been applied to decode various block and convolutional codes based on their tail biting trellises. Simulations results for the AWGN channel show that this algorithm achieves near optimum MLD error performance for all the codes being decoded with

185

a maximum number I_{max} of 2 to 4 iterations. For convolutional codes with $L \geq 6m$ where m is the memory order, $I_{max} = 2$ is enough for the WA-V algorithm to achieve near or virtually optimum error performance. The WA-V algorithm requires much less computational complexity than the optimum VTMLD algorithm. Simulation results for several codes are given in the following to demonstrate the effectiveness of the WA-V algorithm.

Figure 6 compares the error performance of the WA-V algorithm with that of the other existing algorithms described in Section 2 for the (64,32) tail biting code obtained by truncating the rate-1/2 (2,1,7) convolutional code of memory order $m = 7$ with generator polynomials (712,476) (or generator sequences $\mathbf{g}_1 = (1,1,1,0,0,1,0,1)$ and $\mathbf{g}_2 = (1,0,0,1,1,1,1,1))$ [1]. The tail biting trellis for this code has $L = 32$ sections and 128 states at each section boundary location. Since for the other existing algorithms, simulations were performed over a binary symmetric channel (BSC), we compare the WA-V algorithm with these algorithms based on a BSC. From Figure 6, we see that the WA-V algorithm outperforms all the existing algorithms. It achieves virtually optimum error performance with a maximum number of iterations set to 4 and outperforms the Wang-Bhargava and CV algorithms by 0.2 dB at BER's 10^{-3} and 10^{-4}, respectively. It outperforms the Bar-David and Ma-Wolf algorithms by 1.0 dB and 0.8 dB at BER=10^{-3}, respectively. Table 1 gives the decoding complexities of various algorithms in terms of average number of Viterbi trials required for various SNR's. It shows that the WA-V algorithm requires the least number of Viterbi trials, 1.3 on average.

The rest of simulation results for the WA-V algorithm given in the following are obtained based on an AWGN channel. Figure 7 shows the bit error performance of the WA-V algorithm for decoding the (128,64) tail biting code obtained by truncating the rate-1/2 (2,1,6) convolutional code of memory order $m = 6$ generated by generator polynomials (554,744) [1]. The tail biting trellis of this code has $L = 64$ sections and 64 states. We see that the WA-V algorithm achieves virtually optimum error performance with the maximum number I_{max} of iterations set to 2. The average number of iterations required is 1.33 for SNR's over the range 1.0 to 3.0dB. The figure also shows that the algorithm converges very fast.

In [6], a 16-state tail biting trellis with 12 sections for the (24,12)

Golay code has been constructed. Figures 8 and 9 show the bit and frame error performance of the WA-V algorithm for decoding the (24,12) Golay code based on its 16-state tail biting trellis. Again, both figures show that the WA-V algorithm achieves virtually optimum error performance with the maximum number I_{max} of iterations set to 4. With I_{max} set to 2, there is only 0.2 dB performance degradation compared with MLD at BER=10^{-4}. Figure 10 shows the average number of Viterbi updates versus SNR's. For $I_{max} = 4$, it requires an average of 17 Viterbi updates to complete the decoding process at SNR=3dB.

A 64-state 12-section tail biting trellis for the (24,12) Golay code can be constructed by truncating the 64-state trellis of the rate-1/2 $(2, 1, 6)$ convolutional code generated by generator polynomials (414,730) with $L = 12$ [17]. Figure 11 shows the bit error performance of the (24,12) Golay code decoded with the WA-V algorithm based on this 64-state tail biting trellis. Also included in this figure is the bit error performance of a modified CV algorithm devised by Anderson and Hladik [17, 18], called the optimal circular Viterbi algorithm (O-CVA). (This algorithm has not been publicly reported and the simulation results are provided by the authors.) We see that the WA-V algorithm with both $I_{max} = 2$ and $I_{max} = 4$ outperforms the O-CVA. The O-CVA requires 112 Viterbi updates to complete the decoding for each SNR. However, the average numbers of Viterbi updates required by the WA-V algorithm with $I_{max} = 4$ are 31.67 at 1 dB SNR, 25.65 at 2 dB SNR, 20.45 at 3 dB SNR and 16.2 at 4 dB SNR, respectively. For $I_{max} = 4$, the maximum number of Viterbi updates required is 48. Therefore, the WA-V algorithm outperforms the O-CVA with less computational complexity.

4. An Iterative Bidirectional Viterbi Decoding Algorithm

All the algorithms, including the WA-V algorithm presented in the last section, for decoding linear codes based on their tail biting trellises are unidirectional decoding algorithms which process a tail biting trellis in one direction. It is possible to devise a bidirectional decoding algorithm which processes a tail biting trellis from both ends simultaneously using two decoders. If the bidirectional process is carried out properly, not only optimum or near optimum error performance can be achieved but also the decoding delay can be shortened. In this section, such a bidirectional algorithm for decoding linear codes based on their tail biting trellises is presented and is called an **iterative bidirectional Viterbi** (IBD-V) algorithm.

Consider an (n, k) code C with an L-section tail biting trellis T. Let $\mathbf{v} = (v_1, v_2, \cdots, v_n)$ be the codeword to be transmitted. Before its transmission, it is permuted into $\mathbf{v}' = (v_1, v_n, v_2, v_{n-1}, \cdots)$. Let $\mathbf{r} = (r_1, r_n, r_2, r_{n-1}, \cdots)$ be the received sequence. Before decoding, $\mathbf{r}$ is decomposed into two sequences, $\mathbf{r}^{(1)} = (r_1, r_2, \cdots, r_n)$ and $\mathbf{r}^{(2)} = (r_n, r_{n-1}, \cdots, r_1)$. The IBD-V algorithm processes the tail biting trellis T simultaneously from both ends (right and left) with two Viterbi decoders based on the received sequences $\mathbf{r}^{(1)}$ and $\mathbf{r}^{(2)}$, respectively. The decoders that process the tail biting trellis T from the left and right ends are called the left and right Viterbi decoders, respectively. The state space $\Sigma_0(C)$ at boundary location-0 is the starting state space for the left Viterbi decoder and the state space $\Sigma_L(C)$ at boundary location-L is the starting state space for the right Viterbi decoder. The decoding process that the two decoders start from opposite ends, work through the trellis and reach to the other ends is called a decoding iteration. The IBD-V algorithm consists of a sequence of iterations. At the end of each iteration, the two decoders wrap around the tail biting trellis T and then continue the decoding process. The metrics of states at each end of T are used as the starting state metrics for the next iteration. At the beginning of the first iteration, all the starting states in $\Sigma_0(C)$ and $\Sigma_L(C)$ have the same initial state metrics. During each decoding iteration, the two decoders start to make decoding decision jointly as soon as they meet. Iteration process continues until the most likely tail biting path is found or a preset maximum number I_{max} of iterations is reached.

Suppose the two decoders are executing the i-th iteration. For $0 \le t \le L$ and $1 \le k \le q_t$, let $C_{t,k}^{l,(i)}$ and $C_{t,k}^{r,(i)}$ denote the cumulative metrics of the state $s_{t,k}$ at the boundary location-t computed by the left and right Viterbi decoders at the i-th iteration, respectively. There are two surviving paths terminating at the state $s_{t,k}$, one from the left end of the trellis T and the other from the right end of T, denoted $\mathbf{p}_{t,k}^{l,(i)}$ and $\mathbf{p}_{t,k}^{r,(i)}$, and are called left and right surviving paths, respectively. The L-branch path obtained by concatenating the left surviving path $\mathbf{p}_{t,k}^{l,(i)}$ and the right surviving path $\mathbf{p}_{t,k}^{r,(i)}$ is called a **composite path** (CP) through $s_{t,k}$, denoted $\mathbf{p}_{t,k}^{c,(i)}$. A CP that has the same state at both ends is called a **composite tail biting path** (CTP). Let $s_{0,h}$ and $s_{L,j}$ denote the starting states of the left surviving path $\mathbf{p}_{t,k}^{l,(i)}$ and the right surviving path $\mathbf{p}_{t,k}^{r,(i)}$, respectively. Define the metric differences

$$\Delta_{t,k}^{l,(i)} \triangleq C_{t,k}^{l,(i)} - C_{0,h}^{l,(i)}, \tag{9}$$

$$\Delta_{t,k}^{r,(i)} \triangleq C_{t,k}^{r,(i)} - C_{L,j}^{r,(i)}, \tag{10}$$

as the **path metric gains** of the left and right surviving paths, $\mathbf{p}_{t,k}^{l,(i)}$ and $\mathbf{p}_{t,k}^{r,(i)}$, respectively. Then the path metric of the CP through the state $s_{t,k}$ is defined as

$$\Delta_{t,k}^{c,(i)} \triangleq \Delta_{t,k}^{l,(i)} + \Delta_{t,k}^{r,(i)}. \tag{11}$$

As soon as a state $s_{t,k}$ has been visited by the two Viterbi decoders from opposite directions during the i-th iteration, the metric of the CP through this state is computed. The CP at boundary location-t that has the largest metric is called the **best** CP of the i-th iteration at the boundary location-t, denoted $\mathbf{p}_{t,best}^{c,(i)}$. Let $\Delta_{t,best}^{c,(i)}$ denote its metric. Let $\mathbf{p}_{best}^{c}$ and Δ_{best}^{c} denote the best composite path and its metric that have been found and stored up to the moment that $\mathbf{p}_{t,best}^{c,(i)}$ is found. If decoding decision is not made at this moment, $(\mathbf{p}_{t,best}^{c,(i)}, \Delta_{t,best}^{c,(i)})$ is then used to update $(\mathbf{p}_{best}^{c}, \Delta_{best}^{c})$. The pair $(\mathbf{p}_{best}^{c}, \Delta_{best}^{c})$ are updated each time when each of the two decoders has completed processing one section of the tail biting trellis T in opposite directions. If there are CTP's at the boundary location-t, the CTP that has the largest metric is called the **best** CTP of the i-th iteration at boundary location-t, denoted $\mathbf{p}_{t,best}^{T,(i)}$. Let $\Delta_{t,best}^{T,(i)}$ denote its metric. Let $\mathbf{p}_{best}^{T}$ and Δ_{best}^{T} denote the best CTP and its metric that have been found and stored up to the current moment. If decoding decision is not made at this moment, the pair $(\mathbf{p}_{t,best}^{T,(i)}, \Delta_{t,best}^{T,(i)})$ is used to update $(\mathbf{p}_{best}^{T}, \Delta_{best}^{T})$. The pair $(\mathbf{p}_{best}^{T}, \Delta_{best}^{T})$ is updated continuously as the two decoders move in opposite directions one section at a time.

The two decoders process the tail biting trellis T continuously section by section. When they reach the opposite ends of T, they wrap around and start the next iteration. The two decoders collaborate to make a decoding decision. A decoding decision is made when the best CP found by the two decoders is a tail biting path in T or when a preset maximum number of iterations, I_{max}, is reached. For the latter case, the decoder outputs $\mathbf{p}_{best}^{T}$ (if any), otherwise outputs $\mathbf{p}_{best}^{c}$ (this is not a codeword in C).

4.1 The algorithm

During each decoding iteration, the two decoders execute a procedure to find the best CP and the best CPT at each boundary location of T to make a decoding decision. The procedure to be executed is called the **Find-Best(t) procedure**. We use $flag = 1$ to indicate that the best CP is found to be a tail biting path, and $flag = 0$ otherwise. The **Find-Best(t) procedure** at the i-th iteration consists of the following steps:

a) Compute $\Delta_{t,k}^{c,(i)}$ for all the states $s_{t,k}$ in $\Sigma_t(C)$.

b) Find the best composite path $\mathbf{p}_{t,best}^{c,(i)}$ at location-t.

c) If $\mathbf{p}_{t,best}^{c,(i)}$ is a tail biting path, set $flag = 1$ and output $\mathbf{p}_{t,best}^{c,(i)}$ as the decoded codeword. Otherwise, update $(\mathbf{p}_{best}^{c}, \Delta_{best}^{c})$ that are stored in the memory and go to step d.

d) Find the best composite tail biting path, $\mathbf{p}_{t,best}^{T,(i)}$ (if any), update the pair $(\mathbf{p}_{best}^{T}, \Delta_{best}^{T})$ that are stored in the memory.

Set the maximum number of iterations to I_{max}. The IBD-V algorithm consists of the following steps:

A. Set $i = 1$. $flag = 0$, $\mathbf{C}_{0}^{l,(1)} = \mathbf{C}_{L}^{r,(1)} = (-\infty, -\infty, \cdots, -\infty)$ (initial state metrics at both ends of T), and $\Delta_{best}^{c} = \Delta_{best}^{T} = -\infty$.

B. If $i < I_{max}$ and $flag = 0$, execute the following steps:

1) Perform the Viterbi decoding process from both ends of the trellis.

2) When the two decoders meet at boundary location-t_0, set $t_l = t_r = t_0$.

3) Call and execute the **Find-Best(t_0) procedure**. If $flag = 1$, stop the decoding process. Otherwise, go to Steps 4 and 5.

4) Set $t_l = t_l + 1$. If $t_l \le L$, call and execute the **Find-Best(t_l) procedure**.

5) Set $t_r = t_r + 1$. If $t_r \ge 0$, call and execute the **Find-Best(t_r) procedure**.

6) Repeat Steps 4 and 5 simultaneously. If $flag$ is set to 1 by either decoder or by both, decoding stops. For the latter case, the two best composite paths found at boundary

190

location-t_l and -t_r are both tail biting paths. If they are not the same, the one with larger metric is chosen as the decoded codeword. If $flag = 0$, update $(\mathbf{p}_{best}^c, \Delta_{best}^c)$ and $(\mathbf{p}_{best}^T, \Delta_{best}^T)$ and repeat Steps 4 and 5.

7) When the two decoders reach both ends of the trellis, check if $i < I_{max}$. If so, set $i = i + 1$, $\mathbf{C}_0^{l,(i)} = \mathbf{C}_L^{l,(i-1)}$, $\mathbf{C}_L^{r,(i)} = \mathbf{C}_0^{r,(i-1)}$, go to Step B and start the next iteration. Otherwise, go to Step C.

C. If $\Delta_{best}^T > -\infty$, output $\mathbf{p}_{best}^T$ as the decoded codeword; Otherwise output $\mathbf{p}_{best}^c$.

4.2 Analysis

Again, let C_s be the super code of C which consists of the label sequences of all the paths in T as codewords. Assume that transmission is over an AWGN channel. The path in T that has the largest correlation metric with the received sequence $\mathbf{r}$ is the most likely codeword in C_s and is called the **optimum path**, denoted $\mathbf{p}_{opt}$. If $\mathbf{p}_{opt}$ is a tail biting path, it is the most likely codeword in C. In the following, we prove several theorems which characterize the IBD-V algorithm.

Theorem 4.1 *If at the beginning of a decoding iteration of the IBD-V algorithm, all the starting states in $\Sigma_0(C)$ for the left decoder have the same initial state metrics and all the starting states in $\Sigma_L(C)$ for the right decoder have the same initial state metrics, the optimum path $\mathbf{p}_{opt}$ will not be discarded by the decoders during the decoding process.*

Proof: Since all the starting states at each end of T have the same initial state metrics, it follows from (6) that the path terminating at a state $s_{t,k}$ at boundary location-t which has the largest path metric also has the largest cumulative path metric. A path $\mathbf{p}$ in T can be discarded by either the left decoder or the right decoder or by both. Suppose the optimum path $\mathbf{p}_{opt}$ for a given received sequence is discarded at a state $s_{t,k}$ at boundary location-t. If it is discarded by the left decoder, the left survivor into state $s_{t,k}$ from the left has larger path metric than the part of the optimum path $\mathbf{p}_{opt}$ from its starting state in $\Sigma_0(C)$ to state $s_{t,k}$. If it is discarded by the right decoder, the right survivor into state $s_{t,k}$ from the right has larger path metric than the part of the optimum path $\mathbf{p}_{opt}$ from its starting state in $\Sigma_L(C)$ to state $s_{t,k}$. Either case results in a composite path through state $s_{t,k}$ that has a

191

metric larger than the metric of $\mathbf{p}_{opt}$. This is not possible since $\mathbf{p}_{opt}$ has the largest metric with the received sequence. Therefore, $\mathbf{p}_{opt}$ will not be discarded by either decoder. $\triangle\triangle$.

A direct consequence of Theorem 4.1 is Corollary 4.1.

Corollary 4.1 *If at the beginning of a decoding iteration of the IBD-V algorithm, all the starting states in $\Sigma_0(C)$ have the same initial state metrics and all the starting states in $\Sigma_L(C)$ have the same initial state metrics, the best composite path at each boundary location of T is the optimum path. If the best composite path is a tail biting path, it is the most likely codeword in C with respect to the received sequence $\mathbf{r}$.*

Note that at the beginning of the first iteration of the IBD-V algorithm, all the starting states in both $\Sigma_0(C)$ and $\Sigma_L(C)$ are set with the same initial state metrics. It follows from Corollary 4.1 that at the first iteration, the best composite path is found as soon as the two decoders meet at the center of the trellis T and this best composite path is the optimal path in T. If this optimum path is a tail biting path, then it is the most likely codeword in C and the decoding is optimal.

The next theroem simply says that if the condition of Theorem 4.1 does not hold, the best composite path found at any section boundary is not necessarily the optimum path in T for a given received sequence $\mathbf{r}$. The proof of this theorem is similar to the proof of Theorem 3.2.

Theorem 4.2 *If at the beginning of a decoding iteration, not all the starting states in $\Sigma_0(C)$ or in $\Sigma_L(C)$ have the same initial state metrics, the best composite path found at any boundary location of T is not necessarily the optimum path $\mathbf{p}_{opt}$ in T for a given received sequence $\mathbf{r}$, and hence it is not necessarily the most likely codeword in C even if it is a tail biting path.*

Theorem 4.2 implies that for $i > 1$, if decoding decision is made during the i-th iteration, the decoded codeword is not necessarily the most likely codeword in C. Therefore, IBD-V algorithm is not an optimal MLD algorithm. However, simulation results of this algorithm for decoding many codes show that this algorithm achieves virtually optimum error performance with a maximum of only two iterations.

After the first decoding iteration, in general, the starting states at either end of the trellis T do not have the same initial state metrics. As a result, the sets of composite paths at different boundary locations

192

may be different. This fact can be proved readily and is given in the following theorem.

Theorem 4.3 *At the i-th decoding iteration with $i > 1$, the sets of composite paths at different boundary locations may be different.*

This theorem implies that after the first iteration, the best CP's at different boundary locations of the trellis T may be different and the best CTP's at different boundary locations of T may be different. Therefore, to achieve good error performance, we must keep updating $\mathbf{p}_{best}$ and $\mathbf{p}_{best}^{T}$ from section to section, because they are candidates for the decoded codeword when the decoding process is terminated at the end of I_{max}-th iteration.

Since the trellis is processed by two decoders from both directions and the two decoders start to make decoding decision as soon as they meet at the center of the trellis, the IBD-V algorithm has a shorter decoding delay than an unidirectional iterative algorithm, such as the WA-V algorithm. Furthermore, IBD-V algorithm updates its candidates for the decoded codeword continuously section by section rather than waiting until the end of an iteration. As a result, $\mathbf{p}_{best}^{T}$ is chosen from a larger subset of tail biting paths of T than the WA-V algorithm and hence has better chance to be the most likely codeword in C. Therefore, the IBD-V algorithm achieves better error performance than the WA-V algorithm with the same number of iterations and converges faster to the MLD performance.

4.3 Performance and Complexity

The IBD-V algorithm has been applied to decode several convolutional and linear block codes based on their tail biting trellises. Simulation results show that for all the codes being decoded, the IBD-V algorithm virtually achieves optimum error performance with a maximum of 2 iterations. Results for some of these codes are given in the following to show the effectiveness of the IBD-V algorithm.

Figures 12 and 13 show the bit and frame error performance of the IBD-V algorithm for the (68,34) tail biting code obtained by truncating the rate-1/2 (2,1,7) convolutional code generated by polynomials (712,476). We see that the IBD-V algorithm virtually achieves optimum error performance with a maximum of 2 iterations ($I_{max} = 2$). In the same figures, we see that the WA-V algorithm virtually achieves optimum error performance with a maximum of 4 iterations ($I_{max}=4$).

Table 2 gives the percentages of transmitted codewords that are decoded into the most likely codewords with IBD-V and WA-V algorithms for various SNR's. We see that even with SNR=1 dB, the IBD-V algorithm decodes 93% of the transmitted codewords into most likely codewords with $I_{max} = 1$ and 99% with $I_{max} = 2$. The WA-V algorithm achieves almost the same percentages with $I_{max} = 2$ and $I_{max} = 4$, respectively. Table 3 gives the average numbers of Viterbi updates required for the two decoding algorithms with various SNR's. We see that both algorithms require relatively small number of Viterbi updates to complete the decoding even for small SNR's.

Figure 7 shows the bit error performance of the IBD-V algorithm for the (128,64) tail biting codes obtained by truncating the rate-1/2 (2,1,6) convolutional code generated by polynomials (554, 744). Again, the IBD-V algorithm virtually achieves optimum error performance with a maximum of 2 iterations. In fact, for this long code, WA-V is just as effective as the IBD-V algorithm and it achieves optimum error performance with $I_{max} = 2$. Table 4 gives the average numbers of Viterbi updates required for both algorithms with various SNR's.

Figures 8 and 9 gives the bit and frame error performance of the IBD-V algorithm for the (24,12) Golay code based on the minimal 16-state tail biting trellis constructed in [6]. Again, we see that the IBD-V algorithm achieves optimum error performance with a maximum of 2 iterations. Table 5 gives the average number of Viterbi updates for both IBD-V and WA-V algorithms. We see that the number of Viterbi updates required for decoding this code is small even for low SNR's.

Finally, Table 6 gives the computational complexities for decoding the above codes with the VTMLD, WA-V and IBD-V algorithms, respectively. Also included in this table is a recursive MLD (RMLD) algorithm for decoding codes based on their tail biting trellises. This RMLD is simply a generalization of the RMLD devised in [19] for decoding linear block codes based on their conventional trellises. We see that both WA-V and IBD-V algorithms significantly reduce the computational complexity for these codes. The RMLD algorithm also reduces the computational complexity compared with the VTMLD algorithm.

5. Conclusion

In this paper, two new efficient iterative algorithms for decoding linear codes, block or convolutional, based on their tail biting trellises have been presented. One is an unidirectional algorithm and other is a bidirectional algorithm. Both algorithms achieve virtually optimum error performance with a maximum of 2 to 4 iterations with a significant reduction in decoding computational complexity. For short tail biting convolutional codes, the bidirectional algorithm converges to optimum MLD error performance faster and gives better error performance than the unidirectional algorithm. For long tail biting convolutional codes, both algorithms perform equally well and achieve virtually optimum error performance with a maximum of 2 iterations. The bidirectional algorithm reduces decoding delay. Both algorithms outperform all the existing tail biting trellis-based algorithms in performance and decoding complexity.

References

[1] S. Lin and D. J. Costello Jr., *Error Control Coding: fundamentals and applications*, Prentice Hall, Englewood Cliffs, NY, 1983.

[2] S. Lin, T. Kasami, T. Fujiwara and M. P. C. Fossorier, *Trellises and Trellis Based Decoding Algorithms for Linear Block Codes*, Kluwer Academic Publishers, Boston, MA, 1998.

[3] A. Vardy, "Trellis Structure of Codes," the Handbook of Coding Theory, V.S. Pless and W. C. Huffman (Editors), Elsevier, Amsterdam, 1998.

[4] G. Solomon and H. van Tilborg, " A connection between block and convolutional codes", *SIAM J. Appl. Math.*, Vol. 37, No. 2, pp. 358-369, Oct. 1979.

[5] H. H. Ma and J. K. Wolf, "On tail biting convolutional codes," *IEEE Trans. Commun.*, Vol. 34, No. 2, pp. 104-111, Feb. 1986.

[6] A. R. Calderbank, G. D. Forney, Jr., and A. Vardy, "Minimal Tail-Biting Trellises: Golay Code and More," *IEEE Trans. Inform. Theory*, Vol. 45, No. 5, pp. 1435-1455. July 1999.

[7] G. D. Forney Jr., "Coset code - Part II: Binary Lattices and Related Codes," *IEEE Trans. Inform. Theory*, Vol. 34, No. 5, pp. 1152-1188, September 1988.

[8] D. J. Muder, "Minimal trellises for block codes," *IEEE Trans. Inform. Theory*, Vol. 34, pp. 1049-1053, September 1988.

[9] R. Kötter and A. Vardy, "Construction of Minimal Tail-Biting Trellises", in *Proc. 1998 IEEE Inform. Theory Workshop*, pp. 72-74, Killarney, Ireland, June 1998.

[10] ——, "The Theory of tail-biting trellises", in preparation.

[11] R. Shao, S. Lin, and M. Fossorier, "An Iterative Bidirectional Decoding Algorithm for Tail Biting Codes," *Proc. 1999 IEEE Inform. Theory Workshop*, Kruger National Park, South Africa, June 22-25, 1999.

[12] R. Shao, *Decoding of Linear Codes Based on Their Tail Biting Trellises and Efficient Stopping Criteria for Turbo Decoding*, Ph.D. Dissertation, University of Hawaii at Manoa, December 1999.

[13] Q. Wang and V. K. Bhargava, "An Efficient Maximum Likelihood Decoding Algorithm for Generalized Tail Biting Convolutional Codes Including Quasicyclic Codes," *IEEE Trans. Commun.*, Vol. 37, No. 8, pp. 875-879, August 1989.

[14] K. S. Zigangirov and V. V. Chepyshov, "Study of decoding tailbiting convolutional codes," *Proc. 4-th Joint Swedish-Soviet International Workshop Informat. Theory*, pp. 52-55, Gotland, Sweden, August 1989.

[15] B. D. Kudryashov, "Decoding of block codes obtained from convolutional codes," *Problemy Peredachi Informatsii*, Vol. 26, No. 2, pp. 18-26. April-June 1990 (in Russian). English Translation, Plenum Publishing Corporation, October 1990.

[16] R. V. Cox and C. E. Sundberg, " An efficient adaptive circular Viterbi algorithm for decoding generalized tailbiting convolutional codes," *IEEE Trans. Vehicular Tech.*, Vol. 43, pp. 57-68, February 1994.

[17] J.B. Anderson and K. E. Tepe, Private communication.

[18] J.B. Anderson and S. M. Hladik, "An optimal circular Viterbi decoder," in preparation.

[19] T. Fujiwara, H. Yamamoto, T. Kasami and S. Lin, "A Trellis-Based Recursive Maximum Likelihood Decoding Algorithm for Linear Block Codes," *IEEE Trans. Inform. Theory*, Vol. 44, No. 2, March 1998.

Table 1: Decoding complexity of various decoding algorithms in terms of number of Viterbi trials for the (64,32) tail biting convolutional code generated by $\mathbf{g}_1 = (1,1,1,0,0,1,0,1)$ and $\mathbf{g}_2 = (1,0,0,1,1,1,1,1)$ over BSC.

SNR	Bar-David	Two-step	Wang-Bhargava	CVA	WA-V $(I_{max} = 4)$
4.588	116.21	67.42	14.67	2.23	1.43
4.812	72.1	60.17	13.41	2.20	1.35
5.032	67.65	58.24	5.76	2.15	1.32
5.535	62.25	54.27	2.3	2.08	1.21
6.123	56.79	47.11	1.48	2.01	1.13

Table 2: Percentage of transmitted codewords that are decoded into most likely codewords for the (68,34) convolutional tail biting code generated by polynomials (712,476) using the WA-V and the IBD-V algorithms (minimum 10,000 transmitted codewords).

SNR	WA-V			IBD-V	
	$I_{max} = 1$	$I_{max} = 2$	$I_{max} = 4$	$I_{max} = 1$	$I_{max} = 2$
1.0dB	71.65%	93.68%	95.98%	92.91%	98.66%
1.5dB	79.49%	97.65%	99.34%	95.11%	99.81%
2.0dB	84.44%	98.61%	99.54%	96.85%	99.72%
2.5dB	90.54%	99.67%	99.89%	98.71%	99.96%
3.0dB	94.13%	99.90%	99.95%	99.41%	99.99%

Table 3: Average number of Viterbi updates required for decoding the (68,34) convolutional tail biting code generated by polynomials (712,476) using the WA-V and the IBD-V algorithms.

SNR	WA-V		IBD-V		
	$I_{max} = 2$	$I_{max} = 4$	$I_{max} = 1$	$I_{max} = 2$	$I_{max} = 2$ (per decoder)
1.0dB	53.02	79.33	53.02	79.98	39.99
2.0dB	49.61	70.33	49.61	69.92	34.96
3.0dB	45.90	59.96	45.90	60.52	30.26
4.0dB	41.84	50.61	41.84	50.71	25.35
5.0dB	39.17	44.69	39.17	44.66	22.33

Table 4: Average number of Viterbi updates required for decoding the (128,64) convolutional tail biting code generated by polynomials (554,744) using the WA-V and the IBD-V algorithms.

SNR	WA-V		IBD-V		
	$I_{max} = 2$	$I_{max} = 4$	$I_{max} = 1$	$I_{max} = 2$	$I_{max} = 2$ (per decoder)
1.0dB	99.17	145.16	99.17	137.09	68.55
2.0dB	92.18	125.92	92.18	122.36	61.18
3.0dB	83.46	103.99	83.46	103.27	51.64
4.0dB	77.69	92.89	77.69	91.46	45.73
5.0dB	73.17	82.90	73.17	82.35	41.17

Table 5: Average number of Viterbi updates required for decoding the (24,12) Golay code with the 16-state tail biting trellis using the WA-V and the IBD-V algorithms.

SNR	WA-V		IBD-V		
	$I_{max} = 2$	$I_{max} = 4$	$I_{max} = 1$	$I_{max} = 2$	$I_{max} = 2$ (per decoder)
1.0dB	17.79	26.04	17.79	26.42	13.21
2.0dB	16.02	21.26	16.02	21.60	10.80
3.0dB	14.24	16.88	14.24	17.12	8.56
4.0dB	13.09	14.25	13.09	14.35	7.17
5.0dB	12.43	12.87	12.43	12.90	6.45

Table 6: Decoding complexity in terms of number of additions and comparisons with various decoding algorithms at SNR=1.0dB (10,000 blocks).

Code	VTMLD	RMLD	WA-V ($I_{max} = 4$)	IBD-V ($I_{max} = 2$)
Golay (24,12)	9,615	3,379	1,383	1,668
(64,32) ($m = 6$)	397,375	250,043	14,739	17,694
(128,64) ($m = 6$)	794,687	643,323	28,314	32,493
(68,34) ($m = 7$)	1,679,999	1,000,251	32,493	39,761

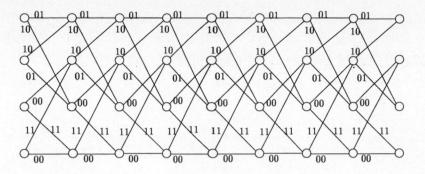

Figure 1: An 8-section tail biting trellis for the rate-1/2 (2,1,2) convolutional tail biting code generated by $\mathbf{g}_1 = (1,0,1)$ and $\mathbf{g}_2 = (1,1,1)$.

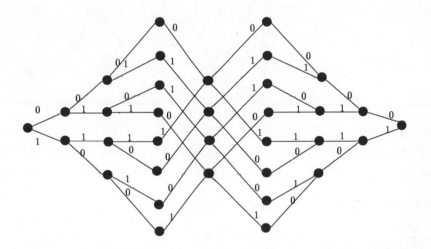

Figure 2: A minimal 8-section conventional trellis for the (8,4,4) RM code.

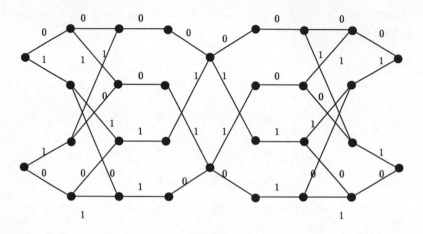

Figure 3: A minimal 8-section tail biting trellis for the (8,4,4) RM code.

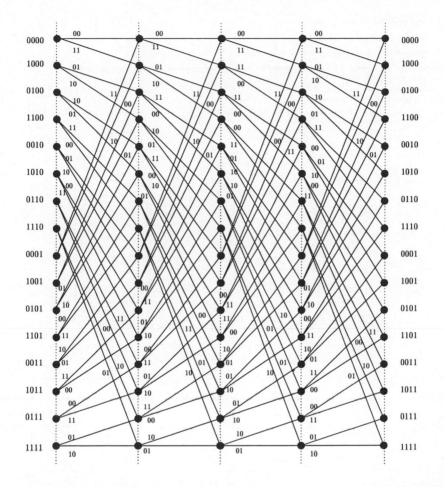

Figure 4: Four sections of the minimal tail biting trellis for the (24,12,8) Golay code.

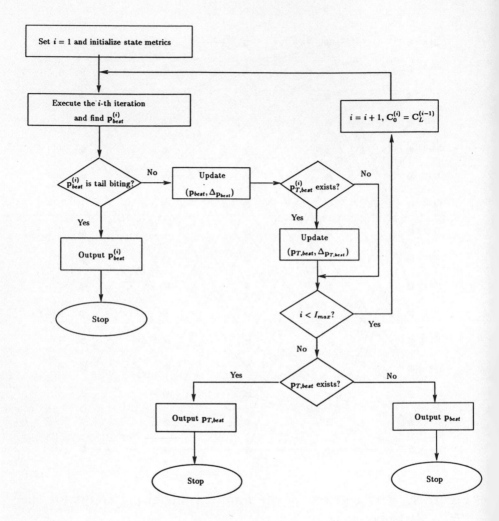

Figure 5: A flow-chart for the Wrap-Around Viterbi algorithm.

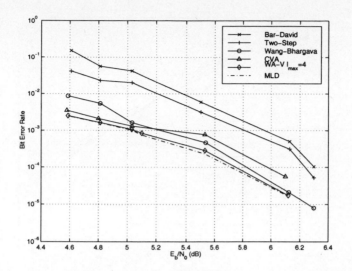

Figure 6: BER performance of various decoding algorithms for the rate-1/2 (64,32) tail biting convolutional code with memory order $m = 7$ and generated by (712,476) over BSC.

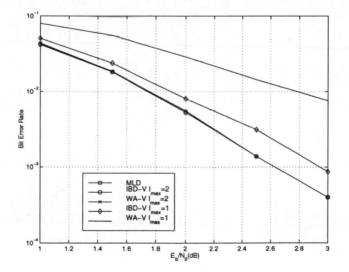

Figure 7: BER performance of the (128,64) tail biting convolutional code generated by (554,744) using the WA-V and the IBD-V algorithms.

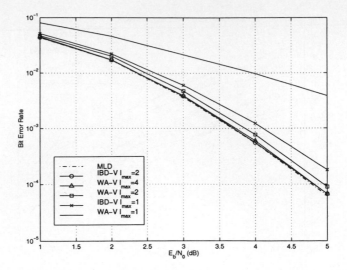

Figure 8: BER performance of the (24,12) Golay code with the 16-state tail biting trellis using the WA-V and the IBD-V algorithms.

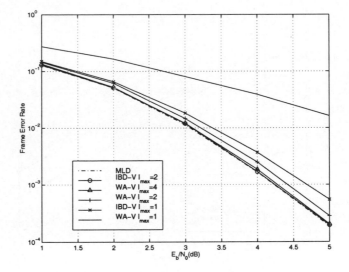

Figure 9: FER performance of the (24,12) Golay code with the 16-state tail biting trellis using the WA-V and the IBD-V algorithms.

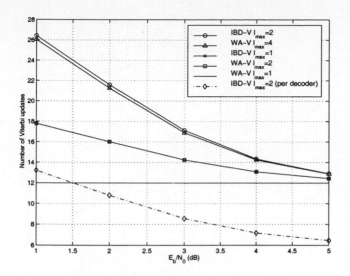

Figure 10: Decoding complexity of the (24,12) Golay code with the 16-state tail biting trellis using the WA-V and the IBD-V algorithms.

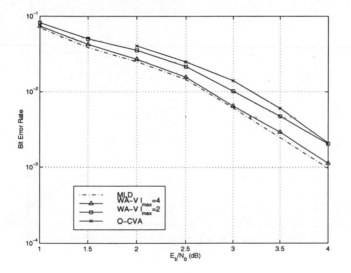

Figure 11: BER performance of the (24,12) Golay code with the 64-state tail biting trellis using the WA-V and the O-CVA algorithms.

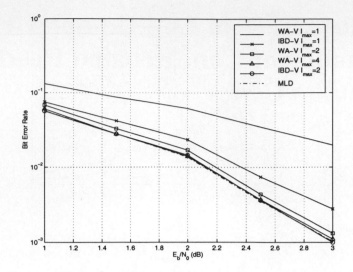

Figure 12: BER performance of the (68,34) tail biting convolutional code generated by polynomials (712,476) using the WA-V and the IBD-V algorithms.

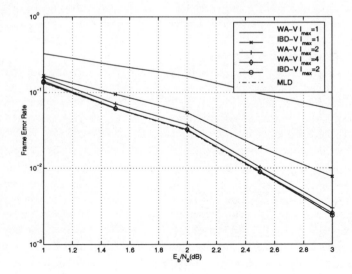

Figure 13: FER performance of the (68,34) tail biting convolutional code generated by polynomials (712,476) using the WA-V and the IBD-V algorithms.

Performance of Low Complexity Decoding of Concatenated Reed-Solomon Codes

Nader Zein
CRC/Engineering Department, Lancaster University,
Lancaster LA1 5YR, United Kingdom
Tel:+44-1524-593016; Fax: +44-1524-592713
email: N.Zein@Lancaster.ac.uk

W. G. Chambers
Department of Electronic and Electrical Engineering,
King's College London, Strand, London WC2R 2LS, United Kingdom
email: w.chambers@kcl.ac.uk

ABSTRACT

The performance of a (255, 223) Reed-Solomon code concatenated with a (9,8) parity-check inner code on a Rayleigh fading channel is simulated. The Welch-Berlekamp algorithm gives a performance over 1dB better than an algorithm which chooses the best set of symbols to be erased.

1. INTRODUCTION

The Welch-Berlekamp (WB) algorithm [1] is a way of carrying out the algebraic decoding of Reed-Solomon (RS) codes, which enables us to choose an optimum out of several decoded possible codewords. Let N denote the number of symbols in a codeword, K the number of information symbols, and $R=N-K$ (assumed even) the number of checks. Let Q denote the total number of symbols. Also we define $T = \lfloor R/2 \rfloor$, which is the maximum number of errors that can be corrected. In the WB algorithm we are free to choose any K symbols in the received word as the information symbols, and so in the decoding process we choose the most reliable. Thereafter we introduce the checks two at a time starting with the most reliable of the received symbols left and working down. The WB algorithm may return several decoded codewords, the correct one is obtained whenever for any l pairs of checks introduced ($0 \le 1 \le T$) there are at most l errors in the $K+2l$ symbols so far processed. In this way a number of codewords may be found, and we can select 'the best'.

2. WEIGHTING DECODED CODEWORDS

We suppose that the RS code is being used as the outer code in a concatenated coding scheme, and that at the receiving end the inner decoder returns the decoded symbols forming the received word $r = \{r_0, r_1, \ldots r_{N-1}\}$ for the outer RS decoder to decode, together with the estimates pi of the probability of decoding error for the ith symbol. These errors are assumed to be statistically independent, which in practice would require some form of interleaving on a fading channel.

Let $t_\alpha = \{t_0, t_1, t_2, \ldots, t_{N-1}\}$ be the αth possible outer codeword at the transmitter. Then the probability that t_α was sent given r was received is

$$p(\mathbf{t}_\alpha \mid \mathbf{r}) = p(\mathbf{r} \mid \mathbf{t}_\alpha) \cdot p(\mathbf{t}_\alpha) / p(\mathbf{r})$$

Take $p(t_\alpha)$ as independent of α. Therefore for maximum likelihood decoding we need to maximise $p(r|t_\alpha)$ with respect to α. Then the probability that r_i was produced by the inner decoder, given that t_i was sent into the inner encoder, is $(1-p_i)$ if $r_i = t_i$, and $p_i/(Q-1)$ if $r_i \neq t_i$. Here Q is the number of symbols, and it is assumed for simplicity that a decoding failure in the inner decoder produces any one of the $Q-1$ erroneous symbols with equal probability. Thus

$$p(\mathbf{r}|\mathbf{t}_\alpha) = \prod_{i:r_i=t_i}(1-p_i) \cdot \prod_{i:r_i \neq t_i}(p_i/(Q-1))$$

So the log of the probability is

$$\sum_i \ln(1-p_i) + \sum_{i:r_i \neq t_i} \ln \frac{pi/(Q-1)}{1-p_i}$$

The first term is independent of α. Thus we choose the decoded codeword that maximises the second sum, which we shall refer to as the measure.

3.   MODEL FOR A RAYLEIGH CHANNEL AND A SIMPLE INNER CODE

We assume that the probability of the inner decoder receiving a bit with energy E is $\exp(-E)$. Here E is greater than or equal to 0. There is no need for a scale factor, since we can incorporate that in E.

If the inner code is very strong, then on a fading channel the decoded symbols have error probabilities very close to either 0 or 1. Thus there is very little point in using anything more than the erasure of the symbols that are almost certainly wrong. If we have a weak inner code, then because of the low Hamming distance the erroneously decoded symbols are still quite close to the original, and there are not very many possibilities for the error patterns (which are themselves codewords in a linear code), so that the RS code is not being used with maximum effectiveness. Thus if we are using 8-bit symbols without coding, the most likely error patterns are 1-bit, and there are only 8 of them. If we are using a (9,8) parity-check code, then there are 36 weight-2 error patterns. But if we were using a

(128,8) biorthogonal code, then there are 254 error patterns of weight 64. Unfortunately in this case there would not be much point in using the WB method.

In consequence we decided to model our trials on the (9, 8) parity-check code, a code that is almost trivially easy to soft-decode using the Wagner algorithm. (Here one uses hard-decision decoding, and if there is a parity failure one flips the least reliable bit.) The outer code is taken as the standard (255, 223) RS code over GF(256). The asymptotic error probability was taken as $[36 \cdot (4 \cdot \pi \cdot (16/9)\beta \cdot E)-1/2] \cdot \exp(-(16/9) \cdot \beta \cdot E)$, where E is the energy per information bit, and β equals $1/N_0$. Since the average energy of the Rayleigh distribution is 1, this β is the E_b/N_0 ratio. This formula does not work at low values of E, and since the error probability for $E=0$ is $1-1/Q$ (with $Q=256$, the number of codewords) we used the formula $p=(255/256) \cdot \exp(y)$, with $y = -x + (1.0-\exp(-x))$ with $x = (16/9) \cdot \beta \cdot E$. This agrees with the above asymptotic form at $E=7.913$, and has zero slope and value $255/256$ at $E=0$.

4.   MODEL FOR DECODING SUCCESS

If for any l from 0 to T, we find that in the first $K+2l$ symbols used there are at most l errors, then we have a correct decode. This may be slightly optimistic as it assumes that the correct decoded codeword always gives the optimum measure. However, it upper bounds the best performance.   This was checked by using the full RS decoding algorithm, although because of the computational complexity very large numbers of trials were not possible.

5.   SEMI-EMPIRICAL TECHNIQUE

We now describe a technique which enables us to obtain the coding performance with the above model (and similar models) without actually carrying out the decoding. Choose an energy E_i for the ith symbol ($i=0 \ldots N-1$) using the Rayleigh distribution.   Put $P_i = p(E_i)$, where $p(E)$ is the error probability described previously. Reorder the symbol numbering so that P_i falls monotonically with i. For $i = 1, \ldots, N$, let $p_i(t)$ denote the probability of t errors in the symbols from 0 to i-1. Set $p_0(t) = 0$ for $t>0$, $p_0(0) = 1$. Then we have for $i=0$ to $N-1$

$$p_{i+1}(t) = (1 - P_i) \cdot p_i(t) + P_i \cdot p_i(t-1) \quad \text{for} \quad t > 0,$$
$$p_{i+1}(0) = (1 - P_i) \cdot p_i(0) \quad \text{for} \quad t = 0.$$

We use these recurrences to compute $p_K(t)$, the probability that there are t errors in the first K symbols. Next we define $q_i(t)$ as the probability that with the first i symbols considered ($i \geq K$)there are no decoding successes and there are t errors.   Thus we set $q_K(t) = p_K(t)$ for $t \geq 1$, $q_K(0) = 0$. The reason for setting $q_K(0)$ to 0 is that we are computing the probability of decoding failure, and any decoding success (in this case because the first K symbols are correct) means that we have eventual success, regardless of what happens afterwards. This is because we have at least one correct decode, and it is assumed that it will have the best measure.

211

(Note that $\Sigma t\, q_K(t)$ is the probability of decoding error using the first K symbols and erasing the rest.)

Then using the same recurrences as for $p_i(t)$ we form $q_{K+2}(t)$ and set $q_{K+2}(1) = 0$, so that $\Sigma_t\, q_{K+2}(t)$ is the probability of decoding failure after the first pair of checks has been included. Note that $q_{K+2}(0)$ is automatically 0 from the recurrence. Again with no more than one error after $K+2$ symbols we are guaranteed success.

Then we iterate by computing $q_{K+2l}(t)$ from $q_{K+2(l-1)}(t)$ using the recurrences and setting $q_{K+2l} = 0$. Finally $\Sigma_t\, q_{K+2T}(t)$ is the final probability for decoding failure, which occurs only when there are no decoding successes at all.

It is worth noting that if there are more than T errors at any stage, then whatever happens afterwards and whatever the number of errors we certainly will not get a later decoding success. So we may save computational effort by accumulating $\Sigma^{\infty}_{t=T+1}\, p_i(t)$ in $p_i(T+1)$; we modify the recurrence by using

$$p_{i+1}(T+1) = p_i(T+1) + P_i \cdot p_i(T)$$

for $t = T+1$ and the previous recurrences only for $t \le T$. We do the same for $q_i(T+1)$. Then the final probability for decoding failure is $q_N(T+1)$.

6.   OTHER DECODING STRATEGIES

At the same time as running the above program we can also test three other strategies:

(i)   Simply ignore the fading levels, and use ordinary error-correction without any erasures. Decoding failure occurs if the number of errors exceeds T. The probability is given by $p_N(T+1)$ if we use $P_i(T+1)$ to accumulate the probability of more than T errors.

(ii)   Use the K most reliable symbols and ignore the rest, so that they can be recomputed by erasure decoding. Decoding failure occurs with probability

$$\sum_{t=1}^{T+1} p_K(t)$$

(iii)   Erase all symbols for which the error-probability exceeds a value just below 0.5. We chose 0.4. Basically this is the 'best-erasure' strategy. The idea is that with s the number of erasures and t the number of unerased errors we need $s+2t$ not to exceed the number of check symbols r. If we unerase two symbols with error-probability p, then with chance p^2 there are two extra errors and so with two fewer erasures $s + 2t$ is increased by 2; with chance $2p(1-p)$ there is one extra error and $s + 2t$ does not change, and with chance $(1-p)^2$ there are no errors and $s + 2t$ is decreased by 2. So the mean change is $2 \cdot p^2 - 2 \cdot (1-p)^2 = 4p-2$, which is negative if $p<0.5$. With l pairs taken from the check symbols the error-probability is

$$\sum_{t=l+1}^{T+1} p_{K-1+2l}(t)$$

We choose l as the lowest non-negative value for which $P_{2K-1+2l}$ exceeds 0.4.

212

7. RESULTS

An average over 106 runs is shown in the Figure 1. We assumed that we were using the (255, 223) code over GF(256), with N=255, K=223, and R=32. In this case it was found that the worst strategy is erasing the R least reliable symbols, and the next is to erase nothing. The best-erasure strategy as described above gives significant improvement and the use of the WB algorithm gives the best performance. The coding gain at a word-error probability around 10^{-6} is over 1dB (about 1.2 dB) when compared with best erasure strategy.

REFERENCE

[1] Berlekamp E, "Bounded distance plus 1 soft-decision Reed-Solomon decoding", IEEE Transactions on Information Theory, 1996, 42, No.3, pp.704-720.

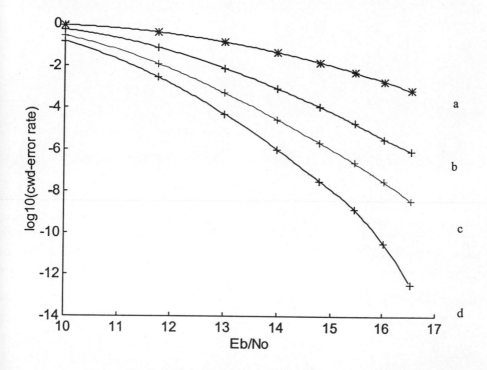

Fig. 1 Codeword error probabilities for four decoding strategies obtained by averaging over 10^6 runs, for Rayleigh fading channel. In order of decreasing error-probability the runs are (a) Erase R weakest symbols; (b) Pure error-correction without erasures; (c) 'Best-erasure' strategy; (d) WB algorithm. We assume an inner (9,8) parity-check code, and an outer (255, 223) RS code over GF(256).

SECTION 2

COMMUNICATIONS

Frequency Domain Equalization for PCC-OFDM with overlapping symbol periods

Jean Armstrong*, Jinwen Shentu* and Chintha Tellambura†
* La Trobe University, Victoria, Australia,
†Monash University, Victoria, Australia

ABSTRACT

Polynomial cancellation coding (PCC) is a coding method for orthogonal frequency division multiplexing (OFDM) in which the information to be transmitted is modulated onto weighted groups of subcarriers rather than onto individual subcarriers. It has previously been shown that compared with ordinary OFDM, PCC-OFDM has very much reduced sensitivity to frequency offset and Doppler spread, lower out-of-band power and reduced intersymbol interference (ISI) due to multipath transmission. In its simplest form PCC-OFDM results in a reduction in overall bandwidth efficiency. One way of retaining the benefits of PCC-OFDM without loss of bandwidth efficiency is to overlap the transmitted symbols. At the receiver an equalizer is used to recover the data. The equalizers are two-dimensional. In this paper the results are presented for simulations of a number of different equalizer structures. It is shown that by using a decision feedback equalizer, the data can be recovered with approximately 1.5dB SNR degradation compared with the ideal case.

1.   POLYNOMIAL CANCELLATION CODED OFDM SYSTEMS

OFDM is the modulation method chosen for many high-speed digital communication systems. This is despite OFDM having a number of well-known disadvantages that include extreme sensitivity to frequency offset, large out-of-band power, and high peak-to-mean power ratio. One of the often-quoted advantages of OFDM is that by using a cyclic prefix it can be made insensitive to multipath transmission. However this is at the cost of some loss in bandwidth efficiency. One technique which has the potential to solve many of the problems of OFDM is Polynomial Cancellation Coding (PCC) [1,2]. In PCC-OFDM the data to be transmitted is mapped onto weighted groups of subcarriers rather than individual subcarriers.

Figure 1.1 shows the block diagram of a PCC-OFDM communication system. Compared with standard OFDM there is an extra block in the transmitter to map the data onto the subcarriers. There is also an extra block in the receiver marked 'weight and add subcarriers'. This combines the received subcarriers in a group and can be

217

shown to result in matched filtering of the received signal [3]. The same weightings are used in the transmitter and receiver and these are chosen so that intercarrier interference (ICI) tends to cancel. The results are completely general and any number of subcarriers can be used in a group. In most practical situations, groups of only two subcarriers are required. In this case the two subcarriers in a group are given relative weightings +1 and −1.

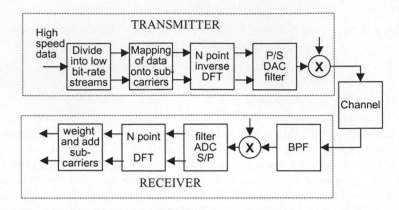

Fig. 1.1   Block diagram of PCC-OFDM communication system

PCC-OFDM has been shown to be much less sensitive to frequency offset and Doppler spread than standard OFDM [1,2]. It has also been shown to have better spectral roll-off and reduced sensitivity to multipath propagation [3]. These properties of PCC-OFDM can be understood by considering the result of weighted pairs of subcarriers in the frequency domain and in the time domain.

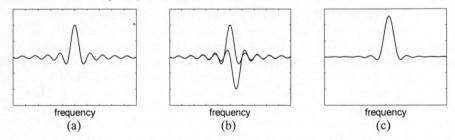

Fig. 1.2   PCC-OFDM in the frequency domain – spectra of subcarriers. (a) One subcarrier, (b) Two adjacent subcarriers, (c) Sum of weighted pair of subcarriers

In OFDM the spectrum of each subcarrier has a $\sin x / x$ form. Figure 1.2 shows how the weighting of a pair of subcarriers in PCC results in a canceling of the sidelobes and a very much faster overall spectral roll-off. As a result the overall power spectrum of a PCC-OFDM signal with mapping onto pairs of subcarriers falls off as $1/(N^3 f^4)$ compared with $1/(Nf^2)$ for standard OFDM.

In the time domain the weighting and adding of pairs of subcarriers results in a windowing effect. The windowing function, which is equivalent to PCC-OFDM, is not identical to any of the windowing functions described in the literature. It is complex, in contrast to all windowing functions previously described, which are real.

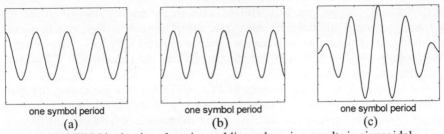

| one symbol period | one symbol period | one symbol period |
| (a) | (b) | (c) |

Fig. 1. 3 PCC-OFDM in the time domain – adding subcarriers results in sinusoidal envelope. (a) One subcarrier, (b) Next subcarrier with opposite polarity, (c) Sum of pair of subcarriers

Figure 1.3 shows the combination of the real components of two adjacent subcarriers with opposite weighting. Note the sinusoidal envelope. This results in most of the energy of a PCC-OFDM symbol being concentrated in the centre of the symbol period. This also means that PCC-OFDM is much less sensitive to ISI due to multipath transmission.

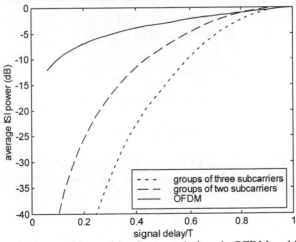

Fig. 1. 4 Power of ISI caused by multipath transmissions in OFDM and PCC-OFDM

219

Figure 1. 4 compares the power of ISI for normal OFDM and PCC-OFDM for the case of a matched filter receiver [3]. For signals delayed by 0.2T, a typical value used in the design OFDM systems, the multipath signal is reduced by approximately 20dB in the system using subcarrier pairs compared with normal OFDM. As a result, for many typical channels, PCC-OFDM does not require the cyclic prefix usually required for OFDM.

2. SPECTRAL EFFICIENCY OF PCC-OFDM

Despite its many advantages, PCC-OFDM used in its simplest form has one major disadvantage - loss in spectral efficiency. The use of two subcarriers, instead of one, to transmit each complex value, reduces the spectral efficiency by half. The elimination of the cyclic prefix, the improved spectral roll-off and the reduction in ICI will make up for some, but not all, of this loss.

Two ways of retaining the benefits of PCC-OFDM, while increasing the spectral efficiency have been explored. These can broadly be described as 'overlapping in frequency' and 'overlapping in time'. It can be shown that 'overlapping in frequency' is a form of the well-known technique called partial-response signaling [4]. A number of groups have independently been researching this and similar approaches [5,6]. However our research has shown that it is not particularly effective. This is because the 'weighting and adding' block in the PCC-OFDM receiver contributes significantly to the improved performance [7] and this block can not readily be incorporated into a partial-response system.

The second approach, 'overlapping in time' in which the symbol periods of adjacent symbols overlap gives much better results. Figure 2.1 shows the basic idea of overlapping in the time domain.

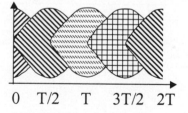

$$0 \quad T/2 \quad T \quad 3T/2 \quad 2T$$

Fig. 2.1 PCC-OFDM with symbols overlapping in time domain

Symbols of duration T are transmitted at intervals of less than T, typically $T/2$. In other words intersymbol interference (ISI) is deliberately introduced at the transmitter to increase the data rate. For the case of an overlap of $T/2$, the transmitted signal at any instant is the sum of components from two symbols. This could be achieved by adding some extra circuitry in the transmitter after the inverse DFT.

Figure 2.2 shows a block diagram for the transmitter. The rate of clocking of the IDFT must also be increased to the new symbol rate.

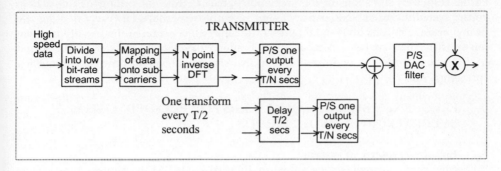

Fig. 2.2 OFDM transmitter with PCC and overlapping symbol periods

Figure 2.3 shows a block diagram for the receiver. An equalizer is required to recover the transmitted data. This can be either a time domain equalizer or a frequency domain equalizer but as will be shown particularly simple and effective frequency domain equalizers can be designed. The rate of clocking of the receiver DFT must also be increased to the new symbol rate. Figure 2.3 also shows the form of the two-dimensional frequency domain equalizer.

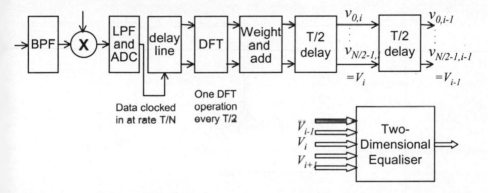

Fig. 2.3 OFDM receiver with PCC and overlapping symbol periods

One way of describing PCC-OFDM with overlapping symbol periods is as a new modulation scheme based on 'almost but not quite' orthogonal functions which are insensitive to time and frequency errors. In contrast, standard OFDM is based on functions which, in the absence of distortion, are absolutely orthogonal but which are very sensitive to these errors. The overlapping of symbol periods destroys the orthogonality, but because of the sinusoidal envelope of PCC-OFDM, this departure from orthogonality is quite small and results in an almost negligible loss in SNR. Partial-response signaling causes a much greater loss in orthogonality and a consequentially greater SNR penalty. Very recently two groups have reported the use of non-orthogonal functions in OFDM. Matheus et al. considered the use of Gaussian pulses [8]. Their analysis included consideration of possible equalizers. Kozek and Molisch considered the optimization of pulse shapes subject to time and frequency spreading [9].

3.   FREQUENCY DOMAIN EQUALIZERS FOR PCC-OFDM WITH OVERLAPPING SYMBOL PERIODS

3.1   Impulse response of system

Frequency domain equalizers are not normally used in OFDM to counteract the effects of multipath transmission. Instead a cyclic prefix is used. This is because the ICI resulting from ISI is spread across a large number of subcarriers and an impractical number of equalizer taps would be required [10]. The polynomial cancellation properties of PCC also work to cancel the interference caused by ISI so that there are only a few significant terms. This means that the equalizer structures can be much simpler. In general the interference is two-dimensional; it is between symbols and also between subcarriers within a symbol. The equalizers, which are being considered for PCC-OFDM, are two dimensional frequency domain equalizers, which operate on the outputs of the 'weighting and adding' block.

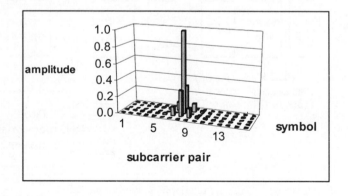

Fig 3.1   Amplitude of two dimensional impulse response for ideal channel

Figure 3.1 shows the outputs from the 'weighting and adding' block in the receiver, which result from one transmitted subcarrier pair in one symbol. It can be considered as a form of two-dimensional impulse response. Because each symbol overlaps in time, only with the preceding and following symbol, the impulse response has non-zero terms only for three symbols: the preceding, the current and the following symbol. In the current symbol, only the wanted subcarrier pair has a non-zero value. In the preceding and following symbols there are three significant terms; these are for the corresponding subcarrier pair and the subcarrier pairs on each side. The total impulse response has only seven terms greater than -20dB, only three of which are above -10dB. In a PCC-OFDM system with overlapping in time and an ideal channel the equalizer in the receiver would to have to equalize this response. For a real channel, the equalizer would also have to compensate for the added distortion in the channel. This would change the details of figure 3.1 but, because of the properties of PCC-OFDM, would still result in an impulse response with only a small number of significant terms.

A number of forms of equalizer have been simulated. The simulations were the simple case of an additive white Gaussian noise (AWGN) channel. To demonstrate the real potential of PCC-OFDM with overlapping symbol periods it will be necessary to consider more realistic channels that introduce significant ISI and ICI. This will be the subject of future work.

In all of the simulations OFDM with 32 subcarriers was used. Each subcarrier pair was modulated with 4QAM. The simulations were for 50000 transmitted symbols. In each case the performance is compared with that of normal OFDM. The results for OFDM are the same as those for any system using a number of orthogonal carriers and so are also identical to the performance of PCC-OFDM with no overlap.

3.2 Zero forcing linear equalizers

By extending well-known equalizer theory to two dimensions, linear zero forcing equalizers operating on three, five and seven symbols were designed. Figure 3.2 shows

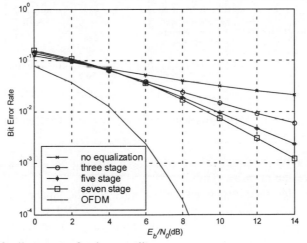

Fig. 3.2 BER for linear zero forcing equalizers.

the bit error rate (BER) as a function of E_b/N_0 for these equalizers. For comparison, the result for no equalizer and the result for normal OFDM with the same AWGN channel are also shown. The results for PCC-OFDM with no overlap are the same as for normal OFDM. The performance improves with the numbers of equalizer stages, but even for seven stages the performance is more than 3dB worse than that for normal OFDM. A better BER performance with the same bandwidth efficiency could be achieved using PCC-OFDM with no overlap, and increasing the size of the constellation.

3.3 Decision feedback equalization with zero forcing feedforward section

Figure 3.3 shows the results for decision feedback equalizers (DFEs) with a varying number of feedforward stages. In other words, decision feedback was used to subtract out the interference from the preceding symbol, linear equalization was used to reduce the interference from the following symbols. The feedforward stages were designed to meet the zero forcing criterion.

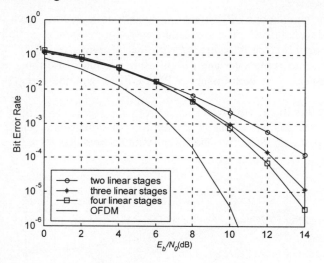

Fig. 3.3. BER for decision feedback equalizers with linear zero forcing feedforward section.

3.4 Decision feedback equalization with zero forcing feedforward section and error correction across a symbol

The results for the DFE are much better than for the linear equalizer, but the degradation compared with normal OFDM, or PCC-OFDM with no overlap is still more than 3dB. In this case the errors in decoding each subcarrier pair are being fed back and as will be shown, this contributes significantly to the BER. One way to reduce this error propagation is to use an error correcting code across each symbol. This would reduce significantly the probability of error for each subcarrier pair and hence the probability of error propagation. Figure 3.4 shows the results where the correct data values are used in the feedback. The performance is improved considerably and the BER is now within approximately 1.5dB of that for normal OFDM.

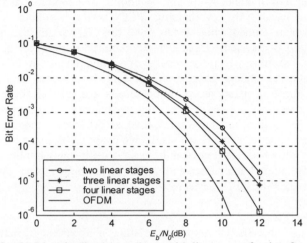

Fig. 3.4 BER for decision feedback equalizers with linear zero forcing feedforward section. Correct decisions fed back.

3.5 Other equalizer structures
By designing the feedforward section using the minimum mean square error criterion (MMSE) further improvements should be possible. The design of the MMSE section must take into account that the noise at the input to the equalizer is not white. The weighting and adding section introduces some correlation between the noise values in adjacent vectors.

Alternatively a maximum likelihood sequence estimator (MLSE) could be designed. Matheus [8] considered this approach for OFDM with Gaussian windowing but it is computationally complex. The properties of PCC-OFDM which concentrate the significant interference in only a few terms, and allow greater choice in the number of subcarriers, may lead to algorithms with significantly reduced complexity.

3.6 Equalization to counteract channel impairments
In any real application equalization would have to counteract the effect of channel impairments as well as correct for the deliberately introduced ISI. A number of papers have considered the use of vector equalization for OFDM [11,12]. The design of

equalizers and the overall performance of PCC-OFDM for typical channels remain topics for further study. However the properties of PCC-OFDM which concentrate the interference in only a few terms should make vector equalization for this case much simpler than for normal OFDM.

4.   CONCLUSIONS

PCC-OFDM is a new method of combining coding and modulation to improve the properties of OFDM. By overlapping PCC-OFDM symbols in time, these improvements can be gained while at the same time *increasing* the overall spectral efficiency of the OFDM system. Equalizers are required in the receiver to recover the transmitted data. In this paper the results of simulations of a PCC-OFDM with frequency domain equalizers have been presented. It has been shown that comparatively simple decision feedback equalizers can cancel the distortion with minimal noise enhancement. Zero forcing linear equalizers have been shown to give very poor results, as they are both ineffective at equalizing the signal and cause considerable noise enhancement. These results indicate that by using PCC-OFDM with overlapping symbol periods, systems can be designed for many applications including mobile telephony, digital television and ADSL with higher data rates and better performance than existing OFDM systems.

5.   REFERENCES

1.   J. Armstong, "Analysis of new and existing methods of reducing intercarrier interference due to carrier frequency offset in OFDM", *IEEE Transactions on Communications*, vol. 47, pp365-369, March 1999.
2.   J. Armstrong, P.M. Grant, G. Povey, "Polynomial cancellation coding of OFDM to reduce Intercarrier interference due to Doppler spread", *IEEE Globecom* , vol 5, pp. 2771-2776, 1998.
3.   J. Armstrong, 'Polynomial Cancellation Coding with Overlapping Symbol Periods', submitted to *IEEE Journal on Selected Areas in Communications*.
4.   J. Armstrong, P.M. Grant, "Polynomial Cancellation Coding of OFDM with mapping of data onto overlapping groups of subcarriers", submitted to *IEEE Communications Letters*.
5.   Yuping Zhao, Jean-Damien Leclercq and Sven-Gustav Häggman: "Intercarrier Interference Compression in OFDM Communication Systems by using Correlative Coding", ", *IEE Comm. Letter*. Vol. 2, pp 214-216. Aug. 1998.
6.   S. B. Slimane, "Performance of OFDM Systems with time-limited waveforms over multipath channels," *IEEE Globecom*, vol 2, pp. 962-967, 1998.
7.   K. Seaton and J. Armstrong, 'Polynomial Cancellation Coding and finite differences', accepted for *IEEE Transactions on Information Theory*.
8.   K. Matheus, K. Knoche, M. Feuersanger and K-D Kammeyer, "Two Dimensional (recursive) channel equalization for multicarrier systems with soft impulse shaping (MCISS)", in *IEEE Globecom conf,* Sydney, November 1998, pp956-961.

9. W. Kozek and A.F.Molisch, "Non-orthogonal pulseshapes for multicarrier communications in doubly dispersive channels", *IEEE J. on Sel. Areas in Comms,* vol. 16, no. 8, October 1998, pp1579-1589.
10. J.A.C. Bingham, "Multicarrier modulation for data transmission: An idea whose time has come," *IEEE Commun. Mag.,* pp. 5-14, May 1990.
11. V. Demoulin and M. Pecot, "Vector Equalization: an alternative approach for OFDM systems," *Ann. Telecomm.,* vol 52, no. 1-2, pp4-11, 1997.
12. W.G. Jeon, K.H. Chang and Y.S. Cho, "An equalization technique for orthogonal frequency-division multiplexing systems in time-variant multipath channels", *IEEE Transactions on Communications*, vol. 47, pp27-32, January 1999.

Lossy 4D Biosemiotic Visual Human Scale Equaliser For TV/Video Image Source Coding

L. R. Atero and R. A. Carrasco

School of Engineering, Staffordshire University, UK
lram@toqui.diinf.usach.cl
r.carras@bss10a.staffs.ac.uk

Abstract
In this chapter a novel biosemiotic visual human scale equaliser (B-*VHSE*) for lossy TV/Video image source coding (*SC*) is presented. This approach uses biological and semiotic concepts on a multilevel 4D orientated genetic machine to induce selective mutation on features of the native colour-space-time image population. The single pseudo-intelligent *heuristic* of B-*VHSE* uses the stochastic nature of its own spatial image frames to place and equivalently prune the search domain, improving the crossover performance with minimum fitness overhead. The B-*VHSE* has been conceived as a *SC*-step, which evolves in an autonomous fashion to generate single and optionally double sided equalisation for dense motion TV/Video image sequences, whilst preserving high visual quality.
Index Terms—Lossy, biosemiotic, genetic, visual human scale, alpha and visual image levels, image equaliser.

1. INTRODUCTION
In the vast majority of compression systems, which employ some form of image coding, the final recipient of the reconstructed visual information is the human eye. It is thus natural that attempts should be made to incorporate a measure of the visual human system features into the source code chain. In the design of digital TV/Video image (*DTVI*) source coding, based on visual quality, one of the most important objectives is to represent, store, transmit and display psychovisual information, which is the *only* visual stimulus that the human eye can perceive.

The matter of human visual response, visual human scale (*VHS*) and image quality in relation to image source coding has been importantly considered in the research literature [1][2][16][3][4][5][6][7]. Two main objectives continue to be addressed for TV/Video image source coding: The first is oriented to ensure that the source code bits are preferentially allocated within the colour space time (*CST*)

229

image levels to which the eye is more sensitive. The second is oriented to achieve numerical measures to apply human perception dynamically in source coding, which should avoid the actual need for extensive subjective testing as a means of generating the *VHS* features and assess the effectiveness of *VHS* based image processing algorithms.   Until now, these attempts have met with limited success [7] and some proprietary methods generated by psychophysical and other experiments have been applied in visual masking for source coding standards such as *MPEG* [8].

A distinctive feature of the new *B-VHSE* technique is that it attempts to reduce peripheral lower and upper invisible and less visible (*alpha*) image levels, preserving the visual resolution inside the fovea, which is analogous to the phenomenological human perception [6]. Research studies show that at the centre of the human field of view there is a high-resolution fovea of 1° in diameter, where acuity is 3-arc min under favorable lighting and contrast. Outside the fovea, acuity degrades peripherally at a uniform rate. At the peripheral limit, acuity is 100 times coarser than in the fovea [10]. This suggests that the colour component resolution can be decreased drastically in the lower and upper peripheral visual, without adversely affecting the image perception, which is central to image equalisation and image source coding methods. Another important visual feature is contrast edge, a local boundary between light and dark neighboring texture regions. Contrast edge is the elementary stimulus for visual acuity, and human vision has the capability of perceiving complex patterns [9] based on sparse contrast edges. The *B-VHSE* source code-step mainly exploits this visual feature by preserving visual borders, texture, edges and fine visual details within its self generated *VHS* domain.

2.   THE NEW LOSSY BIOSEMIOTIC-*VHSE* FORMULATION

The biosemiotic theory (bios=life & semion=sign) is related to biological and semiotic concepts and fundamentally has to do with the biological evolution of genetic individuals based on a pseudo-intelligent communication (semiotic) among them [11]. In this development, the biosemiotic concepts are oriented to generate TV/Video image source coding-steps on the basis of an informed visual human perception of the image population and its evolution within a *4D* colour-space-time domain. In this context, the genetic population allows alpha and visual perception classification and selective mutation. This involves genetic algorithms for processing, directed by autonomous or external forced semiotic signs.

2.1   The Lossy Genetic Image Equaliser Principles
The concept of an equaliser has been mainly used in advanced channel coding strategies for communication systems [12], and involves the estimation and generation of the inverse transfer function of the communication channel. Hence the functional concatenation equaliser-transmission channel generates a virtual unitary transfer function which dynamically allows compensation, by

concatenation code, of distortion and noise induced by nonlinearities and channel variations along the transmission process.

Using a similar principle, the proposed image equaliser is oriented to induce self-similarity degrees within the alpha visual features using its own pseudo stochastic image features but such that minimal perceptible image distortion and noise is induced. Besides, the new lossy equaliser nomination refers to the fact that this image oriented approach of equalisation, can accept numeric quality loss but, is restricted to preserve the whole image information meaning without or with non sensible visual quality loss.

In this context, a main objective within the new methodology is to search for and classify the alpha image levels in the *CS* and *CST* domain. An exhaustive algorithm can be used to find the distribution of lower and upper *VHS* crossing points restricted to an optimal or lossy (suboptimal) quality error evaluation. However the searching procedure can be accelerated by using genetic algorithms [13]. A genetic algorithm outperforms the exhaustive algorithm, since the paths of searching can be heuristically pruned, then the searching depth and fanout tree complexity is much less than in the case of the exhaustive search algorithm. Furthermore, in the latter case, a further check of the code is optionally required to compensate visual image features allowing the algorithmic effectiveness to be investigated in terms of visual quality, mutation areas, reduction of genetic code mass and other performance indexes.

2.2 The Characteristic Steps of the Biosemiotic Image Equaliser Process

The *B-VHSE* equalisation involves an optimisation process which merges image individuals in a pseudo-intelligent process with an informed genetic search, multiple fitness and dynamic crossover points to generate visual population mutation and blind (alpha) and visible image individual classes with a bounded equalised spatial dynamic range scale [14].

The *B-VHSE* equalisation begins with an image population of contending trial solutions brought to the task at hand (*native population*). New solutions (*new population*) are created by heuristically altering the existing solutions by multiple genetic processing. An objective measure of performance (*fitness*) is used to assess the "error" of each trial solution, and a selection mechanism (*crossover*) determines which solutions (*mutations*) should be maintained as "image parents" (*classification*) for the subsequent equalised generation (*recombination*). The differences between the multiple genetic procedures involved are characterised by the types of alterations that are imposed on solutions to create offspring, the methods employed for selecting new image parents, and the data structures that are used to represent solutions. In the proposed *B-VHSE* strategy the children are dynamically created by the stochastic features of blind similarity population levels and global population diversity which belong to their own image population or are optionally forced externally. For visual equalisation purposes, the new generations (*offsprings*) can be selected around and behind lower and upper image population features. In this equaliser, the heuristic *VHS* offspring's crossover are

231

autonomously updated in time instants $t_k = k \cdot M \cdot N \cdot b_i \cdot T_S$, where k is an integer which denotes a frame sampling time instant and M denotes the number of image lines per frame [*lpf*], N the number of genetic pixels per line [*ppl*], b_i the number of bits per '*i*' colour component, and T_S denotes the sampling period. These native image parameters $\{k,M,N,b,T_S\}$ with $b=max\{b_i\}$, are obtained from the involved *TV/Video* image standard and transmission characteristics. By default, the lower side (*LS*) equalisation (*LS-VHSE*) is always provided.

Applying recursively the *LS-VHSE* structure on "complement-to-supreme" population levels saved in a *VHSE^k* buffer, the B-VHSE equaliser generates the optional double sided (*DS*) equalisation (*DS-VHSE*). Hence the equaliser uses a recursive-concatenated multigenetic process to obtain the double sided mutation and classification required. In both models, the *B-VHSE* can generate integer image code. With small modifications *B-VHSE* allows optional single lower, single upper, or double sided visual equalisation with optimisation tuning parameters. These characteristics are for flexible codec-steps functionality, useful to improve multiresolution-based *SC* techniques, layered motion compensation and embedded motion source codes belonging to some new TV/Video image *SC* techniques [15].

2.3 The Native Population Model

The new strategy is based on the consideration of a pseudo stochastic and framed native (*oldest*) population, which macro features are defined either by TV/Video image standards or proprietary formats on biosemiotic image population concepts.

This image population considers visual genetic object encapsulation, mixed with genetic and semiotic methods to classify visual features, visual human scaled object and semiotic inheritance features. In the design, evolutionary objects oriented modelling (*EOOM*) based in object techniques are proposed to model the *B-VHSE* native evolution.

The Fig.2.1 illustrates an example of an oldest genetic image population and its framed biosemiotic structure using *EOOM* techniques. The model represents a framed standard *HDTV* image population, which evolves naturally at a rate of K frames per second [*fps*], with an evolution period between consecutive time instant $k \in [1,K]$. This model considers separable *RGB* colour component image features, with a maximum of 2^{bi} colour image pixels levels per '*i*' colour component (*cc*) and the same planar resolution. The frames have uniform size $M \cdot N$ and embedded visual and alpha *cc* levels, distributed in an assumed pseudo stochastic form.

The referred image population considers planar and colour-space-time (*CST*) visual acuity related to a vertical/horizontal screen aspect ratio v:h, and a native transmission bandwidth *BW*. In addition, at level of frame classification, the model assumes proper sequence methods (*MethTVISc$_i$*) and statistical encapsulation measurements as mean and standard deviation of the genetic levels (*gl*), as well as measurements of the native dynamic range, infimum and supreme magnitude of colour component population.

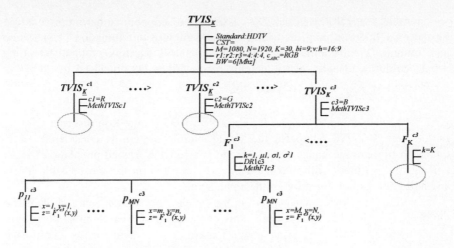

Fig.2.1 The *OLDEST* biosemiotic object population design.

Due to the object modelling bases, any genetic mutation and population reclassification evaluated in a determined evolution period can be easily represented by an *EOOM* model. This representation facility is useful in designing the object *LS-VHSE* and *DS-VHSE* functionality for the *B-VHSE* equaliser, which is shown in Fig.2.5. Complementarily, the formulation of heuristic methods to search for the alpha lower and upper *VHS* levels and recombined new population is provided by using a vector array notation and object principles. In this context, the $TVIS_K$ image population belonging to the oldest representation model shown in Fig.2.1 is defined by an equivalent vector array of framed population matrices, given by **[14][15]**

$$TVIS_K^c = \left| \underline{F}_1^c, \ \underline{F}_2^c, \ \underline{F}_3^c, \quad \underline{F}_k^c, \quad \dots \quad \underline{F}_K^c \right| \tag{2.1}$$

In above formulation, each colour image matrix represents a separable colour component population structured as

$$\underline{F}_k^c = [\underline{F}_k^{c1}, \underline{F}_k^{c2}, \underline{F}_k^{c3}] \tag{2.2}$$

where proper colour component is defined by as **[14][15]**

$$\underline{F}_k^{c}{}^{()} = \begin{bmatrix} F_{11}^{c()} & F_{12}^{c()} & F_{13}^{c()} & \dots & F_{1n}^{c()} & \dots & F_{1N}^{c()} \\ & & & & & & \\ F_{m1}^{c()} & & & & F_{mn}^{c()} & & \\ & & & & & & \\ F_{M1}^{c()} & & & \dots & F_{Mn}^{c()} & \dots & F_{MN}^{c()} \end{bmatrix}_{M \cdot N}^{k} \tag{2.3}$$

233

Also, the *LS-VHSE* and *DS-VHSE* equalised population represented in Fig.2.5 is defined by matrices with a similar structure to expression (2.3). These add *LS* and *DS* distinctive subscripts to the native symbology to differentiate proper evolution. Hence, a new colour image *LS* or *DS* equalised in time k is represented by $\hat{\underline{F}}_{kLS}^{c}$ or $\hat{\underline{F}}_{kDS}^{c}$ respectively.

2.4 The Searching Principles for the *LS* and *DS* Image Equalisation

In the new *B-VHSE* approach, the visual human system is considered as an unknown biosemiotic image object system, where each framed population has an embedded *VHS* mask with maximum linearity centred on the most visible levels and null gradient non-linearity for the alpha levels.

To find the lower and upper alpha levels and visual span, a heuristic multigenetic algorithm is developed. This considers a 4D searching strategy built on the assumption that any visual image feature evolves dynamically within each still and motion image space in a pseudo stochastic form.

The new strategy uses two fitness functions, both based on a heuristic *VHS* mean squared error (*MSE*) quality criterion and two crossover functions which are self generated using population similarity and diversity principles. The algorithm first considers a lower sided *VHS* equalisation and then, using a semiotic link, the double sided *VHS* equalisation is optionally built. In both equalisation steps, an equivalent heuristic general best first (*H-GBF*) searching strategy is used to prune the searching paths.

The following expressions affix the single mutation bases for the heuristic *LS-VHSE* and *DS-VHSE* search strategies.

$$\hat{F}_{ij\ LS}^{ck} = \begin{cases} F_{ij}^{ck} & if \quad F_{ij}^{ck} \geq VHS_{kLS}^{c} \\ VHS_{kLS}^{c} & if \quad F_{ij}^{ck} < VHS_{kLS}^{c} \end{cases} \tag{2.4}$$

$$\hat{\underline{F}}_{ij\ DS}^{ck} = \begin{cases} LS - VHSE & if \quad \underline{F}_{ij}^{ck} < VHS_{kLS}^{c} \\ VHS_{kDS}^{c} & if \quad \underline{F}_{ij}^{ck} > VHS_{kDS}^{c} \end{cases} \tag{2.5}$$

In equations (2.4) and (2.5), VHS_{kLS}^{c} and VHS_{kDS}^{c} represent heuristic visual crossover points which are embedded into the oldest image population F_{k}^{c}, and $\hat{\underline{F}}_{ij\ LS}^{ck}$, $\hat{\underline{F}}_{ij\ DS}^{ck}$ represent the new population generated by the recombination of mutated *LS* and *DS* image levels.

2.5 The *LS-VHSE* Genetic Fitness and Crossover Methods

Equation (2.6) represents the framed likelihood index used to derive the compensated fitness and crossover function for the *LS-VHSE* equalisation algorithm.

234

$$J_{LS}^{k} = \min_{k \in [1,K]} E\{(M_{LS}^{ck} \otimes \underline{F}_{k}^{c} - \underline{\hat{F}}_{kLS}^{c} - \underline{Ce}_{kLS}^{c})^2\} \qquad (2.6)$$

Subject to *R1: Full visual meaning*
R2: MaximumVisual Quality

In the formulation, M_{LS}^{ck} is a self generated *LS* visual mask, $\underline{F}_{k}^{c}$ is the native image frame, $\underline{\hat{F}}_{kLS}^{c}$ is a pseudo stochastic population model, with lower alpha features equalised to the dark VHS_{kLS}^{c} crossover level, and a dynamic range DR_{k}^{c} reduced to the magnitude DR_{kLS}^{c}. The term $\underline{Ce}_{kLS}^{c}$ is an optional regularisation matrix, used mainly to compensate a posteriori, numeric error quality indexes. The symbol '$\otimes$' represents a product masking operation defined by

$$M_{XX}^{ck} \otimes \underline{F}_{k}^{c} = \begin{bmatrix} M_{11}^{ck} \cdot F_{11}^{ck} & M_{12}^{ck} \cdot F_{12}^{ck} & \cdots & M_{1N}^{ck} \cdot F_{1N}^{ck} \\ M_{21}^{ck} \cdot F_{21}^{ck} & & & \\ & & M_{ij}^{ck} \cdot F_{ij}^{ck} & M \\ M_{M1}^{ck} \cdot F_{M1}^{ck} & \cdots & & M_{MN}^{ck} \cdot F_{MN}^{ck} \end{bmatrix}_{M \cdot N}^{ck} \qquad (2.7)$$

where M_{ij}^{ck}, F_{ij}^{ck} are elements of spatial matrices $\underline{M}_{xx}^{ck}$, $\underline{F}_{k}^{c}$, both of size $M \cdot N$ and where $i \in [1,M], j \in [1,N]$ and $xx \in \{LS,DS\}$. The mask $\underline{M}_{xx}^{ck}$ is self-generated as the heuristic pruning function of the *G-BFS* strategy and is also used to generate comparison between visual and numeric *B-VHSE* fitness indexes, within the visual human scale span. In this context, the resultant *LS-VHSE* formulation for the recombination of the $\underline{\hat{F}}_{kLS}^{c}$ genetic population is given by

$$\underline{\hat{F}}_{kLS}^{c} = VHS_{kLS}^{c} \cdot \begin{bmatrix} 1 & 1 & 1 & \cdots & 1 \\ 1 & 1 & 1 & & \\ & & & & \\ 1 & 1 & 1 & \cdots & 1 \end{bmatrix}_{M \cdot N} + DR_{kLS}^{c} \cdot \overline{F}_{kLS}^{c} \qquad (2.8)$$

Here, $\overline{F}_{kLS}^{c} = (\underline{\hat{F}}_{kLS}^{c} - \underline{VHS}_{kLS}^{c})/DR_{kLS}^{c}$ is a normalised dynamic range matrix, whose colour component supreme has unitary magnitude, and $\underline{VHS}_{kLS}^{c}$ is the constant crossover matrix defined in the first term of equation (2.8), both of size $M \cdot N$. In addition, the *LS-VHSE* equalisation dynamic range is given by

$$DR_{kLS}^{e} = \underset{\forall i,j}{Suprem}\{F_{ij}^{ck}\} - VHS_{kLS}^{c} \qquad (2.9)$$

The involved $VHS^c_{k'LS}$ dark crossover level is defined by equation (2.10), where $\lfloor\cdot\rfloor$ means magnitude truncation operation.

$$VHS^c_{k'LS} = \left\lfloor LSsimil^c_{kLS} + LSdiver^c_{kLS} \right\rfloor \qquad (2.10)$$

The terms of expression (2.10) are related to the similarity and diversity features of the dark alpha levels belonging to the assumed embedded genetic visual human scale, and are estimated by

$$LSsimil^c_{kLS} = \Delta^* \cdot \left(\frac{M}{N} \cdot \sum_{j=1}^{N} n^{ck}_j + \sum_{i=1}^{M} m^{ck}_i \right) \qquad (2.11)$$

$$LSdiver^c_{kLS} = \Lambda^* \cdot \left(\sqrt{\sum_{i=1}^{M} \frac{(Nm^{ck}_i - m^*)^2}{M}} + \sqrt{\sum_{j=1}^{N} \frac{(Nn^{ck}_j - n^*)^2}{N}} \right) \qquad (2.12)$$

In the formulation, $n^{ck}_j \in \underline{n}^{ck}$ and $m^{ck}_i \in \underline{m}^{ck}$ are alpha image magnitudes, searched within each framed image $\underline{F}^c_k$ to generate its own lower side crossover point, and $n^* = m^* = \mu_M$ is a mean background genetic index given by

$$\mu_M = \frac{\sum_{i=1}^{M}\sum_{j=1}^{N} F^{ck}_{ij}}{M} \qquad (2.13)$$

The $\underline{n}^{ck}$ vector is expressed as a neighbouring projection array, composed by row's global infimus and defined $\forall i \in [1, M]$ as

$$\underline{n}^{ck} = \min_{j \in [1,N]}\{F^{ck}_{ij}\} = [n_1, n_2, n_3 .. n_j .. n_N]^{ck}_{1-N} \qquad (2.14)$$

Similarly, the $\underline{m}^{ck}$ vector is expressed as a cross neighbouring projection array, composed by column's global infimus and defined $\forall j \in [1, N]$ as

$$\underline{m}^{ck} = \min_{i \in [1,M]}\{F^{ck}_{ij}\} = [m_1, m_2, m_3 .. m_i .. m_M]^{ck}{}^T_{M-1} \qquad (2.15)$$

In addition, Δ^* and Λ^* represent heuristic similarity and diversity tuning parameters, respectively defined by $\Delta^* = \Delta / M$ and $\Lambda^* = \Lambda / N$, where by default $\Delta = 0.5$ and $\Lambda = -0.5$. Finally, the compensation matrix $\underline{Ce}^c_{kLS}$ considering $M^{ck}_{ij\ LS} = 1$ $\forall ij$, is given by equation (2.16)

236

$$\underline{Ce}^\varepsilon_{kLS} = \frac{1}{N}\left(\frac{\sum\limits_{i=1}^{M}\sum\limits_{j=1}^{N}\hat{F}^{ck}_{ij\,LS}}{M} - \mu_M\right)\cdot \underline{Fl}_{M\cdot N} \qquad (2.16)$$

where the matrix $\underline{Fl}_{M\cdot N}$ is defined by

$$\underline{Fl}_{M\cdot N} = \begin{bmatrix} 1 & 1 & 1 & & \cdots & 1 \\ 1 & 1 & 1 & & & \\ \cdot & & & & & \\ \cdot & & & & & \\ \cdot & & & & & \\ 1 & 1 & 1 & & \cdots & 1 \end{bmatrix}_{M\cdot N} \qquad (2.17)$$

2.6　The *DS-VHSE* Genetic Fitness and Crossover Methods

The expression (2.18) represents the framed likelihood index used to derive the compensated fitness and crossover function for the *DS-VHSE* equalisation algorithm.

$$J^k_{DS} = \min_{k\in[1,K]} E\{(M^{ck}_{DS}\otimes\underline{F}^\varepsilon_k - \hat{\underline{F}}^\varepsilon_{kDS} - \underline{Ce}^\varepsilon_{kDS})^2\} \qquad (2.18)$$

Subject to.　*R1: Full visual meaning*
R2: LS-VHSE equalisation
R3: MaximumVisual Quality

The above expression is quite similar in structure and principles to equation (2.6), but has been built on a recursive equalisation base. This means that activating one semiotic link from the *LS-VHSE* mutation, the *DS-VHSE* equaliser searches and generates an equivalent second *OLD* population, which is estimated by

$$\hat{\underline{F}}^\varepsilon_{kOLD2} = (VHS^\varepsilon_{kLS} + DR^\varepsilon_{kLS})\cdot \underline{Fl}_{M\cdot N} - \hat{\underline{F}}^\varepsilon_{kLS} \qquad (2.19)$$

From here, the new *DS-VHSE* recombined population is searched for and formulated, using equations (2.8) to (2.16) but by replacing some notation and involved values. The following expressions show the method used

$$\hat{\underline{F}}^\varepsilon_{kOLD1} = \hat{\underline{F}}^\varepsilon_k \xrightarrow{DS-VHSE} \hat{\underline{F}}^\varepsilon_{kOLD2}, \hat{\underline{F}}^{ck}_{ij} \xrightarrow{DS-VHSE} \hat{\underline{F}}^{ck}_{ij\,OLD2}, \quad (.)_{LS} \xrightarrow{DS-VHSE} (.)_{DS}$$

In this context, the explicit formulation for the recombination $\hat{\underline{F}}^\varepsilon_{kDS}$ genetic population is given by

$$\hat{\underline{F}}^\varepsilon_{kDS} = VHS^\varepsilon_{kDS}\cdot \underline{Fl}_{M\cdot N} + DR^\varepsilon_{kDS}\cdot \overline{\underline{F}}^\varepsilon_{kDS} \qquad (2.20)$$

237

The *DS-VHSE* dynamic range and the upper side crossover level are estimated respectively by

$$DR^{c}_{k\,DS} = \underset{\forall i,j}{Suprem}\{F^{ck}_{ij\,OLD2}\} - VHS^{c}_{k\,DS} \tag{2.21}$$

$$VHS^{c}_{k\,DS} = \left(VHS^{c}_{k\,LS} + DR^{c}_{k\,LS}\right) - \left\lfloor LSsimil^{c}_{k\,DS} + LSdiver^{c}_{k\,DS}\right\rfloor \tag{2.22}$$

The *DS-VHSE* compensation matrix $\underline{Ce}^{c}_{k\,DS}$ considering $M^{ck}_{ij\,DS} = 1 \;\; \forall ij$, is given by

$$\underline{Ce}^{c}_{k\,DS} = \frac{1}{N}\left(\frac{\displaystyle\sum_{i=1}^{M}\sum_{j=1}^{N}\hat{F}^{ck}_{ij\,DS}}{M} - \mu_{M}\right)\cdot\underline{F1}_{M\cdot N} \tag{2.23}$$

From the above formulation, to obtain the compensated lower and higher visual scale borders, a shift of the lower and upper crossover levels i.e. visual span are involved. This is dependent on the compensation error strategy considered and the type of code generation required which can involve integer level resolution or decimal level resolution. In both cases, the upper and lower *VHS* borders coincide with the compensated crossover levels, which are estimated by

$$lowerVHS^{c}_{k\,LS} = \underset{\forall i,j}{Infimum}\{\hat{F}^{ck}_{ij\,LS} + \underline{Ce}^{c}_{k\,LS}\} \tag{2.24}$$

$$lowerVHS^{c}_{k\,DS} = \underset{\forall i,j}{Infimum}\{\hat{F}^{ck}_{ij\,DS} + \underline{Ce}^{c}_{k\,DS}\} \tag{2.25}$$

$$upperVHS^{c}_{k\,DS} = \underset{\forall i,j}{Suprem}\{\hat{F}^{ck}_{ij\,DS} + \underline{Ce}^{c}_{k\,DS}\} \tag{2.26}$$

2.7   The *B-VHSE* Codec-step Structure and Algorithm

The Fig.2.2 to Fig.2.4 represent the functional codec-step structure, equalisation states and design algorithm for the *B-VHSE* equaliser formulated before.

In the proposed structure, the *LS* equalisation functionality is considered by default, but options for *DS* equalisation or forced *LS* and *DS* equalisation are also provided.

This functionality is soft synchronised by the LS/DS Search Control Kernel (*LS/DS-SCK*) unit, which among other things, controls internal or external crossover, equalisation states, and proper *B-VHSE* throughput using two buffer-multiplexers arrays of size *M·N*.

238

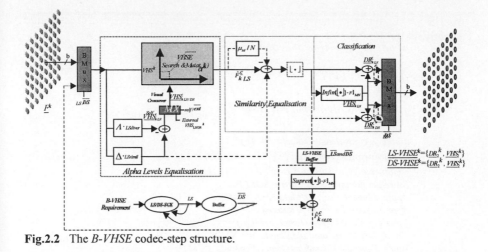

Fig.2.2 The *B-VHSE* codec-step structure.

At the level of biosemiotic processing, the genetic evolution of the new *B-VHSE* aproach is assessed by evaluating performances on the states of mutation for the genetic machine represented in Fig.2.3.

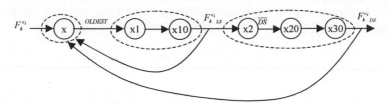

Fig.2.3 The *B-VHSE* mutation states.

In this scheme, state x generates and assesses the *OLDEST* image population. In *LS-VHSE* equalisation, state $x1$ generates and assesses the new visual $\hat{\underline{F}}^{ck}_{LS}$ population and $x10$ the numeric compensated $\widetilde{\underline{F}}^{ck}_{LS}$ population, which is defined by $\widetilde{\underline{F}}^{ck}_{LS} = \hat{\underline{F}}^{ck}_{LS} + \underline{Ce}^{ck}_{LS}$. In the step associated with *DS-VHSE* equalisation, $x2$ defines a new recursive complement to supreme population, $x20$ generates and assesses the new visual $\hat{\underline{F}}^{ck}_{DS}$ population and $x30$ the numerically compensated $\widetilde{\underline{F}}^{ck}_{DS}$ population, which is defined by $\widetilde{\underline{F}}^{ck}_{DS} = \hat{\underline{F}}^{ck}_{DS} + \underline{Ce}^{ck}_{DS}$.

In this context, the basic algorithm of the *B-VHSE* structure is represented in Fig.2.4. The pseudo code considers a generic one colour component TV/Video image sequence equalisation.

```
4DBiosemioticVisualHumanScaleEqualiser_B-VHSE(.)
{
  for (k=1, k=K, k++)
  {
    MultiGeneticAlgorithm B-VHSE^k(.)
    {
      Capture_NativeImageFrameF_k_NIFk(.)
      If VHS^k=NotExternalCross {
        Generate_HeuristicCrossoverPoint_HCP(.)}
      Search_SolutionObjectsPattern_SOP(.)
      Apply_PrunedCrossover/Mutation_1_PCM_1(.)
      Apply_Classif&Recomb_ClaRec(.)
      Generate_VHSE^kImageObject_VHSE_1(.)
      Check_NewMeanPopulationSimilarity_NMPS_1(.)
      Apply_Recomb&Cross&Mut_2ObjectFeatures_RCM_2OF(.)
      Classify_NonVisibleObjectLevels_NVOL(.)
      Classify_PopulationVisualDynamicRange_PVDR(.)
      If opt=LS {
        Generate_MuxNewLSEqualisedObjectPopulation_MNEOP(.) }
    }
    If opt=DS {
      Search_SupremeMNEOPpopulationDiversity_SMPD(.)
      CreateBuffer_Complement-to-RCM_2OFasNativeImageFrameF_kDS_NIFk(.)
      Apply_ VHSE^k /*Recursively*/
      Generate_MuxNewDSEqualisedObjectPopulation_MNEOP(.)}
  }
}
```

Fig.2.4 The *B-VHSE* algorithm.

This algorithm allows a full colour, pseudo colour or grey TV/Video image sequence equalisation to be generated, as well as the particular cases of still full colour, pseudo colour or grey image frame equalisation.

2.8   The Recombination *B-VHSE* Population Model

The Fig.2.5 represents the resultant new colour TV/Video image population recombination, produced after equalisation at a time instant *k*. In fact, this structure represents the object model for the *B-VHSE* equaliser design associated with   the *LS* or *DS* biosemiotic methods and encapsulation.

This model shows that the biosemiotic equalisation of a TV/Video image sequence is produced simply by lossy mutation and recombination of its oldest population, which considers a framed separable colour component representation. The first key of population classification is by the colour component, the second is by the temporal position of colour component frames, and the third is by the *VHS* embedded levels distribution, searched for *LS* or *DS* equalisation methods.

240

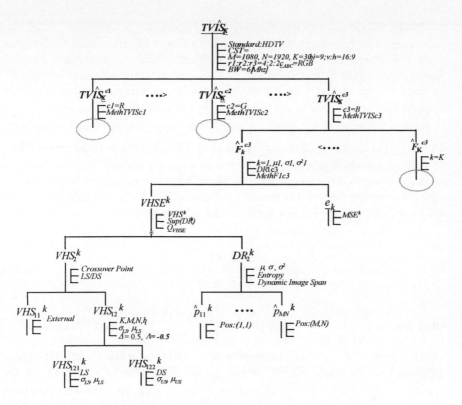

Fig.2.5 The *New* biosemiotic object population design.

In fact, the encapsulation is provided through an informed lower sided or double sided *VHS* crossover, (internal or external), which involves the heuristic search of lower and (optionally) upper alpha image levels. Considering a self reproduction method, which is based on searching for and recombining the similarity and diveristy of dark *VHS* levels, the single lower sided or optional double lower and upper sided equalisation encapsulation is obtained.

The new object population based design represents any colour TV/Video image sequence equalisation, and is also valid to represent the equalisation of pseudo colour, grey or monochrome image sequences and colour, pseudo colour or grey still images, all which represent a particular case of biosemiotic object equalisation. In addition the design includes external semiotic links oriented to force a specific lower or upper crossover point which is useful to generate some fixed (reference) visual human scale, mainly in image sequence processing. In these cases the required crossover is replaced by the reference one which generally diminishes the computational load on the remaining genetic operations.

2.9   The Visual and Genetic Density Based Indexes.

To manage the *CS* visual behaviour and coding load associated to different biosemiotic image populations, the concept of visual indexes, picture gene position density, spatial gene code density and *CST* relative genetic density are introduced. All these can be evaluated on a local or global population area and equivalently defined by an *M*·N** genetic size as for still and motion activity assessment.

The visual indexes are simply generated by applying the visual mask M_{xx}^{ck} $xx \in [LS,DS]$ to the native image, using the $M_{xx}^{ck} \otimes F_k^c$ operation defined previously.

The gene position density is evaluated on a located genetic size, and involves the ratio between the number of individuals with colour component magnitude not null belonging to a new (still or motion) population, and the original number of not null individuals belong to the oldest one. The index is given by

$$\hat{G}PD_k^c = \frac{\sum_{i=1}^{M^*}\sum_{j=1}^{N^*} \hat{pos}_{ij}^{cik}}{\sum_{i=1}^{M^*}\sum_{j=1}^{N^*} pos_{ij}^{cik}} \qquad (2.27)$$

where $pos_{ij}^{cik} = \begin{cases} 1 & if \quad \left|F_{ij}^{cik}\right| > 0 \\ 0 & if \quad F_{ij}^{cik} = 0 \end{cases}$ and $\hat{pos}_{ij}^{cik} = \begin{cases} 1 & if \quad \left|\hat{F}_{ij}^{cik}\right| > 0 \\ 0 & if \quad \hat{F}_{ij}^{cik} = 0 \end{cases}$, $\forall i \in [1, M^*]$, $\forall j \in [1, N^*]$.

The gene code density involves a new (still or motion) genetic colour component image mass and its native spatial code volume evaluated on the equivalent *M*·N** genetic size. The index is built on the consideration that each population position contains a specific gene mass and code volume. The gene mass is defined to be equal to the colour component magnitude involved. In the same context the gene code volume is given by a normalised (unitary) gene visual area shape, and a height defined by the maximum code resolution for the colour component involved. This index is defined by equation (2.28)

$$\hat{G}CD_k^{ci} = \frac{\sum_{i=1}^{M^*}\sum_{j=1}^{N^*} \hat{F}_{ij}^{cik}}{M^*\cdot N^* \cdot 2^{hi}} = \frac{Mass_k^{ci}}{Vol_k^{ci}} \qquad (2.28)$$

The indexes given by equation (2.27) and (2.28) can also be used to define the starting state features at a time *k* to assess the *OLDEST* colour image population. This is achieved by considering that the new (still or motion) population did not have mutations and hence equal position and genetic mass are obtained as a new population. Using the above consideration, the relative genetic density is defined as the ratio between any code or position density to compare, relative to another one used as proper reference. This index is formulated by

$$RGCD_k^{ci} = \frac{GCD_k^{ci}}{GCD_{k\ REF}^{ci}}, \quad RGPD_k^{ci} = \frac{GPD_k^{ci}}{GPD_{k\ REF}^{ci}} \qquad (2.29)$$

242

3.   SIMULATION RESULTS AND DISCUSION

The proposed *B-VHSE* method is applied to *LS*, *DS* and external forced image equalisation. The visual results are evaluated and compared against the primitive image in terms of its image meaning, visual perception, subjective numeric quality and other performance indexes. In every native image, the oldest image quality is normalised to the *PCM* digital quality [16]. For standard image format with 8 bits per colour component, the referential one is fixed to 52.2 [db] given in equivalent *PSNR* units. The stimulus with maximum bitrate per frame (*Pili&Jav*) is selected as the referential one to compare the genetic still and motion load that affect the equalisation process. The **Fig.3.1** presents a sample of the different types of visual image stimuli considered.

Fig.3.1 Synthetic Stimuli. *(1): GT1, (2): GT2, (3): GT3; Natural Stimuli. (4): Lena, (5): Pili&Jav, (6):Mandrill, (7):Image sequence ramHand-frame F07.*

The main differentiation among visual image stimuli shown in **Fig.3.1** is given by the subjective spatial synthetic and natural intraframe texture as well as the pseudo stochastic motion in between the image frames of the TV/Video sequence considered. These features involve the embedded alpha and visual contrast, borders, edges and fine details defined by *cc* image levels variations, contrast distribution and equivalent areas neighbour correlation. Hence they are very difficult to evaluate in line for fast comparation between native and *VHS* processed pictures. However the assessment of internal states of biosemiotic equalisation, enables to investigate the subjective meaning changes and related visual perception, both correlated with numerical performance indexes and with the evaluation of genetic mutation and evolution, controlled by the *B-VHSE* processing options. In comparison with psychophysical, grating and other subjective methods [1][2][3][6][9], this new approach does not require knowledge of either the human cortex transfer function or the normalised contrast sensitivity function to generate visual masks and *VHS* processing. In addition, the autonomous *B-VHSE* behaviour enables generating numeric results and the reduction of alpha levels in line.

243

3.1 The Primitive Still and Motion Image Features

The Table 3.1 summarises *OLDEST* feature population measurements, relative to one colour component for each framed image stimuli.

Table 3.1 The native population macro features

NativFeatures	Texture	M	N	b	BR	Popul	Inf	Supr	Mean	StdDev	GCD	RGCD	H	I
GT1	Synthetic	512	512	8	2,048	262,144	17	251	134.0	82.7	0.523	0.607	6.8	3,252
GT2	Synthetic	512	512	8	2,048	262,144	17	251	134.0	58.5	0.523	0.607	7.8	2,177
GT3	Synthetic	512	512	9	2,304	262,144	0	268	134.0	59.5	0.210	0.245	6.6	2,499
Lena	Natural	512	512	8	2,048	262,144	2	240	134.4	41.5	0.524	0.608	7.2	2,478
Pili&Jav	Natural	512	770	8	3,080	394,240	1	255	146.9	66.8	0.574	1.000	7.5	2,174
Mandrill	Natural	480	500	8	1,875	240,000	1	220	104.8	63.5	0.409	0.434	7.5	1,806
F07	Natural	232	320	8	580	74,240	0	250	97.4	42.1	0.381	0.125	7.2	2,213

Units: BR=Bitrate [Kb/s-frame], Popul=Population [pixels per frame], Inf=Infimum, Sup=Supreme, GCD=Genetic Code Density, RGCD=GCD relative to GCD Pili&Jav.
H=Entropy, I=Information

The Fig.3.2 shows the perceptual intraframe population curves associated with the equalisation state *x0* for the whole set of native images.

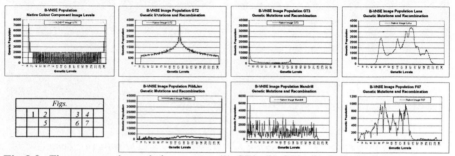

Fig.3.2 The perceptual population curves. *(1):GT1, (2):GT2, (3):GT3, (4):Lena, (5):Pili&Jav, (6):Mandrill, (7):F07.*

3.2 Equalisation of Natural Still Images

As an example of *B-VHSE* processing for natural still images and reference frame for motion images, the Fig.3.3 summarises the perceptual results for the *Pili&Jav* image equalisation. In *(1a)*, the native image to process and the equivalent problem of finding the embedded psychovisual *VHS* borders is illustrated. In *(1c)*, the native spatial population model is presented. In *(2)* and *(3)* the default *LS* and *DS* equalisation results are shown. The curves *(a)* show perceptual population features i.e. genetic mutation produced by the *B-VHSE* equalisation. The volumetric curves *(b)* represent the spatial distribution of genetic levels obtained in the phase of recombination of the equalised population. The pictures *(c)* show the meaning and visual perception obtained after equalisation.

From *(2a)* it can be seen that selective mutation of the dark genetic levels is generated with a lower *LS-VHSE* compensated crossover of 62 *gl*. In the same context from *(3a)* the lower crossover obtained is 61 and the higher is 233 *gl*. The experiment shows that in the *LS* equalisation the visual dynamic range diminishes from 254 to 193 *gl* and in *DS* equalisation it reduces to 172 *gl*. Besides, the generated psychovisual equalisation borders are [62,255] and [61,233] respectively. In both cases an excellent comparative meaning and visual perception is obtained which is corroborated by pictures *(c)*. In the image experiment, no visuals blocking neither distortion nor noise effects are perceived.

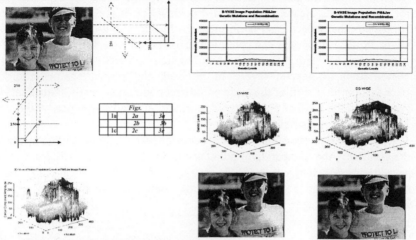

Fig.3.3 Processing results for image *Pili&Jav* equalisation.

The Fig.3.4 represents the evolution of performance indexes for the image *Pili&Jav* processing in the different *B-VHSE* equalisation states.

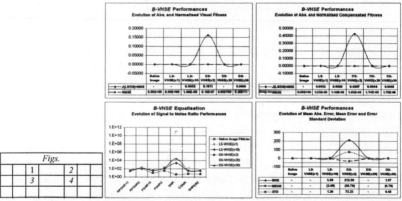

Fig.3.4 Performances for *Pili&Jav* equalisation.

In *(1)* and *(2)*, the evolution of the normalised absolute visual genetic fitness and compensated fitness evaluation in terms of masked *MSE* units are presented. By comparison of curve *(1)* and *(2)*, the uncompensated *LS* and *DS* fitness perform better than the compensated one. This paradoxical effect is obtained due to the biosemiotic compensation that improves the unmasked *MSE* cost function, uses a genetic plane and not the selective visual levels within the *VHS* span when

245

evaluated by the masked fitness function. In *(3)*, the visual *SNR* within the *VHS* span is presented for different signal to noise ratio index versions [6][7][14]. In comparison with the *OLDEST SNR*, the $x1$ and $x20$ state presents equal values of *SNR* and longer than the compensated one. In *(4)*, the evolution of mean absolute error, mean and standard deviation of the visual error are shown. Again, $x1$ and $x20$ presents the better visual performances. In addition it can be observed in the table of figure *(4)* that the compensation error produces a negative offset of error both in the *LS* and *DS* equalisation, which induces a new mutation and recombination of genetic levels. In general, the planar compensation used produces a uniform shift of the mean equalised population levels, with small visual differences at the level of picture perception and masked differences at the level of neighbour contrast distribution.

The Fig.3.5 represents the *Pili&Jav* genetic level evolution and compressibility indexes. In *(a)* the comparative mutated colour levels on the different states of equalisation are shown and in *(b)* the resultant effect of statistical compressibility and visual information effects oriented to combined visual source coding are presented.

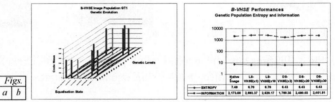

Fig.3.5 *Pili&Jav* Compressibility features: *(a)*: Shifting effects on distribution of genetic population, *(b)*: Entropy and Information.

The figure *(a)* also summarises the effect of population evolution by recombination in the different equalisation states, which shows a novel reposition of genetic code within the embedded *VHS* span. This is because the induced intraframe similarity and neighbouring statistic change from the *OLDEST* to *LS* and from *LS* to *DS* equalisation. However the compensated mutation mainly produces a shift of genetic levels, hence the statistical features are mainained relatively constant within the equalisation states. This effect is corroborated in *(b)*, where curves show the evolution of still entropy and information associated to the compressibility indexes. From the table in *(b)*, it is shown that for the native population, the maximum crossing point of lossless compression is restricted to 7.5 bits per pixel [bpp].However in *LS* equalisation it diminishes to round a mean of 6.7 [bpp] and for *DS* equalisation to 6.43 [bpp], producing a reduction of the less perceptual visual entropy by around 10% and 14% respectively, without blocking effects and distortion.

3.3   Equalisation of Natural *TV/Video* Images
This section presents results of *B-VHSE* equalisation for *TV/Video* images with variable motion. The Fig.3.6 illustrates the generic model of TV/Video image

sequence and also the conceptual problem of finding the embedded psychovisual *VHS* borders.

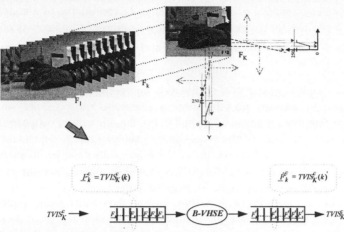

$$F_k^c = TVIS_K^c(k) \qquad \tilde{F}_k^c = TVIS_K^c(k)$$

$$TVIS_K^c \longrightarrow \boxed{F_1 | F_2 | F_3 | F_4 | F_5} \longrightarrow \left(B\text{-}VHSE\right) \longrightarrow \boxed{F_1 | F_2 | F_3 | F_4 | F_5} \longrightarrow TVIS_K^c$$

Fig.3.6 The *B-VHSE* equalisation of TV/Video Image Sequences.

In this context, Fig.3.7 shows a sample of motion image frames belonging to the stimuli *ramHand*. In the pictures *(1)*, the frames *F07* to *F10* represent a section of the oldest framed TV/Video image population. Each population presents a gamma of variable contrast and perceptual genetic features at a time *k,* which now include embedded *visual motion* alpha and visual levels in the time direction.

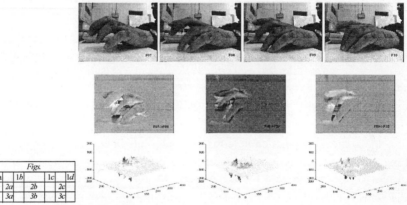

Fig.3.7 The *ramHand* motion features.

In pictures *(2)* the searched visual changes between consecutive image frames are shown. These pictures illustrate the so called interframe motion effect. In this representation, the visual perception is magnified by increasing the motion values using a linearly zoomed mutation with unitary scaling and a lighting translation factor fixed by the infimum value of the involved interframe motion. In pictures

(3) the colour-space-time representation of spatial interframe motion searched at a time $k \in [8,9,10]$ is presented. The spatial values of motion are obtained by a first order predictor **[16][6]** i.e. differential image levels relative to a consecutive time instant k. In the simulation, the interframe motion can be equivalently evaluated between a reference image frame $\underline{F}_k^c$ and a following (forward or backward) image frame $\underline{F}_p^c$, where the null interframe motion and its spatial representation is given by a z-plane of size $M \cdot N$ centered on the zero *CST* component magnitudes.

Hence in pictures *(3)*, the motion textures closest to the referred plane represent fine motion image levels and detail the differences between the reference and the next one. These differences can be visible or alpha, dependent on the *VHS* value of the referential levels. In fact, a plane with positive offset in the colour levels direction means that the next frame will be lighter than the referential one and the inverse will be obtained for negative offsets.

In addition, regions with texture levels above this plane represent lighter textures than the next frame and texture levels below it represent darker ones, the visual effect of which depends on the colour component magnitude of the texture involved. In general, the textures with longer differences of colour magnitudes above or below this plane are associated with uncover or cover motion image regions. These regions are very influential on the motion activity involved in the image sequence. In this investigation the absolute framed code mass relative to the null motion plane is defined as an index of motion activity. The Fig.3.8 shows the motion activity performances associated with the sequence *ramHand*.

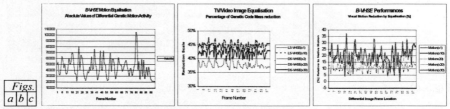

Fig.3.8 The *ramHand* motion activity.

In *(a)* the native motion in terms of its absolute interframe differences in each time instant $k \in [1,101]$ is represented. The curve shows a high non-stationarity produced by pseudo stochastic motion. In *(b)* the perceptual reduction of population code mass for the different equalisation states is shown. It can be observed an average reduction of code mass to around of 45% for *LS* equalisation and 42% for *DS* equalisation. In *(c)* the percentual reduction of motion activity is shown. It can be observed a reduction of alpha motion activity to around of 20% for *LS* equalisation and 23% for *DS* equalisation.

Fig.3.9 shows the mutation of genetic levels i.e. the psychophysical *VHS* borders for the 101 frames of the sequence *ramHand*. In *(a)* the native and *LS* equalisation levels are presented and in *(b)* the native and *DS* equalisation levels are shown. In both cases, it can be seen that there is a significative increasing of the lower spatial genetic level, which in *LS* and *DS* equalisation fixes a lower sided crossover plane at 83 *gl* and a *DS* higher crossover plane at 200 *gl*. This generates a significant reduction of population dynamic range, from 250 to 167 *gl* for *LS* equalisation and 250 to 117 *gl* for *DS* equalisation. Besides, the generated psychovisual equalisation borders are around [83,250] and [83,200] for *LS* and *DS* equalisation respectively.

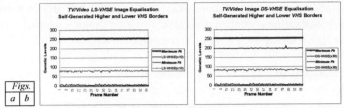

Fig.3.9   Code Levels Reduction by *B-VHSE* Equalisation.

Finally the Fig.3.10 illustrates the evolution of equalised motion, for the 101 frames of the image sequence *ramHand*, using relative visual density indexes.

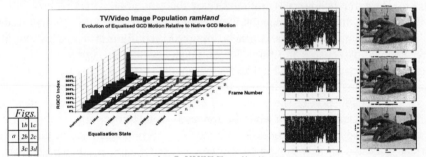

Fig.3.10   Code Levels Reduction by *B-VHSE* Equalisation.

In *(a)* the comparison of mutation levels in terms of relative framed code mass is presented. The measure emphasises better than typical indexes the relative effect of motion compressibility and the significative reduction of framed alpha motion density in each time instant *k*. In *(b) and (c)*   typical   cumulative *x* projection levels and resultant pictures are presented. *In (1)* the *ramHand* native code levels and image before equalisation are shown. In *(2)* and *(3)* the *VHS* effect on genetic levels and image perception for *LS* and *DS* equalisation are illustrated. In general, for *DS* equalisation the lower *VHS* levels are close to the *LS* ones but the higher *VHS* levels are definitively smaller than the *LS* equalisation.

In motion image processing, the *B-VHSE* processing significantly reduces the dynamic range, code mass and motion activity. In this experiment, it enables the generation of a *DS* dynamic range reduction of around 50% of the original one, reduction of code mass of around 40% and reduction of the motion activity to around 20%, mantaining the inheritable characteristics of the more visual motion features without further processing,which is highly required for improved current *DTVI* source coding or designing new combined visual source coding strategies.

In general, a better visual perception is obtained for *LS* equalisation rather than *DS* equalisation. The code mass reduction produced for *DS* equalisation is longer relative to the *LS* one, hence *DS* equalisation is more suitable for combined source coding applications of very low bit rate with options of progressive quality on demand. However considering mixed effects, the combined *LS* equalisation can perform better than the stand-alone *DS* equalisation if a spatial non-linear codec-step or transformations (applied on higher dynamic range values) are concatenated with *LS-VHSE* techniques before further compression processing.

4. CONCLUSIONS

In this chapter a new biosemiotic visual human scale equaliser for lossy combined digital TV/Video image source coding has been presented.

The *B-VHSE* method is conceived as a tuneable pre-processing codec-step, is applicable to colour and grey images with diverse still and motion features and achieves in autonomous form a significative reduction of the involved alpha dynamic range, code mass and motion activity.

For default the B-*VHSE* equaliser generates lower side equalised image codes in an integer spatial format and can be optionally configured in *DS* or external forced modality, reusing the same lower sided equalisation structure. The new method is robust, flexible, and unlike the psychophysical and other qualitative and quantitative visual methods, it does not require knowledge of either the human cortex transfer function or the normalised contrast sensitivity function to generate the required visual masks of equalisation and visual processing. The *B-VHSE* generates framed equalised codes in line, allowing easy concatenation to improve current or designing new combined source coding. Besides, the generation of its codes can be made with integer or decimal pixel resolution which allows a forward concatenation with flexible interworking load for progressive combined source coding applications on demand.

The equalised code population is mutated accordingly to a constant *VHS* crossover surface, which increases neighbouring correlation and diminishes marginal entropy within the embedded alpha image levels. This allows generating a new biosemiotic image model with a simple and equivalent reduced code mass relative to the original one, thereby preserving visual meaning and graceful quality without blocking distortion or noise perception, which is a highly required *CST* codec-step feature for the development of new flexible combined source codes

REFERENCES

[1]   T. N. Cornsweet; "Visual Perception", New York, Academic Press, 1970.

[2] W. F. Schreiber, "Psychophysics and the improvement of television picture quality," SMPTE J., pp. 717-725, Aug. 1984.

[3] F. J. Kolb, Jr., Ed. "Bibliography: Psychophysics of image evaluation", SMPTE J., pp.594-599, Aug. 1989.

[4] J. A. Saghri, P. S. Cheatham, and A. Habibi, "Image Quality Measure based on a Human Visual System Model", Opt. Eng., Vol.28, No.7, pp.813-818, July 1989.

[5] B. Girod; "The information theoretical significance of spatial and temporal masking in video signals", (in Proc. SPSE/SPIE Symp. on Human Vision, Visual Processing and Display), Los Angeles, CA, Jan. 1989.

[6] A.N. Netravali; "Digital Pictures: Representation and Compression", AT&T Bell Laboratories, 1988.

[7] R.J. Clarke; "Digital Compression of Still Images and Video", Academic Press Ltd., 1995.

[8] H. Benoit; "Digital Television MPEG1, MPEG2 and Principles of DVB System", John Wiley & Sons, 1997.

[9] I.P. Howard, B.I. Rogers; "Binocular Vision and Stereopsis", Oxford University Press, UK, 1995.

[10] E. L. Schwartz; "On the mathematical structure of the retinotopic mapping of primate striate cortex", Sci-Ence, pp 277-1066, 1985.

[11] A.A. Sharov, "Biosemiotics: Functional-evolutionary approach to the analysis of the sense of information", Biosemiotics, Mouton de Gruyter, New York, pp.345-373, 1992.

[12] I. Coloma, R.A. Carrasco; "Non Linear Adaptive Algorithms for Equalisation in Mobile Satellite Communications", Neural Computing&Applications, Vol.2, pp.97-110, 1994.

[13] Z. Michalewic;"Genetic Algorithms+Data Structure=Evolution Programs", 3rd Ed., New York: Spring Verlag, 1996.

[14] L.R. Atero, R.A. Carrasco, " New LST Transform for Image Compression", 4th IEE/IEEE International Symposium on Communication Theory and Applications, UK, 1997.

[15] L.R. Atero, R.A. Carrasco, "LST-based Residual Multilayer and Multiresolution Image Compression CODEC with scalable Motion Compensation", 1st IEEE International Symposium on Communication Systems & Digital Signal Processing, CSDSP'98, UK, April 1998.

[16] A.B. Carlson; "Communication Systems: An Introduction to Signals and Noise in Electrical Communications", McGraw Hill Inc., 1986.

Interference Mitigation Using Parsimonious Signal Representations

S. Burley and M. Darnell
University of Leeds, UK

1. INTRODUCTION

The design and performance evaluation of digital communication systems, and their associated signal processing algorithms, has traditionally relied on the assumption of an additive white Gaussian noise (AWGN) channel. However, in numerous circumstances this assumption is not always justifiable, and the communicating medium can be more accurately described using non-Gaussian models. In essence, the reason for this tradition is threefold:

- by central limit considerations, the Gaussian model is approximately valid provided that the noise process includes contributions from a large number of sources;

- the Gaussian model has been extensively studied by mathematicians and engineers alike, and the design of algorithms based on Gaussianity is a well understood procedure;

- the resulting algorithms are usually simple in nature and can be implemented in real-time without the need for advanced hardware and software requirements.

The advantages offered by the Gaussian assumption, however, come at the expense of severe degradation in algorithmic performance when the underlying noise statistics deviate significantly from Gaussianity. In the past, such degradation may have been acceptable due to the lack of sufficient processing capability. However, with today's increased availability of cheap and powerful digital signal processing devices, a loss in algorithmic performance in exchange for simplicity is no longer acceptable. In an effort to transmit information over communication channels that contain Gaussian and non-Gaussian noise components, both military and commercial applications frequently rely upon the use of direct sequence spread spectrum (DSSS) modulation techniques.

An important attribute of DSSS is that it can provide a degree of protection against non-Gaussian interference. This interference rejection capability is brought about by intentionally making the transmission bandwidth far in excess of the minimum bandwidth necessary to send the information. Spectrum spreading is accomplished through the use of a pseudorandom, or pseudonoise (PN) code which is independent of the data. In DSSS, each data bit is used to invert (or not invert) one full period of the PN spreading code. The original information signal is then

253

recovered at the receiver by *despreading* the received signal using a synchronised, locally generated copy of the PN spreading code.

Whilst DSSS is an interference-tolerant modulation scheme, situations may be encountered where the power of an interferer is large enough so that even the advantages offered by spread spectrum are insufficient. Under these circumstances, the interference immunity of a DSSS system can be further improved at the expense of increasing the transmission bandwidth for a given information bandwidth. Practical considerations such as the complexity of transmitter/receiver hardware and the available frequency spectrum can, however, limit the attainable processing gain. Under these circumstances, interference mitigation strategies have to be included within the system architecture to attain the low bit error rates (BER) required by emerging applications. To date, the majority of signal processing techniques developed for interference mitigation purposes have focused exclusively on suppressing narrowband interference. However, there is a need to be able to mitigate more general classes of non-Gaussian interference.

Interference mitigation in DSSS systems is usually accomplished prior to despreading through the use of either adaptive filtering or transform domain processing [1], [2], [3]. Both techniques operate on a discrete-time representation of the received signal, and rely on the assumption that the interferer has a high spectral concentration in a narrow frequency range, while the DSSS signal and background noise are both wideband and spectrally flat. Transform domain processing typically employs the discrete Fourier transform (DFT) as the basic building block for estimating and suppressing interference. Here, the input sample stream to the receiver is typically grouped into blocks of uniform length. Portions of the transform that exceed a predefined threshold are then usually replaced with zero, prior to computing the inverse DFT. As a result, both signal energy and interference are excised in each contaminated frequency bin. Like adaptive filtering, this approach can be employed with reasonable success if the interferer is localised and stationary within the frequency domain. However, severe performance degradation is encountered when the interference is nonstationary. This is due to the fact that the DFT does not yield a representation that explicitly indicates how the spectral components of a signal vary over time. Hence, if a given processing block is contaminated by an interferer occupying disjoint regions in time and frequency (say), thresholding the DFT coefficients will lead to an excessive amount of wanted signal energy being excised. Hence, in order to suppress nonstationary interference more effectively, a transform domain that provides a joint time-frequency description of the received signal is needed.

The chapter is organised as follows: in Section 2, the spread spectrum model is defined; in Section 3, we discuss the linear expansion of discrete-time signals; in Section 4, the concept of signal denoising is introduced; in Section 5, we exploit the concept of denoising and develop a new interference mitigation strategy for

DSSS communication systems; in Section 6, we provide a performance analysis of the proposed technique in terms of the signal-to-noise ratio (SNR) at the correlator output and the bit error rate (BER); finally, in Section 7, conclusions are drawn from the work contained in this chapter.

Notation: The Kronecker delta δ is defined such that $\delta(n-m)=0$, unless $n=m$, in which case $\delta(0)=1$. The superscript * denotes complex conjugation and the symbol i is used to denote the square root of -1.

2.   THE SPREAD SPECTRUM MODEL

In the first instance, the data source at the transmitter generates an information sequence I_j which, during a bit interval T_b, can take on one of two equiprobable binary states $\{+1,-1\}$. This binary information sequence is then used to modulate a PN spreading code comprising L chips per information bit. The resulting information-bearing DSSS waveform is, therefore, of the form

$$s(t)=\sum_{j=0}^{\infty} I_j \, c(t-jT_b),$$ (2.1)

where

$$c(t)=\sum_{m=0}^{L-1} c(m) \, q(t-mT_c).$$

Here, $c(m)\in\{+1,-1\}$ are the chip elements of a random PN spreading code, so that $E[c(m)]=0$ and $E[c(m)\,c(l)]=\delta(m-l)$. The chip waveform $q(t)$ has duration T_c and unit energy.

The information-bearing signal is then transmitted over the channel where it is contaminated by Gaussian and non-Gaussian noise such that the model describing the signal at the DSSS receiver is of the form

$$r(t)=s(t)+w(t)+i(t)$$
$$=\sum_{j=0}^{\infty} I_j \sum_{m=0}^{L-1} c(m) \, q(t-jT_b-mT_c)+w(t)+i(t).$$ (2.2)

Here, $w(t)$ is AWGN having zero-mean and variance σ_w^2, and $i(t)$ is a non-Gaussian component. At the receiver, $r(t)$ is first processed by a chip-matched filter whose output is sampled at the chip rate. The resulting discrete-time signal sample for the mth chip of the jth bit is given by

$$r_j(m)=\int_{jT_b+mT_c}^{jT_b+(m+1)T_c} r(t) \, q(t-jT_b-mT_c) \, dt,$$ (2.3)

so that for the jth bit interval we have

$$r_j(m)=s_j(m)+w_j(m)+i_j(m), \qquad m=0,1,...,L-1,$$ (2.4)

255

and the desired signal is $s_j(m) = I_j\, c(m)$. The receiver then attempts to suppress the non-Gaussian component, prior to recovering the information sequence by cross-correlation with a stored replica of the PN spreading code.

3. LINEAR EXPANSION OF DISCRETE–TIME SIGNALS

In signal processing applications, it is often useful to decompose a discrete-time signal $x(n) \in C^N$ into a collection of elementary building blocks, so that we can write

$$x(n) = \sum_{l=0}^{M-1} C_l^x \, \psi_l(n), \qquad n = 0, 1, \ldots, N-1, \tag{3.1}$$

where

$$C_l^x = \langle x(n), \varphi_l(n) \rangle = \sum_{n=0}^{N-1} x(n)\, \varphi_l^*(n), \qquad l = 0, 1, \ldots, M-1.$$

Of particular importance is the case when: $M = N$; $\psi_l(n) = \varphi_l(n)$, for all l; and $\langle \varphi_l(n), \varphi_k(n) \rangle = \delta(l-k)$, then (3.1) is an orthonormal basis expansion. The motivation here is to choose a complete set of orthonormal basis functions $\{\varphi_l(n)\}$ (or *transform*) so that the expansion coefficients $\{C_l^x\}$ (or *transform domain coefficients*) of a given signal emphasise features that are not easily discernible from the signal in its original form. Important examples of orthonormal bases include the identity $\{\delta(n-l)\}$ and Fourier basis $\{1/\sqrt{N}\, e^{i2\pi nl/N}\}$, which span the discrete-time and discrete-frequency domains, respectively. The collection of basis functions $\{\varphi_l(n)\}$ is usually obtained through a set of transformations that are applied to a single prototype function $\varphi(n)$. For the identity and Fourier bases, these transformations include translation and modulation, respectively. Functions of this nature are often called *self-similar*.

3.1. Time–Frequency Representations

During recent years, the signal processing community have renewed their interest in Gabor's approach to representing signals in a joint time-frequency domain [4]. To appreciate this, we recall that the Fourier basis does not yield a representation that explicitly indicates how the spectral components of a signal vary over time. Gabor's seminal work, however, addressed this problem by introducing temporal information within the continuous-time Fourier transform. In essence, Gabor introduced a *windowing* procedure that partitioned the signal under examination into time intervals of uniform length. Following this, the Fourier transform was computed on each interval, thus providing a description of the frequencies present within each localised region. Gabor's joint time-frequency representation later

256

became known as the short-time Fourier transform (STFT), and its definition encompassed both continuous and discrete-time representations. Since then, a whole range of time-frequency representations have been developed, and [5], [6] provide excellent treatments on recent trends in this field.

The *localisation* of a given basis function in time and frequency is an important consideration when choosing a basis set for the linear expansion of a discrete-time signal. Each basis function has a region in the time-frequency plane where most of its energy is concentrated. If the collection of basis functions is complete and satisfies the orthonormality constraint, these regions in the time-frequency plane are non-overlapping and cover the entire time-frequency plane; if any part of the time-frequency plane were not covered, there would be a *hole* in the basis, and we would not be able to completely represent all signals in the space. The localisation area of a particular basis function should not overlap adjacent basis functions by too much, since this would represent a redundancy in the system.

Choosing a basis set $\{\varphi_l(n)\}$ can be loosely thought as selecting a tiling of the discrete-time discrete-frequency plane. Shown below are tilings induced by various orthonormal bases in C^{32}; the horizontal axis represents discrete-time, whilst the vertical axis represents discrete-frequency. Each tile contains 32 points out of a total 32^{32} (in practice, however, boundaries between these regions will overlap).

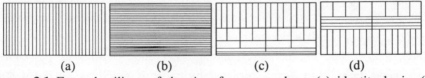

| (a) | (b) | (c) | (d) |

Figure 3.1 Example tilings of the time-frequency plane: (a) identity basis; (b) Fourier basis; (c) wavelet basis; (d) example wavelet packet basis.

3.2. Parsimonious Signal Representations

If the tiling of the time-frequency plane matches the time-frequency content of a signal, the expansion coefficients $\{c_l^x\}$ and their, respective, basis functions $\{\varphi_l(n)\}$ provide valuable local information about the inner structures of a signal. However, if the tiling of the time-frequency plane is poorly matched to the inner structures of a signal, its energy is diluted across the time-frequency plane; for example, the influence of a Dirac function $\delta(n)$ when decomposed onto a Fourier basis is diluted uniformly across the entire basis set. In numerous applications, it is desirable to choose a basis set that yields a sparse representation of the signal under examination; that is, for certain values of l, $c_l^x = 0$. Representations of this nature are often called *parsimonious*. In most applications, it is difficult to choose *a priori* the tiling of the time-frequency plane best suited to represent the local features of a given signal and yield a parsimonious representation. To alleviate this problem, the

257

notion of *signal-adapted* representations have been developed and extensively studied over recent years. A parsimonious signal-adapted representation is typically derived by introducing a procedure that selects an appropriate set of (time-frequency concentrated) waveforms from an overcomplete dictionary D (e.g. matching pursuits [7]) that best match the inner structures of a signal.

4. THE CONCEPT OF SIGNAL DENOISING

The concept of signal denoising has recently emerged as a new method for extracting an unknown but deterministic signal $x(n) \in C^N$ immersed in AWGN $w(n)$, i.e. $y(n) = x(n) + w(n)$. If the observation $y(n)$ is modelled with an orthonormal basis representation

$$y(n) = \sum_{l=0}^{N-1} \langle y(n), \varphi_l(n) \rangle \varphi_l(n) = \sum_{l=0}^{N-1} C_l^y \varphi_l(n), \qquad n = 0,1,\dots,N-1, \qquad (4.1)$$

then, by exploiting linearity of the inner product, we can discern the, respective, contributions of the signal and noise as

$$C_l^y = C_l^x + C_l^w, \qquad l = 0,1,\dots,N-1. \qquad (4.2)$$

The random nature of the noise component holds the implication that it does not correlate highly with any of the basis functions. As a result, the energy of $w(n)$ is diluted uniformly across the coefficients $\{C_l^y\}$, independent of the basis set used. If, however, $\{\varphi_l(n)\}$ yields a parsimonious representation for $x(n)$, then for certain values of l, $C_l^x = 0$, and the corresponding observation coefficients C_l^y capture noise alone, rather than signal corrupted by noise. If exactly K ($< N$) of these coefficients contain signal information, while the remainder only contain noise, we can reindex the set $\{C_l^y\}$ such that

$$C_l^y = \begin{cases} C_l^x + C_l^w, & l = 0,1,\dots,K-1 \\ C_l^w, & l = K, K+1,\dots,N-1. \end{cases} \qquad (4.3)$$

If the signal has a higher power density that is concentrated in time and/or frequency, compared with the noise component, we can introduce a thresholding strategy that excludes those $N-K$ coefficients C_l^y containing only noise from the expansion if $|C_l^y| < \lambda$, and estimate the form of $x(n)$ as

$$\hat{x}(n) = \sum_{l=0}^{K-1} C_l^y \varphi_l(n), \qquad n = 0,1,\dots,N-1. \qquad (4.4)$$

When $\{\varphi_l(n)\}$ corresponds to the wavelet basis, this procedure results in a signal where the AWGN is reduced, and has been shown to be asymptotically optimal in a *minimax* sense for a large class of signal spaces [8]. In most practical applications, however, it is difficult to choose *a priori* a basis that yields a parsimonious representation. To circumvent this problem, we can generalise the notion of denoising to encompass an adaptively chosen basis that provides a parsimonious representation for an unknown but deterministic signal immersed in AWGN [9].

5.   INTERFERENCE MITIGATION IN DSSS USING DENOISING

By exploiting the concept of signal denoising, we can formulate an effective strategy for interference mitigation in DSSS systems which, in effect, performs the converse of procedure outlined in the previous section. Here, each $\{r_j(m)\}$ is regarded as an ordered L-tuple from an L-dimensional vector space C^L. Thus, by modelling the jth bit interval with an orthonormal basis representation

$$r_j(m) = \sum_{l=0}^{L-1} \langle r_j(m), \varphi_l(m) \rangle \varphi_l(m) = \sum_{l=0}^{L-1} C_l^{r_j} \varphi_l(m), \qquad m = 0,1,...,L-1, \qquad (5.1)$$

we can discern the, respective, contributions of $C_l^{r_j}$ as

$$C_l^{r_j} = C_l^{s_j} + C_l^{w_j} + C_l^{i_j}, \qquad l = 0,1,...,L-1. \qquad (5.2)$$

Working on the notion that both $s_j(m)$ and $w_j(m)$ are wideband and spectrally flat, their energy will be distributed uniformly across the coefficients $\{C_l^{r_j}\}$, independent of the basis set used. If on the other hand, $\{\varphi_l(m)\}$ is adaptively chosen so that it yields a parsimonious representation for $i_j(m)$, then for certain values of l, $C_l^{i_j} = 0$, and the corresponding observation coefficients $C_l^{r_j}$ capture signal information and noise alone, rather than the combined sum of all three components. If exactly K ($<$ L) of these coefficients contain signal, AWGN and interference, while the remainder contains signal information and noise alone, we can reindex the set $\{C_l^{r_j}\}$ such that

$$C_l^{r_j} = \begin{cases} C_l^{s_j} + C_l^{w_j} + C_l^{i_j}, & l = 0,1,...,K-1 \\ C_l^{s_j} + C_l^{w_j}, & l = K, K+1,...,L-1. \end{cases} \qquad (5.3)$$

If the interference has a higher power density that is concentrated in time and/or frequency, compared with the wanted signal and background noise components, we can introduce a thresholding strategy that excludes those K coefficients $C_l^{r_j}$ energised by interference from the expansion if $|C_l^{r_j}| > \lambda$, and estimate the form of the received signal as

$$\hat{r}_j(m) = \sum_{l=K}^{L-1} C_l^{r_j} \varphi_l(m), \qquad m = 0,1,...,L-1. \qquad (5.4)$$

In practice, this denoising procedure is implemented using the selective reconstruction

$$\hat{r}_j(m) = \sum_{l=0}^{L-1} \theta_T\left(C_l^{r_j}\right) \varphi_l(m), \qquad m = 0,1,\ldots,L-1, \tag{5.5}$$

where

$$\theta_T(x) = \begin{cases} x, & |x| \leq 3\hat{\sigma}_w \\ 0, & |x| > 3\hat{\sigma}_w, \end{cases}$$

and $\hat{\sigma}_w$ is an estimate of the background noise standard deviation.

Reconfiguration of the basis set $\{\varphi_l(m)\}$ every bit interval ensures that the denoising procedure can adapt in accordance with interbit nonstationary interference. Denoising is carried out at the expense of introducing some distortion to the information-bearing signal. However, if the interference is compressed efficiently into a small subset of expansion coefficients, the distortion introduced to the wanted signal is minimised.

6.   PERFORMANCE ANALYSIS

In this section, we investigate the performance of a DSSS communication system that incorporates denoising within the receiver architecture. In order to demonstrate the effectiveness of the proposed technique, we compare the performance of the receiver with and without denoising. Two performance measures are considered; namely, the signal-to-noise ratio (SNR) at the correlator output, and the bit error rate (BER).

6.1.   Signal–to–Noise Ratio Analysis

First, we recall that if the jth bit interval is modelled with an orthonormal basis representation we can discern the, respective, contributions of $C_l^{r_j}$ as

$$C_l^{r_j} = C_l^{s_j} + C_l^{w_j} + C_l^{i_j}, \qquad l = 0,1,\ldots,L-1. \tag{6.1}$$

Working on the notion that both $s_j(m)$ and $w_j(m)$ are wideband and spectrally flat, their energy will be distributed uniformly across the coefficients $\{C_l^{r_j}\}$, independent of the basis set used. If on the other hand, $\{\varphi_l(m)\}$ is adaptively chosen so that it yields a parsimonious representation for $i_j(m)$, then for certain values of l, $C_l^{i_j} = 0$, and the corresponding observation coefficients $C_l^{r_j}$ capture signal information and noise alone, rather than the combined sum of all three components. If exactly K ($<$ L) of these coefficients contain signal, AWGN and interference, while the remainder contains signal information and noise alone, we can reindex the set $\{C_l^{r_j}\}$ such that

$$C_l^{r_j} = \begin{cases} C_l^{s_j} + C_l^{w_j} + C_l^{i_j}, & l = 0,1,\ldots,K-1 \\ C_l^{s_j} + C_l^{w_j}, & l = K, K+1,\ldots,L-1. \end{cases} \tag{6.2}$$

If the denoising procedure is not activated, the PN correlator produces the decision variable

$$
\begin{aligned}
U_j^{(1)} &= \langle r_j(m), c(m) \rangle \\
&= \langle s_j(m), c(m) \rangle + \langle w_j(m), c(m) \rangle + \langle i_j(m), c(m) \rangle \\
&= I_j \sum_{l=0}^{L-1} C_l^c \langle \varphi_l(m), c(m) \rangle + \sum_{l=0}^{L-1} C_l^{w_j} \langle \varphi_l(m), c(m) \rangle + \sum_{l=0}^{K-1} C_l^{i_j} \langle \varphi_l(m), c(m) \rangle \\
&= I_j \sum_{l=0}^{L-1} C_l^c \ C_l^{*c} + \sum_{l=0}^{L-1} C_l^{w_j} \ C_l^{*c} + \sum_{l=0}^{K-1} C_l^{i_j} \ C_l^{*c} \\
&= I_j L + \sum_{l=0}^{L-1} C_l^{w_j} \ C_l^{*c} + \sum_{l=0}^{K-1} C_l^{i_j} \ C_l^{*c},
\end{aligned}
$$

(6.3)

for the jth bit interval. If on the other hand, only the first P $(<.K)$ coefficients energised by interference exceed the denoising threshold criterion, the PN correlator yields the decision variable

$$
\begin{aligned}
U_j^{(2)} &= \langle \hat{r}_j(m), c(m) \rangle \\
&= \langle \hat{s}_j(m), c(m) \rangle + \langle \hat{w}_j(m), c(m) \rangle + \langle \hat{i}_j(m), c(m) \rangle \\
&= I_j \sum_{l=P}^{L-1} C_l^c \langle \varphi_l(m), c(m) \rangle + \sum_{l=P}^{L-1} C_l^{w_j} \langle \varphi_l(m), c(m) \rangle + \sum_{l=P}^{K-1} C_l^{i_j} \langle \varphi_l(m), c(m) \rangle \\
&= I_j \sum_{l=P}^{L-1} C_l^c \ C_l^{*c} + \sum_{l=P}^{L-1} C_l^{w_j} \ C_l^{*c} + \sum_{l=P}^{K-1} C_l^{i_j} \ C_l^{*c} \\
&= I_j (L-P) + \sum_{l=P}^{L-1} C_l^{w_j} \ C_l^{*c} + \sum_{l=P}^{K-1} C_l^{i_j} \ C_l^{*c},
\end{aligned}
$$

(6.4)

for the jth bit interval. For both (6.3) and (6.4), a decision on the polarity of the jth bit is then made by comparing $U_j^{(k)}$, $k=1,2$, with a threshold of zero, i.e. $\hat{I}_j = \text{sgn}\left(U_j^{(k)}\right)$.

The SNR at the correlator output is a commonly used performance metric and is defined as the ratio of the square of the mean to the variance of the decision variable [10], i.e.

$$
SNR_O^{(k)} = \frac{E^2\left[U_j^{(k)}\right]}{Var\left(U_j^{(k)}\right)} = \frac{E^2\left[U_j^{(k)}\right]}{E\left[\left|U_j^{(k)}\right|^2\right] - E^2\left[U_j^{(k)}\right]}, \qquad k=1,2.
$$

(6.5)

Thus, when the denoising procedure is not activated, the expected mean of $U_j^{(1)}$ is

261

$$E\left[U_j^{(1)}\right] = I_j L,$$ (6.6)

due to the zero-mean property of the noise component and PN spreading code. To obtain the mean-square value, we first find

$$\left|U_j^{(1)}\right|^2 = L^2 + I_j L \sum_{l=0}^{L-1} C_l^{w_j} C_l^{*c} + I_j L \sum_{l=0}^{K-1} C_l^{i_j} C_l^{*c} + I_j L \sum_{k=0}^{L-1} C_k^{*w_j} C_k^c + I_j L \sum_{k=0}^{K-1} C_k^{*i_j} C_k^c$$

$$+ \sum_{l=0}^{L-1} \sum_{k=0}^{L-1} C_l^{w_j} C_k^{*w_j} C_l^{*c} C_k^c + \sum_{l=0}^{K-1} \sum_{k=0}^{K-1} C_l^{i_j} C_k^{*i_j} C_l^{*c} C_k^c$$

$$+ \sum_{l=0}^{L-1} \sum_{k=0}^{K-1} C_l^{w_j} C_k^{*i_j} C_l^{*c} C_k^c + \sum_{l=0}^{L-1} \sum_{k=0}^{K-1} C_l^{*w_j} C_k^{i_j} C_l^{*c} C_k^c .$$

(6.7)

Then, by taking the expectation of (6.7), we obtain

$$E\left[\left|U_j^{(1)}\right|^2\right] = L^2 + L\sigma_w^2 + \sum_{l=0}^{K-1} \left|C_l^{i_j}\right|^2 ,$$ (6.8)

due to the zero-mean property and uncorrelatedness of the noise component and PN spreading code. From (6.6) and (6.8), the correlator output SNR for the case when the denoising procedure is not activated is given by

$$SNR_O^{(1)} = \frac{2L}{N_O + (2/L)\sum_{l=0}^{K-1}\left|C_l^{i_j}\right|^2} ,$$ (6.9)

where $N_O = 2\sigma_w^2$ is the single-sided noise power spectral density. On examining (6.9), we find that the interference energy is reduced by a factor L at the correlator output.

When the denoising procedure is invoked, the expected mean of $U_j^{(2)}$ is

$$E\left[U_j^{(2)}\right] = I_j (L - P),$$ (6.10)

due to the zero-mean property of the noise component and PN spreading code. To obtain the mean-square value, we first find

$$\left|U_j^{(2)}\right|^2 = (L-P)^2 + I_j L \sum_{l=P}^{L-1} C_l^{w_j} C_l^{*c} + I_j L \sum_{l=P}^{K-1} C_l^{i_j} C_l^{*c} + I_j L \sum_{k=P}^{L-1} C_k^{*w_j} C_k^c + I_j L \sum_{k=P}^{K-1} C_k^{*i_j} C$$

$$+ \sum_{l=P}^{L-1} \sum_{k=P}^{L-1} C_l^{w_j} C_k^{*w_j} C_l^{*c} C_k^c + \sum_{l=P}^{K-1} \sum_{k=P}^{K-1} C_l^{i_j} C_k^{*i_j} C_l^{*c} C_k^c$$

$$+ \sum_{l=P}^{L-1} \sum_{k=P}^{K-1} C_l^{w_j} C_k^{*i_j} C_l^{*c} C_k^c + \sum_{l=P}^{L-1} \sum_{k=P}^{K-1} C_l^{*w_j} C_k^{i_j} C_l^{*c} C_k^c .$$

(6.11)

Then, by taking the expectation of (6.11), we obtain

$$E\left[\left|U_j^{(2)}\right|^2\right] = (L-P)^2 + (L-P)\sigma_w^2 + \sum_{l=P}^{K-1}\left|C_l^{i_j}\right|^2, \tag{6.12}$$

due to the zero-mean property and uncorrelatedness of the noise component and PN spreading code. From (6.10) and (6.12), the correlator output SNR for the case when the denoising procedure is invoked is given by

$$SNR_O^{(2)} = \frac{2(L-P)}{N_O + (2/L-P)\sum_{l=P}^{K-1}\left|C_l^{i_j}\right|^2}, \tag{6.13}$$

where $N_O = 2\sigma_w^2$ is the single-sided noise power spectral density. On examining (6.13), we find that the residual interference energy following denoising is reduced by a factor $L-P$ at the correlator output.

6.2   Bit Error Rate Analysis

An approximation of the BER can be derived by assuming that the decision variable $U_j^{(k)}$ is Gaussian distributed having mean $E\left[U_j^{(k)}\right]$ and variance $Var\left(U_j^{(k)}\right)$ [10]. Under this assumption, the BER is given by

$$P_e^{(k)} = p\left(U_j^{(k)} \geq 0 \mid I_j = -1\right)$$

$$= \frac{1}{\sqrt{2\pi\sigma_k^2}}\int_0^\infty \exp\left[-\left(U_j^{(k)} - \mu_k\right)^2 / 2\sigma_k^2\right] dU_j^{(k)}, \quad k=1,2, \tag{6.14}$$

where $\mu_k = E\left[U_j^{(k)}\right]$ and $\sigma_k^2 = Var\left(U_j^{(k)}\right)$. Making the change of variable $z_k^2 = \left(U_j^{(k)} - \mu_k\right)^2 / \sigma_k^2$, we find that

$$P_e^{(k)} = \frac{1}{\sqrt{2\pi}}\int_{\sqrt{\mu_k^2/\sigma_k^2}}^\infty \exp\left[-z_k^2/2\right] dz_k = Q\left(\sqrt{SNR_O^{(k)}}\right), \quad k=1,2, \tag{6.15}$$

where $Q(\cdot)$ is the complementary error function. On substituting (6.9) and (6.13) into (6.15), we obtain approximate BER performance curves for a DSSS communication receiver that does not employ any interference mitigation strategies, and when the interference is suppressed using denoising. For simplicity, we assume that the interference is entirely eliminated through denoising, then from (6.13) we have

$$SNR_O^{(2)} = \frac{2(L-K)}{N_O}. \tag{6.16}$$

On examining (6.16), we find that whilst the interference is eliminated at the correlator output, the distortion incurred to the information-bearing DSSS waveform through denoising manifests itself as a reduction in the correlation peak.

263

This in turn, reinforces the notion that when denoising is used to improve the BER performance of a DSSS system operating in non-Gaussian environments, it is imperative that the interference energy is compressed into as few coefficients $\{C_l^{r_j}\}$ as possible. To see this, consider a length 64 random spreading code. Figure 6.1 illustrates the BER performance of a DSSS receiver (as a function of K) that employs denoising for a given $(E_b/N_o)_{dB}$. Here, we find that as the number of excluded coefficients increases, the energy of the wanted signal at the input to the correlator is insufficient to yield a satisfactory correlation peak for reliable detection.

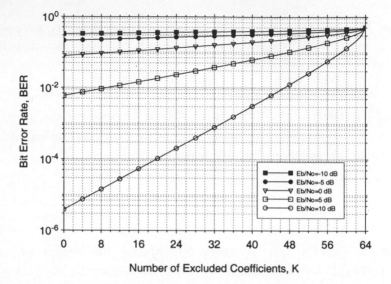

Figure 6.1 BER performance (as a function of K) of a DSSS receiver that employs denoising.

7.   CONCLUSIONS

In this chapter, we have developed a new interference mitigation technique for DSSS communication systems using parsimonious signal representations. The success of this technique (as with any transform domain processing technique), is dependent on the ability of the chosen basis set to compress the interference energy into as few expansion coefficients as possible. To accomplish this, we introduce a procedure   which   selects an appropriate set of (time-frequency concentrated) waveforms from an overcomplete dictionary that best match the inner structures of the   received   signal.

REFERENCES

1. Milstein, L.B., *Interference Rejection Techniques in Spread Spectrum Communications*, Proceedings of the IEEE, Vol. 76, No. 6, pp 657-671, June 1988.
2. Poor, H.V. and Rusch, L.A., *Narrowband Interference Suppression in Spread Spectrum CDMA*, IEEE Personal Communications Magazine, Vol. 1, No. 3, pp 14-27, Third Quarter 1994.
3. Laster, J.D. and Reed, J.H., *Interference Rejection in Digital Wireless Communications*, IEEE Signal Processing Magazine, Vol. 14, No. 3, pp 37-62, May 1997.
4. Gabor, D., *Theory of Communication*, Journal of the IEE, Vol. 93, No. 3, pp 429-457, November 1946.
5. Cohen, L., *Time-Frequency Analysis*, Prentice Hall, 1995, ISBN 0-13-594532-1.
6. Mallat, S.G., *A Wavelet Tour of Signal Processing*, Academic Press, 1998, ISBN 0-12-466605-1.
7. Mallat, S.G. and Zhang, Z., *Matching Pursuits with Time-Frequency Dictionaries*, IEEE Transactions on Signal Processing, Vol. 41, No. 12, pp 3397-3415, December 1993.
8. Donoho, D.L. and Johnstone, I.M., *Wavelet Shrinkage Asymptopia*, Journal of the Royal Statistical Society, Series B, Vol. 57, No. 2, pp 301-369, 1995.
9. Burley, S.J., *Interference Mitigation in Spread Spectrum Communication Systems Using Wavelet Packets*, Ph.D. Thesis, University of Leeds, May 1999.
10. Ketchum, J.W. and Proakis, J.G., *Adaptive Algorithms for Estimating and Suppressing Narrowband Interference in PN Spread-Spectrum Systems*, IEEE Transactions on Communications, Vol. 30, No. 5, pp 913-924, May 1982.

The Complex Finite Field Hartley Transform

R. M. Campello de Souza, H. M. de Oliveira, A. N. Kauffman
CODEC - Communications Research Group
Departamento de Eletrônica e Sistemas - CTG - UFPE
C.P. 7800, 50711 - 970, Recife - PE , Brasil
E-mail: Ricardo@npd.ufpe.br , hmo@npd.ufpe.br , ANK@nlink.com.br

ABSTRACT
Discrete transforms, defined over finite or infinite fields, play a very important role in Engineering. In either case, the successful application of transform techniques is mainly due to the existence of the so-called fast transform algorithms. In this paper, the complex finite field Hartley transform is introduced and a fast algorithm for computing it is suggested.

1. INTRODUCTION

Discrete transforms are a very important tool and play a significant role in Engineering. A particularly striking example is the well known Discrete Fourier Transform (DFT), which has found many applications in several areas, specially in the field of Electrical Engineering. A DFT over Galois fields was also defined [1] and applied as a tool to perform discrete convolutions using integer arithmetic. Since then several new and interesting applications of the Finite Field Fourier Transform (FFFT) have been found, not only in the fields of digital signal and image processing [2-5], but also in different contexts such as error control coding and cryptography [6-8]. In both cases, infinite and finite, the existence of fast algorithms (FFT) for computing the DFT has been a decisive factor for its real-time applications. Another interesting example is the Discrete Hartley Transform (DHT) [9], the discrete version of the symmetrical, Fourier-like, integral transform introduced by R. V. L. Hartley in 1942 [10]. Although seen initially mainly as a tool with applications only on the numerical side and having connections to the physical world only via the Fourier transform, the DHT has proven over the years to be a very useful instrument with many interesting applications [11-13]. Fast Hartley transforms also do exist and play an important role in the use of the DHT.

Recently, a new Hartley transform over finite fields (FFHT) was introduced [14] which has interesting applications in the field of digital multiplexing [15]. However, the FFHT has the restriction that it does not allow blocklengths that are a power of two. In this paper, the complex finite field Hartley transform (CFFHT) is introduced. Thus, in the next section a trigonometry for gaussian integers over a Galois field is introduced. In section 3 the cosine and sine (cas) function over a finite field is introduced and some orthogonality relations are derived. In section

267

4, the complex finite field Hartley transform (CFFHT) is defined using a Galois field gaussian integer argument for the transform kernel which removes the blocklength restriction of the FFHT. Section 5 examines the condition for valid spectra which leads to results that are similar to the conjugacy constraints for the FFFT. An efficient algorithm for computing the CFFHT is presented in section 6. The paper closes with a few concluding remarks and suggestions of some possible areas of applications.

2. A TRIGONOMETRY FOR GAUSSIAN INTEGERS OVER A GALOIS FIELD

The set $G(q)$ of gaussian integers over $GF(q)$ defined below plays an important role in the ideas introduced in this paper (hereafter the symbol := denotes *equal by definition*).

Definition 1: $G(q) := \{a + jb, \ a, b \in GF(q)\}$, $q = p^r$, r being a positive integer, p being an odd prime for which $j^2 = -1$ is a quadratic non-residue in $GF(q)$, is the set of gaussian integers over $GF(q)$.

Let $\otimes$ denote the cartesian product. It can be shown, as indicated below, that the set $G(q)$ together with the operations $\oplus$ and $*$ defined below, is a field.

Proposition 1: Let

$\oplus : G(q) \otimes G(q) \rightarrow G(q)$

$(a_1 + jb_1, a_2 + jb_2) \rightarrow (a_1 + jb_1) \oplus (a_2 + jb_2) =$
$$= (a_1 + a_2) + j(b_1 + b_2)$$

and

$* : G(q) \otimes G(q) \rightarrow G(q)$

$(a_1 + jb_1, a_2 + jb_2) \rightarrow (a_1 + jb_1) * (a_2 + jb_2) =$
$$= (a_1 a_2 - b_1 b_2) + j(a_1 b_2 + a_2 b_1).$$

The structure $GI(q) := \ < G(q), \oplus, * >$ is a field. In fact, $GI(q)$ is isomorphic to $GF(q^2)$.   □

In what follows ζ denotes an element of multiplicative order N in $GI(q)$, the set of gaussian integers over $GF(q)$, $q = p^r$, p an odd prime such that $p \equiv 3$ (mod 4). Trigonometric functions over the elements of a Galois field can be defined as follows.

Definition 2: Let ζ be an element of multiplicative order N in $GI(q)$, $q = p^r$, $p \neq 2$. The $GI(q)$-valued k-trigonometric functions of $\angle(\zeta^i)$ in $GI(q)$ (by analogy, the trigonometric functions of k times the "angle" of the "complex exponential" ζ^i) are defined as

$$\cos_k(\angle\zeta^i) := \frac{1}{2}(\zeta^{ik} + \zeta^{-ik}) \quad \text{and} \quad \sin_k(\angle\zeta^i) := \frac{1}{2j}(\zeta^{ik} - \zeta^{-ik}),$$

for $i, k = 0, 1,...,N-1$. For simplicity ζ is supposed to be fixed. We write $\cos_k(\angle\zeta^i)$ as $\cos_k(i)$. The trigonometric functions above introduced satisfy properties P1-P10 below.

P1. Unit Circle: $\sin_k^2(i) + \cos_k^2(i) = 1.$

268

Proof: $\sin_k^2(\,i\,) + \cos_k^2(\,i\,) = [\frac{1}{2j}(\zeta^{ik} - \zeta^{-ik})]^2 + [\frac{1}{2}(\zeta^{ik} + \zeta^{-ik})]^2 =$

$$= \frac{1}{-4}(\zeta^{2ik} - \zeta^{-2ik} - 2) + \frac{1}{4}(\zeta^{2ik} + \zeta^{-2ik} + 2) = 1. \qquad \square$$

P2. Even / Odd: $\cos_k(\,i\,) = \cos_k(\,-i\,)$
                            $\sin_k(\,i\,) = -\sin_k(\,-i\,)$.

Proof. $\cos_k(-i) = \frac{1}{2}(\zeta^{-ik} + \zeta^{ik}) = \cos_k(\,i\,)$; $\sin_k(\,-i\,) = \frac{1}{2j}(\zeta^{-ik} - \zeta^{ik}) = -\sin_k(\,i\,)$. $\square$

P3. Euler Formula : $\zeta^{ik} = \cos_k(\,i\,) + j\sin_k(\,i\,)$.

Proof. $\cos_k(\,i\,) + j\sin_k(\,i\,) = \frac{1}{2}(\zeta^{-ik} + \zeta^{ik}) + \frac{1}{2}(\zeta^{ik} - \zeta^{-ik}) = \zeta^{ik}$. $\square$

P4. Addition of Arcs :
     $\cos_k(i + t) = \cos_k(\,i\,)\cos_k(\,t\,) - \sin_k(\,i\,)\sin_k(\,t\,)$,
     $\sin_k(i + t) = \sin_k(\,i\,)\cos_k(\,t\,) + \sin_k(\,t\,)\cos_k(\,i\,)$.

Proof. Clearly $\cos_k(\,i + t\,) = \frac{1}{2}(\zeta^{(i+t)k} + \zeta^{-(i+t)k}) = \frac{1}{2}(\zeta^{(i)k}\zeta^{t)k} + \zeta^{-i)k}\zeta^{-t)k}) =$

$= \frac{1}{2}\{[\cos_k(i) + j\sin_k(i)][\cos_k(t) + j\sin_k(t)] + [\cos_k(i) - j\sin_k(i)][\cos_k(t) - j\sin_k(t)]\}$

$= \cos_k(i)\cos_k(t) - \text{sen}_k(i)\text{sen}_k(t)$.
The proof for the sin(.) function is similar. $\square$

P5. Double arc:

$$\cos_k^2(i) = \frac{1 + \cos_k(2i)}{2}; \qquad \sin_k^2(\,i\,) = \frac{1 - \cos_k(2i)}{2}$$

Proof. According to P4,
$\cos_k(\,2i\,) = \cos_k^2(\,i\,) - \sin_k^2(\,i\,) = \cos_k^2(\,i\,) - [1 - \cos_k^2(\,i\,)] = 2\cos_k^2(\,i\,) - 1$.
The proof for the sin(.) function is similar. $\square$

P6. Symmetry:
     $\cos_k(\,i\,) = \cos_i(\,k\,)$
     $\sin_k(\,i\,) = \sin_i(\,k\,)$.
Proof. Follows directly from definition 2. $\square$

P7. Periodicity: $\cos_k(i + N) = \cos_k(\,i\,)$ e $\sin_k(i + N) = \sin_k(\,i\,)$.

Proof. $\cos_k(\,i + N\,) = \frac{1}{2}(\zeta^{i(k+N)} + \zeta^{-i(k+N)}) = \frac{1}{2}(\zeta^{ik}\zeta^{iN} + \zeta^{-ik}\zeta^{iN}) = \cos_k(\,i\,)$, since the

order of ζ is N. $\square$

P8. Complement:
     $\cos_k(\,i\,) = \cos_k(\,t\,)$ where $itk \neq 0$ and $i + t = N$
     $\sin_k(\,i\,) = -\sin_k(\,t\,)$ where $itk \neq 0$ and $i + t = N$.
Proof.

$$2[\cos_k(\,i\,) - \cos_k(\,t\,)] = (\zeta^{ik} + \zeta^{-ik} - \zeta^{tk} - \zeta^{-tk})\left(\frac{\zeta^{kt}}{\zeta^{kt}}\right) = \zeta^{-ik} - \zeta^{tk} = (\zeta^{-ik} - \zeta^{tk})\left(\frac{\zeta^{-kt}}{\zeta^{-kt}}\right) = 0. \qquad \square$$

P9. $\cos_k(\,i\,)$ summation:

$$\sum_{k=0}^{N-1} \cos_k(i) = \begin{cases} N, i = 0 \\ 0, i \ne 0 \end{cases}.$$

Proof. Let $\sigma := \displaystyle\sum_{k=0}^{N-1} \cos_k(i) = \frac{1}{2}\sum_{k=0}^{N-1} (\zeta^{ik} + \zeta^{-ik})$. If $i = 0$ then $\sigma = N$. Otherwise

$$\sigma = \frac{1}{2}\left[\frac{1(\zeta^i)^N - 1}{\zeta^i - 1} + \frac{1(\zeta^i)^N - 1}{\zeta^i - 1}\right] = \frac{1}{2}[0 + 0] = 0. \qquad \square$$

P10. $\sin_k(i)$ summation:

$$\sum_{k=0}^{N-1} \sin_k(i) = 0.$$

Proof. Let $\sigma := \displaystyle\sum_{k=0}^{N-1} \sin_k(i) = \frac{1}{2j}\sum_{k=0}^{N-1} (\zeta^{ik} - \zeta^{-ik})$. If $i = 0$ then $\sigma = 0$. Otherwise

$$\sigma = \frac{1}{2j}\left[\frac{1(\zeta^i)^N - 1}{\zeta^i - 1} - \frac{1(\zeta^i)^N - 1}{\zeta^i - 1}\right] = \frac{1}{2j}[0 - 0] = 0. \qquad \square$$

A simple example is given to illustrate the behaviour of such functions.

<u>Example 1:</u> Let $\zeta = j$, an element of order 4 in GI(3). The $\cos_k(i)$ and $\sin_k(i)$ functions take the following values in GI(3):

Table 1 – Discrete cosine and sine functions over GI(3).

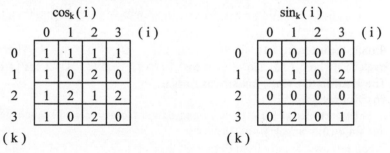

$\cos_k(i)$

(k)	0	1	2	3	(i)
0	1	1	1	1	
1	1	0	2	0	
2	1	2	1	2	
3	1	0	2	0	

$\sin_k(i)$

(k)	0	1	2	3	(i)
0	0	0	0	0	
1	0	1	0	2	
2	0	0	0	0	
3	0	2	0	1	

3. ORTHOGONALITY RELATIONS

The trigonometric functions (definition 2) have interesting orthogonality properties, such as the one shown in lemma 1.

<u>Lemma 1</u>: The k-trigonometric functions $\cos_k(.)$ and $\sin_k(.)$ are orthogonal in the sense that

$$\sum_{k=0}^{N-1} [\cos_k(\angle\zeta^i)\sin_k(\angle\zeta^t)] = 0,$$

where ζ is an element of multiplicative order N in GI(q).

Proof.   From P4, we have $\cos_k(\angle\zeta^i)\sin_k(\angle\zeta^t) = \frac{1}{2}[\sin_k(t + i) + \sin_k(t - i)]$, and

therefore

270

$$\sum_{k=0}^{N-1} [\cos_k(\angle\zeta^i)\sin_k(\angle\zeta^t)] = \frac{1}{2}\sum_{k=0}^{N-1} [\sin_k(t+i) + \sin_k(t-i)].$$

Then, from P10, the result follows. □

A general orthogonality condition, which leads to a new Hartley Transform, is now presented via the $\text{cas}_k(\angle\zeta^i)$ function. The notation used here follows closely the original one introduced in [10].

<u>Definition 3</u>: Let $\zeta \in GI(q)$, $\zeta\neq0$. Then $\text{cas}_k(\angle\zeta^{\,i}) := \cos_k(\angle\zeta^{\,i}) + \sin_k(\angle\zeta^{\,i})$. □

The $\text{cas}_k(.)$ function satisfies properties C1–C5 below:

C1. Addition of Arcs:

   i) $\text{cas}_k(i+t) = \cos_k(i)\,\text{cas}_k(t) + \sin_k(i)\,\text{cas}_k(-t)$.

   ii) $\text{cas}_k(i-t) = \cos_k(i)\,\text{cas}_k(-t) + \sin_k(i)\,\text{cas}_k(t)$.

Proof: i) By definition $\text{cas}_k(i+t) = \cos_k(i+t) + \sin_k(i+t)$, so that from P2 and P4, $\text{cas}_k(i+t) = \cos_k(i)\cos_k(t) - \sin_k(i)\sin_k(t) + \sin_k(i)\cos_k(t) + \sin_k(t)\cos_k(i) =$ $= \cos_k(i)[\cos_k(t) + \sin_k(t)] + \sin_k(i)[\cos_k(-t) + \sin_k(-t)] = \cos_k(i)\text{cas}_k(t) + \sin_k(i)\text{cas}_k(-t)$. □

The proof for (ii) is similar.

C2. Product: $\text{cas}_k(i)\,\text{cas}_k(t) = \cos_k(i-t) + \sin_k(i+t)$

Proof: $\text{cas}_k(i)\,\text{cas}_k(t) = [\cos_k(i)+\sin_k(i)][\cos_k(t)+\sin_k(t)] = \cos_k(i)\cos_k(t)+$ $+\sin_k(i)\sin_k(t) + \sin_k(i)\cos_k(t) + \sin_k(t)\cos_k(i)$, and, from P2 and P4, the result follows.

C3. Symmetry: $\text{cas}_k(i) = \text{cas}_i(k)$

Proof: Direct from P6. □

C4. Quadratic Norm: Let $\text{cas}(\angle\zeta^i)$, with argument $\zeta = \alpha \in GF(q)$. Then

   $[\text{cas}_k(i)]^{q+1} = |\,\text{cas}_k(i)\,|^2 = \cos_k(2i)$.

Proof: With $\text{cas}_k(i) = a+jb$, then $(\text{cas}_k(i))^q = a^q + j^q b^q = a - jb$. Therefore $[\text{cas}_k(i)]^{q+1} = |\,\text{cas}_k(i)\,|^2 = [\cos_k(i)]^2 - [\text{sen}_k(i)]^2 = \cos_k(2i)$ (P1 and P5). □

C5. Periodicity: $\text{cas}_k(i+N) = \text{cas}_k(i)$.

Proof: Direct from P11. □

The set $\{\text{cas}_k(.)\}_{k=0,\,1,\dots,\,N-1}$, can be viewed as a set of sequences that satisfy the following orthogonality property:

<u>Theorem 1.</u> $\displaystyle\sum_{k=0}^{N-1} \text{cas}_k(\angle\zeta^i)\text{cas}_k(\angle\zeta^t) = \begin{cases} N, & i = t \\ 0, & i \neq t \end{cases}$, where ζ has multiplicative

order N.

Proof. From C2 it follows that

$$\sum_{k=0}^{N-1} [\text{cas}_k(\angle\zeta^i)\text{cas}_k(\angle\zeta^t)] = \sum_{k=0}^{N-1} [\cos_k(i-t) + \sin_k(i+t)].$$

Now, using P10, we obtain

$$\sum_{k=0}^{N-1} [\text{cas}_k(\angle\zeta^i)\text{cas}_k(\angle\zeta^t)] = \sum_{k=0}^{N-1} [\cos_k(i-t)], \text{ and, from P9, the result follows. } \square$$

271

4. THE COMPLEX FINITE FIELD HARTLEY TRANSFORM

Let $v = (v_0, v_1, \ldots, v_{N-1})$ be a vector of length N with components over GF(q). The Complex Finite Field Hartley Transform (CFFHT) of v is the vector $V = (V_0, V_1, \ldots, V_{N-1})$ of components $V_k \in GI(q^m)$, given by

$$V_k := \sum_{i=0}^{N-1} v_i \, cas_k(\angle \zeta^i)$$

where ζ is a specified element of multiplicative order N in $GI(q^m)$.

Such a definition extends the definition of the Finite Field Hartley Transform. A signal v and its discrete Hartley spectrum V are said to form a complex finite field Hartley transform pair, denoted by $V = H(v)$ or $v \leftrightarrow V$.

The inverse CFFHT is given by the following theorem.

Theorem 2: The N-dimensional vector v can be recovered from its spectrum V according to

$$v_i = \frac{1}{N(mod\,p)} \sum_{k=0}^{N-1} V_k cas_k(\angle \zeta^i).$$

Proof.

$$v_i = \frac{1}{N(mod\,p)} \sum_{k=0}^{N-1} \sum_{r=0}^{N-1} v_r cas_k(\angle \zeta^r) cas_k(\angle \zeta^i),$$

interchanging the summations

$$v_i = \frac{1}{N(mod\,p)} \sum_{r=0}^{N-1} v_r \sum_{k=0}^{N-1} cas_k(\angle \zeta^r) cas_k(\angle \zeta^i),$$

which, by theorem 1, is the same as

$$v_i = \frac{1}{N(mod\,p)} \sum_{r=0}^{N-1} v_r \begin{Bmatrix} N, & i=r \\ 0, & i \neq r \end{Bmatrix} = v_i. \qquad \square$$

Therefore, as it happens in the continuous Hartley Transform, the CFFHT is symmetrical in the sense that it uses the same kernel for the direct and inverse transforms.

5. CONJUGACY CONSTRAINTS

Theorem 3 states a relation that must be satisfied by the components of the spectrum V for it to be a valid finite field Hartley spectrum, that is, a spectrum of a signal v with GF(q)-valued components.

Theorem 3: The vector $V = \{V_k\}$, $V_k \in GI(q^m)$, is the spectrum of a signal $v = \{v_i\}$, $v_i \in GF(q)$, if and only if $V_k^q = V_{N-kq}$, where indexes are considered modulo N, i, k = 0, 1, ..., N-1 and $N \mid (q^m - 1)$.

Proof: From the CFFHT definition and considering that GF(q), $q = p^r$, has characteristic p, it follows that

272

$$V_k^q = (\sum_{i=0}^{N-1} v_i cas_k(i))^q = (\sum_{i=0}^{N-1} v_i^q cas_k^q(i))$$

If $v_i \in GF(q)\ \forall\ i$, then $v_i^q = v_i$. The fact that $j^2 = -1 \notin GF(q)$ if and only if q is a prime power of the form $4s + 3$, implies that $j^q = -j$. Hence,

$$V_k^q = \sum_{i=0}^{N-1} v_i cas_{N-qk}(i) = V_{N-qk} .$$

On the other hand, suppose $V_k^q = V_{N-qk}$. Then

$$\sum_{i=0}^{N-1} v_i^q cas_{N-qk}(i) = \sum_{i=0}^{N-1} v_i cas_{N-qk}(i)$$

Now, let N-qk = r. Since $GCD(q^m -1, q) = 1$, k and r range over the same values, which implies

$$\sum_{i=0}^{N-1} v_i^q cas_r(i) = \sum_{i=0}^{N-1} v_i cas_r(i)$$

r = 0, 1, ..., N-1. By the uniqueness of the CFFHT, $v_i^q = v_i$ so that $v_i \in GF(q)$ and the proof is complete. □

The cyclotomic coset partition induced by this relation is such that an element and its reciprocal modulo N belong to the same class, which implies that the number of CFFHT components that need to be computed to completely specify the spectrum V is approximately half of the number needed for the Finite Field Fourier Transform.

Example 2 - With q = p = 3, r = 1, m = 5 and $GF(3^5)$ generated by the primitive polynomial $f(x) = x^5 + x^4 + x^2 + 1$, a FFHT of length N = 11 may be defined by taking an element or order 11 (α^{198} is such an element). The vectors v and V given below are an FFHT pair.

$$v = (0, 1, 2, 1, 1, 0, 0, 0, 2, 1, 1)$$
$$V = (0, \alpha^{215} + j\alpha^{46}, \alpha^{241} + j\alpha^{51}, \alpha^{161} + j\alpha^{138}, \alpha^{233} + j\alpha^{96}, \alpha^{239} + j\alpha^{32}, \alpha^{239} + j\alpha^{153},$$
$$\alpha^{233} + j\alpha^{217}, \alpha^{161} + j\alpha^{17}, \alpha^{241} + j\alpha^{172}, \alpha^{215} + j\alpha^{167}).$$

The relation for valid spectra shown above implies that only two components V_k are necessary to completely specify the vector V, namely V_0 and V_1. This can be verified simply by calculating the cyclotomic classes induced by lemma 1 which, in this case, are $C_0 = (0)$ and $C_1 = (1, 8, 9, 6, 4, 10, 3, 2, 5, 7)$.

6. COMPUTING THE CFFHT

A well known transform defined over finite fields is the Finite Field Fourier Transform (FFFT)[1]. Let $v = (v_0 , v_1 , ... , v_{N-1})$ be a vector of length N with components over $GF(q) \subset GI(q)$, $q = p^r$. The FFFT of v is the vector $F = (F_0 , F_1 , ..., F_{N-1})$ of components $F_k \in GF(q^m) \subset GI(q^m)$, given by

273

$$F_k := \sum_{i=0}^{N-1} v_i \alpha^{ki} \ .$$

where α is a specified element of multiplicative order N in $GF(q^m)$. There is a close relation between the FFFT and the FFHT, as it is shown in proposition 2.

<u>Proposition 2</u> - Let $v = \{v_i\} \leftrightarrow V = \{V_k\}$ and $v = \{v_i\} \leftrightarrow F = \{F_k\}$ denote, respectively, a CFFHT and an FFFT pair. Then

$$V_k = \frac{1}{2}\left[(F_k + F_{N-k}) + j(F_{N-k} - F_k)\right] = F_e + jF_o$$

where F_e and F_o denote the even and odd parts of F respectively.

Proof:

$$F_{N-k} = \sum_{i=0}^{N-1} v_i \alpha^{(N-k)i} = \sum_{i=0}^{N-1} v_i \alpha^{-ki} \ ,$$

so that

$$\frac{1}{2}\left[(F_k + F_{N-k}) + j(F_{N-k} - F_k)\right] = \sum_{i=0}^{N-1} v_i \cos_k(\angle\alpha^i) + \sum_{i=0}^{N-1} v_i \sin_k(\angle\alpha^i) =$$

$$= \sum_{i=0}^{N-1} v_i \operatorname{cas}_k(\angle\alpha^i) = V_k \qquad \qquad \square$$

Based on this result an efficient scheme can be devised to compute V as shown below. It is necessary only to compute the FFFT of v, which can be done via a Fast Fourier Transform algorithm.

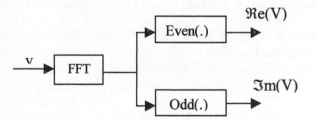

Fig. 1- Computing the CFFHT

The existence of fast algorithms (FFT) for computing the CFFHT is a decisive factor for its real-time applications such as digital multiplexing, which makes it attractive for DSP implementations.

7. CONCLUSIONS

In this paper, a trigonometry for gaussian integers over a Galois field was introduced. In particular, the k-trigonometric functions of the *angle* of the *complex exponential* ζ^i were defined and some of their basic properties derived.

From the $\cos_k(\angle\zeta^i)$ and $\sin_k(\angle\zeta^i)$ functions, the $\mathrm{cas}_k(\angle\zeta^i)$ (cosine and sine) function was defined. It was then shown that the set $\{\mathrm{cas}_k(.)\}_{k=0,\ 1,\dots,\ N-1}$, can be viewed as a set of sequences that satisfy an orthogonality relation, which in turn was used to introduce a new Hartley Transform, the Complex Finite Field Hartley Transform (CFFHT).

Two important relations that have implications as far as the computation of the CFFHT were established. Firstly it was shown that the CFFHT components satisfy the so-called conjugacy constraints, which implies that only the leaders of the conjugacy classes need to be computed. Secondly, a simple relation between the CFFHT and the Finite Field Fourier Transform was established, which meant that FFT type algorithms can be used to compute the CFFHT.

The CFFHT seems to have interesting applications in a number of areas. Specifically, its use in Digital Signal Processing, along the lines of the so-called number theoretic transforms (e.g. Mersenne transforms) should be investigated. In the field of error control codes, the CFFHT might be used to produce a transform domain description of the field, therefore providing, possibly, an alternative to the approach introduced in [6]. Digital Multiplexing is another area that might benefit from the new Hartley Transform introduced in this paper. In particular, new schemes of efficient-bandwidth code-division-multiple-access for band-limited channels based on the FFHT are currently under development.

REFERENCES

[1] J. M. Pollard, *The Fast Fourier Transform in a Finite Field*, Math. Comput., vol. 25, No. 114, pp. 365-374, Apr. 1971.

[2] C. M. Rader, *Discrete Convolution via Mersenne Transforms*, IEEE Trans. Comput., vol. C-21, pp. 1269-1273, Dec. 1972.

[3] I. S. Reed and T. K. Truong, *The Use of Finite Field to Compute Convolutions*, IEEE Trans. Inform. Theory, vol. IT-21, pp. 208-213, Mar. 1975.

[4] R. C. Agarwal and C. S. Burrus, *Number Theoretic Transforms to Implement Fast Digital Convolution*, IEEE Proc., vol. 63, pp. 550-560, Apr. 1975.

[5] I. S. Reed, T. K. Truong, V. S. Kwoh and E. L. Hall, *Image Processing by Transforms over a Finite Field*, IEEE Trans. Comput., vol. C-26, pp. 874-881, Sep. 1977.

[6] R. E. Blahut, *Transform Techniques for Error-Control Codes*, IBM J. Res. Dev., vol. 23, pp. 299-315, May 1979.

[7] R. M. Campello de Souza and P. G. Farrell, *Finite Field Transforms and Symmetry Groups*, Discrete Mathematics, vol. 56, pp. 111-116, 1985.

[8] J. L. Massey, *The Discrete Fourier Transform in Coding and Cryptography*, accepted for presentation at the 1998 IEEE Inform. Theory Workshop, ITW 98, San Diego, CA, Feb. 9-11.

[9] R. N. Bracewell, *The Discrete Hartley Transform*, J. Opt. Soc. Amer., vol. 73, pp. 1832-1835, Dec. 1983.

[10] R. V. L. Hartley, *A More Symmetrical Fourier Analysis Applied to Transmission Problems*, Proc. IRE, vol. 30, pp. 144-150, Mar. 1942.

[11] R. N. Bracewell, *The Hartley Transform*, Oxford University Press, 1986.

[12] J.-L. Wu and J. Shiu, *Discrete Hartley Transform in Error Control Coding*, IEEE Trans. Acoust., Speech, Signal Processing, vol. ASSP-39, pp. 2356-2359, Oct. 1991.

[13] R. N. Bracewell, *Aspects of the Hartley Transform*, IEEE Proc., vol. 82, pp. 381-387, Mar. 1994.

[14] R. M. Campello de Souza, H. M. de Oliveira and A. N. Kauffman, *Trigonometry in Finite Fields and a New Hartley Transform*, Proceedings of the 1998 International Symposium on Information Theory, p. 293, Cambridge, MA, Aug. 1998.

[15] H. M. de Oliveira, R. M. Campello de Souza and A. N. Kauffman, *Efficient Multiplex for Band-Limited Channels*, Proceedings of the 1999 Workshop on Coding and Cryptography - WCC '99, pp. 235-241, Paris, Jan. 1999.

Turbo Coded Image Transmission over Noisy Channels

P. Chippendale, C. Tanriover, B. Honary
Lancaster University

1. Abstract

This paper explores the application of an error resilient coding scheme to image transmission over noisy channels. To improve performance at low signal-to-noise ratios turbo coding is applied. Demonstrated through simulations, this novel combination is shown to correct and restrict errors incurred during transmission over Additive White Gaussian Noise (AWGN) and Rayleigh channels.

2. Introduction

2.1 APEL Coding

Absolute addressed Picture ELement coding (APEL) [1,2] is a lossless, robust image coding system which translates variable sized pixel areas of pre-defined dimensions into independent picture blocks (pels). Each pel is issued with two co-ordinates, x and y, establishing an absolute location with respect to an origin.

As the APEL coding technique operates on a binary level, the encoding of n-bit grey-scale or colour images employs a Bit Plane Coding (BPC) [2] stage. The BPC stage furnishes the APEL encoder with a colour coding sequence to represent a given source image in n binary planes.

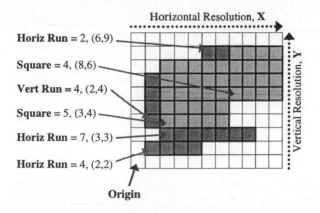

Fig. 1 APEL coded section of an image

Taking each extrapolated binary plane in turn, a recognition algorithm searches through each image looking for square areas of black pixels; starting with large square pels during the first scan, then repeating this process in multiple passes selecting pels of decreasing magnitude. The maximum size of the initial pel is limited according to the anticipated nature of the channel, consequently less information is lost should corruption occur. Once all of the square pels of an efficient size have been removed from the plane, run-lengths of various geometries are used to encode the residue. Fig. 1 illustrates an APEL encoded section of an image. Here, it can be seen how (x,y) co-ordinates are assigned to pels of various geometries.

The data-stream created from this process can be pictured as a succession of (x,y) addresses, grouped according to pel size and interspersed with control symbols (see Fig. 2). These symbols not only serve to provide synchronisation markers, but in addition convey pel geometry metrics to the decoder [2].

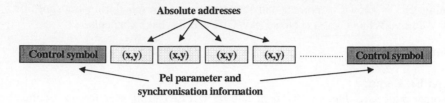

Fig. 2 Breakdown of APEL data stream

The APEL scheme alleviates the need for End Of Line (EOL) symbols and, as each codeword is independent, offers a solution to the problems of horizontal and vertical error propagation. Additionally, as each pel has its own address, it is possible to interleave them within the transmitted data-stream. This versatility can be utilised in many ways, for example: pels pertaining to important image detail can either be dispersed throughout the data-stream or transmitted at the start depending on channel conditions or operator preference.

2.2 Application of Turbo Coding to APEL

Turbo codes [3] are forward error correction schemes which employ concatenated component codes, interleaving and iterative decoding principles to achieve bit error rate performance close to the Shannon limit. Decoding is performed by the sub-optimal log-Maximum Aposteriori Probability (MAP) algorithm [4], which improves the accuracy of the decoded information symbols through a set of iterations where soft extrinsic information is passed between the component decoders.

In this paper, a turbo encoder with parallel concatenation is incorporated into an APEL system. The turbo codec implemented is composed of two recursive systematic convolutional component codes, of rate ½ and constraint length 3. In general, the use of systematic convolutional codes provides robustness against decoding errors by decreasing the minimum free distance of the code. As a consequence of minimising the free distance, the error correction capability of the system improves. It is this feature of systematic convolutional codes that prevents catastrophic error propagation.

It should also be noted that the turbo decoder used in this coding scheme is designed to correct random errors only, hence the majority of burst errors encountered during transmission cannot be corrected.

3. Results

To demonstrate the benefits gained and also to provide benchmarks for comparison, in addition to incorporating turbo coding into an APEL system, we also concatenated the aforementioned turbo coder onto JPEG [5] and bitmap (BMP) file formats. Simulations over AWGN channel, at various signal-to-noise ratios, attest to the excellent performance of the APEL-turbo combination compared to the application of turbo coding onto JPEG and BMP file formats. The results presented in this paper were obtained from simulations conducted using an interleaver length of 8000 bits and 16 decoding iterations.

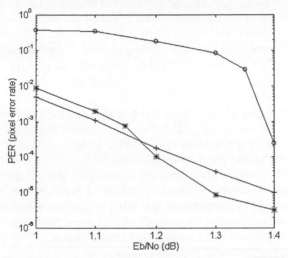

Fig. 3 Turbo coded image transmission over AWGN channel

The calculation of the Pixel Error Rate (PER) in Fig. 3 is performed on a subjective basis. Through the analysis of the ith received pixel's variance from its transmitted value, a measure of visual disturbance, Δ_i, can be quantified as in (1), where t_i and r_i represent the transmitted and received pixel colours respectively, for an n colour image.

$$\Delta_i = \frac{|r_i - t_i|}{n} \qquad (1)$$

From (1) it follows that the PER is calculated as in (2),

$$PER = \frac{1}{XY} \sum_{i=0}^{XY} \Delta_i \qquad (2)$$

where X and Y are the horizontal and the vertical resolution of the image, respectively.

279

As Fig. 3 shows, the performance of the Turbo-JPEG scheme is very poor in the 1.0 – 1.4 dB range. This is due to the inherent fragility of the JPEG structure and its inability to correct or restrict the propagation of any errors.

As expected, the performance of the BMP-turbo scheme is good throughout the range. This results from the complete independence of all pixels from one another. Hence, when errors cannot be repaired by the turbo decoder, only pixels with corrupted bits are affected.

Finally, as Fig. 3 clearly indicates, performance close to, and, as the channel improves, surpassing that of the BMP-turbo model is achieved by the turbo coded APEL. In the region after 1.175 dB, the post-processing techniques employed by APEL [2] recover many of the damaged pixels which could not be corrected in the case of BMP.

To observe the visual impact of data errors, samples of the various file formats have been decoded at a signal-to-noise ratio of 1.175 dB. To provide a qualitative reference for comparison, Fig. 4 also includes an uncoded version of the BMP file transmitted over the same channel.

In this example, although the PER is the same for images 'c' and 'd', the subjective quality of the latter is slightly better. This results from the less frequent and clustered nature of the pixel errors in the APEL image , and the effects can be seen in more detail in the magnified areas of 'c' and 'd'.

Since the APEL image coding scheme is lossless, the compression level relating to the JPEG format was reduced to provide a fair comparison, although even at this minimal level of compression the JPEG image was found to be greatly modified pixel-wise from that of the source. The attained compression ratio for these two formats, APEL and JPEG, was nevertheless still around 3 to 1, offering a substantial reduction over uncompressed BMP data.

Turbo coded JPEG, bitmap and APEL images were also transmitted over a Rayleigh channel with a maximum of 300 burst errors introduced per interleaver block. Figure 5 illustrates the system performance in the presence of burst errors. The uncoded BMP image has also been included to provide an insight into channel conditions. Unlike the Gaussian channel, errors in the more severe Rayleigh case made for unreliable and inconsistent PER plots. It was observed that the dynamic range of the decoded image quality was wide.

Due to the severe effects of burst errors, Turbo-JPEG fails to maintain data integrity and synchronisation after decoding (Fig. 5b). The fragile structure of Huffman coding stage makes it almost impossible to withstand such channel conditions. In addition, since the turbo decoder is unable to correct burst errors, image transmission with Turbo-JPEG becomes very unreliable.

As illustrated in Fig. 5a, channel errors are introduced as both randomly and in bursts. The Turbo-BMP scheme (Fig. 5c) was observed to eliminate the majority of random errors effectively, however burst errors remained uncorrected. In other words, this scheme behaved like a 'burst-pass filter', where erroneous pixels appeared as trails of various lengths after decoding.

Turbo-APEL (Fig. 5d) performance in the presence of burst errors is visually comparable to that of Turbo-BMP (recall that the APEL image has 3:1

compression!). Channel errors which affect pels from various bit planes can be corrected through an analysis of the other planes. In other words, the post-processing techniques introduced by APEL coding provide a powerful means of interpolating pixels using valid image information. Hence, the output of the 'burst-pass filter' can be further processed to correct more pixel errors than in the other cases.

Secondly, the interleaving stage in APEL coding distributes pixel errors across the entire image (Fig. 5d). Visually, small clustered errors are less disturbing to the eye than erroneous pixel trails (Fig. 5c).

4. Conclusions
We have proposed the combination of APEL and turbo coding in order to produce an enhanced image transmission system for low signal-to-noise ratios. Moreover, images 'c' (Fig. 4 and Fig. 5) require more bits to encode and transmit than images 'd' (Fig. 4 and Fig. 5); further underlining the advantages of the APEL turbo scheme outlined here.

Even though APEL coding is used with a Turbo decoder that is not powerful enough to correct burst errors, the second interleaving stage in APEL is seen to minimise the visual impact of errors.

In addition, within the APEL image, whilst the majority of bit errors are corrected via iterative decoding, any which evaded detection (and thus perhaps falsely inserted as erroneous pixels) are restricted as a result of the robust data structure.

The novel combination of source/channel image coding technique, in this case APEL, with additional channel protection provides not only a resilience to Gaussian type errors, but also offers a powerful tool for the restriction and correction of burst errors.

To conclude, this approach can be further explored to develop integrated coding techniques, which could provide more reliable image communication means for noisy channels.

5. Acknowledgements
The authors wish to thank DERA Malvern and NDS Ltd for their financial and technical support.

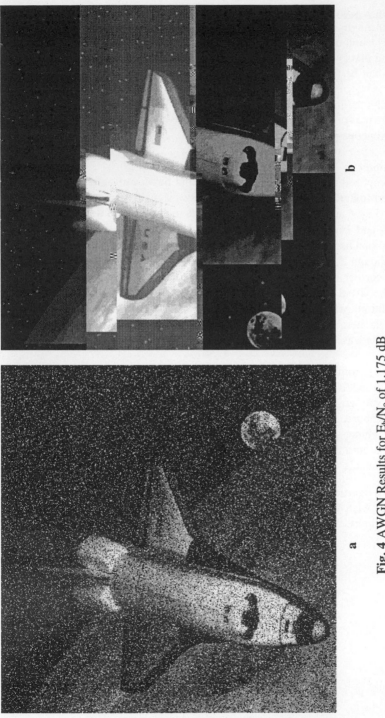

Fig. 4 AWGN Results for E_b/N_o of 1.175 dB
a Uncoded BMP
b Turbo Coded JPEG

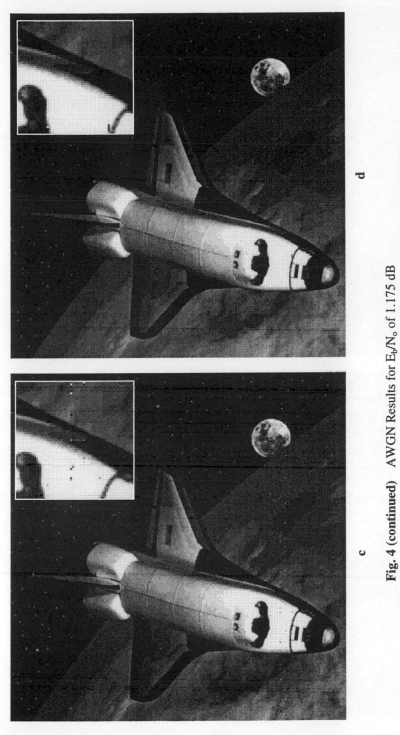

c   d

Fig. 4 (continued)   AWGN Results for E_b/N_o of 1.175 dB

c Turbo Coded BMP
d Turbo Coded APEL

283

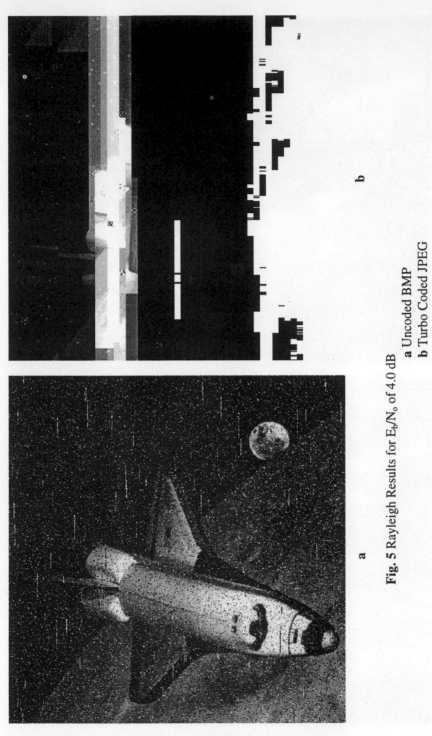

Fig. 5 Rayleigh Results for E_b/N_o of 4.0 dB

a Uncoded BMP

b Turbo Coded JPEG

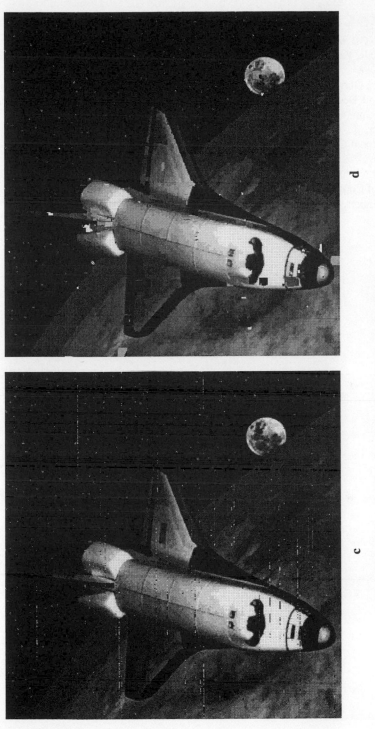

c

d

Fig. 5 (continued) Rayleigh Results for E_b/N_o of 4.0 dB

c Turbo Coded BMP
d Turbo Coded APEL

285

References

1. Chippendale, P., Honary, B., Arthur, P. and Maundrell, M.: International Patent Ref.: PCT GB 98/01877, 'Data Encoding System', 1999 `
2. Chippendale, P.: 'Transmission of images over time-varying channels', PhD Thesis, August 1998
3. Berrou, C., Glavieux, A., Thitimajshima, P.: 'Near Shannon Limit Error Correcting Coding and Decoding: Turbo-Codes', IEEE Proc. ICC '93 Geneva, Switzerland, May 1993, pp. 1064-1070
4. Hagenauer, J., Offer, E., Papke, L.: 'Iterative Decoding of Binary Block and Convolutional Codes', IEEE Transactions on Information Theory, Vol. 42, No. 2, March 1996
5. International Organisation for Standardisation.: 'JPEG Digital Compression and Coding of Continuous-Tone Still Images'. Draft ISO 10918, 1991
6. NewScientist: ' The sky's the limit', No.2193, 03.07.1999, pp. 6

DATA TRANSFER IN THE PIERRE AUGER OBSERVATORY

P.D.J. Clark*, M. Darnell*, A. Bartlett*, V. Tunnicliffe* and A.A. Watson**
*Institute of Integrated Information Systems
**Department of Physics and Astronomy
University of Leeds, Leeds LS2 9JT, UK

Abstract

The Pierre Auger Observatory has been conceived to measure the energy spectrum, anisotropy and mass composition of the highest energy cosmic rays with unprecedented statistical precision. It is envisaged as comprising 2 instruments - one in Mendoza, Argentina, and one in Utah, USA - each with a physical aperture of 3000 km². This paper provides a brief description of the physical basis of the Observatory, together with a description of the communication system designed to allow the necessary data transfers within the Observatory.

1. The Scientific Task of the Observatory

Data currently available on ultra high energy cosmic rays (UHECRs) present an enigma: the most energetic particles observed considerably exceed the cut-off above about 5×10^{19} eV, expected as a result of interactions with the 2.7 K cosmic background radiation. The absence of this cut-off leads to the conclusion that the UHECR sources are relatively near in cosmological terms (<150 million light years). Moreover, the arrival directions of the events are not associated with known nearby energetic objects; in fact, the most consistent hypothesis to date is that the events are isotropic. It is now certain that cosmic rays with energies $>10^{20}$ eV exist, but what type of particles they are, how they acquire their energy, and where they emanate from are all unknown.

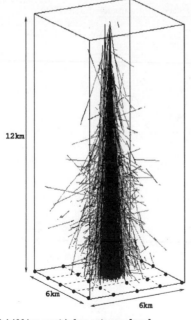

12km

6km

6km

100 billion particles at sea level
photons, electrons (99%), muons (1%)

• Ground Array stations

Figure 1 Shower development

The major objective of the Pierre Auger Observatory (PAO) is to determine the source of such UHECR events and measure their energy spectrum, anisotropy and mass composition. The PAO comprises two instruments - one in the southern hemisphere in Mendoza, Argentina, and the other in the northern hemisphere in Utah, USA. Initially, the southern site is being implemented; the northern site will be implemented at a later date, subject to the output of the southern site and the availability of funding. The complete PAO design is being developed by groups from 19 countries, with a funding requirement of the order of $50M.

A key parameter of the PAO is the effective aperture required to give a reasonable probability of detecting UHECR events. Figure 1 shows the effect of a cosmic ray entering the earth's atmosphere and, by an avalanche of collisions, generating a shower of various types of particles. With high energy events of the type to be detected, this shower can be several kilometres across at the surface of the earth.

Thus, in order to give a reasonable probability of detecting such events (statistically, in a given 1km square, approximately one event would be expected per century), a large aperture detection system must be employed. In the PAO, detector elements covering an area of 3000 km² will be installed at each of the southern and northern sites, corresponding to an average probability of one event per fortnight.

287

A 10^{20} eV shower would typically comprise of the order of 10^{11} particles in total; of these, the electromagnetic particles (electrons, positrons and photons), with a mean energy of about 10 MeV, are approximately 100 times more numerous than the muons, whose mean energy is about 1 GeV. The particles of greatest relevance to the PAO design are those at a distance of more than 1 km from the core of the shower. In the time domain, the shower particles arrive over an interval of several microseconds.

The PAO design incorporates a hybrid detector system comprising 1600 particle detector elements and 3 fluorescence detector elements at each of the two sites. The shower particles will be detected by Cerenkov light produced in water tank surface detectors, each having a surface area of 10 m² and depth of 1.2 m with an efficient diffusely-reflecting lining; the Cerenkov light is then viewed by multiple photomultipliers. The electronic particles incident on the water tanks produce a continuum of small overlapping pulses having the duration of several microseconds mentioned previously, whilst the less numerous muons produce a much smaller number of larger pulses. The muons penetrate the full tank depth, whilst the lower electromagnetic particle energies are almost completely absorbed; thus, analysis of the flash-ADC output derived from the tank allows a reasonable determination of the ratio of the energies of the muonic and electromagnetic components in the shower, and hence an estimation of the nature and mass composition of the primary (causal) event.

The 3 fluorescence detectors will operate on approximately 10% of the events on clear moon-less nights; they will measure the longitudinal development of the shower and provide calorimetric estimates of shower energies by integrating the amount of light observed, since this is related absolutely to the energy dissipated by ionisation in the atmosphere. The surface detector array will be efficient for cosmic rays with energies exceeding 4×10^{19} eV, when 5 detector elements are activated simultaneously. The energy of the primary beam can then be measured to within ± 10%, and its direction to approximately 1.5°. For the 10% of events where simultaneous information is available from both the surface array and the fluorescence detector, the direction can be found to a precision of 0.3°.

2. Data Transfer in the Observatory

Figure 2 is a schematic diagram of the format of the communications infrastructure for the PAO.

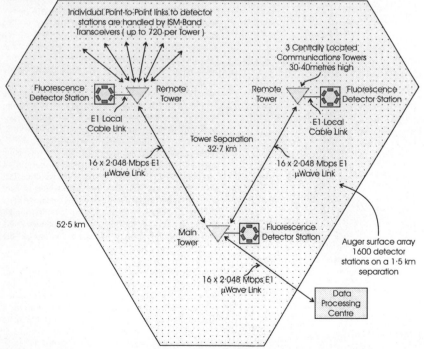

Figure 2 Schematic Layout of a POA Site Communications Infrastructure

The essential requirement of the data transfer system in the PAO is to deliver data from all 1600 detector elements over an area of 3000 km² to the Data Processing Centre (DPC) so that a continuous search for, and analysis of, possible UHECR events can be carried out. It is estimated that a total capacity to the DPC of approximately 2 Mbps is necessary. All data from all detectors must also be time-stamped by means of a Global Positioning System (GPS) receiver co-located with each surface detector

To meet this requirement, the only economically viable means of transfer is line-of-sight radio. A 2-layer hierarchical design has been completed; the two layers are the "concentrator" layer and the "backbone" layer. The concentrator layer is to be implemented by means of a fully customised wireless local area network (WLAN), the transceivers for which are currently under development at the University of Leeds. The concentrator WLAN places a "subscriber" transceiver unit at each surface array detector location, with a number of higher power "base station" units deployed on communications concentrator towers at appropriate locations throughout the array. Each base station unit collects the traffic from up to 80 local subscriber units and forwards it, in a concentrated data stream via the backbone layer, to the DPC.

The backbone layer is a semi-customised design which forwards data from the base station units on the concentrator towers by means of COTS microwave link equipment, thus ensuring that all 1600 surface array detector units are provided with a reliable data link of sufficient capacity to the DPC. The data from the 3 fluorescence detectors is transferred directly by cable to the nearest concentrator tower, where it is multiplexed with the surface array detector data and passed to the DPC. The GPS timing data from all the detector units is also multiplexed with the data and forwarded to the DPC.

An extensive propagation analysis of the southern hemisphere site has been carried out to establish the optimum locations for the concentrator towers, together with the necessary radio frequency (RF) parameters for the transceiver units which will allow the data transfer specification to be met. Figure 3 shows the way in which the communications system interfaces with the data processing sub-system at the DPC.

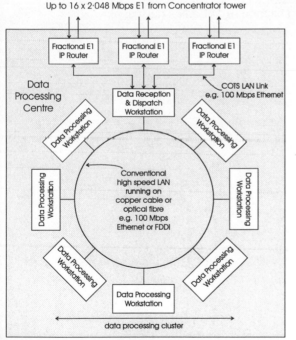

The WLAN transceiver unit is essentially a long-range digital transmitter/receiver system that uses DSP technology to permit a large number of units to co-operate in a digital wireless data network. The design is ruggedised to withstand the wide range of operating conditions likely to be encountered in high-altitude, desert locations. The DSP-based architecture, essentially a software radio, makes extensive use of readily available ICs; it enables flexible configuration of the data formatting, modem, channel codec and synchronisation functions. An operating frequency of 915 MHz in the industrial, scientific and medical (ISM) band has been cleared for use in the observatory. Figure 4 is a simplified schematic diagram of the transceiver unit.

Figure 3 Communications System Interfaces at the DPS

289

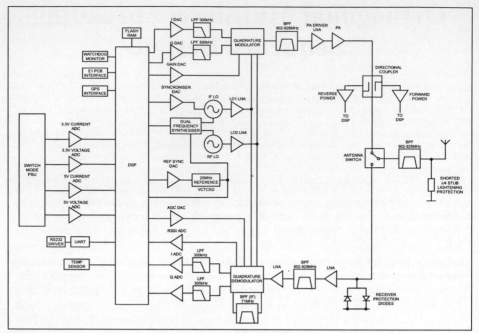

Figure 4 Simplified Schematic Diagram of WLAN Transceiver

Orthogonal Multilevel Spreading Sequence Design

H.M. de Oliveira, R.M. Campello de Souza
CODEC - Communications Research Group
Departamento de Eletrônica e Sistemas - CTG- UFPE
C.P. 7800, 50711-970, Recife-PE, Brazil
E-mail: {hmo,ricardo}@npd.ufpe.br

ABSTRACT

Finite field transforms are offered as a new tool of spreading sequence design. This approach exploits orthogonality properties of synchronous non-binary sequences defined over a complex finite field. It is promising for channels supporting a high signal-to-noise ratio. New digital multiplex schemes based on such sequences have also been introduced, which are multilevel Code Division Multiplex. These schemes termed Galois-field Division Multiplex (GDM) are based on transforms for which there exist fast algorithms. They are also convenient from the hardware viewpoint since they can be implemented by a Digital Signal Processor. A new Efficient-bandwidth code-division-multiple-access (CDMA) is introduced, which is based on multilevel spread spectrum sequences over a Galois field. The primary advantage of such schemes regarding classical multiple access digital schemes is their better spectral efficiency. Galois-Fourier transforms contain some redundancy and only cyclotomic coefficients are needed to be transmitted yielding compact spectrum requirements.

1. INTRODUCTION

Digital multiplex usually concerns Time Division Multiplex (TDM). However, it can also be achieved by Coding Division Multiplex (CDM) which has recently been the focus of interest, especially after the IS-95 standardisation of the CDMA system for cellular telephone [QUAL 92]. The CDMA is becoming the most popular multiple access scheme for mobile communication. Classical multiplex increases simultaneously the transmission rate and the bandwidth by the same factor, keeping thus the spectral efficiency unchanged. In order to achieve (slight) better spectral efficiencies, classical CDMA uses waveforms presenting a nonzero but residual correlation. It is well known that spread spectrum sequences provide multiple-access capability and low probability of interception. We introduce here a new and powerful topic on CDMA techniques that can be implemented along with fast transform algorithms.

In this paper a design of spreading spectrum sequences is introduced which is based upon Galois field Transforms (GFT) such as the Finite Field Fourier Transform (FFFT) introduced by Pollard [POL 71], so they seem to be attractive from the implementation point of view. The FFFT has been successfully applied to perform discrete convolution and image processing [REE et al. 77, REE&TRU 79], among many other applications. In this paper we are concerned with a new finite field version [CAM et al. 98] of the integral transform introduced by R.V.L.

291

Hartley [HAR 42, BRI 92]. More details can be found in the companion paper "The Complex Finite Field Hartley Transform". Alike classical Galois-Fourier transforms [BLA 79], the Finite Field Hartley Transform (FFHT), which is defined on a Gaussian integer set $GI(p^m)$, contains some redundancy and only the cyclotomic coset leaders of the transform coefficients need to be transmitted. This yields new *"Efficient-Spread-Spectrum Sequences for band-limited channels"*. Trade-offs between the alphabet extension and the bandwidth are exploited in the sequel. Tributaries are rather stacked instead of time or frequency interleaved. This paper estimates the *bandwidth compactness factor* relatively to Time Division Multiple Access (TDMA) showing that it strongly depends on the alphabet extension. The synchronous spreading provides a null inter-user interference.

Another point to mention is that the superiority of the spreading spectrum sequences is essentially due to   their low implementation complexity.

2. NEW SYNCHRONOUS MULTILEVEL SPREADING SPECTRUM SEQUENCES

Given a signal v over a finite field, we deal with the Galois domain considering the spectrum V over an extension field which corresponds to the Finite Field Transform (Galois Transform) of the signal v [BLA 79, CAM *et al.* 98]. Let $v = (v_0, v_1, ..., v_{N-1})$ be a vector of length N with components over $GF(q)$, $q = p^r$. (hereafter the symbol := denotes *equal by definition*). The FFFT of v is the vector $F = (F_0, F_1, ..., F_{N-1})$ of components $F_k \in GF(q^m)$, given by

$$F_k := \sum_{i=0}^{N-1} v_i \alpha^{ki},$$

where α is a specified element of multiplicative order N in $GF(q^m)$. The FFHT of v is $V = (V_0, V_1, ... , V_{N-1})$ of components $V_k \in GI(q^m)$, given by

$$V_k := \sum_{i=0}^{N-1} v_i \operatorname{cas}_k(\angle \alpha^i)$$

where α is a specified element of multiplicative order N in $GF(q^m)$. The cas(.) is the Hartley "cosine and sine" kernel defined over a finite field [CAM *et al.* 98].

Each symbol in the ground field $GF(p)$ has duration T seconds. Spreading waveforms can be used to implement an N-user multiplex on the extension field $GF(p^m)$ where $N \mid p^m-1$. For the sake of simplicity, we begin with m=1 and consider a (p-1)-channel system as follows. Typically, we can consider GF(3) corresponding to Alternate Mark Inversion (AMI) signalling.

Definition 1. A Galois modulator (figure 1) carries a pairwise multiplication between a signal $(v_0,v_1,...,v_{N-1})$, $v_i \in GF(p)$ and a carrier $(c_0,c_1,...,c_{N-1})$, with $c_i \in GI(p)$. ∎

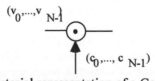

Fig. 1. A pictorial representation of a Galois modulator.

292

A (p-1)-CDM considers, as digital carrier sequences per channel, versions of the cas function $\{cas_i k\}_{k=0}^{p-1}$ over the Galois (complex) field GI(p). The cas (cos and sin) function is defined in terms of finite field trigonometric functions [CAM et al. 98] according to $cas_i k := \cos_i k + \sin_i k$.

carrier 0:

$\{cas_0 0 \ cas_0 1 \ cas_0 2 \ ... \ cas_0(N-1)\}$

carrier 1:

$\{cas_1 0 \ cas_1 1 \ cas_1 2 \ ... \ cas_1(N-1)\}$

...

carrier j:

$\{cas_j 0 \ cas_j 1 \ cas_j 2 \ ... \ cas_j(N-1)\}$

...

carrier N-1:

$\{cas_{N-1} 0 \ cas_{N-1} 1 \ cas_{N-1} 2 ... \ cas_{N-1}(N-1)\}$.

The cyclic digital carrier has the same duration T of an input modulation symbol, so that it carries N slots per data symbol. The interval of each cas-symbol is T/N and therefore the bandwidth expansion factor when multiplexing N channels may be roughly N.

A spread spectrum multiplex is showed in figure 2: The output corresponds exactly to the finite field Hartley Transform of the "user"-vector $(v_0, v_1,...,v_{N-1})$. Therefore, it contains all the information about all channels. Each coefficient V_k of the spectrum has duration T/N.

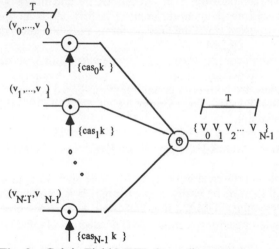

Fig. 2. Galois-Field MUX: Spreading sequences.

These carriers can be viewed as spreading waveforms [MAS 95]. An N-user mux has N spreading sequences, one per channel. The requirements to achieve Welch's lower bound according to Massey and Mittelholzer [MAS&MIT 91] are achieved by $\{cas_i k\}_{k=0}^{p-1}$ sequences. The matrix $[\{cas_i k\}]$ presents both orthogonal rows and orthogonal columns having the same "energy".

3. IMPLEMENTATION OF A SPREADING SPECTRUM SCHEME BY FINITE FIELD TRANSFORMS

3.1 Transform Spreading Spectrum

As an alternative and attractive implementation of the spread spectrum system described in the previous section, the spreading can be carried out by a Galois Field Transform (FFFT/FFHT) of length N | p^m-1 so the de-spreading corresponds exactly to an *Inverse Finite-Field Transform* of length N.

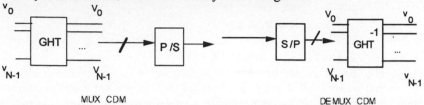

MUX CDM   DEMUX CDM

Fig. 3. Implementation of Galois Field Transform (GFT) spreading spectrum.

Discrete Fourier transforms (DFT) have been applied in the multicarrier modulation schemes [WEIN&EBER 71] referred to as Orthogonal Frequency Multiplexing (OFDM). Although OFDM presents a very similar block diagram regarding GDM [compare fig. 1 in URI&CAR 99 and figure 3 above], the true nature of these schemes is quite different. The first one is an analogue, discrete-time, frequency division while the later performs a digital Galois division, i.e.,

	OFDM	GDM
	Fourier spectrum	*Finite Field Spectrum*
DIVISION	(frequency domain)	(Galois domain)

However, they are both orthogonal transform-based schemes that support fast algorithms (Fast Fourier Transforms) being thus very attractive from the complexity viewpoint.

3.2 Interpreting Galois-Hartley Transform over GF(5) as Spreading Waveforms

A naive example is presented in order to illustrate such an approach. A 4-channel CDMA over GF(5) can be easily implemented. It is straightforward to see that such signals are neither FDMAed nor TDMAed. The GI(5)-valued cas(.) function is shown on Table I assuming α equal to 2, an element of GF(5) of order four.

Table I. Cas function on GI(5) with α=2, an element of order 4.

$cas_0 0 = 1+j0$	$cas_0 1 = 1$	$cas_0 2 = 1$	$cas_0 3 = 1$
$cas_1 0 = 1+j0$	$cas_1 1 = j3$	$cas_1 2 = 4$	$cas_1 3 = 2j$
$cas_2 0 = 1+j0$	$cas_2 1 = 4$	$cas_2 2 = 1$	$cas_2 3 = 4$
$cas_3 0 = 1+j0$	$cas_3 1 = 2j$	$cas_3 2 = 4$	$cas_3 3 = j3$

294

A 4-channel complex spreading waveforms over GF(5) can be chosen as (figure 4):

$\{cas_0k\} = \{1, 1, 1, 1\}$ $\{cas_1k\} = \{1, j3, 4, j2\}$

$\{cas_2k\} = \{1, 4, 1, 4\}$ $\{cas_3k\} = \{1, j2, 4, j3\}$.

If channels number 1, 2, 3, and 4 are transmitting $\{4, 0, 1, 2\}$ respectively, the mux output will be $(2, 3+4j, 3, 3+j)$, which corresponds to

$$\{4,0,1,2\} \otimes \{1,1,1,1\} \equiv 2 \bmod 5$$
$$\{4,0,1,2\} \otimes \{1,j3,4,j2\} \equiv 3+4j \bmod 5$$
$$\{4,0,1,2\} \otimes \{1,4,1,4\} \equiv 3 \bmod 5$$
$$\{4,0,1,2\} \otimes \{1,j2,4,j3\} \equiv 3+j \bmod 5$$

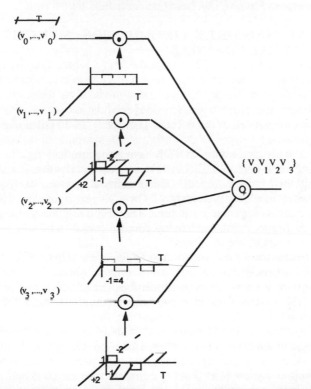

Fig. 4 Interpreting Galois-Hartley Transform over GF(5) as spreading waveforms.

The digital carriers are defined on a complex Galois field GI(p) where the elements may or may not belong to GF(p), although the original definition [CAM et al. 98] considers -1 as a quadratic non-residue in GF(p). Two distinct cases are to be considered: p=4k+1 and p=4k+3, k integer. For instance, considering $j \in GF(5)$ then $2^2 \equiv -1 \pmod 5$ so $j = \sqrt{-1} \equiv 2 \pmod 5$. Two-dimensional digital carriers then degenerated to one-dimensional carriers. Considering the above example, carriers are reduced to Walsh carriers!

$$\{cas_0 k\} = \{1, \ 1, 1, 1\} = \{1,1, 1, 1\}$$
$$\{cas_1 k\} = \{1, \ 1, 4, 4\} = \{1,1,-1,-1\}$$
$$\{cas_2 k\} = \{1, \ 4, 1, 4\} = \{1,-1,1, -1\}$$
$$\{cas_3 k\} = \{1, \ 4, 4, 1\} = \{1,-1,-1, 1\}.$$

In the absence of noise, there is no cross talk from any user to any other one, which corresponds to orthogonal carrier case. Considering the above example, carriers are reduced to Hadamard carriers. Therefore,these spreading sequences can be interpreted as some kind of generalisation (multilevel and 2-dimensional) of classical synchronous orthogonal Hadamard spreading spectrum sequences. There is *no gain* when the transform is taken without alphabet extension. However, we have a nice interpretation of CDM based on finite field transforms.

4. EFFICIENT-BANDWIDTH CODE-DIVISION MULTIPLE ACCESS FOR BAND-LIMITED CHANNELS

The main title of this section is, apart from the term CDMA, literally identical to a Forney, Gallager and co-workers paper issued more than one decade ago [FOR *et al.* 84], which analysed the benefits of coded-modulation techniques. The large success achieved by Ungerboeck's coded-modulation came from the way redundancy was introduced in the encoder [UNG 82]. In classical channel coding, redundant signals are *appended* to information symbols in a way somewhat analogous to time division multiplex TDM (envelope interleaving). It was believed that introducing error-control ability would increase bandwidth. An efficient way of introducing such ability without either sacrificing rate or requiring more bandwidth consists in adding redundancy by an alphabet expansion. This technique is particularly suitable for channels in the narrow-band region. A similar reasoning occurs in the multiplex framework: many people nowadays believe that multiplex must increase bandwidth requirements.

In the present work, the coded-modulation idea [UNG 82] is adapted to multiplex: Information streaming from users is not combined by interleaving (like TDM) but rather by a *signal alphabet expansion*. The mux of users' sources over a Galois Field GF(p) deals with an expanded signal set having symbols from an extension field $GF(p^m)$, $m>1$. As a consequence, the multiplex of N band limited channels of identical maximal frequency B leads to *bandwidth requirements less than* N B, in contrast with TDMAed or FDMAed signals. It is even possible multiplexing without requiring bandwidth expansion or multiplexing with bandwidth compression provides that the signal-to-noise ration is high enough.

So far we have essentially considered Finite Field Transforms from GF(p) to GF(p). Extension fields can be used and results are much more interesting: The Galois-Field Division Multiple Access schemes. The advantage of the new scheme named GDMA over FDMA / TDMA regards its higher spectral efficiency.

The new multiplex is carried out over the Galois domain instead of the "frequency" or "time" domain. As an attractive implementation, the multiplex can be carried out by a Galois Field Transform (FFFT/FFHT) so the DEMUX corresponds exactly to an Inverse Finite-Field Transform of length N | p^m-1. Transform-based multiplexes by spreading spectrum perform as follows. First, the Galois spectrum of N-user GF(p)-signals is evaluated. The spectral compression is achieved by eliminating the redundancy: only the leaders of cyclotomic cosets are transmitted.

Figure 5 exhibits a block diagram of transform-based multiplexes. First, the Galois spectrum of N-user GF(p) signals is evaluated. Demultiplex is carried out (after signal regeneration) first recovering the complete spectrum by "filling" missing components from the received coset leaders. Then, the inverse finite field transform is computed so as to obtain the de-mux signals. Another additional feature is that GDM implementations can be made more efficient if fast algorithms for computing the involved transforms are used.

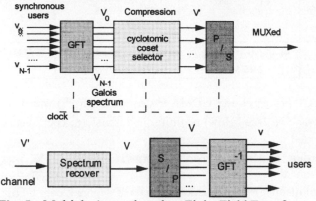

Fig. 5. Multiple Access based on Finite Field Transforms.

Suppose that users data are p-ary symbols transmitted at a speed $B:=1/T$ bauds. Let us think about the problem of multiplexing N users. Traditionally the bandwidth requirements will increase proportionally with the number N of channels, i.e., $B_N = NB$ Hz.

Thereafter the number of cyclotomic cosets associated with a Galois-Fourier (or Galois-Hartley) spectrum is denoted v_F (respectively v_H). The clock driving multilevel (finite field) symbols is N/v times faster than the input baud rate. The bandwidth requirements will be $(N/v)B$ instead of NB.

Definition 2. The bandwidth compactness parameter γ_{cc} is defined as $\gamma_{cc}:=N/v$. ∎

It plays a role somewhat similar to the coding asymptotic gain γ_c on coded modulation [UNG 82].

The processing gain, G, of these multilevel CDMA systems is given by the number of cyclotomic cosets, that is, $G=N/\gamma_{cc}=v$.

Another point that should be stressed is that instead of compressing spectra (eliminating redundancy), it is possible to use all the coefficients to introduce some error-correction ability. The valid spectrum sequences generate a multilevel block code.

Transform-multiplex, i.e., digital multiplex based on finite field transforms are very attractive compared with FDM/ TDM due to their better spectral efficiency as it can be seen in Table II.

Table II. A Spectral Efficiency Comparison for Multiple Access Systems.

	one-user	N-users TDMAed	N-users GDMAed
Transmission Rate	$R_{i-user} = \dfrac{\log_2 p}{T}$	$R = \sum_i R_{i-user} =$ $N\dfrac{\log_2 p}{T}$ bps	$R = \sum_i R_{i-user} =$ $N\dfrac{\log_2 p}{T}$ bps
Bandwidth requirements	$B_1 = \dfrac{1}{T}$ Hz	$B_N = \dfrac{1}{T/N} =$ NB_1 Hz	$B_{GDM} = \dfrac{1}{T/(\gamma_{cc}^{-1}N)}$ $\dfrac{1}{\gamma_{cc}}(NB_1)$ Hz
Spectral Efficiency	$\eta_{i-user} = \log_2 p$ bits/s/Hz	$\eta_{mux} = \log_2 p$ bits/s/Hz	$\eta_{GDM} = \gamma_{cc}\log_2 p$ bits/s/Hz

<u>Proposition 1</u>.   For an N-user GDMA system over $GI(p^m)$ with $N \mid p^m$-1, only a number $v = \gamma_{cc}^{-1}N$ (see below) of finite-field transform coefficients are required to be transmitted.

Proof. According to Mœbius' inversion formula, $I_k(q) = \dfrac{1}{k}\sum_{d \mid k}\mu(d)q^{k/d}$ gives the number of distinct irreducible polynomials of degree k over GF(q), where μ is the Mœbius function [McE 87]. Therefore, the number v_F of cyclotomic sets on the Galois-Fourier transform $(V_0, V_1, ..., V_{N-1})$ is given by $v_F = \sum_{k \mid m}I_k(p)-1$.

Since each pair of cosets containing reciprocal roots is clustered, then

$$v_H = \frac{v_F - (N \bmod 2)}{2} + 1 \cdot \quad\blacksquare$$

As a rule-of-thumb, the number of cosets in the case of block-length $N=p^m$-1 is roughly given by $v_F \approx \left\lceil \dfrac{N}{m} \right\rceil$ and $v_H \approx \left\lceil \dfrac{1}{2}\left\lceil \dfrac{N}{m} \right\rceil + 1 \right\rceil$, where $\lceil x \rceil$ is the ceiling function (the smallest integer greater than or equal to x). A simple example over $GF(3) \rightarrow GI(3^3)$ is presented below: Factoring x^{26}-1 one obtains v_F=10 and v_H=6. For the FFHT, $V_k^3 = V_{26-k\,3}$ (indexes modulo 26) according to [CAM et al. 98, Lemma 1].

FFFT cosets
C0=(0)
C1=(1,3,9)
C2=(2,6,18)
C4=(4,12,10)
C5=(5,15,19)
C7=(7,21,11)

FFHT cosets
C0=(0)
C1=(1,23,9,25,3,17)
C2=(2,6,18,8,24,20)
C4=(4,14,10,22,12,16)
C5=(5,11,19,21,15,7)
C13=(13).

C8=(8,24,20)
C13=(13)
C14=(14,16,22)
C17=(17,25,23).

By way of interpretation, Hartley transforms can be seen as some kind of Digital Single Side Band since the number of cyclotomic cosets of the FFHT is roughly half that of the FFFT. We can therefore say, "*GDM/FFFT is to FDM/AM as GDM/FFHT is to FDM/SSB.*"

Proposition 2. (GDM Gain) The gain on the number of channels GDMed regarding to TDM/FDM over the same bandwidth is N-ν, which corresponds to $g\%:=100(1 - \gamma_{cc}^{-1})\%$.

Proof. The bandwidth gain is $g_{band}=B_{TDM}/B_{GDM} = \gamma_{cc}$ and the saved Bandwidth is given by $B_{TDM} - B_{GDM}$. Calculating how many additional B_1-channels (users) can be introduced:

$$(B_{TDM} - B_{GDM})/B_1 = (1 - \frac{1}{\gamma_{cc}})N. \qquad \blacksquare$$

In the previous example, a 26-user GDM furnishes a 20-channels gain ($\approx 77\%$) regarding to TDM.

What can one tell about the alphabet extension? A simple upper bound on the bandwidth compactness factor can be easily derived. The greatest extension that can be used depends on the signal-to-noise ratio, since the total rate cannot exceed Shannon Capacity over the Gaussian channel. Therefore,

$$B_{GDM}\,\gamma_{cc}\,\log_2 p \leq B_{GDM}\,\log_2\left(1 + \frac{S}{N}\right) \text{ bps, or } \gamma_{cc} \leq \log_p\left(1 + \frac{S}{N}\right).$$

5. CONCLUSIONS

Finite field transforms are offered as a new tool of spreading sequence design. New digital multiplex schemes based on such transforms have been introduced which are *multilevel* Code Division Multiplex. They are attractive due to their better spectral efficiency regarding to classical TDM/CDM which require a bandwidth expansion roughly proportional to the number of channels to be multiplexed. This new approach is promising for communication channels supporting a high signal-to-noise ratio. Although optical fibres are not yet band-limited channels, the new CDM introduced can be adopted on satellite channels or even on cellular mobile communications. Moreover, a Digital Signal Processor (DSP) can easily carry out the Galois-Field Division implementation. A number of practical matters such as imperfect synchronisation, error performance, or unequal user power are left to be investigated. Combined multiplex and error-correcting ability should be investigated. Another nice payoff of GDMA is that when Hartley Finite Field transforms are used, the spreading and de-spreading hardware is exactly the same.

ACKNOWLEDGMENTS
This first author expresses his deep indebtedness to Professor Gérard Battail whose philosophy had a decisive influence on his way of looking to coding and multiplex. The authors also thank Professor Paddy Farrell for his constructive criticism.

REFERENCES

[BLA 79] R.E. Blahut, Transform Techniques for Error Control Codes, *IBM J. Res. Develop*, **23**, n.3, pp. 299-314, May, 1979.

[BRI 92] J. Brittain, Scanning the past: Ralph V.L. Hartley, *Proc. IEEE,* vol.**80**, p. 463, 1992.

[CAM *et al.* 98] R.M. Campello de Souza, H.M. de Oliveira, A.N. Kauffman and A.J.A. Paschoal, "Trigonometry in Finite Fields and a new Hartley Transform", *IEEE International Symposium on Information Theory*, ISIT, MIT Cambridge, MA, THB4: Finite Fields and Appl., p. 293, 1998.
(see http://lids.mit.edu/ISIT98)

[CAM&FAR 85] R.M. Campello de Souza and P.G. Farrell, Finite Field Transforms and Symmetry Groups, *Discrete Mathematics*, **56**, pp. 111-116, Elsevier pub., 1985.

[FOR et al. 84] G.D. Forney Jr, R.G. Gallager, G.R. Lang, F.M. Longstaff and S.U. Qureshi, Efficient modulation for Band-limited channels, *IEEE J. Select. Areas Commun.*, SAC **2**, pp. 632-646, Sept., 1984.

[HAR 42] R.V.L. Hartley, A more symmetrical Fourier analysis applied to transmission problems, *proc. IRE*, vol **30**, pp. 144-150, 1942.

[HON&VET 93] J.J. Hong and M. Vetterli, Hartley Transforms over Finite Fields, *IEEE Trans. Info. Theory*, **39**, n.5, pp.1628-1638,Sept.,1993. Also Computing m DFT's over GF(q) with one DFT over GF(q^m), *IEEE Trans. Info. Theory*, **29**, n.1, pp. 271-274, Jan., 1993.

[MAS 95] J.L. Massey, *Towards an Information Theory of Spread-Spectrum Systems, in: Code Division Multiple Access Communications*, Eds S.G. Glisic and P.A. Leppnen, Boston, Dordrecht and London, Kluwer, pp. 29-46, 1995.

[MAS&MIT 91] J.L. Massey and T. Mittelholzer, Welch's bound and sequence sets for Code-Division-Multiple-Access Systems, *Proc. of Sequences'91*, Springer-Verlag, 1991.

[McE 87] R.J. McEliece, Finite Fields for Computer Scientist and Engineers, Kluwer Ac. Pub., 1987.

[POL 71] J.M. Pollard, The Fast Fourier Transform in a Finite Field, *Math. Comput.*, **25**, pp. 365-374, Apr., 1971.

[QUAL 92] Qualcomm, *The CDMA Network Engineering Handbook*, Qualcomm Inc., San Diego, CA, 1992.

[REE et al. 77] I.S. Reed, T.K. Truong, V.S. Kwoh and E.L. Hall, Image Processing by Transforms over a Finite Field, *IEEE Trans. Comput.*, **26**, pp. 874-881, Sep., 1977.

[REE&TRU 79] I.S. Reed and T.K. Truong, Use of Finite Field to Compute Convolution, *IEEE Trans. Info. Theory*, pp. 208-213, Mar., 1979.

[SIL&SHA 96] C.A. Siller and M. Shafi, Eds., *SONET/SDH: A Sourcebook of Synchronous Networking*, IEEE press, 1996.

[UNG 82] G. Ungerboeck, Channel Coding with multilevel/phase signals, *IEEE Trans. Info. Theory*, IT **28**, pp. 55-67, Jan., 1982.

[URI&CAR 99] R. Uribeetxeberria and R.A. Carrasco, Multicarrier Code Division Multiple Access Schemes for Mobile Radio Communication, *Proc. of the IEE 5th Int. Symp. on Comm. Theory and Appl.*, pp.112-113, Ambleside, 1999.

[WEI&EBER 71] S.B. Weinstein and P.M. Ebert, Data Transmission by Frequency Division Multiplexing using Discrete Fourier Transform, *IEEE Trans. On Comm. Techn.*, COM **19**, n.5, Oct., 1971.

Modelling and Simulation of High Pincount Connector Systems

T. Gneiting and H. Khakzar
Stuttgart University of Applied Sciences, Germany

1   Introduction

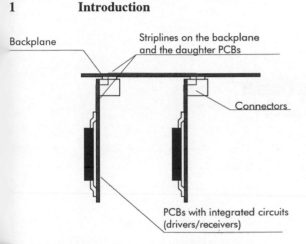

Fig. 1 Backplane of a communication system

- The tremendous increase of the data transmission rate requires the simulation of whole signal paths in communications systems (e.g. ATM switches, Compact PCI buses etc.).
- The signal integrity e.g. the reflections and the cross coupling between different lines must be evaluated.
- The timing requirements must be fulfilled.

Requirements for simulation models

- Macro model for the use in every commercial available SPICE based simulator.
- The model must be evaluated for rise times of 150ps and frequencies up to 3.0GHz.

- ➢ The evaluation includes the transmission and reflection behaviour of single pins and the far and near end crosstalk. All these effects are measured in the time domain with a TDR (time domain reflectometer) and a network analyzer in the freqency domain.
- ➢ The model represents a 5x5 pin matrix of the connector system.
- ➢ The shields on the top and the bottom of the connector are included.

3   **Structure of a SPICE macro model**

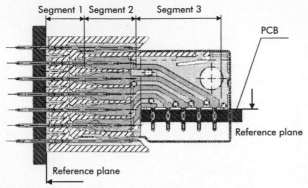

Fig. 2   Cross section of connector

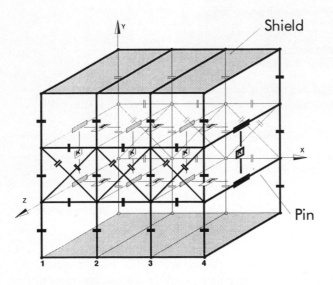

 **Fig. 3   Basic connector segment with 4 rows, 2** 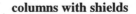 **columns with shields**

> 4 subcircuits for connector segments and series resistance
> Totally 2.500 primitive elements (L,C,R,K)

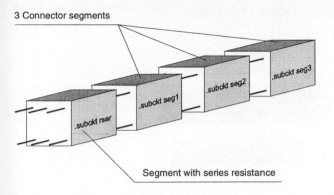

3 Connector segments

.subckt rser

.subckt seg1

.subckt seg2

.subckt seg3

Segment with series resistance

Fig. 4 Modular structure of the connector model

4 Test Structures

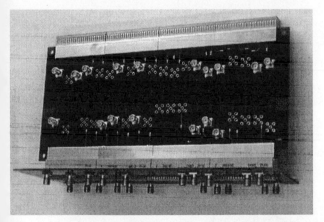

Fig. 5 PCB with 2.0mm metric high pincount connectors

> The high pincount connectors are mounted on multilayer PCBs.
> SMA connectors and microstriplines are used to connect the measurement equipment.
Calibration structures are included to model the parasitics and for de-embedding.

5   **Modelling Procedure**

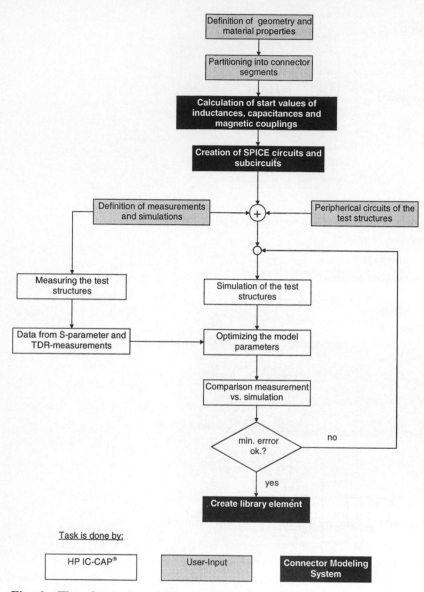

Fig. 6   Flowchart of modelling procedure

Transmission

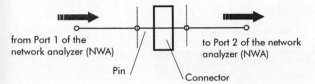

from Port 1 of the
network analyzer (NWA)

to Port 2 of the network
analyzer (NWA)

Pin

Connector

Crosstalk
Near end

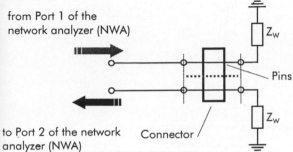

from Port 1 of the
network analyzer (NWA)

Z_W

Pins

to Port 2 of the network
analyzer (NWA)

Connector

Z_W

Far end

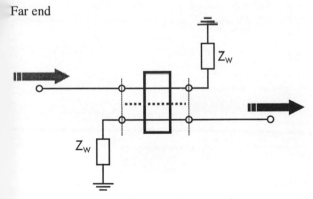

Z_W

Z_W

7 Results

7.1 Transmission through one pin

transmission |S.21|

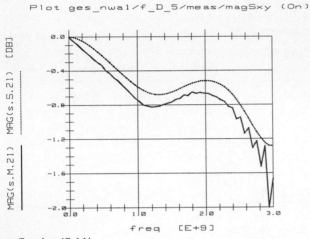

reflection |S.11|

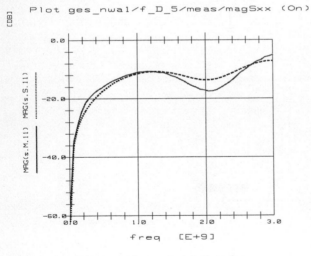

Fig. 7 Measured and simulated data

7.2   Crosstalk between two pins

Pin configuration:

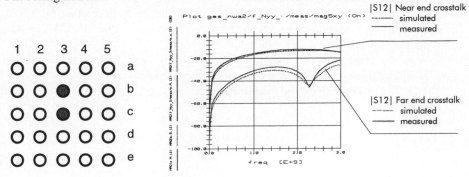

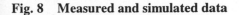

Fig. 8   Measured and simulated data

7.3   Results Time Domain

Crosstalk between two pins

Pin configuration:

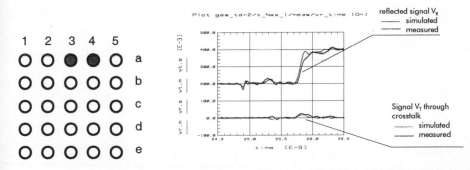

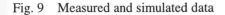

Fig. 9   Measured and simulated data

8   Summary

➤   In this paper, the modelling of a complex passive device - a 2.0mm metric high
     pincount connector was demonstrated.

➤   A program, the "Connector Modelling System" has been developed for a fully
     automatic   creation of structured SPICE netlists and IC-CAP model
     parameter files.

➤   With the created model, the full high frequency behaviour of the connector
     including far end and near end crosstalk can be simulated.

➤   The comparison between measurements and simulations showed good
     agreements.

Low-Complexity Design and Realization of Two-Channel Linear-Phase Biorthogonal FIR Filter Banks: An Algebraic Approach

Min-Chi Kao and Sau-Gee Chen
Department of Electronics Engineering and Institute of Electronics
National Chiao Tung University
Hsinchu, Taiwan, ROC

ABSTRACT

A novel iterative design methodology for two-channel linear-phase biorthogonal FIR filter banks is proposed. This approach builds low-complexity biorthogonal filter banks by simple algebraic composition means, using short half-band filters as basic building elements. The proposed design method, unlike other existing design methods that involve complicated filter optimization procedures, is free of complicated generalized spectral factorization and filter optimization processes. Linear-phase biorthogonal FIR filter banks with good frequency responses and high performance are obtained in only a few iterations. Moreover, the designed filter banks can be realized as a forward multi-stage structure, composed of several short half-band filters and delay elements in cascade and/or parallel forms. Since its building elements are low-complexity and repetitively shared, the overall computational complexity of the structure is very low. Furthermore, the structure is highly modular, repetitive in all stages, in addition, structurally PR under finite-precision realization. As such, the structure is very suitable for VLSI implementation.

1. INTRODUCTION

Recently, discrete perfect-reconstruction (PR) filter banks have gained great popularity in a wide range of applications on video coding, audio coding, communication transmultiplexing, and waveform coding in BPSK and QPSK systems [1-6]. PR filter banks are divided into two categories: paraunitary/orthogonal filter banks and biorthogonal filter banks. For the two-

311

channel case, the linear-phase property is in conflict with the paraunitary property [1-2]. In contrast with orthogonal filter banks, biorthogonal filter banks achieve linear-phase by imposing additional degrees of freedom in the design of linear-phase analysis and synthesis filters.

The generalized spectral factorization technique, one well-known approach for the design of biorthogonal filter banks, is to factorize a long half-band filter into two linear-phase factors and then use them to define analysis and synthesis filter banks. However, the difficulties are that the factorization is sensitive to small changes in zeros on or near the unit circle, multiple zeros particularly, and that finite accuracy of the factorization also destroys PR. Additionally, the existing spectral factorization methods fail easily when the half-band filter to be factorized is long. Two favorable alternatives are lifting scheme [3] and iterative decomposition scheme [4]. However, these schemes require complicated filter optimization.

Another crucial issue commonly encountered in PR filter banks realization is to have high numerical stability in frequency response. For the existing designs, a small change (due to the coefficient quantization) of a single coefficient to be optimized actually causes a global distortion of the overall frequency response. Yet another crucial design issue is to have low computational complexity.

To tackle the mentioned problems, in this paper we take an alternative approach using simple algebraic composition based on entirely short half-band filters. The results are high-performance linear-phase biorthogonal filter banks realized in multi-stage cascade and/or parallel forms, which have low computational complexity and good numerical stability.

The following notations are used for convenience.

$\hat{H}_{hb}(z)$: short linear-phase FIR half-band filter of length $\hat{N}$,

$$\hat{H}_{hb}(z) = 0.5z^{-(\hat{N}-1)/2} + \hat{H}_{hb0}(z^2).$$

k: iteration index.

$H_{hb}^{(k)}(z)$: the kth-iteration linear-phase half-band filter of length $N^{(k)}$,

$$H_{hb}^{(k)}(z) = 0.5z^{-(N^{(k)}-1)/2} + H_{hb0}^{(k)}(z^2).$$

$[H_0^{(k)}(z),\ H_1^{(k)}(z)]$: the kth-iteration linear-phase analysis filter pair of lengths $N_0^{(k)}$ and $N_1^{(k)}$.

2. NEW ITERATIVE DESIGN

Here we propose a new iterative design methodology. The idea is that we combine the design of half-band pair filter banks with the means of algebraic composition. The new iterative construction consists of two following steps:

Step 1. Construct the lowpass filter $H_0^{(k+1)}(z)$.

$$H_0^{(k+1)}(z) \leftarrow H_{hb}^{(k+1)}(z) \equiv H_0^{(k)}(z)H_1^{(k)}(-z).$$

Step 2. Compose the highpass filter $H_1^{(k+1)}(z)$ with $\hat{H}_{hb}(z)$ (or $H_{hb}^{(k+1)}(z)$) and delay elements (to be detailed later).

312

By successive applications of this scheme, we can construct a sequence of low-complexity linear-phase analysis filter pairs $[H_0^{(k+1)}(z),\ H_1^{(k+1)}(z)]$. As shown in Design examples later, such evolved analysis filter pair will be a better pair than its predecessor. Furthermore, starting from a short filter pair with mild constraints on the spectral shapes, a significant improvement in the frequency responses can be obtained in only a small number of iteration times.

It is desired to construct a low-complexity filter pair $[H_0^{(k+1)}(z),\ H_1^{(k+1)}(z)]$. For low complexity, we can refine $H_1^{(k+1)}(z)$ in two modes, as follows.

(*Mode I*). Refine by $\hat{H}_{hb}(z)$:

Provided that

$$\begin{pmatrix} H_0^{(k)}(z) \\ H_1^{(k)}(z) \end{pmatrix} = \begin{pmatrix} 1 & 0 \\ z^{-(\hat{N}-1)/2} - 2\hat{H}_{hb}(z) & z^{-(N_0^{(k)}+\hat{N}-2)/2} \end{pmatrix} \begin{pmatrix} H_{hb}^{(k)}(z) \\ 1 \end{pmatrix} \tag{1}$$

where $H_{hb}^{(k)}(z)$ is entirely composed of identical building elements $\hat{H}_{hb}(z)$ and delay elements.

Define a refined pair

$$H_0^{(k+1)}(z) = H_{hb}^{(k)}(z)H_1^{(k)}(-z), \tag{2}$$

$$H_1^{(k+1)}(z) = z^{-(N_0^{(k)}+\hat{N}-2)} + [z^{-(\hat{N}-1)/2} - 2\hat{H}_{hb}(z)]H_{hb}^{(k)}(z)H_1^{(k)}(-z). \tag{3}$$

The biorthogonality and linear-phase properties are certainly preserved.

From (1), it is easy to see that

$$H_1^{(k)}(-z) = 2z^{-(N_0^{(k)}-1)/2}\hat{H}_{hb}(z) + z^{-(\hat{N}-1)/2}H_{hb}^{(k)}(z) - 2\hat{H}_{hb}(z)H_{hb}^{(k)}(z). \tag{4}$$

Examining (2), (3) and (4), we find that both $H_0^{(k+1)}(z)$ and $H_1^{(k+1)}(z)$ are also entirely composed of identical low-complexity building elements $\hat{H}_{hb}(z)$ and delay elements. Furthermore, the filter pair $[H_0^{(k+1)}(z),\ H_1^{(k+1)}(z)]$ shares $H_{hb}^{(k)}(z)$ and $\hat{H}_{hb}(z)$. Thus the overall computational complexity is substantially reduced. Fig. 1 shows a polyphase realization of two-stage structure, from the kth-iteration to the $(k+1)$th-iteration, in cascade and/or parallel form. The above technique can be extended to arbitrary stage structures.

(*Mode II*). Refine by $H_{hb}^{(k)}(z)$:

Putting more zeros at $\omega = \pi$ for lowpass filter $H_0^{(k+1)}(z)$ and at $\omega = 0$ for highpass filter $H_1^{(k+1)}(z)$ would improve their regularities. In some situations, filter pairs having sharp frequency responses under certain regularities are necessary. Provided that

313

$$\begin{pmatrix} H_0^{(k)}(z) \\ H_1^{(k)}(z) \end{pmatrix} = \begin{pmatrix} 1 & 0 \\ z^{-(N_0^{(k)}-1)/2} - 2H_{hb}^{(k)}(z) & z^{-(N_0^{(k)}-1)} \end{pmatrix} \begin{pmatrix} H_{hb}^{(k)}(z) \\ 1 \end{pmatrix}, \tag{5}$$

we define another refined pair

$$H_0^{(k+1)}(z) = H_{hb}^{(k)}(z)H_1^{(k)}(-z), \tag{6}$$

$$H_1^{(k+1)}(z) = [z^{-(N_0^{(k+1)}-1)/2} - H_0^{(k+1)}(z)][z^{-(N_0^{(k+1)}-1)/2} + 2H_0^{(k+1)}(z)]. \tag{7}$$

The biorthogonality and linear-phase properties are certainly also preserved.

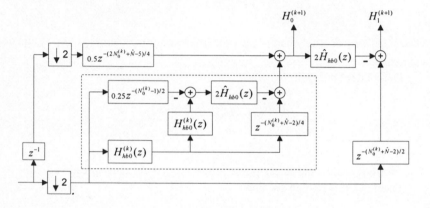

Fig. 1. A polyphase realization of two-stage structure, from the kth-iteration to the $(k+1)$th-iteration.

Note that the new design methodology is nonlinear and different from lifting scheme in construction. The major advantages of the new one over the existing technologies are: (1) simple algebraic construction steps, (2) no filter optimization required, (3) half-band and biorthogonal properties inherent in structure, (4) PR under finite-precision realization, (5) forward multi-stage cascade implementations of high-performance filter banks.

3. DESIGN EXAMPLES

Two filter bank design examples based on Lagrange half-band filters and common FIR half-band filters are simulated as follows.

Design Example 1 (based on a Lagrange half-band filter). Let's choose the shortest Lagrange half-band filter $\hat{H}_{hb}(z) = (1 + 2z^{-1} + z^{-2})/4$ as the building element, and start from the short low-complexity biorthogonal filter pair,

$$H_0^{(0)}(z) = (1 + 2z^{-1} + z^{-2})/4, \; H_1^{(0)}(z) = [-1 + 2z^{-1} - z^{-2}][1 + 4z^{-1} + z^{-2}]/8,$$

which have fairly poor frequency selectivity. The simulated responses of the analysis filters are shown in Fig. 2. In this example, good design results occur by taking only a few iteration times. In addition, the design has a much smaller coefficient dynamic range than a direct-form realization, thus a better numerical property is obtained. Moreover, the resulting multi-stage design is multiplierless.

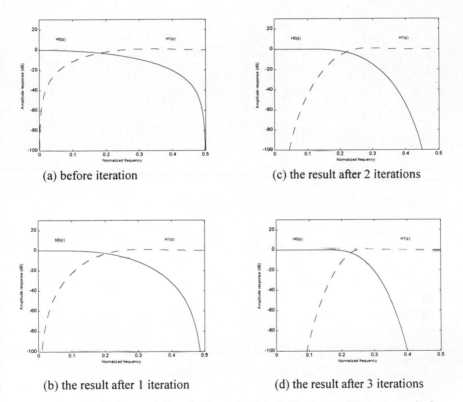

(a) before iteration   (c) the result after 2 iterations

(b) the result after 1 iteration   (d) the result after 3 iterations

Fig. 2 Design of biorthogonal filter banks using Mode-II scheme: (a) responses before iteration, and responses after (b) 1 iteration, (c) 2 iterations, and (d) 3 iterations.

315

Design Example 2 (based on a common FIR half-band filter). This example arbitrarily tries a poor and rough lowpass half-band filter $\hat{H}_{hb}(z)$

$$\hat{H}_{hb}(z) = (-2 + 10z^{-2} + 16z^{-3} + 10z^{-4} - 2z^{-6})/32,$$

which is inferior to the 6th-order Lagrange half-band filter $H_{hb}(z) = (-1 + 9z^{-2} + 16z^{-3} + 9z^{-4} - z^{-6})/32$. The results of the first 3 iterations are demonstrated in Fig. 3. As shown, the responses are getting better with increasing iteration numbers.

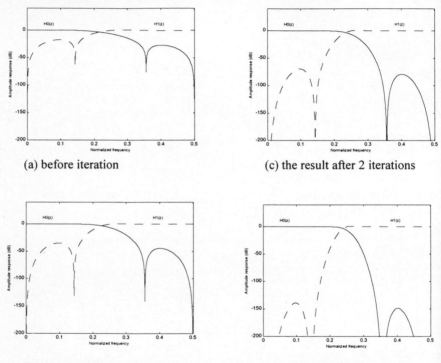

(a) before iteration

(c) the result after 2 iterations

(b) the result after 1 iteration

(d) the result after 3 iterations

Fig. 3 Design of biorthogonal filter banks using Mode-II scheme: (a) responses before iteration, and responses after (b) 1 iteration, (c) 2 iterations, and (d) 3 iterations.

316

4. CONCLUSION

An algebraic approach to the low-complexity design of biorthogonal filter banks was developed. It can be extended to the design of filter banks based on Butterworth IIR half-band filters. It can also be extended to the design of 2-D biorthogonal filter banks, which is under investigation.

References

[1] Vaidyanathan, P. P., *Multirate Systems and Filter Banks*, Prentice-Hall, 1993.

[2] Strang, G. and Nguyen, T. Q., *Wavelets and Filter Banks*, Wellesley-Cambridge, 1996.

[3] Sweldens, W., "The lifting scheme: A custom-design construction of biorthogonal wavelets", *Journal of Appl. and Comput. Harmonic Analysis*, vol. 3, pp. 186-200, 1996.

[4] Pinchon, D. and Siohan, P., "Analysis, design, and implementation of two-channel linear-phase filter banks: a new approach," *IEEE Trans.*, SP-46, (7), pp. 1814-1826, 1998.

[5] C. W. Kim and R. Ansari, "Subband decomposition procedure for quincunx sampling grids," *Proc. SPIE Conf. Visual Commun. And Image Processing,* vol. 1605, pp. 112-123, Boston, MA, Nov. 1991.

[6] M.-C. Kao and S.-G. Chen, "Low-complexity perfect-reconstruction biorthogonal filter banks," submitted for publication.

A Binary Sequence Pair with Zero Correlation Zone Derived from Complementary Pairs

Shinya Matsufuji*, Naoki Suehiro+, Noriyoshi Kuroyanagi*
and Kenji Takatsukasa*

*Saga University, Japan, +Tsukuba University, Japan
*Tokyo University of Technology, Japan

1. INTRODUCTION

For cellular CDMA mobile communication systems, if the base station in a cell transmits a sync signal to users in the cell, synchronization among the users can be controlled within permissible time difference (PTD). Such a system has been called the approximately synchronized CDMA (AS-CDMA) system. The PTD depends on cell size and chip duration of spreading sequences.

Suehiro proposed AS-CDMA system, so that co-channel interference or influence of multipath is entirely free[1]-[4]. It permits use of different orthogonal carriers and the same spreading sequence, which are assigned to the users. The orthogonal carriers, which can remove co-channel interference, can be realized by a signal design, so that within PTD, a spreading sequence has comb-shaped spectrum and a matched filter to recover binary data detects only periodic correlation values. The spreading sequence is constructed by repeats of a periodic one. In order to remove influence of multipath, an orthogonal sequence is used as the periodic one.

The signal design naturally raises a new sequence one for AS-CDMA system with non use of the orthogonal carriers. The AS-CDMA system without co-channel interference nor influence of multipath can be realized by using a sequence set, whose periodic auto/cross-correlation functions take 0 for continuous shifts corresponding to PTD. It is now called as a sequence set with zero correlation zone (ZCZ), or a ZCZ set, shortly.

In this paper we discuss a binary ZCZ pair which is a fundamental ZCZ set. We first explain that a ZCZ set gives AS-CDMA system without co-channel interference nor influence of multipath. We next show that a pair with half length ZCZ is easily derived from a perfect complementary pair [5][6]. It seems to have the maximum ZCZ for binary pairs. As a special case, functions for binary ZCZ pairs of length 2^n are formulated, and it is shown that the ZCZ pairs are also complementary pairs.

2. A ZCZ SEQUENCE SET FOR AS-CDMA SYSTEM

We now consider a binary ZCZ set and its application to AS-CDMA system.

Let $S = \{a, b, \cdots\}$ be a binary sequence set of length N expressed by

$$a = (a_0, \cdots, a_x, \cdots, a_{N-1}), \quad a_x \in \{1, -1\}.$$

319

The periodic correlation function between a and b within S at a shift τ is defined by

$$R_{ab}(\tau) = \sum_{x=0}^{N-1} a_x b_{(x+\tau) \bmod N} = C_{ab}(\tau) + C_{ab}(\tau - N),$$

where $C_{ab}(\tau)$ denotes the aperiodic correlation function expressed by

$$C_{ab}(\tau) = \begin{cases} \displaystyle\sum_{x=0}^{N-1-\tau} a_x b_{x+\tau} & \text{for } 0 \leq \tau < N, \\ \displaystyle\sum_{x=0}^{N-1+\tau} a_{x-\tau} b_x & \text{for } -N < \tau < 0, \\ \qquad 0 & \text{for } |\tau| \geq N. \end{cases}$$

They are regarded as auto-correlation functions for $a = b$ and cross-ones for $a \neq b$.

For asynchronous CDMA systems influence of co-channel interference or multipath must be investigated by use of aperiodic correlation functions. They can not be decided uniquely, and appear high values certainly. But for AS-CDMA system which guarantees synchronization among users within PTD, we can discuss without consideration of them, as follows.

Let $S' = \{a', b', \cdots, \}$ be a binary sequence set of length $N + 2T$ derived from $S = \{a, b, \cdots, \}$ of length N, that each sequence is expressed by

$$a' = (a_{N-T}, \cdots, a_{N-1}, a_0 \cdots, a_{N-1}, a_0, \cdots, a_{T-1}),$$

where T corresponds to PTD. If we use a sequence within the set S' as a spreading sequence, and recover binary information data from correlation between it and one within S, the correlation takes periodic correlation values for shifts, $-T \leq \tau \leq T$, even if binary information data change. And also, if we use a sequence set with $2T$ ZCZ, which satisfies

$$R_{ab}(\tau) = \begin{cases} N & \text{for } \tau = 0, a = b, \\ 0 & \text{otherwise}, \end{cases}$$

for $-T \leq \tau \leq T$, as shown in Fig. 1, the correlation has an impulse response for the shifts.

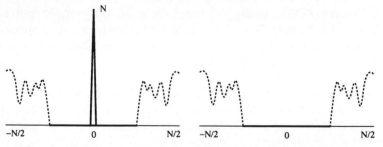

Fig. 1 Periodic auto/cross-correlation properties of a ZCZ set.

This means that the peak value seemingly decreases by $N + 2T$ to N, but co-channel interference or influence of multipath is entirely free. Note that the above method can be applied to both of up-link and down-link.

3. CONSTRUCTION OF A ZCZ PAIR

We now consider a binary ZCZ pair, which is a fundamental ZCZ set.

From exhaustive research we have

Conjecture 1   The maximum ZCZ for binary pairs of length N is half length, i.e., $2T = N/2$.

We give a construction of binary ZCZ pairs satisfying Conjecture 1.

Let $[c, d]$ be a binary complementary pair of length M defined by

$$C_{cc}(\tau) + C_{dd}(\tau) = \begin{cases} 2M & \text{for } \tau = 0, \\ 0 & \text{otherwise.} \end{cases}$$

It is known that a complementary pair of length $M = K2^n$ can be easily derived from one of length $K = 2, 10$, or 26 called a kernel, in order [5][6]. Let $[c', d']$ be a complementary pair of length M derived from $[c, d]$ which is expressed by

$$\begin{aligned} c' &= (d_{M-1}, d_{M-2}, \cdots, d_0), \\ d' &= (-c_{N-1}, -c_{N-2}, \cdots, -c_0). \end{aligned}$$

It is known that a set of $[c, d]$ and $[c', d']$ satisfy

$$C_{cc'}(\tau) + C_{dd'}(\tau) = 0.$$

The set is called a perfect complementary pair.

We have

Theorem 1   Let $\{[c, d], [c', d']\}$ be a perfect complementary pair of length $N/4$. A binary pair of length N given by

$$a = \pm(c, d, c, \bar{d}), \quad b = \pm(c', d', c', \bar{d}'),$$

has $N/2$ ZCZ, where $\bar{x}$ denotes the inversion of a sequence x, i.e., $\bar{x} = -x$.
Proof: Let $C_{x,y}(\tau)$ be the aperiodic correlation function between sequences of length $N/4$, x and y. For $\tau = \pm N/4$, we have

$$R_{ab}(\tau) = C_{cd'}(0) + C_{dc'}(0) + C_{c\bar{d}'}(0) + C_{\bar{d}c'}(0) = 0,$$

since $C_{x\bar{y}}(\tau) = -C_{xy}(\tau)$. Similarly, for $|\tau| < N/4$, we can derive

$$R_{ab}(\tau) = 2(C_{cc'}(\tau) + C_{dd'}(\tau)).$$

From the aperiodic auto/cross-correlation properties of the perfect complementary pairs, we obtain the final result.

QED.

Note that length N is the same as the smallest value for $a_x = a_{x+N}$, i.e., period, since it can be shown that $R_{aa}(\tau) \neq N$ except $\tau = 0$.

We consider functions generating pairs of period $N = 2^n$ with $N/2$ ZCZ, in order to understand the construction in Theorem 1.

Let $\vec{x} = (x_0, x_1, \cdots, x_{n-1}) \in V_n$ be a vector of order n over $GF(2)$, whose elements are coefficients expressed by the binary expansion of an integer $x (0 \leq x \leq N - 1)$, i.e., $x = x_0 2^0 + x_1 2^1 + \cdots + x_{n-1} 2^{n-1}$. The functions $f_n(\vec{x})$ and $g_n(\vec{x})$ are defined by

$$a_x = (-1)^{f_n(\vec{x})}, \ b_x = (-1)^{g_n(\vec{x})},$$

which map V_n to $GF(2)$.

Theorem 2 The binary pair of length $N = 2^n$ with $N/2$ ZCZ given in Theorem 1 is produced by

$$
\begin{aligned}
f_n(\vec{x}) &= x_{i_0} x_{i_1} \oplus \cdots \oplus x_{i_{n-4}} x_{i_{n-3}} \oplus x_{i_0} x_{n-2} \oplus \\
&\quad x_{n-2} x_{n-1} \oplus \alpha_0 x_0 \oplus \cdots \oplus \alpha_{n-2} x_{n-2} \oplus e, \\
g_n(\vec{x}) &= f_n(\vec{x}) \oplus x_{i_{n-3}} \oplus e',
\end{aligned}
$$

where x_{i_j} is an element of $\vec{x} \in V_n$ defined by $x_{i_j} \neq x_{i_k}$ for $0 \leq i_j \neq i_k \leq n-3$, $\alpha_j (0 \leq j \leq n - 2)$ are elements of $GF(2)$ to produce different pairs, e and e' are elements of $GF(2)$ to give the inversion of sequences, and $\oplus$ denotes addition over $GF(2)$, i.e., EXOR.

Proof: From the references [7]-[8], functions for a binary complementary pair $[c, d]$ of length $N/4$ can be written as

$$
\begin{aligned}
\hat{f}_{n-2}(\vec{x}') &= x_{i_0} x_{i_1} \oplus \cdots \oplus x_{i_j} x_{i_{j+1}} \oplus \cdots \oplus x_{i_{n-4}} x_{i_{n-3}} \\
&\quad \oplus \alpha_0 x_0 \oplus \cdots \oplus \alpha_{n-3} x_{n-3} \oplus m, \\
\hat{g}_{n-2}(\vec{x}') &= \hat{f}_{n-2}(\vec{x}') \oplus x_{i_0} \oplus m',
\end{aligned}
$$

where $m, m' \in V_1$, and $\vec{x}' = (x_0, x_1, \cdots, x_{n-3}) \in V_{n-2}$. Let $\bar{x}_{i_k}$ be the inversion of x_{i_k}, i.e., $\bar{x}_{i_k} = 1 \oplus x_{i_k}$. From consideration of the truth table for $f_n(\vec{x})$, we can write

$$
\begin{aligned}
f_n(\vec{x}) &= \bar{x}_{n-2} \bar{x}_{n-1} \hat{f}_{n-2}(\vec{x}') \oplus x_{n-2} \bar{x}_{n-1} \hat{g}_{n-2}(\vec{x}') \\
&\quad \oplus \bar{x}_{n-2} x_{n-1} \hat{f}_{n-2}(\vec{x}') \oplus x_{n-2} x_{n-1} (\hat{g}_{n-2}(\vec{x}') \oplus 1) \oplus l \\
&= x_{n-2} (\hat{f}_{n-2}(\vec{x}') \oplus \hat{g}_{n-2}(\vec{x}')) \oplus \hat{f}_{n-2}(\vec{x}') \oplus x_{n-2} x_{n-1} \oplus l \\
&= \hat{f}_{n-2}(\vec{x}') \oplus x_{n-2} m' \oplus x_{n-2} x_{n-1} \oplus l.
\end{aligned}
$$

Setting $m' = \alpha_{n-2}$ and $e = m + l$ gives $f_n(\vec{x})$ in Theorem 1.

We consider functions for the complementary pair $[c', d']$ of length $N/4$ expressed by $c'_x = d_{N/4-1-x}$ and $d'_x = -c_{N/4-1-x}$. Let $\hat{f}_{n-2}(\vec{x}')$ and $\tilde{g}_{n-2}(\vec{x}')$ be the functions for c' and d', respectively. Since x corresponds to $\vec{x}'$, on the other hand $N/4 - 1 - x$ does to

$$\bar{\vec{x}}' = (\bar{x}_0, \bar{x}_1, \cdots, \bar{x}_{n-3}),$$

322

the function for d' can be given as

$$
\begin{aligned}
\tilde{g}_{n-2}(\vec{x}') &= \hat{f}_{n-2}(\vec{\bar{x}}') \oplus 1, \\
&= (x_{i_0} \oplus 1)(x_{i_1} \oplus 1) \oplus \cdots \oplus (x_{i_{n-4}} \oplus 1)(x_{i_{n-3}} \oplus 1) \\
&\quad \oplus \alpha_0(x_0 \oplus 1) \oplus \cdots \oplus \alpha_{n-3}(x_{n-3} \oplus 1) \oplus m, \\
&= \hat{f}_{n-2}(\vec{x}') \oplus x_{i_0} \oplus x_{i_{n-3}} \oplus l',
\end{aligned}
$$

where $l' = \alpha_0 \oplus \cdots \oplus \alpha_{n-3} \oplus (n-3) \oplus 1$. Similarly, we have

$$
\begin{aligned}
\tilde{f}_{n-2}(\vec{x}') &= \hat{g}_{n-2}(\vec{\bar{x}}'), \\
&= \hat{f}_{n-2}(\vec{x}') \oplus x_{i_0} \oplus l'.
\end{aligned}
$$

As well as the derivation of $f_n(\vec{x})$, we can obtain $g_n(\vec{x})$.

QED.

Theorem 2 shows that the pairs with half length ZCZ are also complementary pairs, since functions for complementary pairs include all for the new pairs.

4. CONCLUSION

We have proposed binary pairs with the maximum ZCZ, which can be applied to AS-CDMA system without co-channel interference nor influence of multipath. We will report sequence sets, which are derived from ZCZ sets, for AS-CDMA systems with high data capacity and non co-channel interference, elsewhere.

ACKNOWLEDGMENT

The authors wish to thank JSPS/NSFC and International Communication Foundation for their support.

REFERENCES

[1] N. Suehiro, "Approximately synchronized CDMA system without co-channel interference using pseudo-periodic sequences," Proceedings of International Symposium on Personal Communications '93-Nanjing, pp.179-184, July 1994.
[2] N. Suehiro, "A signal design without co-channel interference for approximately synchronized CDMA systems," IEEE Journal of Selected Areas in Communications, vol.12, pp. 837-841, June 1994.
[3] N. Suehiro, "Binary or quadriphase signal design for approximately synchronized CDMA systems without detection sidelobe nor co-channel interference," Proceedings of ISSSTA'96, pp.650-653, Sept. 1996.
[4] N. Suehiro, H. Torii, "Quadriphase M-ary CDMA signal design without co-channel interference for approximately synchronized mobile systems," Proceedings of ISCC'98, pp. 110-114, June 1998.
[5] M.J.E.Golay, "Complementary series," IRE Trans. Inform. Theory vol.IT-7, pp.82-87, 1961.

323

[6] P. Fan, M.Darnell, *Sequence design for communieations applications,* Research studies Press LTD, 1997.

[7] J. A. Davis, J. Jedwab, "Peak -to-mean power control in OFDM, Golay complementary sequences and Reed-Muller codes," HP Laboratories Technical Report, HPL-97-158, Dec. 1997.

[8] S. Matsufuji, N. Suehiro, "Functions for even-shift orthogonal sequences," Proceedings of ISCTA'97, pp.168-171, July 1997.

Efficient Turbo Coded ARQ for Low Earth Orbit Microsatellites

Yusep Rosmansyah, Peter Sweeney, Martin N. Sweeting*
Centre for Communication Systems Research (CCSR)
*Surrey Space Centre (SSC)
University of Surrey, Guildford GU2 5XH, U.K.
Tel. (+44 1483) 873606, Fax. (+44 1483) 259504

Abstract — A proposed turbo coded hybrid ARQ designed for UoSAT/SSTL LEO microsatellite downlink communications is presented. The good error correcting capability of turbo codes is incorporated adaptively into the existing PB-ARQ protocol. Throughput of over 84% was shown from simulation at channel bit error rate of $5 \cdot 10^{-3}$, at which the current protocol gives nearly zero.

0.1   Introduction

This paper*assesses the hybridization of turbo codes (TCs) with the PACSAT Broadcast Automatic Retransmission Request (PB-ARQ) currently in use by Surrey Satellite Technology Limited (UoSAT/SSTL) low Earth orbit (LEO) microsatellites for the downlink communication subsystems. It is an improvement to a similar scheme based on convolutional codes [11]. Performance, compatibility, simplicity, and customizability are important design criteria. Therefore, the description is oriented towards optimization of practical constraints and requirements.

Several studies concerning the hybridization of TCs to ARQ have appeared in publications [4, 7, 9, 12]. These are, however, general treatises.

Definition and overview of the existing system will be described in the next section. In Section 0.3, the design of the proposed scheme will be underlined. Simulation results along with brief analysis are presented in Section 0.4. The paper concludes in Section 0.5.

---

*The research was carried out at and supported by Surrey Space Centre, and sponsored by Institut Teknologi Bandung (ITB), Indonesia.

0.2 System Description

0.2.1 Definition

Conventionally, throughput efficiency (for brevity: throughput) is defined as the ratio of the amount of "information" successfully received to the amount of "raw data" received in attempts of transferring the "information". Apart from parity bits for error correction and detection, all other data items are classified as "information", whereas data items allocated for frame synchronizations are not taken into account.

0.2.2 The Existing Protocol and Communication Link Characteristics

The currently operational PB-ARQ can be thought of as a special type of selective repeat (SR-) ARQ. During a file downloading, the receiving ground station maintains a list of the packets that are received erroneously, representing "holes" in the received file, hence the name "hole-filling-ARQ" . The retransmission is not requested until the file transfer is complete. Two nested CRC-16's are used for error detection.

In favor of timing recovery at the receiver, packets are scrambled prior to modulation. There are two undesirable consequences as far as soft-decision error control coding (ECC) is concerned: bit error rate (BER) multiplication effect and the need for soft-decision descrambling (soft-descrambling) .

Note that LEO communication links are established only during passes. A pass — a state where a ground station is under the footprint of the microsatellite — typically lasts for 12-20 minutes and the interval between passes is approximately 4-6 hours. This characteristic will be exploited by properly scheduling the iterations of the TC.

0.3 Scheme Design

The TC used as a mother code in the proposed scheme is that based on parallel concatenation of recursive systematic convolutional (RSC) encoders, pseudorandom interleaver, and maximum a posteriori (MAP) decoders [1]. A TC(1, 35/23, 35/23) is chosen as a result of trade-off among the error correcting capability, complexity, and the ease of handling within a byte-oriented protocol. The simplified MAP decoding algorithm [10] is adopted and modified appropriately. Likewise, as suggested in [5], pseudorandom interleaver and full trellis termination strategies are adopted. Further, taking a constant value of 0.25 for channel noise variance resulted in insignificant degradation in performance.

One solution to overcome the compatibility requirement, the decoding

Table 0.1: Scheme parameters for practical implementation over unscrambled link (Legend: TC_Q16).

Number of retranmissions	0	1	2	3
Max. num. of iterations	0	0.5	6	6
Code rates approx.	1	8/9	8/11	8/15
Puncturing matrices	$\begin{pmatrix} FF \\ 00 \\ 00 \end{pmatrix}$	$\begin{pmatrix} FF \\ 80 \\ 00 \end{pmatrix}$	$\begin{pmatrix} FF \\ 81 \\ 80 \end{pmatrix}$	$\begin{pmatrix} FF \\ 85 \\ A1 \end{pmatrix}$
Effective for BER $\leq$	0	$1 \cdot 10^{-3}$	$5 \cdot 10^{-2}$	$1 \cdot 10^{-1}$

delay of TC, and the delayed-link characteristic of LEO channel is by hybridizing TC into the existing ARQ such that it allows two modes of operation:

1. *Conventional uncoded ARQ mode for transmission session (0th retransmission):* The protocol acts as if there were no added-in capability. This implies the use of uncoded-and-scrambled link. This mechanism is made possible due to the systematic nature of the TCs.

2. *Turbo coded ARQ mode for retransmission session (1st, 2nd, ... n^{th} retransmissions):* The mode of ARQ operation is switched to this mode by the retransmission request from the ground station. No scrambling-descrambling are necessary, since the coded sequences themselves have been inherently scrambled by the RSC encoders. Meanwhile, filling the "holes" is now replaced by retransmitting a portion of the parity corresponding to these erroneous packets.

With regard to the soft-descrambling of the quantized values, the principle of log-likelihood ratio (LLR) summation [3] has been adopted.

Computer search was performed to find a good set of parameters, the result of which is listed in Table 0.1.

0.4 Simulation Results and Discussions

0.4.1 Throughput Performance

Figure 0.1 shows the performance of the proposed scheme. To maintain the compatibility of comparison with other authors, the shown curves are those from simulations without scrambler-descrambler. However, when the scrambler-descrambler are involved, the proposed scheme does also outperform the others. Referring to the legend of the figure from top to bottom, the first two curves labelled by Uncoded and Convol are taken from [11] for comparison. These correspond respectively to the throughput of the uncoded ARQ and the hybrid convolutional coded ARQ with Viterbi decoding and code combining. The remaining two curves are variations of the basic proposed scheme: the

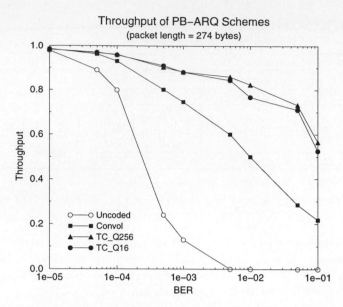

Figure 0.1: Throughput performance of various PB-ARQ schemes simulated over AWGN channels.

third one, TC_Q256, corresponds to the one of which parameters are optimized solely for maximum throughput; and the last one, TC_Q16, is that optimized for the unscrambled channel with the number of quantization levels of demodulator output reduced to 16.

Both variations of turbo coded schemes outperform the rest remarkably. While throughput of the uncoded scheme starts dropping close to 0% at BER 5×10^{-3}, those based on turbo code still give more than 84%.

Similarly, these schemes also give better throughput performance compared to the schemes based on convolutional codes [8] and indirectly [6], block codes [13], or product codes [2]. Comparisons with similar schemes based on TCs require careful analysis, since the authors may use different TC parameters as well as measure of merits. Assuming binary phase shift keying (BPSK) modulation schemes are used and plotting the curve with E_b/N_0 for x-axis, it can be shown that the proposed schemes give better throughput performance than those in [4, 7]. With regard to the similar schemes in [9], comparison is not straightforward, as they use frame error rate (FER) for assessing the performance. The performance of the proposed schemes look slightly better than that in [12], but the TC parameters are different.

0.5   Conclusions

The proposed scheme has shown a promising performance. Further refinement of parameters is possible for the actual implementation and when operational channel characteristic is known.

Bibliography

[1] C. Berrou, A. Glavieux, and P. Thitimajshima, "Near Shannon limit error correcting coding and decoding: Turbo-Codes", *Proc. Int. Conf. Commun. (ICC '93)*, Geneva, Switzerland, pp. 1064-1070, May 1993.

[2] Y. Chang, "A new adaptive hybrid ARQ scheme", *IEEE Trans. Commun.*, vol. 43, no. 7, pp. 2169-2171, July 1995.

[3] J. Hagenauer, "Iterative decoding of binary block and convolutional codes", *IEEE Trans. Info. Theory*, vol. 42, no. 2, pp. 429-445, Mar. 1996.

[4] J. Hamorsky, U. Wachsmann, J.B. Huber, and A. Cizmar, "Hybrid automatic repeat request scheme with turbo codes", *Proc. Int. Symp. on Turbo Codes and Related Topics*, (Brest, France), pp. 247-250, Sept. 1997.

[5] P. Jung and M. Nasshan, "Dependence of the error performance of turbo codes on the interleaver structure in short frame transmission systems", *Elec. Letters*, vol. 30, pp. 287-288, Feb. 17, 1994.

[6] S. Kallel, "Efficient hybrid ARQ protocols with adaptive FEC", *IEEE Trans. Commun.*, vol. 42, no.2/3/4, pp. 281-289, Feb./Mar./Apr. 1994.

[7] J. Li and H. Imai, "Performance of hybrid-ARQ protocols with rate compatible turbo codes", *Proc. Int. Symp. on Turbo Codes and Related Topics*, (Brest, France), pp. 188-191, Sept. 1997.

[8] S. Lin and P.S. Yu, "A hybrid ARQ scheme with parity retransmission for error control of satellite channel", *IEEE Trans. Commun.*, vol. 30, no.7, pp. 1701, July 1982.

[9] K.R. Narayanan and G.L. Stuber, "Turbo decoding for packet data systems", *Proc. IEEE Global Telecommun. Conf. (GLOBECOM), Commun. Theory Mini Conf.*, Nov. 1997.

[10] S.S. Pietrobon and A.S. Barbulescu, "A simplification of the modified Bahl decoding algorithm for systematic convolutional codes", *Proc. Int. Symp. on Info. Theory and Applications*, (Sydney, Australia), pp. 1073-7, Nov. 1994.

[11] Y. Rosmansyah and M. Allery, "Improving the throughput of a low Earth orbit microsatellite protocol", *Proc. Int. Conf. on Inform. Commun. and Sig. Proc. (ICICS)*, vol. 1, pp. 10-14, Singapore, Sept. 1997.

[12] D.N Rowitch and L.B. Milstein, "Rate compatible punctured turbo (RCPT) codes in a hybrid FEC/ARQ system", *Proc. IEEE Global Telecommun. Conf. (GLOBECOM), Mini Conf.*, pp. 55-59, 1997.

[13] A. Shiozaki, "Adaptive type-II Hybrid Broadcast ARQ system", *IEEE Trans. Commun.*, vol. 42, no. 4, pp. 420-422, Apr. 1996.

[14] Y.M. Wang, "A modified selective-repeat type-II hybrid ARQ system and its performance analysis", *IEEE Trans. Commun.*, vol. 31, no. 5, May 1983.

Non-data-aided and decision-directed synchronization of turbo coded modulation schemes

Piotr Tyczka[1] and Stephen G. Wilson[2]

[1]Institute of Electronics and Telecommunications
Poznań University of Technology
ul. Piotrowo 3A, 60-965 Poznań, Poland

[2]Department of Electrical Engineering, University of Virginia
Charlottesville, VA 22903, USA

1.   INTRODUCTION

Introduced in 1993 a new coding technique named turbo codes [1, 2] gained much research and practical interest in recent years. Reported in [1] performance of turbo codes which are capable of approaching the Shannon capacity limit on an AWGN channel using simple constituent codes and a reasonable level of decoder complexity employing an iterative procedure, makes turbo codes attractive for applications in various digital wireless communication systems, including satellite and mobile communications [3].

One of the issues of practical interest for coherent turbo-coded modulation systems is their synchronization. The main difficulty with synchronization comes from the fact that turbo codes are designed to operate in the region of low SNR. Some results on data-aided maximum-likelihood (ML) joint phase and timing synchronization for turbo codes have been reported in [4]. In this paper we deal with carrier phase estimation for turbo-coded BPSK and QPSK signals and study both approaches: non-data-aided (NDA) and decision-directed (DD) synchronization.

The paper is organized as follows. In Section 2 description of the communication system considered and brief turbo coding overview are given. Section 3 presents the Viterbi and Viterbi algorithm [5] for NDA phase recovery and next, in Section 4, a decision-directed synchronizer structure is introduced. Numerical results of the application of these phase recovery schemes to turbo-coded BPSK and QPSK signals are reported and discussed in Section 5. Section 6 contains conclusions.

331

2.   SYSTEM DESCRIPTION

The communication system considered in this paper is shown in Fig. 1. The binary data stream is first differentially encoded and then, in frames of size N, passed to the turbo encoder. The output of the turbo encoder is fed to a BPSK or QPSK modulator. The channel is an AWGN one which introduces an unknown phase shift θ. After the received signal is demodulated, the phase recovery circuit estimates the unknown phase shift and phase correction is made to channel observations which are then fed to the turbo decoder. Finally, the turbo decoder outputs are differentially decoded to obtain the estimates of sent data bits.

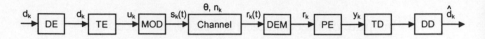

Fig. 1.   Communication system with turbo coding: DE - differential encoder,
TE - turbo encoder, MOD - modulator, DEM - demodulator,
PE - phase estimator, TD - turbo decoder, DD - differential decoder.

Turbo codes [1, 2] are parallel concatenation of recursive systematic convolutional (RSC) codes separated by interleaving stage. Typically, two simple rate-1/2 RSC codes and pseudo-random interleaving are used. In order to achieve desired code rates puncturing of parity bits is done. A turbo encoder operates in a frame-oriented fashion accepting blocks of N data bits, where N is the interleaving size. Additionally, in the scheme of Fig. 1 it is required the turbo code be rotationally invariant to a 180 degree ambiguity for BPSK modulation and to a 90 degree ambiguity for QPSK.

The turbo decoder performs iterative, suboptimal, soft-output decoding procedure which operates in the trellis graphs of the constituent encoders separately, yet shares symbol-likelihood information provided by each constituent decoder. The constituent decoders proceed with a maximum a posteriori (MAP) bit estimation rule.

3.   THE VITERBI AND VITERBI SYNCHRONIZATION ALGORITHM

For M-PSK signals at low SNR when no reliable data estimates exist, NDA approach to carrier phase recovery can be employed. An efficient structure of the NDA carrier synchronizer for M-PSK signals is the Viterbi and Viterbi (V&V) synchronizer [5]. It is a feedforward phase tracking scheme, i.e. the estimate is derived from the received signal before it is corrected in the phase rotator. The structure of the V&V synchronizer is depicted in Fig. 2. The V&V carrier phase estimate is given by:

$$\theta = \frac{1}{M} \arg\left(\sum_{k=1}^{K} F\left(|r_k|\right)\exp(jM \arg(r_k)) \right) \tag{1}$$

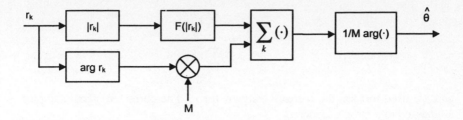

Fig. 2. The Viterbi and Viterbi algorithm for NDA phase recovery.

According to derivations of [5], we have chosen the nonlinear function $F(|r_k|)$ as:

$$F(|r_k|) = |r_k|^2 \qquad (2)$$

to minimize error variance at low SNR.

4. DECISION-DIRECTED SYNCHRONIZER

The decision-directed synchronizer which we consider in this paper is shown in Fig. 3.

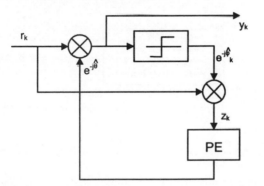

Fig. 3. Decision-directed synchronizer structure: PE - phase estimator.

In this structure, based on received samples r_k tentative decisions on data are made and then used to remove data from the received signal. The phase estimates $\hat{\theta}$ are then obtained from samples z_k using ML rule:

333

$$\hat{\theta} = arctan \frac{\sum\limits_{i=1}^{L} z_{k-i}^{Q}}{\sum\limits_{i=1}^{L} z_{k-i}^{I}} \qquad (3)$$

and are used to form the corrective signal for r_k. The corrected signal samples y_k are passed to a turbo decoder.

5.   NUMERICAL RESULTS AND DISCUSSION

For performance analysis of turbo-coded schemes with considered synchronizers, computer simulations were performed. In Fig. 4 results for BPSK combined with rate-1/2 turbo code with generator 31/37 and block length of 1024 bits are presented. Fig. 5 shows results for the same turbo code combined with QPSK.

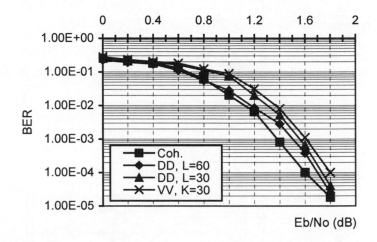

Fig. 4.   BER of turbo-coded BPSK using V&V and DD synchronizers (N=1024).

From the obtained results one may conclude that with sufficient window size of our DD synchronizer (for instance 30 samples for coded BPSK and 60 for coded QPSK in a scheme with block length of 1024 bits) the performance degradation compared to perfect synchronization case is only of 0.1-0.2 dB for BPSK schemes and 0.3-0.4 dB for QPSK schemes at BER=10^{-4}. The V&V synchronizer with comparable window size yields additional loss of 0.1-0.7 dB, depending on the scheme. This degradation is due to greater phase jitter resulting from self-noise.

To verify simulation results, the analysis of cycle slipping in the DD synchronizer was also performed. Fig. 6 shows curves of the number of cycle slips observed for a data block of length 10^6 versus window size of the synchronizer for coded modulation systems of Figs. 4 and 5. It can easily be seen that QPSK requires substantially larger window size compared to BPSK to have similar level

334

of cycle slipping. Moreover, the curve for QPSK decreases with much smaller slope than BPSK. Based on these observations suitable values of window size may be chosen for achieving required performance of coded system. For example, to have almost no cycle slipping for this data block length the BPSK would require window of length 30 samples and QPSK window of length 60 samples. It may be concluded that the cycle slipping analysis confirms performance results obtained and gives indications for DD synchronizer design.

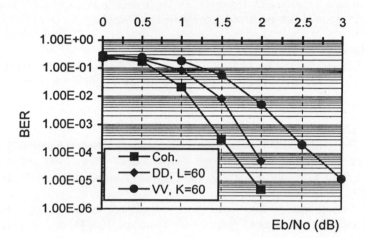

Fig. 5. BER of turbo-coded QPSK using V&V and DD synchronizers (N=1024).

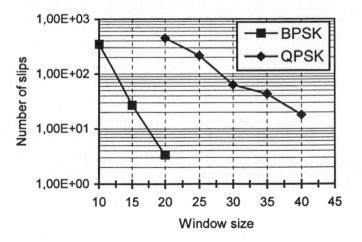

Fig. 6. Number of cycle slips in DD synchronizer for a data block of length 10^6 bits and various window sizes for turbo coded modulation schemes of Figs. 4 and 5.

335

6. CONCLUSIONS

In this paper the study of two phase recovery schemes for turbo-coded signals in the AWGN channel has been conducted. The BER simulation results confirmed the superiority of decision-directed synchronizer over the NDA structure at low SNR where turbo codes operate. In terms of energy penalties versus coherent reception with perfect synchronization, the use of considered DD synchronizer with a reasonable window size incurs only a fraction of dB loss. For the V&V synchronizer with comparable averaging time 0.5-1 dB degradation in error performance is experienced. However, an improvement of the V&V synchronizer performance can be achieved with increasing its window size.

ACKNOWLEDGMENT

This work was done in part while P. Tyczka was on the Fulbright Fellowship in the Department of Electrical Engineering, University of Virginia, Charlottesville, VA, USA.

REFERENCES

[1] C. Berrou, A. Glavieux, and P. Thitimajshima, "Near Shannon limit error-correcting coding and decoding: Turbo codes," *Proc. 1993 IEEE Internat. Conf. on Commun. (ICC'93)*, Geneva, Switzerland, May 1993, pp. 1064-1070.

[2] C. Berrou and A. Glavieux, "Near optimum error correcting coding and decoding: Turbo-codes," *IEEE Trans. Commun.*, vol. 44, pp. 1261-1271, Oct. 1996.

[3] C. Heegard and S. B. Wicker, *Turbo Coding*, Kluwer Academic Publishers, Boston / Dordrecht / London 1999.

[4] L. Lu and S. G. Wilson, "Synchronization of turbo coded modulation systems at low SNR," *Proc. 1998 IEEE Internat. Conf. on Commun. (ICC'98)*, Atlanta, GA, USA, June 1998.

[5] A. J. Viterbi and A. M. Viterbi, "Nonlinear estimation of PSK-modulated carrier phase with application to burst digital transmission," *IEEE Trans. Inform. Theory*, vol. IT-29, pp. 543-551, July 1983.

Polyphase Chirp Sequences for Wireless Applications

Beata J. Wysocki , Tadeusz A. Wysocki
University of Wollongong, School of Electrical, Computer & Telecommunications Engineering, Northfields Avenue, NSW 2522 Australia
email: tad_wysocki@uow.edu.au

1.   INTRODUCTION

There are several families of binary and complex spreading sequences proposed in literature [1], [2], [3], [4], [6], [7], with some of them, e.g. sequences proposed in [6] allowing for a good compromise between mean square aperiodic crosscorrelation and mean square aperiodic autocorrelation for the whole set. There are, however, no clear ways how to chose appropriate values of parameters to achieve the desired spectral characteristics, and to avoid high peaks in crosscorrelation functions (CCFs). In this paper, we propose a method to design a useful set of sequences for DS CDMA wireless data networks. Based on the fact that use of complex spreading codes introduces a phase modulation into the band-pass signal, we look into the properties of sequences obtained on the basis of a linear combination of baseband chirps [9], which are among the analogue signals having very good autocorrelation properties. The similar approach has been used by Popovic [7] in design of his P3 and P4 sequences, utilising a single-chirp like sequence . Here, however, we will look into design of sequences for any given length N. Ability to do so, is very important from the viewpoint of applying such sequences in wireless data networks for variable data rates

2.   CHIRP SEQUENCES

2.1   Design method

Chirp signals are widely used in radar applications for pulse compression [10], and were also proposed for use in digital communications by several authors, e.g. [11]. They refer to creation of such a waveform where an instantaneous frequency of the signal changes linearly between the lower and upper frequency limits. This is

337

graphically illustrated in Figure 1, which presents the two basic types of chirp pulses and their instantaneous frequency profiles.

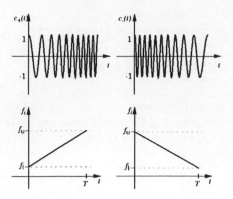

Figure 1: Positive and negative chirp pulses and their instantaneous frequency profiles.

For the positive chirp $c_+(t)$, the instantaneous frequency $f_i(t)$ increases during the pulse duration, according to the formula:

$$f_i(t) = f_l + (f_u - f_l)\frac{t}{T} \tag{1}$$

where f_l and f_u are the lower and the upper frequency limits, respectively, and T is the duration of the chirp pulse. In the case of the negative chirp $c_-(t)$, the instantaneous frequency $f_i(t)$ decreases during the pulse duration, accordingly:

$$f_i(t) = f - (f_u - f_l)\frac{t}{T} \tag{2}$$

Introducing a modulation index h, defined as for binary frequency shift keying (FSK), $h = (f_u - f_l)T = \Delta f T$, we can express $f_i(t); 0 < t \le T$, as:

$$f(t) = \begin{cases} \left[\left(f_c - \dfrac{h}{2T}\right) + \dfrac{ht}{T^2}\right], & \text{for} \quad c_+(t) \\[3mm] \left[\left(f_c + \dfrac{h}{2T}\right) - \dfrac{ht}{T^2}\right], & \text{for} \quad c_-(t) \end{cases} \tag{3}$$

where f_c denotes the central frequency of the chirp pulse, sometimes referred to as the carrier frequency.

Hence, we can describe the waveform $c_+(t); 0 < t \le T$, having an amplitude A, by means of:

$$c_+(t) = A\cos\left[2\pi\int_0^t f_i(\tau)d\tau + \phi_0\right] = A\cos\left[2\pi\int_0^t\left(f_c - \frac{h}{2T} + \frac{h\tau}{T^2}\right)d\tau + \phi_0\right] \quad (4)$$

which after performing an integration yields:

$$c_+(t) = A\cos\left[2\pi\left(f_c - \frac{h}{2T}\right)t + \frac{\pi h t^2}{T^2} + \phi_0\right] \quad (5)$$

By a direct analogy, the $c_-(t)$; $0 < t \le T$ waveform is given by:

$$c_-(t) = A\cos\left[2\pi\left(f_c + \frac{h}{2t}\right)t - \frac{\pi h t^2}{T^2}\phi_0\right] \quad (6)$$

In equations (4), (5), and (6), ϕ_0, being an initial phase value, is a real constant $0 \le \phi_0 < 2\pi$.

Using a bandpass signal notation, and for simplicity assuming $A = 1$, we can express $c_+(t)$ as:

$$c_+(t) = \begin{cases} \exp[j2\pi h q_p(t)]\exp[j(2\pi f_c t + \phi_0)], & 0 < t \le T \\ 0, & \text{otherwise} \end{cases} \quad (7)$$

where $q_p(t)$ is an elementary phase pulse given by [9]:

$$q_p(t) = \begin{cases} \dfrac{t^2}{2T^2} - \dfrac{t}{2T}, & 0 < t \le T \\ 0, & \text{otherwise} \end{cases} \quad (8)$$

Using the same notation, we have:

$$c_-(t) = \begin{cases} \exp[-j2\pi h q_p(t)]\exp[j(2\pi f_c t + \phi_0)], & 0 < t \le T \\ 0, & \text{otherwise} \end{cases} \quad (9)$$

Therefore, the baseband chirp pulses are given by:

$$b_+(t) = \begin{cases} \exp[j2\pi h q_p(t)], & 0 < t \le T \\ 0, & \text{otherwise} \end{cases} \quad (10)$$

$$b_-(t) = \begin{cases} \exp[-j2\pi h q_p(t)], & 0 < t \le T \\ 0, & \text{otherwise} \end{cases} \quad (11)$$

Discretising the analog chirp pulse by substituting n for t, and N for T in (10), we can write a formula defining a complex polyphase chirp sequence

339

$$\left\{ \hat{b}_n(h) \right\} = \left(\hat{b}_n(h); \quad n = 1,2,...,N \right) \tag{12}$$

where:

$$\hat{b}_n(h) = \exp[\, j2\pi h b_n\,], \quad n = 1,2,...,N, \tag{13}$$

$$b_n = \frac{n^2 - 1}{2N^2} \tag{14}$$

and h can take any arbitrary nonzero real value.

Certainly, both periodic and aperiodic autocorrelation functions (ACFs) strongly depend on the value of h. To illustrate this dependency, the plots of magnitudes of aperiodic ACFs for chirp sequences are given in Figure 2 for three values of parameter h.

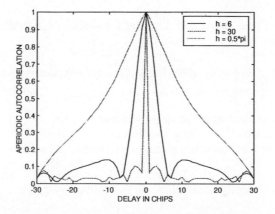

Figure 2: Magnitudes of aperiodic autocorrelation functions for example chirp sequences, $N = 31$.

The chirp sequences exhibit also good crosscorrelation properties for some pairs of parameter h values. This is illustrated in Figure 3, where the magnitude of aperiodic CCF is plotted for an example pair of chirp sequences $(h_1 = 6, h_2 = 30)$.

The main advantage of chirp sequences compared to other known sets of sequences, lies in that we can easily generate the set for any given length N. On the other hand, most of the known sets of sequences can be generated only for a certain values of N. The values of parameter h for the sequences can be optimised to achieve:

    i.   minimum multiaccess interference - by minimising the mean square aperiodic crosscorrelation, R_{CC} [6],

    ii.   the best synchronisability - by minimising the mean square aperiodic autocorrelation R_{AC} [6], *iii.* minimum peak interference - by minimising the maximum value for the aperiodic CCFs, $ACCF_{max}(d)$, over the whole set of the sequences.

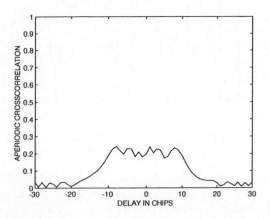

Figure 3: Magnitudes of aperiodic crosscorrelation function between a pair of chirp sequences, $N = 31, h_1 = 6, h_2 = 30$.

Usually, by improving one of the above features the other two need to be compromised. Therefore, while searching for the optimum values of parameter h for the whole set of sequences, the acceptable compromise needs to be achieved.

2.2 Example

Let us design a set of 16 polyphase chirp sequences $\{\hat{b}_n^{(r)}\}$ of length $N = 16$. Because the parameter h can take any real non-zero value, we chose them according to the following pattern[1]

$$h^{(r)} = \begin{cases} (r-9)d, & \text{for} \quad r = 1,2,...,8 \\ (r-8)d, & \text{for} \quad r = 9,10,...16 \end{cases} \tag{15}$$

To find the proper value of d, we then calculate the values of R_{CC}, R_{AC}, and $ACCF_{max}$ for $1 \le d \le 20$ with a step of 0.1, calculated for a single sample per chip. A reasonable compromise can be reached for $d = 7.3$, with $R_{CC}(7.3) = 1.0041$, $R_{AC}(7.3) = 0.7405$, and $ACCF_{max}(7.3) = 0.4824$. For the

---

[1]. Certainly, any other choice can be considered, and may even lead to better performance.

341

comparable set of 16 sequences, i.e. Gold-like sequence set of length $N = 15$, we have the following values: $R_{CC} = 0.9627$, $R_{AC} = 0.7490$, and $ACCF = 0.6000$.

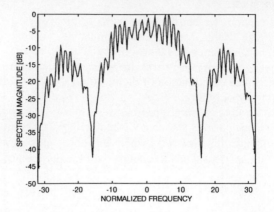

Figure 4: Power spectrum magnitude for signal obtained by spreading a random bipolar signal by the use of the chirp signature of length 16, and parameters h defined by the use of equation (15) with $d = 7.3$, $r = 6$.

Additional comparison of these two sets needs to be done from the viewpoint of spectral characteristics of the sequences. There are several different methods of estimating power spectrum of complex signals. We have decided to use here the nonparametric Welch method to estimate power spectrum of the spread signal. The method is implemented in a standard MATLAB Signal Processing Toolbox as a function *'psd'* [5].

To obtain a good spectral resolution, we simulated random bipolar, {+1, -1}, data sequences of length 64 bits spread by the spreading sequences, and applied sampling of four samples per chip. For other parameters of the *'psd'* function we used MATLAB default parameters [5], i.e.: FFT length - 256, Hanning window of length 256, 50% overlapping. An example plot of the obtained power spectrum is given in Figure 4.

3.   SEQUENCES DESIGNED BY THE USE OF MULTIPLE CHIRPS

3.1   Design method

In the previous section, we showed that using sequences based on the baseband chirp pulses we can design useful sets of spreading sequences of any arbitrary length. Here, we will consider an extension to this idea, i.e. design of sequence sets comprising sequences designed on the basis of baseband chirp pulses of higher order or even the linear combination of them. To do so, we first introduce a definition of the chirp pulse of order s.

A pulse is referred to as a chirp pulse of the order s, if and only if the first time derivative of its instantaneous frequency (the angular acceleration) is a step function with the number of time intervals where it is constant is equal to s. In addition, if the integral of the instantaneous frequency over the duration of the pulse is equal to zero:

$$\int_0^T f_i(t)dt = 0 \qquad (16)$$

then such a pulse is called a baseband chirp pulse of the order s.

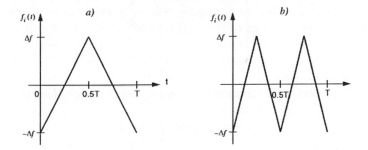

Figure 5: Example baseband chirp pulses of the order: a) 2, b) 4.

As an example, baseband chirp pulses of orders 2 and 4 are shown in Figure 5. The presented pulses are symmetrical, in general however the chirp pulses do not need to be so regular.

The instantaneous frequency function $f_i(t)$ for the chirp pulse of order 2, depicted in Figure 5 is given by:

$$f_i(t) = \begin{cases} \dfrac{4t}{T}\Delta f - \Delta f, & 0 < t \le \dfrac{T}{2} \\ -\dfrac{4t}{T}\Delta f + 3\Delta f, & \dfrac{T}{2} < t \le T \\ 0, & \text{otherwise} \end{cases} \qquad (17)$$

Substituting h/T for Δf and performing integration gives the following expression for the elementary phase pulse $q_p(t)$ for the chirp pulse of order 2:

$$q_p(t) = \begin{cases} \dfrac{2t^2}{T^2}h - \dfrac{th}{T}, & 0 < t \le \dfrac{T}{2} \\[2mm] -\dfrac{2t^2}{T^2}h + 3\dfrac{th}{T} - 1, & \dfrac{T}{2} < t \le T \\[2mm] 0, & \text{otherwise} \end{cases} \tag{18}$$

Substituting n for t, and N for T to discretise the pulse $q_p(t)$ given by equation (18), we obtain the formula for the elements d_n of a normalised ($h = 1$) double chirp sequence $\{d_n\}$:

$$d_n = \begin{cases} \dfrac{2n^2}{N^2} - \dfrac{n}{T}, & 0 < t \le \dfrac{N}{2} \\[2mm] -\dfrac{2n^2}{N^2} + 3\dfrac{n}{N} - 1, & \dfrac{N}{2} < t \le N \\[2mm] 0, & \text{otherwise} \end{cases} \tag{19}$$

The complex double chirp sequence elements $\hat{d}_n$ are therefore given by:

$$\hat{d}_n = \exp[\,j2\pi h d_n\,]; \quad n = 1,2,...,N \tag{20}$$

In the same way, we can find the formula of the elements q_n of a normalised quadruple chirp sequence $\{q_n\}$, corresponding to the chirp pulse of the order 4. The elements q_n are expressed as:

$$q_n = \begin{cases} \dfrac{4n^2}{N^2} - \dfrac{n}{N}, & 0 < t \le \dfrac{N}{4} \\[2mm] -\dfrac{4n^2}{N^2} + 3\dfrac{n}{N} + 1, & \dfrac{N}{4} < t \le \dfrac{N}{2} \\[2mm] \dfrac{4n^2}{N^2} - 5\dfrac{n}{N} - \dfrac{3}{2}, & \dfrac{N}{2} < t \le \dfrac{3N}{4} \\[2mm] \dfrac{4n^2}{N^2} - 7\dfrac{n}{N} - 3, & \dfrac{3N}{4} < t \le N \\[2mm] 0, & \text{otherwise} \end{cases} \tag{21}$$

and the elements of the complex quadruple chirp sequences are given by:

$$\hat{q}_n = \exp[\, j2\pi h q_n \,]; \quad n = 1,2,...,N. \tag{22}$$

Analogically, one can develop the formulae describing any, even irregular, chirp sequences.

Another class of higher order chirp sequences, can be obtained if a superposition of chirp sequences of different orders is used to create the complex polyphase sequence. In the following example, we will show that by using such a superposition we can create sequence sets having better performance.

3.2 Example

Let us consider a set of 16 complex sequences $\{\hat{s}_n^{(r)}\}$, $r = 1,2,...16$, of length 16 obtained by the use of a superposition of a single and double chirp sequences. Therefore, their elements $\hat{s}_n^{(r)} (h_1^{(r)}.h_2^{(r)})$ are given by:

$$\hat{s}_n^{(r)} (h_1^{(r)}.h_2^{(r)}) = \exp[\, j2\pi(h_1^{(r)}b_n + h_2^{(r)}d_n)]; \quad r = 1,...16, n = 1,...16, \tag{23}$$

where the coefficients $h_1^{(r)}$ and $h_2^{(r)}$ can be any real numbers, with the only exception that they cannot be equal both to zero for the same r.

In order to find the acceptable values for the coefficients $h_1^{(r)}$ and $h_2^{(r)}$ for all 16 sequences; let us define them in the following way:

$$h_1^{(r)} = \begin{cases} d_1(r-9), & r = 1,2,...,8 \\ d_1(r-8), & r = 9,10,...16 \end{cases} \tag{24}$$

$$h_2^{(r)} = rd_2, \quad r = 1,2,...,16, \tag{25}$$

and compute the values of $R_{CC}(d_1,d_2)$, $R_{AC}(d_1,d_2)$, and $ACCF_{max}(d_1,d_2)$ with a grid of 0.2.

Since the average mean aperiodic crosscorrelation is generally regarded as the most important parameter from the viewpoint of multiaccess interference in DS CDMA systems, we decided here to choose those values of d_1 and d_2, where the minimum of $R_{CC}(d_1,d_2)$ appears, i.e. $d_1 = 14.2$, and $d_2 = 7.6$.

This results in $R_{CC}(14.2,7.6) = 0.9057$, $R_{AC}(14.2,7.6) = 1.7439$, and $ACCF_{max}(14.2,7.6) = 0.6085$. The full list of corresponding values of $h_1^{(r)}$ and $h_2^{(r)}$ for all 16 sequences is given in Table 1, and the plot of $ACCF_{max}(\tau)$ for $d_1 = 14.2$, and $d_2 = 7.6$ is given in Figure 6.

Table 1: List of the coefficients $h_1^{(r)}$ and $h_2^{(r)}$.

r	$h_1^{(r)}$	$h_2^{(r)}$	r	$h_1^{(r)}$	$h_2^{(r)}$
1	-113.60	7.60	9	14.20	68.40
2	-99.40	15.20	10	28.40	76.00
3	-85.20	22.80	11	42.60	83.60
4	-71.00	30.40	12	56.80	91.20
5	-56.80	38.00	13	71.00	98.80
6	-42.60	45.60	14	85.20	106.40
7	-28.40	53.20	15	99.40	114.00
8	-14.20	60.80	16	113.60	121.60

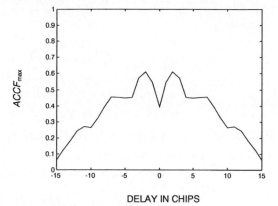

DELAY IN CHIPS

Figure 6: Plot of $ACCF_{\max}(\tau)$ for $d_1 = 14.2$, and $d_2 = 7.6$.

Another important set of characteristics for a spreading sequence set is power spectral densities of signals spread by these sequences. An example plot of the magnitude of power spectrum for signal spread by the sequence $\{\hat{s}_n^{(14)}\}$ is given in Figure 7. The plot was obtained using the same method as described in the previous section.

Further improvement in the value of R_{CC} can be obtained if coefficients $h_1^{(r)}$ and $h_2^{(r)}$ are optimised for all 16 sequences from the viewpoint of reaching minimum of R_{CC}. Several different methods of optimisation can be used for this purpose, and determining which one is the most efficient exceeds the scope of this thesis. To show however, that reduction in R_{CC} is possible, we have applied the Nelder-Meade simplex search implemented in MATLAB as the function *'fmins'* [5], choosing the values given in Table 1 as a starting point.

After completing this optimisation, we were able to achieve $R_{CC} = 0.8441$. However, as expected the gain was counteracted by deterioration in the synchronisability performance due to $R_{AC} = 2.4875$. The list of the optimised coefficients $h_1^{(r)}$ and $h_2^{(r)}$ is given in Table 2.

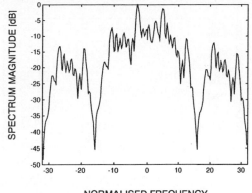

Figure 7: Plots of power spectrum magnitudes for signals obtained by spreading a random bipolar signal by the use of the sequence $\{\hat{s}_n^{(14)}\}$.

Table 2: List of the optimised coefficients $h_1^{(r)}$ and $h_2^{(r)}$.

r	$h_1^{(r)}$	$h_2^{(r)}$	r	$h_1^{(r)}$	$h_2^{(r)}$
1	-112.6513	7.5972	9	13.2249	69.7038
2	-96.7127	15.2773	10	28.2715	78.1511
3	-84.1755	23.5579	11	42.2284	85.7450
4	-71.0210	31.3700	12	57.6174	92.8630
5	-56.8045	36.4517	13	70.2810	98.7896
6	-44.9827	44.2826	14	85.4777	105.8105
7	-27.9950	49.9497	15	96.5492	112.4437
8	-14.5283	63.7458	16	114.0881	121.3066

In Figure 8 we present two example plots of the magnitude of aperiodic CCF between the sequences (1,2) and (1,16), having their parameters $h_1^{(r)}$ and $h_2^{(r)}$ according to Table 2.

Even though the value of $R_{AC} = 2.4875$, the aperiodic ACFs for all of the sequences are still reasonable, exhibiting significant peaks at zero. The example plots of the magnitudes of ACFs for three different sequences are given in Fig. 9.

Certainly, one can optimise the coefficients $h_1^{(r)}$ and $h_2^{(r)}$, to minimise other parameters like R_{AC}. Also, one can choose different starting point for the optimisation.

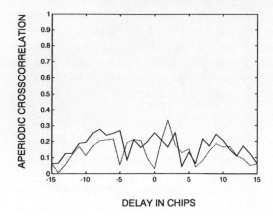

Figure 8: Magnitudes of the aperiodic CCFs between the sequences: (1,2) - solid line, and (1,16) - dotted line, having their parameters $h_1^{(r)}$ and $h_2^{(r)}$ according to Table 2.

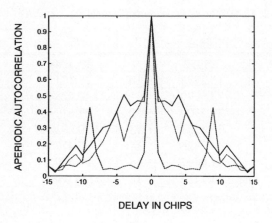

Figure 9: Magnitudes of aperiodic ACFs for $r = 1$, 8 and 16.

4. CONCLUSIONS

In this work we have introduced the new methods of designing polyphase spreading sequences for DS CDMA wireless networks. Both methods are based on application of discretised baseband chirp pulses or pulses containing multiple chirps or even linear combinations of them. The example sets of designed sequences exhibit good correlational properties, which is reflected in the values of mean square aperiodic crosscorrelation, R_{CC}, and mean square aperiodic autocorrelation, R_{AC}. The major benefit of the methods lies in the fact that we can design sequences of any arbitrary length, and optimise their parameters to achieve reasonable level of multiaccess interference and/or good synchronisation properties.

REFERENCES

[1]   P. Fan and M. Darnell: *"Sequence Design for Communications Applications,"* John Wiley & Sons, New York, 1996.

[2]   R.L. Frank: "Polyphase codes with good nonperiodic correlation properties", *IEEE Trans. on Info. Theory*, vol. IT-9, pp.43-45, 1963.

[3]   H. Fukumasa, R. Kohno, and H. Imai: "Design of pseudonoise sequences with good odd and even correlation properties for DS/CDMA", *IEEE Journ. on Selected Areas in Communications*, vol. JSAC-12, pp.828-836, 1994.

[4]   P.V. Kumar and O. Moreno: "Polyphase sequences with periodic correlation properties better than binary sequences", *IEEE Trans. on Info. Theory*, vol. IT-37, 1991.

[5]   MATLAB: *"Signal processing toolbox: user's guide,"* The Math Works, 1996.

[6]   I. Oppermann and B.S. Vucetic: "Complex spreading sequences with a wide range of Correlation Properties", *IEEE Trans. on Commun.*, vol. COM-45, pp. 365-375.

[7]   B.M. Popovic: "GCL polyphase sequences with minimum alphabets", *IEE Electronics Letters*, vol. 30, pp.106-107, 1994.

[8]   M.B. Pursley: "Performance Evaluation for Phase-Coded Spread-Spectrum Multiple-Access Communication - Part I: System Analysis", *IEEE Trans. on Commun.*, vol. COM-25, pp. 795-799, 1977.

[9]   T.A. Wysocki: "Chirp Modulation," in G.Webster ed.: *"Electrical Engineering Encyclopedia"*, John Wiley & Sons, vol.3, February 1999.

[10]   C.E. Cook: "Pulse compression – key to more efficient radar transmission," *Proc. of IRE*, vol.48, pp.310-316, 1960.

[11]   A.K. Elhakeem and A. Targi: "Performance of hybrid chirp/DS signals under Doppler and pulsed jamming," *Proc. of GLOBECOM'89*, vol.3, pp.1618-1623, 1989.

SECTION 3

BROADCASTING

Optimised COFDM waveform and coding schemes for digital terrestrial radio Broadcasting

Cédric DEMEURE, Pierre-André LAURENT,
Thomson-CSF Communications, 66 Rue du Fossé Blanc, 92231 Gennevilliers Cedex, France

Bernard LeFLOCH, Dominique LACROIX
France Telecom/CNET, 4 Rue du Clos Courtel, BP 59, 35512 Cesson Sévigné, France

1. INTRODUCTION

This paper presents a new coherent COFDM (Coded Orthogonal Frequency DeMultiplex) modem for use in high quality audio broadcasting in the frequency bands below 30 MHz, proposed as a candidate to replace the current AM modulation format. The main characteristics of this system are to be compatible with existing channelisation within these bands and with high power transmitter technology. Therefore it should be a better alternative than satellite broadcasting at higher frequencies, while opening the door for much better quality by offering net bit rate compatible with up-to-date audio compression techniques like MPEG 4. Such a broadcasting scheme may even be implemented using existing power transmitters in a transmission mode named Simulcast [2]. This mode consists in transmitting a program in a given frequency channel by using simultaneously the new digital signal and an AM compatible analogue waveform.

This broadcasting system is currently elaborated within the NADIB consortium (European Eureka 1559 project : NArrow Band DIgital Broad-casting) and within the DRM consortium (Digital Radio Mondiale) as a candidate for international normalisation at ITU. Real transmission on a 100 kW short wave transmitter was demonstrated at the 1997 IBC conference in Amsterdam.

Thomcast, Thomson-CSF Communications and France Telecom-CCETT are working together on designing such a broadcasting system and are proposing it as a candidate to be used world wide as a new high quality sound broadcasting system [2]. Recently an agreement with Deutsche Telecom was reached to propose and optimise within DRM a single solution based on OFDM. A wider expert group is currently optimising the proposed solution and studying various additional features (alternate frequency search, better coding scheme, multiplexing, ...). Such a standard should speed up acceptance of this new technology and renew interest in terrestrial radio broadcasting at frequencies below 30 MHz.

Going for digital broadcasting allows the introduction of new services such as program associated data (PAD), RDS type alternative frequency management,

353

single frequency network (SFN), simultaneous data channels for various services such as picture transmission, etc.

The system has been designed taking into account a number of constraints, among which are : short access time, maximum quality in the allowed transmission bandwidth, robustness against distortions (multipaths, doppler, noise, …), parametrability and flexibility (including operating modes that can be used in the transition phase where simultaneous broadcasting-Simulcast- of an AM compatible signal is required), minimum disturbance of AM users, low receiver complexity, user-friendly system (not necessary to be an HF specialist), graceful degradation, …

The paper is organised as follows : section 2 describes the system architecture and main features, section 3 gives a view of some variations, section 5 contains performance evaluations together with the description of the simulators used (propagation and transmitter) and finally section 6 details the existing demonstrator. Finally some concluding remarks and future work close this paper.

2. SYSTEM DESCRIPTION

The proposed system is based upon a multicarrier modulation (OFDM) [1]: it can be seen as a regular juxtaposition in the frequency domain of K elementary narrow band modems (carriers), each of them conveying a bit rate of D/K if D is the overall bitrate of the system. This choice comes from the very good robustness of such a waveform when a high spectral efficiency is necessary while at the same time severe propagation conditions must be endured. Similar choices were made for higher frequency terrestrial radio broadcasting (DAB [8]) and TV broadcasting (DVB-T [9]) in Europe.

This leads to an optimum occupancy of the available bandwidth since the frequency spectrum of the signal is (almost) rectangular. This is possible because the signal conveyed by each carrier is orthogonal to the others. This property enables the signal conveyed by the different carriers to be separable, even if the narrow band carrier spectra overlap. The adjustment of the system bandwidth is obtained *via* the modification of the number K of carriers, without any other change, especially at the receiver hardware and software level.

The following definitions are used hereafter : the system conveys symbols that are located at known instants and frequencies. A carrier is the set of symbols that are located at the same frequency. A frame is the set of symbols that are synchronously transmitted on all the used carriers. Hence, the number of symbols in a frame is the number of used carriers. The frames are grouped in a complete pattern which appears periodically with the same format, i.e. the same repartition of references and useful symbols. The short access time is obtained by means of a few dedicated carriers that the receiver looks for in a first step for fast frequency synchronisation. In addition, another set of carriers always carry the same information at a given instant : this corresponds to a constant known waveform/pattern which is used for pattern synchronisation. The maximum quality is obtained by the use of multilevel Quadrature Amplitude Modulation (QAM): the proposed QAMs have 8, 16, 64 or 256 states, the number of states being chosen as a function of the desired level of robustness. For this type of modulation, coherent demodulation is required (at each instant and at each frequency, it is necessary to estimate the complex gain of the transmission channel). In order to evaluate the channel response, some of the symbols (at pre-defined frequencies and instants) are sent with a pre-defined amplitude and phase (references), so that the gain of the channel can be evaluated at any instant and any frequency by interpolation.

Robustness is achieved by the use of Trellis Coded Modulation (TCM) [1], [3], or Block Turbo-Codes (BTC) [4], [5] : both are an association of modulation and convolutional encoding leading to an optimisation of the transmission efficiency. Other alternate coding schemes are under study such as Multilevel RS coding. In conjunction with coding, time and frequency interleaving are used, which have the effect of spreading perturbations (frequency selective fading, flat fading, interference) on distant symbols, so that decoding is more efficient. An external Reed-Solomon (RS) block code may also be used to correct the remaining error bursts at the output of the TCM or Turbo-code decoder or, if not possible, to detect them so that the source decoders (audio, images, data) be able to minimise the subjective effects of these disturbances.

Parametrability is obtained by an incremental design of the broadcast signal : it contains a standard kernel group of carriers (occupying 3 kHz) which is common to all versions, and the required bandwidth/bit rate is obtained by adding additional groups of carriers (each 1.5 kHz wide) on either side of the kernel group. During the analog to digital transition phase, a small number of additional groups may be used. The unused spectrum will be occupied by an AM compatible waveform which can be received by classical AM receivers, without any modification. Flexibility is also due to the fact that the overall bit stream is divided in a main stream for conveying standard audio or audio + still pictures and a data stream with a much lower bit rate conveying any data, for example program associated date (PAD similar to RDS). With up-to-date audio coders, the ratio audio/pictures may be instantaneously variable in the main stream, and the significance of the data bit stream can vary *ad libitum*.

Low complexity is inherent to the system principle. Since the signal can be seen as a number of elementary carriers uniformly spaced in frequency, the main digital signal processing is done by the mean of several Fast Fourier Transforms or Inverse Fast Fourier Transforms (FFT, IFFT) which are known for their very efficient implementation. At the receiver, the FFT is equivalent to a large filter bank, each filter selecting one and only sub-carrier. The complexity level is only proportional to the occupied bandwidth, and it is independent of the channel quality.

Finally, the easiness to use (user-friendly/transparency for the listener) of the system is obtained by the use of automatic Remote Control (RC) of the receiver, dedicated highly protected symbols convey all the necessary configuration parameters : any change in the transmission characteristics (bandwidth, coding, interleaving...) is automatically taken into account by the receiver. The RC symbols are always located at the same time/frequency positions in the common kernel group of carriers.

3. SYSTEM VARIATIONS

The system exists in two compatible versions : a ground version, designed for good propagation channels (especially ground wave propagation hence its name) and a sky version, especially designed for skywave HF propagation. Each symbol has a duration of T_s = 36 ms (ground) or 24 ms (sky). This duration is the sum of a useful time T_u = 32 ms or 18 ms and a guard time T_g = 4 or 6 ms. Other options for the values of the useful time and guard time are considered for a further optimisation stage in the standardisation process. Each symbol is modulated independently from its neighbours by choosing a given point in a pre-defined constellation according to the value on an information word (3 to 8 bits) (useful symbol).The reference symbols are transmitted with a pre-defined amplitude and phase. A reference symbol is used either for synchronisation purposes or for channel complex response estimation. A useful symbol has to be demodulated and decoded in order to recover the original information it conveys.

The different carriers are located at offsets form the centre frequency that are multiples of $\Delta f = 1/T_u$, i.e. 31.25 Hz (ground system) or 55 $^5/_9$ Hz (sky system). By convention, in the complex baseband representation, the k-th carrier is at an offset of k Δf from the Direct Current (DC) component; k can be positive (at the "right" of the reference carrier) or negative (at the "left" of the reference carrier). The 0-th carrier is the DC itself. In the ground system, the pattern contains 8 frames, and has duration 8x36 ms = 288 ms. In the sky system, the pattern contains 12 frames, and has also duration 12x24 = 288 ms. As already mentioned above, the carriers are grouped in :

- a kernel group of carriers, which is common to all transmission modes and which conveys all the reference symbols which are necessary for time and frequency synchronisation, as well as the Remote Control (RC) symbols which describe the current mode ; the kernel group is immediately above the carrier at frequency F_0, and does not contain it. The kernel group contains only a main stream, and no data stream. Its bandwidth is exactly 3.0 kHz between the zeros of its frequency spectrum.
- additional groups of carriers (possibly none, in the 3 kHz version) which number is defined according to the desired bit rate. An additional group does not contain any synchronisation or RC symbol. If there are additional groups below the carrier, their number is always such that the frequency spectrum of the signal is symmetrical around the carrier. The bandwidth of each additional group is exactly 1.5 kHz between the zeros of its frequency spectrum.

The system uses TCM or BTC with 64 QAM with a rate 2/3 inner code, and no external RS code, for a total bandwidth of 9 kHz (Mode 3, described below). In this case, and in the ground mode:

- The kernel group conveys exactly 8 kbits/s of audio and no data.
- Each additional group conveys a main stream of exactly 4 Kbits/s and a data stream of 666.7 bits/s.
- There is 1 (one) kernel group and 4 additional groups
- The total bandwidth is 9 kHz between the zeros of the frequency spectrum.
- The total bit rate is 27166.7 bits/s, a spectral efficiency higher than 3 bits/Hz/s.

In the current definition of the system, there exist 8 different versions for transmission, depicted in figure 1. In this figure, the grey area shows the bandwidth doubling due to AM transmission of a baseband digital signal, each small block has a bandwidth of 1.5 kHz except for the kernel which is 3 kHz wide. Some of them (versions 1,3,5,7) are pure digital versions where the entire available bandwidth is devoted to the transmission of digital streams, the other versions (0,2,4,6) use only half of the bandwidth for digital transmission, the other half being used :

- either by a replica of the digital carriers, so that the signal can be transmitted by an AM compatible transmitter (depicted in grey in figure 1)
- or by an AM compatible analog audio signal (VSB,Vestigial Side Band) which can be received by standard current AM radio receivers. The position of the analog carrier is chosen to be as far as possible from the digital section of the signal so as to minimise cross interference.

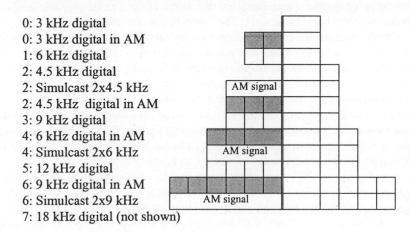

0: 3 kHz digital
0: 3 kHz digital in AM
1: 6 kHz digital
2: 4.5 kHz digital
2: Simulcast 2x4.5 kHz
2: 4.5 kHz digital in AM
3: 9 kHz digital
4: 6 kHz digital in AM
4: Simulcast 2x6 kHz
5: 12 kHz digital
6: 9 kHz digital in AM
6: Simulcast 2x9 kHz
7: 18 kHz digital (not shown)

Fig. 1: The 8 modes of transmission

4. CAPACITY

In order to take into account the imperfections of most transmitters and to simplify the design of receivers, the central carrier corresponding to DC is not used.

The various versions currently defined for the standard mode for example used in its 64 QAM version are depicted in table 1.

Table 1: Bandwidths and bit rates (standard system with 64 QAM constellation)

Version number	Useful digital Bandwidth (kHz)	Main stream Net bit rate (bits/s)	Data stream	
			Net bit rate (bits/s) RS in use	Net bit rate (bits/s) RS not in use
0	3 kHz	5000	0	500
2	4.5 kHz	12000	541	1041
1 and 4	6 kHz	16000	1083	1833
3 and 6	9 kHz	24000	2166	3166
5	12 kHz	32000	3250	4500
7	18 kHz	72000	8125	10750

357

5.   PERFORMANCES

The Nadib and DRM consortium normalised laboratory testing conditions in order to get a fair comparison between various proponents. The transmitter and channel models which have been selected are described hereafter.

5.1 Propagation model

The approach is to use stochastic time-varying models with a **stationary statistics** and define models for good, moderate and bad conditions by taking appropriate parameter values of the general model with stationary statistics. One of those models with adaptable parameters is the *wide sense stationary uncorrelated scattering model* (WSSUS model). The justification for the stationary approach with different parameter sets is justified by the fact that results on real channels lead to BER curves between best and worst cases found in the simulation.

A tapped delay line model is then used for multipaths generation [6] [10]. The time-variant tap weights are zero mean complex-valued stationary gaussian random processes. The magnitudes are Rayleigh-distributed and the phases are uniformly distributed. For each weight, there is one stochastic process, characterised by its variance and power density spectrum (PDS). The variance is a measure for the average signal power which can be received via this path and the PDS determines the average speed of variation in time.

The width of the PDS is commonly referred to as the Doppler spread of that path. There might be also a non-zero centre frequency of the PDS, which can be interpreted as an average frequency shift (or Doppler shift).

It is common to assume a Gaussian amplitude statistics for the processes, which is a reasonable assumption for the ionospheric channel. The stochastic processes belonging to every individual path then become Rayleigh processes. WSSUS does not define the shape of the PDS. For ionospheric channels, Watterson has shown a Gaussian shape to be a good assumption [11] [12]. The one-sided Doppler spread is then defined as the standard deviation (σ) of the shape of the PDS.

Five channels are currently used by Nadib and DRM :

CH 1.   AWGN : one path of constant amplitude (for ground wave propagation).

CH 2.   Rice with delay : one constant path of unit amplitude , a second with half amplitude delayed 1 ms, with 0.1 Hz doppler spread (for flat fading at MW and SW).

CH 3.   US Consortium : 4 paths of amplitudes (1, 0.7, 0.5, 0.25), delay (0, 0.7 ms, 1.5 ms, 2.2 ms) doppler spread (0.1 Hz, 0.5 Hz, 1 Hz, 2 Hz) and frequency shifts (0.1 Hz, 0.2 Hz, 0.5 Hz, 1 Hz).

CH 4.   CCIR poor : 2 paths of equal amplitude delayed 2ms and equal 1 Hz doppler spread (SW propagation).

CH 5.   Similar as channel 4 but 4 ms delay, and 2 Hz doppler spread (bad SW propagation).

In such conditions, the proposed modem has the performances depicted in figure 2. In 9 kHz bandwidth, both the normal and sky modes are shown used leading to 27 or 20.5 kb/s overall output rate. Here 2s interleaving is used for the sky mode and 0,3s for the normal mode. Only the TCM mode performances with external RS coding are given in figure 2, as the Turbo-code optimisation is still under way, and so its performances are not given in this paper. Channel 1 and 2 are tested with the normal mode and channels 3, 4 and 5 with the sky mode.

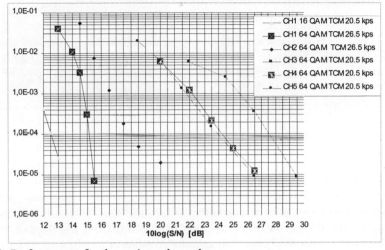

Fig. 2: Performances for the various channels

5.2 Transmitter model

In order to assess the impact on the modem performance of all the impairments implied by the use of very high power transmitters, a simple simulator model was designed for tube type architectures. The mathematical model is based upon the separation of the signal in its amplitude and phase components (actually the constant amplitude signal with the phase : $\exp(j\phi)$). The amplitude path is subject to non-linearities and frequency band limitations. The phase path is also limited in bandwidth. The final output tube is modelled by a feed-through part incorporating a hard limiter that correspond to the maximum power delivered and a feed-back loop for the anode-cathode interactions. A variable differential delay is added to tune the overall delay between the two paths before recombination.

A real time version of this model was developed on a PC using a simple digital AES-EBU board for input/ouput interfaces. Over-sampling is used internally to perform the computation of the model without aliasing effects. An over-sampling rate of a factor 16 was chosen. An external converter box was used to get perfect match between the I and Q signals so that no image spectra are generated by the converters (in a 80 dB dynamic range at least).

Figure 3 shows the transmitter model with its man-machine interface and the resulting signal difference. For easy use, a simple mouse-click on the given parameter allows for the access for change. Fig. 3 also contains the picture of the man-machine interface showing the input and output signals and spectrum.

In practice a sufficiently high sampling rate must be used to avoid effects not desired in the model itself.Various bandwidths were used during the tests showing that the spectrum shoulders could come as high as 40 dB below the main spectrum

359

without any noticeable effects on the bit error rate. Only bandwidth limitations were tried. Non linearity effects are still under investigation.

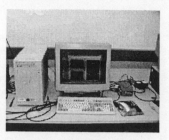 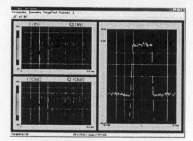

Fig. 3: Transmitter simulator model and real-time setup

6. DEMONSTRATOR

Since 1996, several versions of a real time demonstrator were developed with increasing performance and capability. From the 3rd Radio Symposium in Montreux, June 1996 to the fourth in June 1998, with IBC 96, and 97, and NAB 97 as intermediate versions [7], the demonstrator consists in :

- a pair of PCs with DSP boards containing source coding and modem functions,
- a real time transmitter simulator that allows simulation of various impairments encountered in real power transmitters (typically using tubes).
- a real time wideband SW propagation simulator to show the insensitivity of the digital part of the system to multipath, whereas at the same time the analogue part is seriously perturbed. The simulator may only generate a maximum of 3 paths due to CPU limitations (a new version is under way). All the characteristics (amplitude, average power, frequency offset, Doppler spread, time spread) are adjustable in real time using a natural Man-Machine interface. Narrow band interference may be added for system tests.
- a combined analogue/digital low power exciter
- a standard short waves consumer receiver used to receive the analogue program,
- a modified short waves consumer receiver dedicated to receive the digital program. The modification consists only in the implementation of a second IF output with a wider filter.

Such a configuration allows for the test of various sets of parameters (standard AM Double Side Band, SSB either lower or upper, simulcast and full digital). In the last two cases, various bandwidths may be tested from a nominal ITU 9 kHz allotment, to an extended 12 kHz value compatible with modern transmitters. This demonstrator was developed to show the highest quality achievable with current sound compression techniques and the possibility to add new digital data services.

The demodulator side and its man-machine interface are shown in Figure 4.

The latest version of this demonstrator includes MPEG II layer 3 audio codec running at rates 8 to 32 kbits/s with 1 kbits/s steps. Provision for later introduction of an MPEG 4/AAC codec has been taken. At the modulation level, both TCM and Turbo codes are included for comparison.

Fig. 4: Picture of the demodulator, and its man-machine interface.

7.   CONCLUSION

This paper presented a complete system proposal for terrestrial audio broadcasting that shows the current state of the art in COFDM modem technology. COFDM was chosen because of its very good compromise between extreme robustness and a high spectral efficiency. At the same time severe propagation conditions must be endured, while maintaining receiver complexity well within current DSP technology reach. Such a system should restore interest in short wave broadcasting, and existing transmitters can be used for such broadcasts. This new modem opens the road for good quality and robust audio broadcasting at an overall price much lower than present satellite projects.

This system proposal has been being tested (real time demonstrator measurements) in the Fraunhofer Institute laboratory in Germany during February 1999, and a system choice in favour of OFDM has been taken in March 1999 for a first standard proposal at ITU around October 99. Simultaneously real time on-air broadcasting measurements should take place during summer 99. A reference receiver is currently under development for such experiments.

REFERENCES

[1]   Pittet, Pirez "Modulations codées adaptées au fading de Rayleigh : Performances sur canal HF ionosphérique", GRETSI meeting, sept 93, Juan-les-Pins, France.
[2]   P.A. Laurent, C. Demeure, D. Castelain, B. Le Floch, " Thomson–CCETT Common Proposal for a Digital Audio Broadcasting System at Frequencies below 30 MHz", Nadib, june 1998.
[3]   Schlegel, Costello, "Bandwidth efficient coding for fading channels : code construction and performance analysis,", IEEE Journal on selected area on Com., Vol. 7, n°9, 1989, pp. 1356-1368.

[4] C. Berrou et M. Jézéquel, "Frame-oriented convolutional turbo-codes", Electronics Letters, July 18 1996, Vol. 32, N° 15.

[5] C. Berrou, A. Glavieux, P. Thitimajshima, "Near Shannon limit error-correction coding : Turbo-codes", in Proc. IEEE ICC'93, Geneva, Switzerland, pp. 1064-1070, May 1993.

[6] J. Lindner, D. Castelain, F. Nicolas, " Specification of a ionospheric channel model for am radio broadcasting bands," Nadib report , march 1998.

[7] C.J. Demeure, P.A. Laurent, "A new Modem for High Quality Sound Broadcasting at Short Waves," IEE 4441, 7th Conf. on Radio Systems and Techniques, Nottingham, UK, pp. 50-54, july 1997.

[8] DAB system : ETSI norm, ETS 300 401 ed.2, May 1997.

[9] DVB -T system : ETSI norm, ETS 300 744, March 1997.

[10] Annex B to STANAG 4285, Evaluation of modems employing the stanag 4285 WAVEFORM.

[11] CC. Watterson, J.R. Juposher and W.B. Bensema, "Experimental Verification of an Ionospheric Mode, "ESSA Tech. Report, ERL 112-ITS, 1969.

[12] CCIR Recommendation 520, Use of High frequency Ionospheric Channel Simulators.

[13] C.Demeure, P.A. Laurent, B. LeFloch, D. Lacroix, "A COFDM Waveform for Digital Terrestrial Radio Broadcasting to replace AM Modulation", IES 99 conf., Alexandria, VA, USA, may 1999.

Modulation and coding scheme using serial transmission for digital radio broadcast in the HF-Band

J. Egle [1], A. Brakemeier [2], D. Rudolph [3]

[1] Department of Information Technology, University of Ulm, Germany
[2] Research and Technology, Daimler-Chrysler AG, Ulm, Germany
[3] Deutsche Telekom Berkom GmbH, Berlin, Germany

E-mail: jochem.egle@e-technik.uni-ulm.de

1 Abstract

A spectral efficient modulation and coding scheme, suitable for digital radio broadcast in the AM bands, together with an adaptive detection method is introduced. The scheme is based on a serial transmission combined with a multilevel coded 16 APSK scheme. Simulation results for different shortwave specific channel models are shown.

2 Introduction

A new digital modulation and coding scheme based on a single carrier approach is introduced. The aim is to replace the traditional analogue AM modulation scheme in long, medium, and short wave. The work presented in this paper has been carried out by Deutsche Telekom together with the Daimler Chrysler Research Center and the University of Ulm as a contribution to the Eureka project NADIB (**NA**rrow Band **DI**gital **B**roadcast and the worldwide DRM project (**D**igital **R**adio Mondiale) [2].

The main requirements concerning the new digital system which were elaborated in these two projects may be summarized as follows:

- Fit into the analogue carrier spacing
- Re-use of analogue transmitters for the digital system
- Support of simultaneous broadcast of analogue and digital transmission
- Support of data transmission
- Short time delay in the receiver
- Low out-of-band radiation to meet the protection ratios defined by the ITU
- Robustness against doppler spread and multipath spread

363

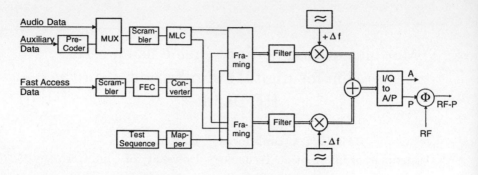

Figure 1: Model of the modulator (including framing and coding)

- Low cost receivers
- Improved audio quality

Taking all this objectives into account Deutsche Telekom pursued an approach based on a single carrier transmission. As a compromise between availability, bandwidth demand and audio quality the net bit rate has been fixed to 20.5 kbit/s in a 10 kHz wide short wave channel. This net datarate combined with new audio compression techniques such as MPEG 4 offers audio quality comparable to analogue FM radio which outperforms today's quality of short wave radio broadcast by far.

3 Transmission Scheme

The basic modulator model is shown in figure 1. The audio data from the source encoder is multiplexed with the auxiliary data and scrambled. The scrambled data stream is encoded using multi level codes (MLC) and interleaved. This will be discussed in more detail in section 3.1.

After dividing the encoded interleaved datastream onto two parallel five kHz channels a 2 PSK test sequence is added as well as the Fast Information Channel (FIC), which is a low rate data channel. Since the FIC is determined to be used for data which is needed at the receiver immediately after tuning in, e.g. identification of the transmit station, no interleaving is applied to this data stream. The length and the frequency of the test sequence depends on the desired capable delay and Doppler spread. Therefore various parameter sets for the different scenarios are proposed [6].

The output of each framing block passes a transmit filter that uses a root raised cosine with roll off 0.25. With a symbol rate of 4000 baud on each carrier the roll off guarantees orthogonality between the two 5 kHz subchannels. After summing the two subchannels the resulting I/Q baseband signal is converted into an Amplitude/Phase (A/P) signal. The A signal and the phase modulated RF-P signal are required to reuse the already existing

364

transmit stations. The consequences of this nonlinear conversion are still subject to various investigations and will not be considered in this paper.

3.1 Channel Coding

The multi level coding concept uses the benefits of coded modulation. It is based on a set partitioning tree, e.g. figure 2 shows the partitioning tree of the 16 APSK constellation used. In multi level coding the numbering of the

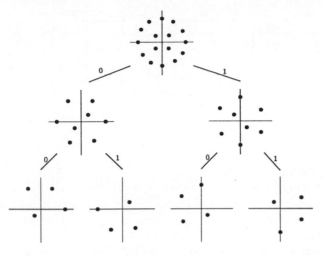

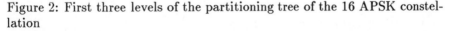

Figure 2: First three levels of the partitioning tree of the 16 APSK constellation

subpartitions is protected by individual codes. The properties are described in more detail in [3].

The structure of a MLC encoder is shown in figure 3. It consists of $m = \log_2(M)$ independent encoders, each of them determining one bit of a constellation. With $\Theta(\cdot)$ denoting the mapping function and c_{ji} denoting the jth code symbol of level i equation 1 the mapping procedure is described by

$$x_j = \Theta(c_{j0}, \dots, c_{jm-1}) \, . \tag{1}$$

4 Detection Scheme

On the receiving side the two parallel subchannels are separated using appropriate bandpass filters. Each bandpass filter output is equalized using a decision feedback type equalizer. This equalizer is adapted by the estimates of the channel impulse response gained by the test sequence. In order to improve performance a combined equalization and decoding strategy is applied (cf. section 4.2).

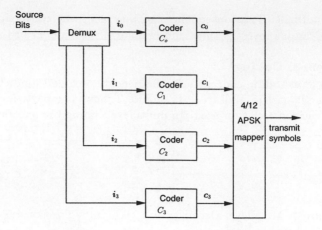

Figure 3: Multilevel Encoder for a 16 point signal constellation

4.1 Decoder

A straightforward approach in decoding multilevel codes is the multistage decoder. This scheme is optimum under the assumption having no error propagation in level direction. The structure of a multistage decoder for a 16 point constellation is shown in figure 4. It consists of $m = 4$ independent decoders matched to the corresponding encoders. When receiving the symbol vector r the MAP decision rule in the decoder of the jth bit of the information word i_i in level i, $\hat{i}_{ji}$, is:

$$\hat{i}_{ji} = \arg\left\{\max_{i_{ji}}\left(P(i_{ji}|r, C_0, \ldots, C_i)\right)\right\} \tag{2}$$

Assuming no error propagation, i.e. $\hat{c}_i$ is the correctly decoded codeword of level i, equation 2 transforms to

$$\hat{i}_{ji} = \arg\left\{\max_{i_{ji}}\left(P(i_{ji}|r, \hat{c}_0, \ldots, \hat{c}_{i-1}, C_i)\right)\right\}$$

$$= \arg\left\{\max_{i_{ji}}\left(\frac{\displaystyle\sum_{c_i \in C_i \cap i_{ji}=c_{ji}} p(r|\hat{c}_0, \ldots \hat{c}_{i-1}, c_i) \cdot P(i_{ji})}{\displaystyle\sum_{c_i \in C_i} p(r|\hat{c}_0, \ldots \hat{c}_{i-1}, c_i)}\right)\right\} \tag{3}$$

Under the assumption of equiprobable transmit bits ($P(i_{ji} = 0) = P(i_Pji = 1) = 1/2$) and omitting the common divisor equation 3 simplifies to:

$$\hat{i}_{ji} = \arg\left\{\max_{i_{ji}} \sum_{c_i \in C_i \cap i_{ji}=c_{ji}} p(r|\hat{c}_0, \ldots \hat{c}_{i-1}, c_i)\right\} \tag{4}$$

366

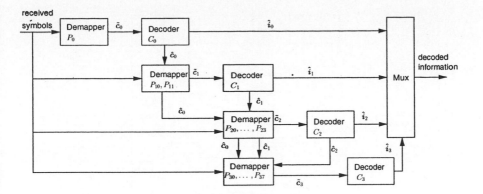

Figure 4: Multilevel Decoder for a 16 point signal constellation

4.2 Combined equalization and decoding

It is well known that an optimum detection scheme for a concatenated transmission scheme is a detector that exploits all dependencies in a single step. This is optimal but in most cases, even under ideal assumptions, by far too complex. Therefore in [1] an iterative solution using independent component detectors was proposed. The original application was in the field of coding but as it turned out later iterative solutions are applicable in many other fields. However, the iterative solution depends on the availability of soft-in soft-out component detectors which are not realizable for the used Reed Solomon level codes. Therefore we followed a slightly different approach and used a combination of equalizer and multistage decoder and modified   the decision function of the equalizer. In each stage $P(x_j|C_0, \ldots, C_{i-1})$ is determined by previous decoding results and therefore contains the constraints of the previous level codes.

$$\hat{x}_j = \arg\{\max_{x_j \in \mathcal{A}}(P(x_j|r) \cdot \underbrace{P(x_j|C_0, \ldots, C_{i-1})})\} \tag{5}$$
$$\text{extrinsic information}$$

Assuming hard decisions $P(x_j|C_0, \ldots, C_{i-1}) = P(x_j|\hat{c}_0, \ldots, \hat{c}_{i-1}) \in \{0; 1\}$ in the previous decoder stage the size of the modulation alphabet in the decision device is decreased from level to level and enables the equalizer to make more reliable decisions. The mechanism of modifying the decision device is depicted in figure 5 for one stage of the combined multistage decoder/equalizer.

5   Simulation Results

For DRM and NADIB five different test channels have been specified. The parameters of these channels are specified in table 1. They represent typical propagation conditions in the AM bands.

367

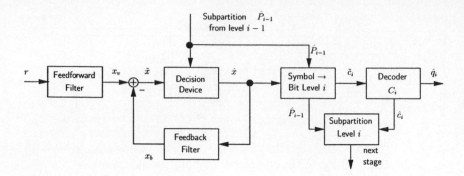

Figure 5: Combined Equalizer and Decoder for one stage of the Multistage Decoder and Equalizer

Channel No.	No 1 AWGN	No. 2 Rice
rel. path amp.	1.0	1.0 / 0.5
Delay spread [ms]	0.0	0.0 / 1.0
Doppler spread [Hz]	0.0	0.0 / 0.1

(a) Channel Parameters of Channel No. 1 and 2

Channel No.	No 3 US Cons.	No.4 CCIR poor	No 5
rel. path amp.	1.0 / 0.7 / 0.5 / 0.25	1.0 / 1.0	1.0 / 1.0
Delay spread [ms]	0.0 / 0.7 / 1.5 / 2.2	0.0 / 2.0	0.0 / 4.0
Doppler spread [Hz]	0.1 / 0.5 / 1.0 / 2.0	1.0 / 1.0	2.0 / 2.0
Doppler shift [Hz]	0.1 / 0.2 / 0.5 / 1.0		

(b) Channel Parameters of Channel No. 3, 4, and 5

Table 1: Channel models proposed in DRM and NADIB

The results were obtained with a simulation of a fully operational modem with all necessary parts including channel estimation, tracking and synchronization and a maximum interleaver delay of 2s. The waveform parameters are listed in table 2.

Bandwidth [Hz]	5000
Symbol rate [Baud]	4000
Blocks per frame	33
Structure ratio	51:189
Bits per symbol	4
Frame length [s]	1.96
Block length [ms]	40
Number of levels	4
Level 0 code C_0	Convolutional and rs-code
Level 1 code C_1	RS-Code $(2^8, 252, 208, 45)$
Level 2 code C_2	RS-Code $(2^8, 252, 234, 19)$
Level 3 code C_3	RS-Code $(2^8, 252, 242, 11)$
Code rate	208:252
Net bit rate [bit/s]	10250

Table 2: Parameter set of one subchannel

In figure 6(a) the performance results for the channels 1 and 2 are depicted. Additionally the 2 PSK AWGN curve is shown as a reference. Comparing channel 1 and 2 the asymptotic loss is about 2.5 dB, which is caused by the time variance and frequency selectivity of channel 2.

In figure 6(b) the results for the three fading channels are drawn. Comparing the three curves shows that channel 3 has the best asymptotic performance, due to the path diversity caused by four independent fading paths. Comparing the two path channels shows that channel 5 outperforms channel 4 which is a consequence of differences in the doppler spread and the resulting larger time diversity gain. Hence, the equalizer setup is more difficult for channel 5.The curves are also a measurement for the robustness and ability of the modem to adapt to quickly changing channels. This capability is crucial for a detection scheme of a serial transmission in short wave.

6 Conclusions

This paper presented a digital transmission scheme aiming to replace the old analogue AM modulation schemes in short, medium and long wave. To achieve the required high bandwidth efficiency higher order modulation schemes together with multilevel codes and a combined decoding and equalization strategy are applied. Simulation results proved the suitability of the proposed scheme to replace analogue AM transmissions. Additionally a real time testbed based on a DSP implementation was implemented by Berkom

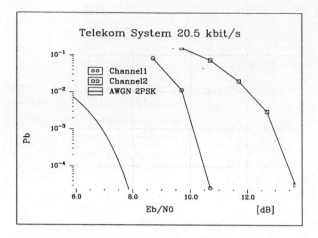

(a) Channel 1 and 2

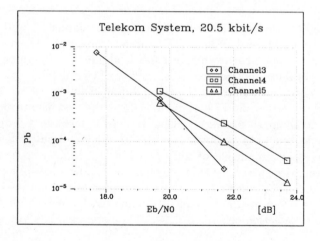

(b) Channel 3, 4 and 5

Figure 6: Performance of the transmission scheme in the test channels, net bit rate 20.5 kbit/s, interleaver delay 2s

which showed comparable performance.

References

[1] BERROU, C.; GLAVIEUX, A.; THITIMAJSHIMA, P.: *Near Shannon Limit Error-Correcting Coding and Decoding: Turbo Codes(1)*, Proc. ICC93, Geneva, Switzerland, 1064–1070, 1993.

[2] Digital Radio Mondiale, Homepage; http://www.drm.org

[3] HUBER, J.; WACHSMANN, U.; FISCHER, R.: *Coded Modulation by Multilevel-Codes: Overview and State of the Art*, ITG-Fachbericht: Codierung für Quelle, Kanal und Übertragung, 255–266, March 1998.

[4] IMAI, H.; HIRAKAWA, S.: *A New Multilevel Coding Method Using Error-Correcting Codes* IEEE Trans. on Information Theory, vol.23 (no.3), 1977.

[5] WACHSMANN, U.; HUBER, J.: *Power and Bandwidth Efficient Digital Communication Using Turbo Codes in Multilevel Codes*. European Transactions on Telecommunications, vol.6 (no.5): pp. 557–567, Sept-Oct 1995.

[6] DEUTSCHE TELEKOM: *System Proposal for a Digital Broadcast Transmission System for the Bands Below 30 MHz*, 1999.

MPEG AUDIO IN DIGITAL BROADCASTING - AN OVERVIEW

OLIVER KUNZ

Fraunhofer Institute for Integrated Circuits, Erlangen, Germany
`kunz@iis.fhg.de`

ABSTRACT

The audio compression methods developed and standardized within the Moving Pictures Expert Group of the International Standardization Organization (ISO/MPEG) take a leading role within digital broadcasting. The numerous schemes that have been standardized over the last years are widely used in different broadcasting systems. The paper will present an overview over the different MPEG audio coding methods, focussing on the latest state-of-the-art achievements contained in MPEG-2 Advanced Audio Coding (AAC) and MPEG-4 Audio. It will describe the respective key features, the resulting usage profiles and will highlight the digital broadcasting systems that profit from using MPEG audio coding schemes.

1   INTRODUCTION

Digital audio broadcasting and digital perceptual audio coding are closely linked together. In fact, the former has at least for some time been the driving factor for the development of digital audio coders. Digital modulation and coding schemes are offering new transmission capabilities, but without audio coding it would not be possible to take advantage from that, because the bitrate needed for the audio would be much too high. This paper describes several MPEG standardized audio coding schemes used for digital broadcasting today or in the near future as well as digital broadcasting systems using these coders.

2   MPEG AUDIO CODING

All the coding schemes mentioned later in this paper have been developed and standardized in the framework of the Moving Pictures Expert Group (MPEG) of the International Organization for Standardization (ISO). MPEG-1 was finished in 1992 [1], MPEG-2 in 1994 (for Layer-2 and 3) [2] and in 1997 (for AAC) [3]. Figure 1 shows the evolution of the MPEG audio coders.

Several tests have been conducted inside and outside of MPEG to evaluate the audio quality of the MPEG coders and other competing algorithms. The probably most thorough test on stereo audio codecs ever conducted is documented in [7].

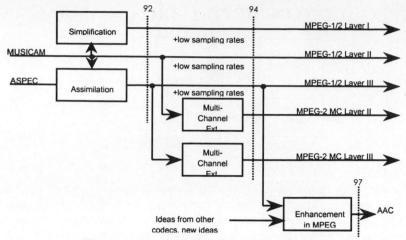

Figure 1: Genesis of MPEG Audio Coders

3 THE MPEG CODING SCHEMES

The following subsections describe the key features of those MPEG audio coding schemes that are already used in digital sound broadcasting systems or that are currently under consideration for use in novel systems.

3.1 MPEG Layer-2

Layer-2 is a frequency domain coder based on a 32 band polyphase filterbank [1][8]. A Layer-2 frame comprises 36 spectra and representing 1152 PCM samples. After a scaling process, the subband samples are uniformly quantized based on the results of the psychoacoustic model and coded using a block companding method (see Figure 2). For stereo coding, Layer-2 provides means to perform intensity stereo coding. Layer-2 does not use short time buffering, so that the audio frames are of constant length.

In stereo broadcasting, Layer-2 is mostly used at bitrates of 192 kbit/sec or below, although the recommended bitrate for stereo broadcasting is 256 kbit/sec. Layer-2 has been extended in MPEG-2 to offer a means for multichannel and multilingual coding backwards compatible to Layer-2 stereo coding [2].

3.1.1 Special provisions for broadcasting

In systems like Eureka 147, unequal error protection is applied to Layer-2. Layer-2 has highly sensitive data such as bit allocation, scalefactor select information and the scalefactors themselves. Since the latter is not covered by the CRC check provided by MPEG, an additional scalefactor CRC check has been introduced for broadcasting scenarios. An error indicated by the ISO CRC will invoke frame concealment, whereas a scalefactor CRC failure will result in special scalefactor concealment. The polyphase sample data itself is relatively insensitive to errors and is therefore less protected.

374

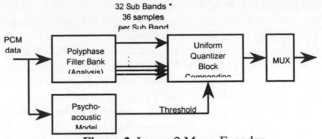

Figure 2: Layer-2 Mono Encoder

3.2 MPEG Layer-3

Layer-3 has been standardized during the same standardization phases as Layer-1 and -2 [1][2]. In contrary to these, however, Layer-3 uses a high frequency resolution filterbank of 576 lines (Figure 3). To avoid speech artifacts, the coder provides the capability to switch to a lower frequency / higher time resolution. For reasons of compatibility, the filterbank is a hybrid filterbank, further analyzing the output of the Layer-2 polyphase filterbank with MDCT transforms. The spectral coefficients are scaled, non-uniformly quantized and entropy coded. For stereo coding, Layer-3 offers Mid-Side (MS) stereo coding as well as intensity coding. A Layer-3 frame comprises 1152 samples at sampling rates greater or equal 32 kHz and 576 samples at lower sampling rates. Short time buffering is implemented in Layer-3, however a special buffering technique still allows for constant rate headers [8].

In case of Layer-3, the CRC check covers all side information including the scalefactors. A CRC failure will cause frame concealment. The coded spectral data itself is of higher error sensitivity than the polyphase sample data of Layer-2 due to error propagation within the Huffman code.

Layer-3 has become very popular as MP3 in the internet. 128 kbps is viewed to offer good audio quality for most stereo signals.

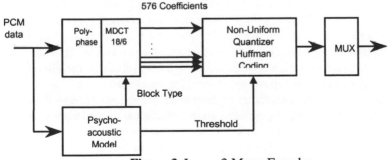

Figure 3: Layer-3 Mono Encoder

3.3 MPEG-2 Advanced Audio Coding (AAC)

AAC (Advanced Audio Coding) currently is the most efficient high quality audio coding algorithm, standardized by MPEG in 1997 [3] [9]. Three profiles are available, of which the Low Complexity (LC) profile is used in digital broadcasting so far. AAC uses a 1024 point MDCT to transform the signal into frequency domain (Figure 4). For time critical signals, the frequency resolution can be reduced by a factor of 8 by means of a blockswitching algorithm. As in Layer-3, the frequency coefficients are scaled, nonuniformly quantized based on psychoacoustic requirements and entropy coded. Huffman coding in AAC is much more flexible than in Layer-3, such are the stereo coding methods. In extension to Layer-3, AAC has a new tool called temporal noise shaping (TNS). TNS allows for intra-frame noise shaping, reducing the need for switching to the short transform length. This increases the bitrate efficiency of the coding algorithm. AAC frames represent 1024 samples and are of variable framelength to enable short time buffer control. AAC permits the use of application specific transport formats, yet the ADTS format defined in the AAC standard is becoming the de-facto standard for broadcasting systems with low error rates.

AAC offers excellent stereo quality at 128 kbit/sec. At 96 kbit/sec it performs equally to Layer-2 at 192 kbit/sec [7]. Due to this good performance, AAC was selected to build the high quality coding part of MPEG-4.

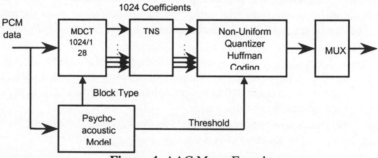

Figure 4: AAC Mono Encoder

3.4 MPEG-4 Audio

MPEG-4 ([4], [5])is the latest in the MPEG series of audio coding standards. The main idea in the standardization process of MPEG-4 was to assemble a toolbox of state-of-the-art coding algorithms to cover the whole range of audio-visual applications from very low bitrates up to broadcast quality. To achieve this goal a number of different coding algorithms were collected and fitted into a common framework. On the audio coding side this toolkit ranges from parametric coding over LPC-based speech coders to high-quality transform coding schemes, namely AAC. A detailed overview of MPEG-4 can be found in [6].

MPEG-4 Audio adds a number of features to AAC that make it very attractive for the use within a digital radio system. Two of them will be described in a little more detail in the following.

3.4.1 Hierarchical Coding

One of the most significant improvements over the previously existing audio coding algorithms is a feature called hierarchical coding or scalability. Hierarchical coding enables applications to create coded representations of audio information that inherently carry multiple quality levels that can be decoded independently. These coding schemes are called hierarchical because every higher layer exploits the results that all lower layers achieved. The range of applications that can possibly profit from hierarchical coding is very widespread. Multimedia databases, accessible via different bandwidth connections, do not have to store multiple representations of the same item, saving storage on the server side. Music on demand services could embed a pre-listen option at lower quality and lower download time to every track, allowing customers to get a first impression in real-time without additional effort in content production. In digital radio systems, a combination of hierarchical coding and multilevel channel coding could increase receptibility even under difficult channel conditions.

Scalability can be achieved in a number of different ways. These ways are

- SNR scalability:
  Could be called subjective quality scalability as well. Here the scalability is achieved by building representations with different demands to the signal to noise ratio.
- Bandwidth scalability:
  This scalability method adds additional audio bandwidth in the higher layers. Especially if high subjective quality in all layers is required like in digital radio systems, this mode is preferable over the SNR scalability.
- Mono/stereo scalability:
  In this case the higher layers in a scalable bitstream add stereo information to the mono part in the lower layer. This mode is useful if the low layer has high audio quality requirements and the bitrate is too low to encode a stereo signal. However, to exploit this scalability mode efficiently the system has to apply certain restrictions to the use of joint stereo techniques.
- Algorithm scalability:
  Different coding algorithms (e.g. a speech coder and an audio coder) can be combined in a single bitstream. This method is especially efficient if the bitrate of the lowest layer is too low for a generic audio coding scheme. And even in this case, the higher layer(s) can exploit the fact that a part of the original signal is already encoded.

3.4.2 Error Resilience

Audio coding schemes achieve a high compression ratio by exploiting both irrelevancies and redundancies in the input signal. Especially the redundancy reduction can create problems on error prone channels. The optimum redundancy reduction, which state-of-the-art audio coding schemes are not too far away from, would result in a bitstream that would not allow the prediction of any erroneous bit in it. The encoded signal would be white noise. This would result in an extreme sensitivity against transmission errors and no possibility for unequal error protection (UEP).

To overcome this problem at least to some extent, MPEG-4 defines a modified bitstream format for AAC in MPEG-4 version 2 [5]. The two main parts of this approach are a resorting of the huffman coded spectral data (HCR) and a reversible variable length code (RVLC) for the scalefactor data.

3.4.2.1   Huffman Code Resorting

The spectral data is transmitted using a huffman code. To optimize this huffman code the spectral data is divided into parts that may use different huffman code books. The problem regarding the spectral data is twofold. On the one hand, huffman codes always bear the risk of error propagation, on the other hand there is one critical codebook in which errors can reach a very annoying level.

By resorting the spectral values the error propagation can be limited and moved into a spectral region with lower sensitivity to errors. This is achieved by placing the low frequency lines at special points inside the datafield (see Figure 5) so that the starting point of the appropriate huffman code word is known in advance. Thus, biterrors that change the length of a previous codeword do not propagate the error into these sensitive spectral regions.

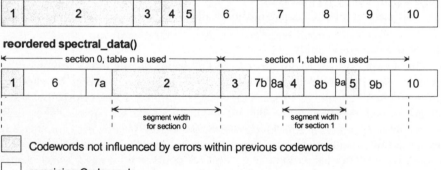

Figure 5: Reordering of spectral values for enhanced error robustness

3.4.2.2   Scalefactor RVLC

The scalefactors play an important role in an AAC bitstream. They are responsible for the frequency selective adjustment of the quantization noise. In the original AAC bistream syntax this data is differentially coded and huffman coded. This type of coding results in an extreme error sensitivity and the risk of error propagation due to the differential encoding. Additionally, erroneous scalefactors can create extremely annoying coding artifacts.

The proposed solution in MPEG-4 version 2 is to replace the huffman code by a similar code that can be decoded from both the beginning and the end of the

378

datafield. This is achieved by a special feature of that code. All codewords are symmetrical.

Using an RVLC allows to limit error propagation and to detect single biterrors. This increases the stability of the scalefactors against transmission errors significantly.

The drawback of this technique is some additional overhead caused by the higher redundancy in the RVLC compared to a usual Huffman code. However, this overhead is acceptable if it leads to a significantly lower amount of annoying artifacts.

4 BROADCASTING SYSTEMS USING DIGITAL AUDIO CODING

In the past years, several digital broadcasting systems using perceptual audio coding have been developed. In the following some of these systems are highlighted.

4.1 Eureka 147 DAB

Eureka is a European initiative for research and development. The development of a digital audio broadcasting system, DAB, turned out to be project number 147 and started in 1987. Since then it is called Eureka 147 [10][11].

Eureka DAB has been designed to replace existing FM broadcast service. Special care has been taken to optimize the system for mobile reception. Consequently, Coded Orthogonal Frequency Division Multiplex (COFDM) has been chosen; the carriers are DQPSK (Differential Quadrature Phase Shift Keying) modulated. Channel coding uses convolutional coding allowing adjustable code rates. For audio coding, MPEG Layer-2 was chosen.

The Eureka system is synchronous to the audio framing (1152 samples = 46 msec @ 48 kHz). This allows usage of unequal error protection by choosing different Viterbi code rates for each class within a frame. Eureka DAB uses 1.536 MHz spectrum, resulting in a net bit rate of up to 1.5 Mbit/sec payload. This would allow for 6 channels at 256 kbit/sec; single frequency networks are possible. However, the ensemble can be configured in a flexible way so that more programs or data services can be transmitted as well – of course by trading audio quality. Eureka DAB has proven to be very robust in mobile reception.

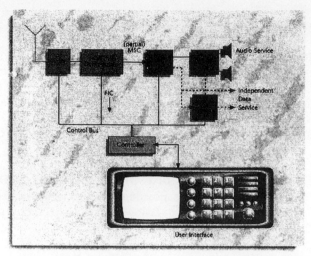

Figure 6: DAB conceptual decoder

In Europe, pilot phases have been conducted in several European countries, now being changed into commercial operation. Yet the system lacks   sufficient numbers of receivers and availability of spectrum. Due to the long take-up time of Eureka DAB, the audio coding involved is no longer state-of-the-art technology. The number of channels could be increased by a factor of up to 2 by using the latest audio coding technology, e.g. MPEG-2 AAC.

Attempts to have Eureka DAB adopted in the U.S. have yet failed, since the U.S. want to establish "InBand" systems in the existing FM band to avoid problems involved with switching to new frequencies. However, Eureka DAB will be used in several other countries outside Europe.

4.2 WorldSpace

WorldSpace is a privately financed company with the goal to establish a satellite broadcasting system for Africa, South-America and Asia. The first satellite, AfriStar, has been launched in October 98. The system is currently under test, has already been demonstrated and will soon go into commercial use. The WorldSpace system uses Quadrature Phase Shift Keying (QPSK) modulation and concatenated channel coding, i.e. convolutional coding followed by a block code (from the viewpoint of the decoder). Each satellite supports three regions, each region is covered by two beams with 96 primary channels á 16 kbit/sec (+0.5 kbit/sec for auxiliary information) each. These primary channels can again be combined to form higher bitrates up to 128 kbit/sec. WorldSpace uses MPEG Layer-3 for audio coding, this allows audio qualities from "similar to shortwave" up to "CD-like" [12][13]. Following the requirements for satellite broadcasting in the countries covered, it is possible to uplink each broadcast channel independently. The satellite is not just a simple transponder, but performs on-board processing to combine the different uplinks to the beams.

380

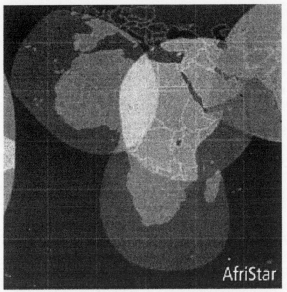

Figure 7: AfriStar coverage area

Similar to most line-of-sight digital satellite broadcasts based on concatenated coding, the error statistics show a "brick-wall" characteristic: As long as the signal is good enough, the error rate is very low. Starting at a certain SNR value, the channel quality drops rather quickly to a very high error rate. Therefore, such a channel basically shows only two states: "signal perfect" or "signal destroyed". In such an environment, bitstream error robustness is of limited importance, since almost all information is distorted and can therefore not be recovered. Of course correct behavior in such cases (e.g. concealment) is still necessary.

4.3 Digital Video Broadcasting (DVB)

DVB is a consortium set up for the development of digital video broadcasting mainly in Europe. Nowadays, however, the system is not only important in Europe, but also in America, Africa and Asia. Broadcasters, consumer electronics manufacturers, regulatory bodies and other entities are members of DVB [14].
DVB specifies three different systems:

- **DVB-S (Satellite)**: This system is based on QPSK modulation and concatenated channel coding (Convolutional coding and Reed Solomon block coding). The code rate can be adjusted, one typical example is around 40 Mbit/sec through one 36 MHz transponder [15].
- **DVB-C (Cable)**: Uses 64 Quadrature Amplitude Modulation (QAM) and Reed Solomon FEC (higher and lower QAMs also possible). An 8 MHz channel can carry 38.5 Mbit/sec if 64 QAM is used [16].
- **DVB-T (Terrestrial)**: Uses COFDM (Coded Orthogonal Frequency Division Multiplexing). 1705 carriers (2k-mode) or 6817 carriers (8k-mode) modulated

381

by QPSK or QAM are used. Channel coding uses concatenated coding similar to the other DVB modes [16]. Being similar to DAB, DVB-T can offer high robustness in case of multipath reception and allows for single frequency networks. DVB-T is highly configurable in terms of channel robustness vs. bitrate. Possible configurations for *stationary* receivers used in tests allow a net bitrate of 19.35 Mbit/sec through a 7 MHz channel. For mobile reception, however, spectral efficiency is much lower (i.e. similar to Eureka DAB).

To match current "NTSC/PAL/SECAM quality" on most television material probably requires operation at between 2.5 and 6 Mbit/s, depending upon the program material.

With the exception of audio coding in some countries, DVB Source Coding is based on MPEG-2 Video, MPEG-1/2 Audio Layer-2 and MPEG-2 Systems. The standard provides stereo as well as multichannel capabilities.

4.4 Systems in Japan defined by the Association of Radio Industries and Businesses (ARIB)

Several standards for digital broadcasting are developed in Japan and defined by ARIB [18]. These systems use MPEG-2 systems and video and MPEG-2 AAC, mainly the LC profile for audio coding.

ISDB (Integrated Services Digital Broadcasting, Satellite):

This system will launch in 2000 and will provide SDTV and HDTV television via Satellite. Exact information on the technical specification of this system is difficult to obtain, but it can be assumed that modulation and channel coding follow the basic concept of other satellite broadcasting systems.

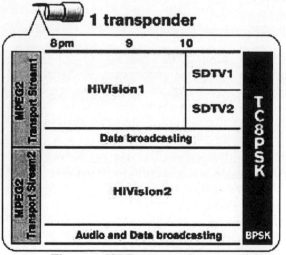

Figure 8: ISDB transponder (example)

382

ISDB-T (ISDB-Terrestrial):
Defines SDTV and HDTV for terrestrial broadcasting. The system uses OFDM based on QPSK, DQPSK or QAM and concatenated coding. Depending on the configuration, between 4 and 27 Mbit/sec can be achieved in a 7 MHz channel [19][20].

ISDB-T sound:
This system is based on ISDB-T, but provides an audio only service using MPEG-2 AAC [19]. It seems to be the first direct competitor for Eureka DAB.

4.5 The Mobile Satellite Broadcasting (MSB) System in Japan
MSB is promoted by Toshiba, Toyota and Fujitsu. Its purpose is sound and multimedia broadcasting from satellite to mobile receivers. MSB will use MPEG-2 AAC for audio coding [20].

4.6 In Band on Channel (IBOC) in the US
The broadcasting infrastructure in the US is quite different from that in Europe. While Europe has many governmental broadcasters, which are transmitting several programs in larger areas or even in the whole country, broadcasters in the US are mainly private and local. While they would certainly like to go digital, a smooth transition period from analog to digital is very important to them. As far as possible they would like to keep their frequencies and operational independence. This led to the development of "In band on channel" systems, which place the digital signal in the same and/or next adjacent channel of the existing analog signal. Using this technology, both the analog and the digital signal coexist in the same frequency area. Thus transition to digital becomes very easy: No new frequency allocations are required and the analog and the digital version can be transmitted simultaneously for several years.

Technically however, IBOC implementation is not a simple task. A test of older IBOC/IBAC systems several years ago showed that technology was not advanced enough at this time to allow such a system to work. However, technology has advanced since then, especially in audio coding. For example, AAC coding is up to a factor 2 more efficient than what was used in some of the older systems (Layer-2).

As of now, three companies in the US are developing IBOC systems, two of them considering AAC as their audio coding system of choice. All systems are supposed to have a mode for medium wave AM and for FM. USA Digital Radio (USADR) uses Orthogonal Frequency Division Multiplex (OFDM) and Reed Solomon FEC. For Audio Coding, MPEG AAC is used. Special care is taken for error robustness and error concealment [22].

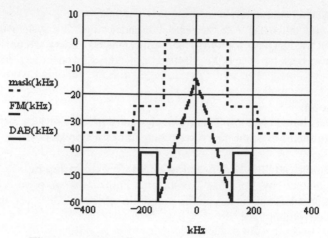

mask(kHz)

FM(kHz)

DAB(kHz)

kHz

Figure 9: USADR FM Hybrid IBOC Spectrum

Lucent Digital Radio also proposes an OFDM based system, but intends to use a special version of Lucent EPAC for audio coding [23]. Finally, Digital Radio Express (DRE), the smallest of the three competitors, has its own system proposal, as well using MPEG AAC for audio coding.

4.7 Digital Radio Mondial (DRM)

Like DVB, DRM is a consortium consisting of broadcasters, equipment manufacturers, receiver manufacturers, research organizations and other bodies. DRM has been established to develop a new digital service for the current analog AM services in long-, medium- and shortwave (i.e. below 30 MHz).

Different proposals for channel coding and modulation have been tested and are under evaluation now. For Audio coding, DRM selected MPEG AAC. Since the channel characteristic especially in short wave bands is very difficult, special care will be taken that the AAC source coding is as error robust as possible within the given channels. Based on this requirement, the above mentioned features for error robustness, defined in MPEG-4 version 2, are under consideration in DRM. Additionally, for future extensions of the DRM system based on channel combining, an AAC solution with scalability features (i.e. MPEG-4 AAC) might be the most appropriate solution.

5 CONCLUSIONS

Although we are already in the middle of the "digital revolution", using Computers, CD-Players and cellular phones, most audio or video (=TV) broadcasting systems in the world are still analog. There are two main reasons for that. First of all, establishment of a new broadcasting system is a complex long-term procedure. Regulatory steps need to be taken, studio and transmitter equipment needs to be modified, and upgraded receivers need to be built and sold. All this takes time.

The second reason is the so-called chicken-and-egg problem. Without customers being equipped with receivers, broadcasters are not interested in setting up expensive services, but without programs the receiver manufacturers don't want to produce receivers because of insufficient market acceptance.

The systems mentioned in the previous sections are tackling this problem with different methods, market success will show in the mid-term future how good their respective concepts were.

The technological basis for establishment of digital broadcasting systems exists since quite some time, but has been improved significantly recently, e.g. because of the availability of highly efficient audio coders such as MPEG AAC.

Even if most audio and TV transmission are still analog today: The digital broadcasting "age" took off and will change the consumers' impression of broadcasting rapidly.

There is no doubt that sooner or later most broadcasting systems will become digital, either because of the added value they offer (e.g. more programs) or simply because the digital systems will become cheaper. The conversion process has already started, but it will take some more time.

REFERENCES

[1]   ISO/IEC JTC1/SC29/WG11 MPEG, International Standard ISO 11172 "Coding of moving pictures and associated audio for digital storage media up to 1.5 Mbit/s", Part 3: Audio

[2]   ISO/IEC JTC1/SC29/WG11 MPEG. International Standard IS 13818-3 Information Technology - Generic Coding of Moving Pictures and Associated Audio, Part 3: Audio, 1994

[3]   ISO/IEC JTC1/SC29/WG11 MPEG. International Standard IS 13818-7 Information Technology - Generic Coding of Moving Pictures and Associated Audio, Part 7: Advanced Audio Coding, 1997

[4]   ISO/IEC JTC1/SC29/WG11 (MPEG), International Standard ISO/IEC IS 14496-3: "Coding of Audio-Visual Objects: Audio", 1999

[5]   ISO/IEC JTC1/SC29/WG11 (MPEG), Committee Draft ISO/IEC 14496-3 Amd 1: "Coding of Audio-Visual Objects: Audio", 1999

[6]   ISO/IEC JTC1/SC29/WG11 (MPEG) Document N2725, "Overview of the MPEG-4 Standard", Seoul, 1999

[7]   G. A. Soulodre, T. Grusec, M. Lavoie, L. Thibault, "Subjective Evaluation of State-of-the-Art 2-Channel Audio Codecs", Journal of the AES, March 1998, pp. 164-177

[8]   K. Brandenburg, G. Stoll, Y.F. Dehery, J.D. Johnston, L.v.d. Kerkhof, E.F. Schröder: "The ISO/MPEG-Audio Codec: A Generic Standard for Coding of High Quality Digital Audio", JAES 42, 780-792

[9]   Bosi, Brandenburg, Quackenbush, Fielder, Akagiri, Fuchs, Dietz, Herre,

Davidson, Oikawa, "ISO/IEC MPEG-2 Advanced Audio Coding", 101st AES Convention, Los Angeles, November 1996

[10] ETSI Publication ETS 300 401 ed.2, "Radio broadcasting systems; Digital Audio Broadcasting (DAB) to mobile, portable and fixed receivers", May 1995 (www.etsi.org)

[11] Website of Eureka DAB, www.eurekadab.org, and website of World DAB, www.worlddab.org, July 99

[12] R. Buchta, S. Meltzer, O. Kunz, "The WorldStar sound format", Preprint 4385, 101st AES convention, Los Angeles, November 1996

[13] Website of WorldSpace, www.worldspace.com, July 99

[14] Website of the Digital Video Broadcasting (DVB) consortium, www.dvb.org, July 99

[15] ETSI Publication EN 300 421 V1.1.2, "Digital Video Broadcasting (DVB); Framing structure, channel coding and modulation for 11/12 GHz satellite services",August 1997

[16] ETSI Publication EN 300 429 V1.2.1, "Digital Video Broadcasting (DVB); Framing structure, channel coding and modulation for cable systems", April 1998

[17] ETSI Publication EN 300 744 V1.2.1, "Digital Video Broadcasting (DVB); Framing structure, channel coding and modulation for digital terrestrial television", Draft, February 1999

[18] Website of the Associaton of Radio Industries and Business (ARIB), www.arib.or.jp, July 1999

[19] Website of the Digital Broadcasting Experts Group (DiBEG), www.dibeg.org, July 1999

[20] M. Takada, "Draft Standard of Digital Terrestrial Audio Broadcasting in Japan", NAB 99, Las Vegas, 1999

[21] S. Hirakawa, "The broadcasting-Satellite service (Sound) Using 2.6 GHz Band in Japan", NAB 99, Las Vegas, 1999

[22] Website of USA Digital Radio, www.ibocradio.com, July 1999

[23] A. Pate, "The Implementation of Digital Audio Broadcasting Using IBOC, A Complete System View"; NAB 99, Las Vegas, 1999

[24] Website of the Digital Radio Mondial (DRM) consortium, www.drm.org, July 1999

Methods for Digital Transmission below 30 MHz: What are the Possibilities?

J. Lindner

Department of Information Technology,
University of Ulm, Germany

1   Introduction

There is no doubt about the advantages of transmission and storage of information in digital format. Wired services for speech and data went already this way. Computer to computer communication and the internet has been digital since its beginning. CD and DVD are examples in the field of storage of audio, video, and still pictures. The term *multimedia* is accepted to describe all these different sources of information.

The same trend to multimedia can also be seen in wireless transmission. Although speech is the main application for mobile and cordless communication (GSM, DECT e.g.) at the moment, multimedia will be the future. Digital broadcast services like satellite TV and radio went also in the digital direction. Moreover, DAB will replace FM radio and DVB-T will be introduced in near future.

The only area left seems to be the broadcast below 30 MHz, i.e. in the LF, MF and HF bands. Of course, here one can also profit from going digital. For this reason the NADIB (NArrowband DIgital Broadcast) group was founded in Europe in 1996. Two candidate systems for digital transmission have been discussed in the NADIB group: one proposal originating from french partners and one from german. At the moment only audio is considered and there was no discussion about the encoding scheme: it should be an advanced version of MPEG audio encoding. There is a special contribution in this book [1] and further contributions concerning the two digital transmission schemes [2], [3].

In 1997 the world-wide group DRM (Digital Radio Mondiale) was founded with the same intention as NADIB, and the technical contributions already developed by NADIB were taken as a basis for DRM. At the moment it is the task of the DRM *coding and modulation group* to define the coding and modulation part of a candidate system for digital broadcast which will be taken then as input for a world-wide standardisation by the ITU.

In the following some basic considerations are made with regard to digital transmission schemes (i.e. coding and modulation) suitable for those frequency regions below 30 MHz.

2 Going digital in frequency regions below 30 MHz

From a theoretical point of view, the reason for replacing analog transmission schemes by digital ones is quite clear for long. Since Shannon's early work it is known that all physical transmission channels have a certain capacity and that only digital transmission with a rate below this capacity has the potential to be error-free. In a first step, speech, music, pictures and movies lead to analog source signals, so they have to be digitised and source encoded before digital transmission. Shannon showed that source and channel coding can be separated without any loss. This means in a first step source encoding (or compression) to remove redundancy. In the second step the channel coding adds redundancy, which is needed to stay below channel capacity and which gives the capability for error correction. The only loss in case of transmission of analog source signals is an unavoidable loss due digitisation, usually called *irrelevance*. In the mean time it has also proven in practice, that for a given physical channel the quality of audio and video transmission by an inner digital transmission will be much better than a direct analog transmission. But the gain in quality depends on the properties of the physical channel as well as on the available transmit power. In practice it is also necessary to look carefully at the interface between source and channel coding. It might be of advantage to have unequal error protection or to benefit from hierarchical coding/modulation. There is one contribution in this book dealing with this topic [4].

In frequency bands below 30 MHz the physical channel exhibits some difficulties, because propagation of electromagnetic waves in this frequency region involves the ionosphere with its time-varying multipath nature.To develop transmission methods which transmit as fast and error-free as possible for the given bandwidths and transmit powers,a modeling of this ionospheric channel is needed. Since the early work of Bello in the sixties appropriate models have been available. In the HF region they are called *Watterson models* because Watterson did pioneering work in this field [5]. Those models can easily be extended to LF and MF. In [2] there is a table with a brief description of the channel models NADIB and DRM agreed on.

Good audio coding schemes can compress the data rate down to less than 30 kbit/s [1]. Because bandwidth and channel allocation will not change compared with existing analog services, a digital transmission scheme with bandwidth efficiency in the order 2 bit/s/Hz to 3 bit/s/Hz must be realised.

3   Digital transmission schemes

There are two basic digital transmission techniques, which are always in discussion if a new transmission scheme shall be defined: multicarrier transmission (MC), especially OFDM (Orthogonal Frequency Division) and single carrier (SC) transmission together with appropriate coding. Both are also candidates for the digital broadcast considered here.They will be assumed in the following, as common, only in connection with linear modulation methods, i.e. quadrature amplitude modulation (QAM) or combinations of amplitude and phase shift keying (ASK/PSK), respectively. Other methods have no potential to reach the goal, to be as bandwidth and power efficient as possible. So further alternatives will not be considered.

It is not the intention of this contribution to explain OFDM and SC transmissions in detail, but differences and commonalities will be considered with regard to broadcast below 30 MHz. More about SC and OFDM transmission can be found e.g. in textbooks like [6]. For OFDM a vast amount of papers have been written. One impetus to consider this old technique again was given by Bingham [7].

3.1   Coded OFDM and coded SC transmission

OFDM divides a given bandwidth into a set of very narrowband *subchannels.* The stream of data symbols to be transmitted is split   into parallel streams which are transmitted then over those subchannels to the receiving side, of course with slower speed. At the receiving side the parallel incoming streams are converted back to one single stream. The advantage of this technique is, that in case of multipath propagation channels with frequency-selective behaviour no equalization is required at the receiving side. Each data symbol is multiplied by a factor (which is complex-valued in general) only. This is in contrast to SC transmissions, where each data symbol covers the whole bandwidth, and, as a consequence, equalization is needed.

Both methods have advantages and disadvantages which depend on the frequency-selectivity of the physical channel as well as on practical restrictions with respect to the complexity allowed for realization. Early comparisons have been made in connection with the development of advanced shortwave radio (HF) modems, long before the term OFDM was used. The result in the beginning of the eighties was that SC is better than those parallel schemes which we call today OFDM. There were two reasons. The first was that OFDM suffers from the frequency-selective behaviour of the channel more than SC and the second was that OFDM has a higher crest factor in the transmit signal, which restricts the transmit power more than in case of SC, because HF radio transmitters are peak-power limited.

Today we can use more advanced coding schemes and for code rates in the order of 1/2 both methods can have similar bit error rate performance for slowly time-varying frequency selective channels. And for the crest factor reduction of OFDM, methods are under discussion for some time. But for code rates close to 1 (i.e. only little redundancy added) there might be differences which still favour SC. The following description shall allow a basic understanding of these facts. More can be found in [8], although this paper treats the same topic in a more general multiuser system context. The original ideas   are published already in [9].

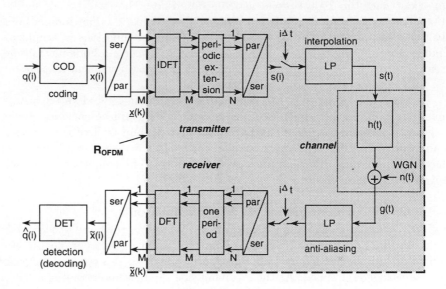

Figure 1: COFDM transmission model

3.2   Model of a coded OFDM transmission

OFDM is a block-wise transmission scheme; Fig. 1 shows a basic model. The coding block in this figure means a mapping of the sequence of source symbols $q(i)$ into a sequence of transmit symbols $x(i)$, which are in general complex-valued, e.g. $x(i)\epsilon\{\pm 1 \pm j\}$ in case of QPSK. The serial-parallel conversion forms *blocks* or *vectors* $\underline{x}(k)$ with these symbols as components. The $\underline{x}(k)$ are then transmitted by the OFDM scheme:inverse discrete fourier transform (IDFT), periodic extension over the guard interval and construction of the continuous-time transmit signal $s(t)$. The coding has to be defined in close relation to the size of the vectors. Then it is common to use the term COFDM (coded OFDM).

The channel is assumed to be time-invariant or only slowly time-variant with impulse response $h(t)$. After sampling, serial-parallel conversion, extraction of one period and discrete fourier transform (DFT) an estimate $\underline{\tilde{x}}(k)$ for $\underline{x}(k)$ with soft values as components results. The detection, which is soft decision decoding only in normal OFDM, produces decisions $\hat{q}(i)$ with respect to the transmitted source symbols $q(i)$. An optimum detector is identical with an optimum soft decision decoder in this case.

3.3 COFDM and coded SC transmission: A common model

For channels like those considered here, a block-wise transmission is also common in case of SC. OFDM uses the gap between two consecuitive blocks for a periodic or cyclic repetition of the signal, while in the SC case it is common to use it for the transmission of a channel sounding sequence.

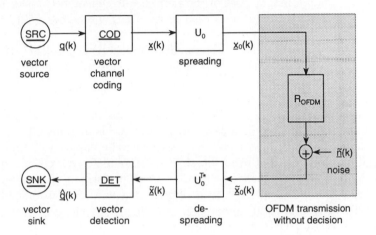

Figure 2: Model for a COFDM and Coded Single Carrier Block Transmission

Fig. 2 shows a model which includes OFDM and a SC transmission within the block as two special cases. Compared with Fig. 1, the sequence of source symbols $q(i)$ is now a sequence of source symbol vectors $\underline{q}(k)$. Of course, in practice the vectors will be formed by serial-parallel conversion which is included now in the vector source. Consequently, the sequence of source symbol vectors $\underline{q}(k)$ will be transformed by *vector coding* (COD) into a sequence $\underline{x}(k)$ of transmit symbol vectors which were described before. The mapping from $\underline{x}(k)$ to $\underline{\tilde{x}}(k)$ is a discrete-time *vector channel*, which is here identical with a simple matrix R_{OFDM}, being defined already in Fig. 1. k is a discrete time variable which counts the blocks $\underline{q}(k)$, $\underline{x}(k)$ and $\underline{x}_0(k)$. Their scalar components are $q_i(k)$, $x_i(k)$ and $x_{0i}(k)$, respectively. The component sequences $x_{0i}(k)$ are transmitted in parallel, which defines the subchannels of the OFDM scheme. So the number M of components in $\underline{x}_0(k)$ is identical with the number of subchannels.

The matrix U_0 is new. It maps the vector sequence $\underline{x}(k)$ to be transmitted into another vector (or block) sequence $\underline{x}_0(k)$, which is the key in this model. If U_0 is assumed to be an identity matrix, a COFDM transmission results and

391

if it is a fourier matrix F (DFT), a coded SC transmission within the block is given.

At the receiving side there is a corresponding vector sequence $\tilde{\underline{x}}_0(k)$ of estimates for $\underline{x}_0(k)$:

$$\tilde{\underline{x}}_0(k) = R_{OFDM} \cdot \underline{x}_0(k) + \tilde{\underline{n}}(k)$$

Due to the guard time between OFDM blocks, the cyclic repetition and the use of only one period at the receiving side, R_{OFDM} is a diagonal matrix. The entries are squared magnitudes of the periodically repeated transfer function of the channel at the frequencies used in the OFDM scheme. $\tilde{\underline{n}}(k)$ is a noise vector.

After multiplication with the conjugate complex transpose of U_0 the detection (DET) gives a sequence $\hat{\underline{q}}(k)$, which corresponds to $\underline{q}(k)$ at the transmitting side. In contrast to Fig. 1, in general DET is no longer the counterpart of COD at the transmitting side. Depending on U_0 it may consist of equalisation and decoding connected in a complicated manner. If COD and U_0 are defined well, the DET algorithms at the receiving side may have the potential to produce an overall best result, i.e. to reach the capacity bound for the physical channel. On the other hand, if it is not defined well, an optimum DET algorithm has no chance to produce good performance, because it cannot correct things which have been done wrong at the transmit side. But the definition of COD and U_0 has also an influence on the complexity of the algorithms used for DET at the receiving side.

Multiplication of the transmit symbol vectors with $U_0 = F$ may also be interpreted as *spreading*, because each individual symbol to be transmitted is spread by this transformation over all OFDM subchannels, i.e. over the total bandwidth used on the physical channel. At the receiving side the multiplication with the conjugate complex transpose of this matrix is then identical with *despreading* and the detection should be a proper combination of equalisation and decoding. Because there is no basic difference between a transmission system with different users or different subchannels as it is considered here, the detection can also be understood as *multiuser detection* (MUD). So MUD algorithms can also be used in this context. For further explanations see [8].

3.4 Spreading and coding

A frequency-selective behavior of the physical transmission channel, which is the normal case in the broadcast regions below 30MHz, can cause zero-entries on the main diagonal of R_{OFDM}. Without any coding, i.e. with code rate 1 or close to 1, OFDM then has no chance to become error-free, even with the noise absent. The reason is that some components in $\tilde{\underline{x}}(k)$ can be faded out in that case. With $U_0 = F$, i.e. in the SC case, this is different. Because all components in $\tilde{\underline{x}}(k)$ can be non-zero then, an error-free transmission is possible, also with code rates 1.

Fig. 3 tries to illustrate this fact for a BPSK transmission with two OFDM

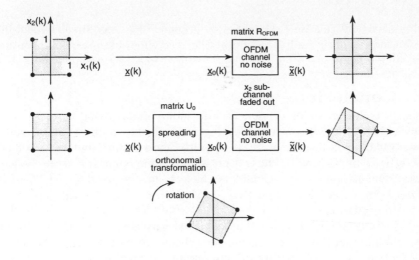

Figure 3: The Effect of Spreading

subchannels, where one subchannel is faded out. Spreading with orthogonal matrices (like F) means a rotation of the constellation in the two-dimensional space in this example. Without this rotation the four points collapse to two, and because this means that two euclidean distances become zero, no error-free transmission is possible. With rotation (i.e. with spreading) the 4 points at the receiving side have a remaining euclidean distance, so error-free transmission is possible. In another way one can also say that SC uses some kind of frequency diversity, OFDM doesn't.

To get this diversity effect, in general it is not necessary to spread the transmit symbols over all OFDM subchannels, i.e. over the whole bandwidth. Because the width of the spreading has an influence on the complexity of the detection algorithm at the receiving side, spreading over a few subchannels might be sufficient. Such a scheme shall be given the name *SOFDM* (spread OFDM). In a multiuser context this scheme is called *MC-CDMA* (multicarrier code division multiple access) or OFDM-CDMA.

Of course, in practice there will be coding with code rates less than one. Then the code can take the role of spreading to some extent and the decoding can use the diversity. But the difference between COFDM and a coded spread OFDM (CSOFDM) transmission depends on the details, i.e. the code, the code rate, the channel, and the complexity allowed at the receiving side. In any case, coding (COD) and the transformation with U_0 may also be considered as a concatenated coding scheme consisting of COD followed by coding with rate 1, which is the transformation or spreading with a proper chosen matrix U_0. Of course, this second code with rate 1 is in the field of real or complex numbers. So, obviously any coding scheme used for OFDM can also

393

be replaced by this new concatenated scheme. But, as already mentioned above, despreading and detection at the receiving side are no conventional decoding scheme.

4 Conclusions

From a technical point of view digital audio broadcasting in frequency regions below 30 MHz is a challenging task. Today, audio coding with less than 30 kbit/s is feasible and gives already good results, but the number of bit/s/Hz to be realised by the transmission scheme remains a great challenge. Two transmission scheme candidates have been discussed so far: COFDM (Coded Orthogonal Frequency Division Multiplexing) and coded single carrier (SC) transmission.

The intention of this contribution was to give some basic insight into the relation between these two transmission schemes and to sketch a way how the two existing proposals can merge into one proposal, which is the intention of DRM. Because standardisation is with respect to the "air interface" only, the methods to be defined at the transmit side should have a potential, allowing a receiver to reach theoretical performance limits.

With respect to coding and modulation there is still some work to be done. But it can be stated already now, that the result of the work in DRM will lead to an advanced system for digital broadcast in frequency regions below 30 MHz, which is up to date from a theoretical point of view and which takes also into account restrictions coming from practice.

References

[1] O. Kunz. MPEG-4 Scalable Audio Coding for Digital Radio Systems. *Proc. 5th International Symposium on Communication Theory and Applications, Ambleside 1999*, these proceedings, 1999.

[2] J. Egle, A. Brakemeier, and D. Rudolph. Modulation and Coding Scheme using Serial Transmission for Digital Radio Broadcast in the HF Band. *Proc. 5th International Symposium on Communication Theory and Applications, Ambleside 1999*, these proceedings, 1999.

[3] C.J. Demeure, P. A. Laurent, B. Le Floch, and D. Lacroix. Optimised COFDM Waveform and Coding Schemes for Digital Terrestrial Radio Broadcasting. *Proc. 5th International Symposium on Communication Theory and Applications, Ambleside 1999*, these proceedings, 1999.

[4] D. F. Yuan, D. Schill, and J. Huber. Robust Hierarchical Broadcasting for AWGN and Flat Rayleigh Fading Channels using Multilevel Codes. *Proc. 5th International Symposium on Communication Theory and Applications, Ambleside 1999*, these proceedings, 1999.

[5] C.C. Watterson, J.R. Juposher, and W.D. Besema. Experimental Verification of an Ionospheric Channel Model. *ESSA Tech. Rept. (US Government Printing Office)*, ERL 112-IST, 1969.

[6] J. G. Proakis. *Digital Commmunications*. McGraw-Hill, New York, 1989.

[7] J.A.C. Bingham. Multicarrier Modulation for Data Transmission: An Idea Whose Time has Come. *IEEE Commun. Mag.*, pages 5–14, 1990.

[8] J. Lindner. MC-CDMA in The Context of General Multiuser / Multisubchannel Transmission Methods. *European Transactions on Telecommunications (ETT)*, page will appear in fall 1999, 1999.

[9] J. Lindner. Channel Coding and Modulation for Transmission over Multipath Channels. *AEÜ, No. 3*, 49:110–119, 1995.

Channel Coding in DVB: State of the Art and Future Developments

G. Markarian, A. Mason, K. Pickavance and S. Waddington

Tandberg Television, Stoneham Rectory, Stoneham Lane,
Eastleigh, Hampshire, SO50 9NW, UK

E-mail: gmarkarian, amason, kpickavance, swaddington@tandbergtv.com

Introduction

In view of the increasing demand for digital video broadcasting services, more efficient utilisation of the existing resources is required. For example, in the case of digital satellite broadcasting this means more efficient utilisation of bandwidth, power and orbit location.

Although digital video broadcasting (DVB) standards have been accepted recently, it is expected that second generation of the DVB systems must have efficiency significantly closer to the Shannon bound when compared to the existing systems. In real terms this means that these systems must satisfy the following demands:

- Maximise the rate of data transmission;
- Maximise data reliability;
- Minimise required energy, bandwidth and system complexity.

In this paper we describe the major DVB standards, estimate their efficiency and show the feasibility of their improvement. In particular we consider novel modulation and error control coding schemes, which, when applied to the DVB systems, could provide up to 3.5 dB additional gain. We also show that this gain can transferred into higher information rates through the same bandwidth or to the smaller antenna dishes as could be the case for DVB over satellites. We concentrate our attention on the use of recently introduced turbo-codes, as one of the most powerful tools that allows the achievement of the above mentioned goals. However, our study indicates that direct application of the known turbo-codes (both turbo-product codes and turbo-convolutional codes) to the digital video broadcasting systems is not possible, due to a number of problems:

- Existing error floor at low bit error ratio;
- The need for external synchronisation;
- The difficulties with the carrier and clock recovery at the demodulator.

In the transmission of digital information over a communications channel, the mapping of digital data into analogue waveforms that match the characteristics of the channel is performed by the modulator. Therefore, the right choice of modulation format for a given channel environment represents one of the most important problems in the communications system design. In future TV broadcasting systems it is desired that the modulation system should meet the following demands:

(i) High information rate, in terms of bits/symbol. It is anticipated that information rates of order $R>4bit/symbol$ would be required;

(ii) Constant envelope. This is because envelope variations in the signal at the input of a non-linear device (such as on-board amplifier) produce distortion of the signal (and therefore the signal spectrum) at the output of the device. This effect leads to spectral spreading which may give rise, ultimately, to adjacent channel interference. The use of constant envelope modulation schemes can help to minimise spectral spreading in non-linear channels.

(iii) Simple (or relatively simple) synchronisation procedure for both carrier and symbol synchronisers.

(iv) Possibility for real-time channel evaluation without additional overhead sequences.

(v) Low complexity (and cost) of the implementation.

In the following Sections of the paper we describe the existing modulation techniques and analyse the feasibility of their implementation in the next generation of DVB-S.

DVB (Digital Video Broadcasting)

In 1991, broadcasters and consumer equipment manufacturers discussed the idea of having a European wide development of digital terrestrial TV. At the end of that year the European Launching Group (ELG) was formulated as a group to oversee this development. A Memorandum of Understanding (MoU) was drafted that established the rules to gain success in this venture. This MoU needed the trust and mutual respect of each of the commercial competitors. The MoU was signed in September 1993, and the launching group became DVB. Around this time the Working Group on Digital Television prepared a study of the prospects and possibilities for digital terrestrial TV in Europe. This introduced proposals to allow several different consumer markets to be served at the same time. In conjunction with this, the existing MAC satellite broadcasting industry was destined to be replaced to digital technology. DVB therefore provided a means to bring together all the major European television interests in one group.

It was soon to become clear that satellite and cable would be delivered first, ahead of terrestrial, due to simpler technical problems, and an easier regulatory climate.

By 1997, the DVB project was into its second stage promoting the open standards globally. The standards were set, and published through European Television Standards Institute (ETSI).

To date DVB includes over 220 well known organisations in more than 30 countries worldwide. Members include broadcasters, manufacturers, network operators and regulatory bodies. Numerous broadcast services using DVB standards are now operational in Europe, North and South America, Africa, Asia and Australasia. There are three main standards that we are mainly concerned with.

DVB-S [DVB-S] is the standard for satellite broadcasting, available in all five continents.
DVB-C [DVB-C], the cable standard. Services are planned or available in the USA, Scandinavia, France, Germany, Brazil, Italy, Spain, Argentina, Australia and the UK.
DVB-T [DVB-T], the terrestrial standard. In the UK the system went live on 15th November 1998, and has been set in the 15 members of the European Union, together with Australia and New Zealand.

There is a different standard for terrestrial set in Japan, ISDB-T [ISDB-T], an additional satellite service DSS, proprietary to Hughes in the USA, and an additional cable standard, OpenCable, developed by US CableLabs in the USA.

Further there is a standard from the group Advanced Television Systems Committee (ATSC), which developed the US terrestrial system [ATSC-DTS]. The differences between these and DVB standards will be explained later.

DVB standards were developed with interoperability in mind, so that the delivery medium was not a problem. There is no interoperability between ATSC, DSS and CableLabs.

Digital Requirements

If we were to simply digitise a television picture and try to use this digitised sequence as the data to send we would have created a much larger problem and so compression was needed. Many compression algorithms exist, for example H.262, H.263 and MPEG-1 and MPEG-2. The latter at the time was deemed to be the most advanced and provided the best quality for the particular problem.

If we simply digitise the picture we get the following:

Signal Component	Symbol	Sampling Frequency
Luminance	Y	13.5 MHz
Colour difference signal B-Y	C_B	6.75 MHz
Colour difference signal R-Y	C_Y	6.75 MHz
Total number of samples/sec		27.00 Mbits/sec
Total bit rate at 8 bits/sample	27×8	216 Mbits/sec
Basic Transmission Bandwidth (using PCM)		108 MHz

Table 1: The Size of the Digital TV problem

The figure of 108 MHz is obviously far too high to be using even the best modulation and coding techniques, so compression must be used to reduce this.

MPEG-2 compression is a varying rate lossy compression algorithm, enabling the broadcaster to have differing qualities of picture at each part of the broadcast chain However, in Table 2 we see that the compression ratios that give the expected results for each part of the chain, still provide significant improvements over the analogue domain.

Picture	Degradation	Bit Rate	Compression Ratio
625 Line Studio Original	Professional Quality – "Perfect Picture"	200 Mbits.s	1
625 Line Compressed	Professional Distribution Quality	8-10 Mbits/s	25-30
625 Line Compressed	Domestic Quality	4-5 Mbits/s	40-50
312 Line Compressed	Domestic VHS	1-2 Mbits/s	100-200

Table 2: Compression Ratios for differing quality of picture

So we have for the same quality as existing domestic TV sets a required bit rate of 4-5 Mbits/s, enabling the broadcaster to fit approximately 6 digital channels in the same 24MHz bandwidth that the existing analogue signal would occupy.

Digital Television

To explain the advantages of digital TV, we could think of the analogy that digital TV is to analogue TV what compact disk was to vinyl records. Of course that is only part of the advantage. This explains fully the quality and convenience advantages. That is, the picture will be of a better quality and more TV channels can be put in the same bandwidth of transmission.

This is not the only advantage that was made available in the standards produced for digital. There is also the facility of interactivity built into the systems. That is, more of the user having the choice to do things. This could be choice of camera angles, returning the result for a quiz or the purchase of merchandise from a televised store.

Further we have the chance of High Definition TV (HDTV) as well as the traditional format of Standard Definition TV (SDTV). This gives the broadcaster the ability to transmit either a single HDTV channel or several SDTV channels along side one another.

Also as the digitised picture is now binary bits, that is the same as computer data or indeed any other data, so embedding other data medium in the stream is no problem.

Along side the superior pictures is the far higher quality sound that can now be achieved using digital technology. Indeed, one attraction is for the home cinema experience, that is 5.1 surround sound. DVB chose the MPEG Layer II (MUSICAM), the audio coding scheme associated with the MPEG-2 video coding system at the time. MPEG also added Advanced Audio Coding (AAC) to the specification of MPEG-2, and this being superior to MUSICAM is being adopted as the audio coding layer for the Japanese market when ISDB-T is launched. One further audio coding layer that has an important place in the digital TV revolution is Dolby AC-3. The ATSC has chosen this as the audio coding layer for the US standard for terrestrial broadcasting.

For a concise but full explanation of the technical aspects of these audio coding layers see [Dietz].

The Broadcast Chain

The broadcast chain may be pictorially displayed along with the picture quality at each stage as seen in Figure 1.

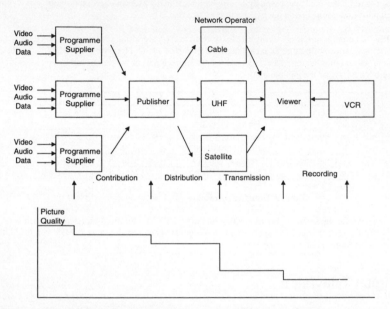

Figure 1: The Broadcast chain with associated picture quality

The Standards Documents

We will now give a brief description of the contents of the three DVB standards ([DVB-S], [DVB-T] and [DVB-S]) and then explain the main differences to the other standards documents mentioned above ([ISDB-T] and [ATSC DTS]).

We will not be too concerned with most of the standards. Our main aim of this paper is to concentrate on the coding and modulation schemes used, and we will only mention other aspects of the standard when totally necessary.

As a precursor to the explanation of the standards we give a pictorial overview of how the systems will see the MPEG-2 data streams. If the error coding and modulation blocks were considered as black boxes then the stream entering them is of the form given in Figure 2.

Sync Byte	187 Bytes

Figure 2: Simplified MPEG-2 Data Stream

400

It must be noted here that the reason for including the sync byte is primarily for the MPEG-2 decoder, however a particular implementation of decoding or demodulation may use it. The sync bytes are not all the same. There are seven packets with the Sync Byte as 47HEX followed by one packet with a B8HEX (inverted 47HEX) sync byte. This will provide a means of synchronisation over one packet and over eight packets.

So in all we have a packet of 188 bytes (called an MPEG frame). By using a pseudo random binary sequence exclusively or'd to the data stream, the data held in the 187 bytes can be considered random. This is to avoid, among other problems associated with long streams of identical symbols, modulation jitter and for spectrum shaping.

DVB-S

This standard is concerned with transmission over the satellite, using 11/12GHz bandwidth. The overall coding and modulation scheme can be seen as a typical concatenated coding scheme with an interleaver placed in between the outer and inner code, see Figure 3.

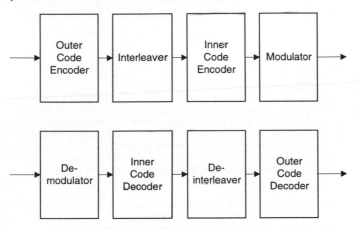

Figure 3: Simplified Satellite Scheme

We will now look closer and in more detail at the scheme. The outer code used is a (204,188,8) Reed-Solomon (RS) code over GF(256). This is a systematic code with bytes (8 binary bits) as symbols. This code is actually constructed using the (255,239,8) RS code, by appending 51 zeros to the input stream before encoding then removing them after encoding. This method is possible as the code is systematic. The interleaver is a convolutional interleaver (as opposed to block interleaver). This will be explained a little more later.

Then in Figure 3 we can see the convolutional code. This is a 64 state convolutional code, with rate ½. Other rates are achievable by puncturing the output stream. The allowed rates are 2/3, ¾, 7/8 and 8/9. The puncturing pattern is fixed and given in [DVB-S].

The modulation scheme used is conventional Gray-coded quadratic phase shift keying (QPSK), with no differential coding.

DVB-C

Similar to the DVB-S standard, the coding scheme used in DVB-C is the same (204,188,8) RS code, together with the same interleaver/deinterleaver, however no convolutional code is used. This is because the cable channel is less severe. Also the modulation is quite different in that there is a choice

401

from 16, 32, 64, 128 and 256QAM, all with differential coding of the two most significant bits (MSB). Figure 4 shows a block diagram for this. In the diagram q is 2 for 16QAM, 3 for 32QAM, 4 for 64QAM, etc.

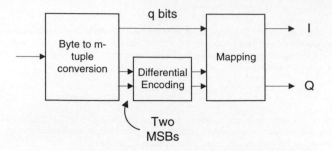

Figure 4: Byte to m-tuple and differential encoding of the cable system

DVB-T

Since the DVB-T system was designed to operate within the existing UHF spectrum allocation for analogue transmissions, the scheme adopted must have sufficient protection against high levels of Co-Channel Interference and Adjacent Channel Interference from existing analogue transmissions. It is with this in mind that the coding and modulation scheme employed was that of concatenated coding (as in DVB-S) with Orthogonal Frequency Division Mulitplexing (OFDM).Three modes of modulation where considered, that of QPSK, 16QAM and 64QAM, depending on the robustness of the particular scheme.

OFDM is a multicarrier modulation where the carriers are separated by a multiple of 1/T, where T is the modulation period and are characterised by the fact that spectrum of different carriers overlaps. Assuming that the carriers are modulated in an independent way, the power spectral density of the transmitted signal is obtained by the sum of the power of all carriers. It is apparent that the transmitted spectrum will tend to have a rectangular shape when the number of carriers increases: this reduced the requirements to channel filters. In the DVB-T standard two modes are defined, which correspond to the number of carriers being used in the OFDM signal. The basic "2k" mode is suitable for single transmitter operation and small single frequency networks (SFN) with limited transmitter power, while the "8k" mode is suitable for both single transmitter operation and small and large SFNs. These carrier frequencies are generated using inverse Fourier transform and accounts for the very robust characteristics of the OFDM signal in the mutipath environment.

Further within the OFDM section of the scheme there is bit and symbol (modulation symbol) interleaving, that will spread errors accounted for by the OFDM scheme drop outs and bursts.

ATSC-DTS

The ATSC-DTS scheme was developed after the above DVB standards. It is mainly to be used as transmission for HDTV. In deciding this standard the COFDM scheme was replaced by a Pragmatic Trellis Coded Modulation (PTCM) scheme incorporating a Vestigial Side Band (VSB) technique. PTCM in one basic form can be considered how to use a rate ½ coding scheme in higher rate systems. The trellis encoder scheme can be seen in Figure 5 .

402

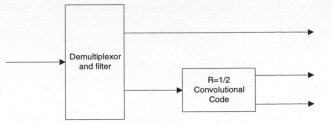

Figure 5 : Rate = 2/3 trellis encoder scheme used in the ATSC DTS standard

The concatenated scheme is much the same in that an outer RS code is used. However this RS code is a (207,187,8) code. The method used is to drop the sync byte of the MPEG-2 packet before encoding and place back on after. There is also an interleaver placed between the coding schemes, but again this is slightly different although still a convolutional interleaver.

Following the trellis encoder is the VSB modulator. This takes in the three bits from the trellis encoder and after mapping and further interleaving produces a modulated signal that can take 8 levels. The VSB modulator provides a filtered (root-raised cosine) IF signal at a standard frequency (44 MHz in the U.S.), with most of one sideband removed. Finally, the RF upconverter translates the signal to the desired RF channel.

ISDB-T

This standard can be thought of a cross between ATSC-DTS and DVB-T. It uses the similar coding and modulation scheme to DVB-T (concatenated coding and OFDM modulation) but is mainly aimed at HDTV in the first instance, with support for multi-channel SDTV.

Coding Introduction

The main problem brought about in relation to the channel coding for digital TV is that due to the high compression rates errors can propagate catastrophically throughout the data. This is such that one error can develop into many errors, thus destroying or causing serious artefacts in the picture. Also when comparing to a *good quality* analogue TV the standards have specified a bit error rate (BER) at the working point of the system as 10^{-11} (this is known as quasi error free, or QEF). This is very low BER and obtaining a coding scheme to achieve this was a near impossible task if only to prove that a scheme was indeed achieving this rate.

At 40Mbits/sec, a BER of 10^{-11} is about one error an hour and for statistical purposes many thousands of errors are required to prove a system is robust. For most simulation schemes achieving anywhere near 40Mbits/sec was near impossible and so together with long simulation runs, the theoretical aspects of the code were investigated. At the time of developing the standards, NASA had completed much work on concatenated coding schemes for space flight models. This information and data were invaluable in choosing the schemes for digital TV. We now give a brief explanation of the constituent parts of the coding schemes used.

Convolutional Codes

The inner code used in the DVB systems (when used) is a constraint length 7 convolutional code, with generators (171_{OCT}, 133_{OCT}). In diagrammatic form this can be seen in Figure 6.

403

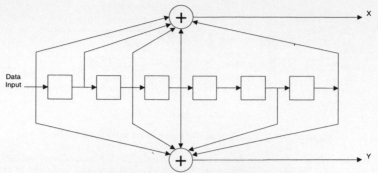

Figure 6.: The mother convolutional code of rate 1/2

As can be seen in Figure 6 this *mother* code is a rate ½ code. Obtaining other rates as required by the standards is performed by puncturing the output. A table of the puncturing patterns can be found in Table 3.

Code Rate	Puncturing Pattern
½	X: 1 Y: 1
2/3	X: 1 0 Y: 1 1
¾	X: 1 0 1 Y: 1 1 0
5/6	X: 1 0 1 0 1 Y: 1 1 0 1 0
7/8	X: 1 0 0 0 1 0 1 Y: 1 1 1 1 0 1 0

Table 3: Table of the puncturing patterns for DVB standards

Concerning the decoder a Viterbi decoder is used on the *mother* code. The punctured patterns are replaced simply by zeros at the input to the decoder. The actual workings of the decoder are not specified in the standard but generally ASIC implementations are of the form of a sliding window of length greater than six times the constraint length.

Interleaver

It is well known that the Viterbi decoder produces burst errors at its output. These bursts cannot fully be taken care of by the RS burst error decoding capabilities, and so an interleaver is used to spread the bursts even more. As the RS code works on 8 bit symbols it was decided that the interleaver should also work on 8 bit symbols. The interleaver used is a convolutional interleaver (as opposed to a block type interleaver). This requires little memory storage and so at the time of specifying was capable of being produced to work at the speeds required. The interleaver is shown in Figure 7.

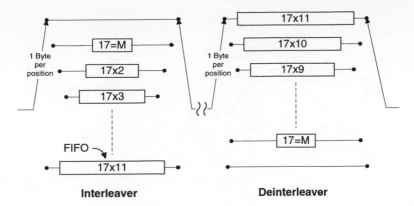

Interleaver   **Deinterleaver**

Figure 7: Convolutional Interleaver and Deinterleaver

Reed-Solomon Codes

Reed Solomon codes were chosen among other reasons for their burst error correction capabilities. With MPEG-2 packets being made up of 8 bit (byte) symbols it was natural to consider RS codes over $GF(2^8)$. The standard RS code over $GF(2^8)$ is of length 255. The length of a MPEG-2 being 188 bytes would naturally lead to the dimension of the RS code being 188 and therefore the code (255,188). This however has a coding rate of 188/255, far too low for the use. It was therefore decided after performance evaluations were completed to use a shortened code. The full size code (255, 239) was shortened to (204,188). This offered a high enough rate together with an acceptable performance in the concatenated system.

The way the encoding is usually done is that a (255,239) RS code is used, and the incoming 188 byte packet is appended with 51 zeros which are removed after encoding as the code used is systematic. The decoder works in a similar way.

Error Performance of the existing Schemes

In this section we will give the error performance of the uncoded schemes representing the modulation schemes used in the standards described. In Figure 8 we can see a graph of BER against E_b/N_0 for PSK schemes, including in particular QPSK and 8PSK (both normal and Gray mapped).

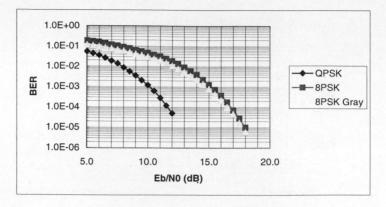

Figure 8 : Graph of Uncoded PSK schemes

In Figure 9 we can see graphs for uncoded QAM schemes, including 16QAM and 64QAM (both normal and Gray mapped) and 256QAM Gray mapped.

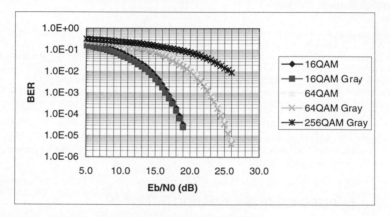

Figure 9 : Graph of Uncoded QAM schemes

It can be seen for all cases that by using Gray mapping, we gain additional performance over the normal mapping. This performance increase is provided without additional complexity.

For the coded schemes we are considering BERs of 10^{-11} and as such graphs are not easily obtainable. We can however consider for the concatenated schemes the point of the system just after the Viterbi decoder. We can thus get for QEF performance of the entire system the following tables of values of E_b/N_0 for a Gaussian channel. The code rate indicates the rate of the convolutional code used to achieve the BER of 2×10^{-4}. In Table 4 we see the values for the terrestrial scheme and Table 5 is for the satellite channel, this using QPSK modulation only.

Modulation	Code Rate	E_b/N_0 for BER=2×10^{-4}
QPSK	½	3.1
QPSK	2/3	4.9
QPSK	¾	5.9
QPSK	5/6	6.9
QPSK	7/8	7.7
16QAM	½	8.8

406

16QAM	2/3	11.1
16QAM	¾	12.5
16QAM	5/6	13.5
16QAM	7/8	13.9
64QAM	½	14.4
64QAM	2/3	16.5
64QAM	¾	18.0
64QAM	5/6	19.3
64QAM	7/8	20.1

Table 4: Values of E_b/N_0 for varying modulation and inner code rates for terrestrial channel

Code Rate	E_b/N_0 for BER=2×10^{-4}
½	4.5
2/3	5.0
¾	5.5
5/6	6.0
7/8	6.4

Table 5: Values of E_b/N_0 for varying modulation and inner code rates for satellite channel

Shannon's Limit

How is system performance estimated?

The conventional criterion for communication systems optimisation is the criterion of minimum probability of error (or maximum a posteriori probability)[Wozen]. However, this criterion is applicable only for receiver optimisation, since the transmitted side is assumed to be specified. Therefore, the conventional criteria are not directly applicable when modulation and coding schemes are to be chosen.

In [Zyuko] the following efficiency criterion has been suggested. Let our aim be to optimise a communication system with information rate R bit/sec, bandwidth B, and E_b/N_o. We define the bandwidth and channel capacity efficiencies as follows :

$$\gamma = R/B \qquad \eta = R/C$$

where C is the channel capacity specified as:

$$C = B\log_2(1 + SNR)$$

and the signal-to-noise ratio in the channel can be expressed as [Wozen]:

$$SNR = \frac{E_b R}{N_o B} = \gamma \frac{E_b}{N_o}$$

Thus, channel capacity efficiency can be re-written as:

$$\eta = \frac{R}{B\log_2(1 + SNR)} = \frac{\gamma}{\log_2(1 + \gamma E_b/N_o)}$$

It follows from the Shannon theory that the maximum value for channel capacity efficiency

407

Thus, for optimum communication system:

$$\eta_{max} = 1$$

$$\gamma = \log(1 + \gamma \, E_b/N_o)$$

$$2^\gamma = 1 + \gamma \, E_b/N_o$$

and the optimum trade-off between the E_b/N_o and frequency efficiency, also known as Shannon Limit can be derived as:

$$E_b/N_o = \frac{2^\gamma - 1}{\gamma}$$

This is presented in Figure 10 which also illustrates the efficiencies some of the DVB-S systems as specified in [DVB-S].

It can be observed that the efficiency of the current standard is at least 4.5 dB away from the Shannon bound.

Shannon Efficiency for DVB schemes

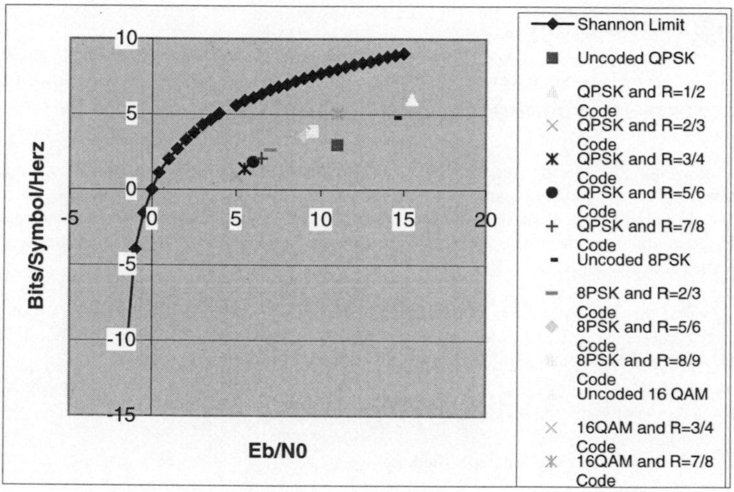

Figure 10:The Shannon Efficiencies of the schemes specified in [DVB-S]

The Future

What does the future hold for digital broadcasting. Diagram 1 indicates the problems and solutions needed for coding. Basically we need a coding scheme that is both bandwidth and power efficient but not complex. This of course is hard and for many years thought of as impossible.

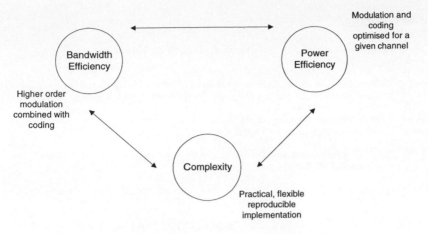

Diagram 1: The problems and solutions to the coding problem

In 1993 at the IEEE International Conference on Communications, Berrou et al. proposed their system of parallel concatenated convolutional codes, also known as "turbo-codes" [Berrou].

The first simulated turbo codes were a parallel concatenation of two simple binary recursive systematic convolutional codes, one being interleaved, and only one systematic bit being sent. The system could achieve (if the parity bits are punctured to achieve an overall coding rate of one half) a BER of 10^{-5} at an $E_b/N_0 = 0.7$dB. This remarkable result was achieved for BPSK modulation under additive white Gaussian channel conditions using 18 iterations of an iterative decoding algorithm.

The insertion of turbo codes into digital broadcasting schemes is non-trivial, and much work is needed on this front. However, since their introduction, turbo-codes have found application in a number of different areas. Two standardisation bodies, responsible for the introduction of the third generation mobile telephone systems (UMTS) and deep-space communications (CCSDS), have already accepted turbo-codes as a standard in their latest proposals. Concerning the area of digital broadcasting and digital TV broadcasting in particular, DVB is considering the use of turbo-codes in the return satellite channels. Therefore the use of them in the broadcasting arena is close.

Of course with these new coding schemes performing so much better than the existing schemes we are able to achieve at similar SNR a higher throughput by using higher order modulation schemes. That is it may be possible to use, 16QAM, 32QAM, etc on satellite, for example. Also possible improvements in existing schemes may be to have hierarchical modulations where we place one carrier on top of another, so that there is more information for a given signal. These, and others, are important and interesting topics that are currently being investigated around the world at leading research establishments.

Conclusions

In this paper we have presented a summary of the current standards for digital broadcasting, including DVB, ATSC and ISDB. We have tried to explain the schemes from a coding and modulation point of view as there are many references for the MPEG-2 side of the systems.

For the future we presented the idea of turbo codes and explained a little of what is possible. These are probably the most important invention since the inception of information theory in 1948 by its founder, Claude Shannon [Shanon].

References

[Dietz] Audio Coding in Digital broadcasting, Martin Dietz, AES 17th International Conference on High Quality Audio Coding, 1999

[ISDB-T] Channel Coding, Frame Structure and Modulation Scheme for Terrestrial Integrated Services Digital Broadcasting (ISDB-T), draft from http://www.dibeg.org/Documents/ISDB-T_Jxx.PDF

[DVB-S] Digital Video Broadcasting (DVB); Framing Structure, channel coding and modulation for digital 11/12GHz satellite systems, ETS 300421

[DVB-C] Digital Video Broadcasting (DVB); Framing Structure, channel coding and modulation for digital cable systems, ETS 300429

[DVB-T] Digital Video Broadcasting (DVB); Framing Structure, channel coding and modulation for digital terrestrial television, ETS 300744

[ATSC-DTS] Advanced Television Systems Committee (ATSC) Digital Television Standard, A/53, from http://www.atsc.org/Standards/A53/a_53.pdf

[MPEG] Coding of moving pictures and associated audio, ISO/IEC 13818-1 (November 1994)

[Wozen] J. Wozencraft and I. Jacobs – Principles of Communications Engineering, Wiley, NY 1965

[Zyuko] A. Zyuko, A. Falko, I. Panifilov, V. Banket and P. Ivachenko – Noise Immunity and efficiency of Communications Systems. Moscow, "Radio and Sviaz", 1985 (*in Russian*)

[Berrou] Berrou, C., Galvieux, A. and Thitimajshima, P. Near Shannon Limit Error-Correcting Coding and Decoding: Turbo Codes (1), Proc. IEEE International Conference on Communication (ICC), Geneva, Switzerland, pp. 1064-1070 , May 1993

[Shannon] Shannon, C., 1948. A Mathematical Theory of Communication, Bell Syst. Tech. J., Vol. 27, pp. 379-423 and 623-656

New Opportunities for Broadcasting below 30 MHz

Jonathan Stott, BBC R&D, UK

1. INTRODUCTION

Various frequency bands below 30 MHz are allocated for broadcasting; as amplitude modulation (AM) is currently used in all of them, they are, perhaps misleadingly, collectively known as the 'AM bands'. Broadcasters now have new opportunities for using them differently, which this paper introduces after a historical review.

2. BROADCASTING HISTORY

2.1. AM beginnings

Broadcasting started because it was *possible*. A way was found to modulate radio waves with the human voice — using *amplitude modulation* (AM) — and enthusiasts realised that this offered something that the general public might be interested to receive — unlike Morse code! The adventure began of discovering the types of programme material and styles of presentation that worked. Some of the early examples appear rather quaint to our sophisticated ears today, but we must remember that in those pioneering days there was no precedent to follow.

Initial services used the lower frequencies that we now call LF/MF. With advances in transmitter power, and the development of the infrastructure for networking, coverage of broadcasts could increase from local to national in scale. Later the possibility was exploited of broadcasting to far-off countries using HF.

I do not believe anyone originally sat down in a committee to propose the standard for AM broadcasting — the basic concept was simple enough, and the bandwidth at first was probably whatever the equipment at the transmitter and receiver could manage. Until the advent of the superhet, the bandwidth of the receiver was in any case difficult to control. Subsequently, as stations multiplied it became necessary to regulate which frequencies they used, leading to plans which minimised mutual interference, and introducing the concepts of defined channel spacing and bandwidth.

2.2. FM, TV and the transistor radio

Frequency modulation (FM) was developed in order to improve sound quality and reduce the impact of interference. It shared an appetite for bandwidth with the pioneering medium of television, and both therefore were introduced using still-higher VHF frequencies. At a time when reception was essentially static, in the home, TV and radio competed for the same audience.

The invention of the transistor, and the consequent development of small, efficient portable battery-powered receivers, changed the face of radio. Radio was now the medium that could accompany you wherever you were, unlike television, and programme offerings gradually adjusted to exploit this difference. A side effect was to slow the acceptance of FM, as early transistor technology was not up to VHF operation. Eventually this difficulty was overcome and, aided by the option of stereo, the popularity of FM grew, although FM receivers gained a reputation with many listeners of being difficult to tune.

2.3. Start of the digital age

Broadcasters first used digital techniques within their own infrastructure, then various 'add-ons' to existing broadcast services were made: RDS (Radio Data System) to assist tuning and add features to FM receivers, and Teletext and digital sound accompanying (analogue) television.

Finally, all-digital broadcasts have been introduced. Digital radio to the Eureka 147 DAB (Digital Audio Broadcasting) standard is broadcast at VHF (and higher) frequencies; it is designed to work well in a mobile environment. Digital television is broadcast in many ways: terrestrially, from satellite or by cable, e.g. using one of the DVB (Digital Video Broadcasting) family of standards. Individual sound-only programmes can also be transmitted by these means.

Alternative forms of distribution, using the Internet, have become possible as more efficient schemes of bit-rate reduction are developed.

2.4. Competition — where now for 'AM bands/broadcasters'?

Not for the first time, broadcasts in AM face competition. Listeners in many cases have the option of better audio quality from FM (or even DAB) broadcasts, placing those AM broadcasters without access to either of these at a disadvantage. This is one trigger for the development of a digital alternative to AM.

3. FEATURES OF THE 'AM BANDS'

3.1. Strengths

To make good use of the 'AM bands' for broadcasting it is important to identify their strengths.

At frequencies in the VHF range (or higher), propagation cannot be guaranteed much beyond line-of-sight. FM or DAB can therefore only cover large areas by the use of extensive transmitter networks which are usually only economically feasible where the population density is fairly high. Large countries therefore often have FM coverage only in major cities.

Ground-wave propagation at LF/MF covers much greater areas. A single transmitter can cover a small country, while medium-size countries can be covered by a modest network at these frequencies. Sky-wave (night-time) propagation at MF/LF can even be used to reach nearby countries if the frequency is clear of interference.

HF can be used for still greater coverage. Vertical-incidence broadcasting (in which a signal is sent straight up to the ionosphere from which it is 'reflected') is useful for covering large countries from within, using a single transmitter. This method is popular in tropical regions, where the interference caused by tropical storms renders MF less attractive, and extensive FM networks are prohibitively expensive.

However, HF is perhaps best known for facilitating *international* broadcasting by oblique ionospheric 'reflection'. Uniquely, it enables another country to be reached without needing the assistance of third parties — satellite operators or relay stations within the target country. HF is therefore especially useful for reaching audiences in 'closed societies' or in times of turmoil.

In summary, the prime advantage of the 'AM bands' is *coverage*.

3.2. Challenges
These bands impose some significant technical challenges.

The total capacity of the bands is limited, and therefore the present channel bandwidth and spacing are kept small to maximise the possible number of users. (This is why present-day AM is limited in audio bandwidth, especially in Europe).

Propagation is variable — especially so at HF, where, in addition, significant multipath and Doppler effects can occur (adding characteristic distortions to AM sound quality).

Because their use dates back to the birth of broadcasting, a certain old-fashioned stigma perhaps attaches to them — does AM perhaps stand for *Ancient Modulation*?

4.   A DIGITAL ALTERNATIVE

4.1.   What is technically possible
Advances in digital bit-rate reduction have brought the bit rate needed for an audio signal of quite reasonable quality into the range that might be supported within the customary 9 or 10 kHz channel by using sufficiently advanced digital modulation. Furthermore, advanced digital modulation/channel coding can cope with adverse propagation conditions, as demonstrated by DAB and DVB-T (the terrestrial variant of DVB).

Once signals are conveyed in digital form, it is possible to send other sorts of data as well, both that needed to make the receiver easier to use, and also to offer new facilities.

4.2.   What is needed from it
To be competitive, the new digital system must offer a significant improvement in audio quality compared with present-day AM. This must apply to the spoken word in a wide variety of languages, as well as to music. Remember that the system must be introduced in the face of competition from existing FM stations, and in an environment where yet other sources of good audio quality (such as CDs) may be available to the listener.

This improvement must also apply to the way the system copes with propagation disturbances. (Indeed, it is the noise, fading and distortion often heard on AM, as well as the limited audio bandwidth, which are together responsible for listeners' perception of poor quality).

A new digital system should have a spectral efficiency as least as great as AM — but this could perhaps be achieved at greater channel bandwidth, if fewer channels were needed in total to achieve the same coverage. (For example, this might be possible at MF, if the system facilitated the use of Single-Frequency Networks, as used in DAB. At HF, multiple frequencies are currently often used to combat poor propagation — it may perhaps be possible to reduce the number used if the new system is robust enough.)

The new digital system must share the ubiquity of AM. The parameters of the radiated signal may need to vary to suit different requirements (both regulatory and technical, e.g. propagation characteristics at different frequencies), implying the use of a range of 'modes', as is done in DAB and DVB-T. Nevertheless, a single receiver design should receive them *all*. This is desirable anyway to maximise sales volume and thus reduce costs, but is essential for international broadcasting.

Receivers must be affordable, both to purchase and to run. Batteries may be expensive or difficult to obtain in some parts of the world, so power consumption must be limited — which may also permit the use of solar or clockwork power instead. This will place an upper limit on the complexity of processing.

Receivers must be much easier to use, especially in comparison with present HF AM receivers, many of which have given HF the reputation of being difficult. New system features will therefore have to be built into the specification so that the signal will contain some data specifically intended for this purpose.

For example, there could be data to identify the station (e.g. BBC), the programme strand or 'channel' (e.g. BBC World Service), perhaps further sub-divisions, especially for international broadcasters (e.g. BBC service to Sub-Saharan Africa in Hausa) and the programme name (e.g. News at Six).

Additional data could, where appropriate, indicate to the receiver a list of alternative frequencies (as in RDS) on which the same programme could be found. This would help the receiver to maintain reception automatically in the presence of very slow fading or interference, and to follow daily or weekly changes in the frequencies used. Any frequency changes should ideally be made seamlessly, without the listener hearing the join. This should be achieved, despite the fact that signals on different frequencies may arrive at different times (they may come from transmitters in very different places). The range of arrival times to be accommodated is of the order of 30 ms.

Other data could give details about other programmes by the same broadcaster (i.e. a schedule) or give further information relating to the present programme (e.g. a recipe, medical advice, details of a musical item, contact details for further information about a subject ...).

Ease of use of the receiver will also require a short 'lock-up' time, so that the receiver can respond quickly to the listener's request for a different programme.

While clearly remembering that the total data capacity will not be large, other uses may be envisaged for data accompanying the programme, or even perhaps for an all-data broadcast without any audio. Indeed, perhaps the real challenge for 'AM' broadcasters is to find imaginative ways to use the data 'pipe' that a digital modulation system provides — they might be the key to success or failure!

5. THE FUTURE
The 'specification' for AM was not written beforehand — it simply evolved. The same cannot be true for its digital replacement. For mutual interoperability it is essential for all relevant parties — broadcasters, transmitter operators, and manufacturers of receivers and transmitting equipment — to come together to develop a *single* world-wide standard. A world-wide consortium, Digital Radio Mondiale (DRM) has been formed with the objective of doing this. It has more than forty members, who are pooling their efforts with the intention of preparing a draft standard by the end of 1999.

The re-use of the AM bands faces a possible threat in the form of *interference*. Various systems have been proposed for using existing cables into people's homes to convey data, particularly for Internet access. There are proposals for both mains cables (power-line transmission, PLT) and telephone cables (various forms of DSL), which, by using these cables in ways for which they were not designed, have the potential to cause interference to all forms of radio communication in the LF/MF/HF spectrum. In particular, PLT systems could increase the noise floor in parts of the HF spectrum by the order of 60 dB. This is clearly incompatible with broadcasting and other uses of the HF bands. It would be a tragedy if PLT systems, offering limited-capacity short-distance communication in circumstances where there are better alternatives, were to sterilise the HF bands which have a unique long-distance capability.

AM broadcasting began over 80 years ago, so the challenge in terms of 'future-proofing' its digital replacement is considerable. Producing a credible strategy for the transition from AM to digital modulation and retention of viable spectrum will be vital to success.

6. CONCLUSIONS
The frequency bands presently used for AM broadcasting are of special value because propagation at these frequencies can readily provide large-area coverage for national or international broadcasting. Indeed, for international broadcasting they are unique in making it possible to reach other countries without the intervention of intermediaries who may act as gatekeepers.

Propagation at these frequencies can suffer fading and multipath, which, taken together with the limited audio bandwidth of present AM, means that the overall quality perceived by the listener does not compare well with that of FM or CDs.

Better audio quality and reliability could be achieved if a digital system were used instead in these bands. Furthermore, features could be facilitated to make reception more user-friendly — especially in comparison with the present 'knob-twiddling' image of HF reception. Automatic selection of alternative frequencies (similar to RDS in modern FM receivers) is a particular example.

The DRM consortium is actively seeking to make this 'digitisation' happen, with a draft specification scheduled for the end of 1999. The aim is to have a single world standard able to meet the needs of all kinds of broadcasters and all kinds of listeners.

7. ACKNOWLEDGEMENT
The author wishes to thank the BBC for permission to publish this paper.

Robust Hierarchical Broadcasting for AWGN and Flat Rayleigh Fading Channels using Multilevel Codes

Dong-Feng Yuan[1]*, Dietmar W. Schill[2]† and Johannes B. Huber[2]

[1]Shandong University, Jinan, P. R. China, E-mail: dfyuan@jn-public.sd.cninfo.net
[2]Lehrstuhl für Nachrichtentechnik II, Universität Erlangen-Nürnberg, Germany,
E-mail: schill@sony.de

1. ABSTRACT

Coded modulation schemes for hierarchical broadcasting employing multilevel coding (MLC) are considered for both AWGN and flat Rayleigh fading channels. Special emphasis is put on good performance in both classes of channels, thus resulting in robust modulation schemes with respect to channel characteristics. Design rules for signal constellations and codes are discussed.

2. INTRODUCTION

With the introduction of digital modulation techniques to the broadcast media of television and audio the theoretical description of the broadcast channel, which first was discussed by Cover [1], has regained considerable interest. The key element is the question of the maximal possible data rates that can be transmitted in a point to multi-point communication environment if the varying receivers exhibit differing propagation conditions. These differences can be due to varying receiver qualities because of differing antennas e.g. or due to the differing physical channel propagation conditions when transmitting to spacially separated receivers. Whatever the reason for the differing signal to noise ratio (SNR) at the input of the demodulator is, a hierarchical system offers the possibility to efficiently transmit data streams decodable at multiple SNRs. One example for a coded modulation scheme capable of performing hierarchical modulation is multilevel coding (MLC) [2] [3] [4]. Another solution, more frequently used up to date, is time-sharing, that is the fragmentation of the available transmission ressources (time, frequency e.g.) into several orthogonal transmission schemes that each have their proper level of protection. In [5] MLC is shown to be far superior to time-sharing in terms of power-bandwidth efficiency. Below, we address the problem of robustness of a MLC-scheme under varying signal propagation

---

*Supported by Deutscher Akademischer Austauschdienst
†Supported by Fraunhofer Institute for Integrated Circuits, Erlangen, Germany

conditions. As examples, the additive white Gaussian noise (AWGN) and the flat Rayleigh fading channel are chosen.

3. MULTILEVEL CODING

The key feature of MLC is the mechanism of splitting the transmission channel into several logical subchannels, with the number of such subchannels depending on the size of the signal constellation of the underlying modulation scheme. Due to the separated subchannels, a multi-stage decoder can be used which asymptotically reaches the performance of an optimal maximum likelihood decoder (MLD) but requires considerable lower decoding complexity [6]. MLC has three major degrees of freedom for its designer. Firstly, the partitioning strategy for the signal constellation. Secondly the choice for the code rates on the individual levels of the MLC-scheme and thirdly, the signal constellation itself with respect to the number of points and their spacing.

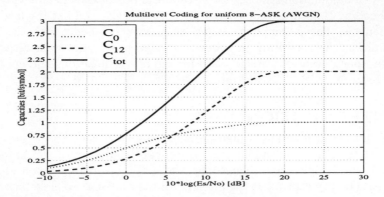

Fig. 1: Capacities for BP on lowest level for 8-ASK
(AWGN, uniform distribution of signal points)

A discussion of the effects for all three choices in the AWGN channel can be found at [7]. Here we only want to recall some of the most important definitions. Throughout this paper, 8-ASK is used as an example constellation. Of course the results are also applicable to 64-QAM using 8-ASK for the inphase and the quadrature channels. Figure 1 gives the theoretically achievable capacities for an 8-ASK constellation with equiprobable signal points using block partitioning (BP) at the first partitioning step in order to render, here for the AWGN channel, the transmission of two levels of protection possible. Applying the capacity rule [6], we set the coding rates on the individual levels by choosing them equal to the capacities at the desired SNRs of operation. The split of the signal constellation into two sub-groups due to BP can be seen from figure 2, where x^0 represents the label associated with the lowest level of the MLC scheme.

The partitioning at the second and third level is yet not specified and

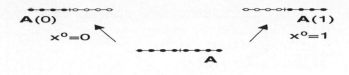

Fig. 2: BP on lowest level for 8-ASK

will be addressed subsequently. Therefore, only the combined capacity of the two higher levels is plotted which is independent from the partitioning strategy. The SNR is defined as average energy per symbol over the one-sided spectral noise power density (Es/No). With respect to the non-uniform ASK-constellations we follow the symmetric approach of [8]. Figure 3 gives the definitions for 8-ASK, where it has to be noted that all constellations used are normalized to the same average energy per symbol Es.

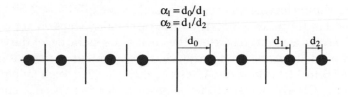

Fig. 3: Non-uniform signal constellation for 8-ASK

4. ROBUST PERFORMANCE

As mentioned above, the code rates have to be chosen according to the capacity rule in order to achieve a power and bandwidth efficient transmission. Therefore, care has to be taken that the distribution of code rates throughout the levels remains constant under all channel conditions. As it was shown by Schramm [9] for non-hierarchical constellations Gray partitioning (GP) of the signal constellation achieves this requirement, whereas the classical Ungerböck partitioning (UP), maximizing the intra-subset Euclidean distance, does not. GP should therefore be used for the partitioning of the levels that are to be decoded at the same SNR. We suggest to combine it with bit-interleaved coded modulation (BICM) as proposed by Caire [10] in order to have a robust method. In our example for 8-ASK, the two upper levels are concerned, which have their accumulative capacity plotted as C_{12} in figure 1.

To see the effect of channel variations on BP we examine figure 4, that shows the same signal constellation and mapping as figure 1 but for the flat Rayleigh fading channel.

Taking desired rates of 0.5 for the lowest level and 1.5 for the upper two

419

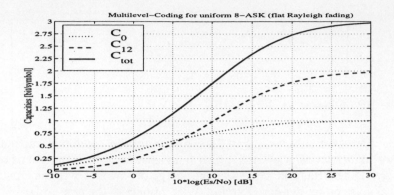

Fig. 4: Capacities for BP on lowest level for 8-ASK
(flat Rayleigh fading, uniform distribution of signal points)

levels, and thus achieving an overall transmission capacity of 2 bits/symbol, we can see that the necessary SNR for the two quality steps do not change by exactly the same amount. Therefore the energetic separation of the levels will change by a small amount for differing channels. For our example it increases from 12.4 dB to 13.1 dB for the AWGN and the flat Rayleigh fading channel respectively. Clearly this is neither a problem for the decoder nor for the system design.

Allowing for non-uniform signal constellations in order to increase the degrees of freedom for the system design, we have to verify that the same constellations are power efficient for both types of channels. As figure of merit for a constellation we take the definition of the loss in performance as introduced in [7]. Loss is defined as the accumulative difference in required SNR between the non-uniform constellation, characterized by its values α_i and the uniform constellation ($\alpha_i = 1$) over all quality levels l, as given by equation 1.

$$Loss(\alpha_1, \alpha_2) = \sum_{i=0}^{l-1} E_s N_0(\alpha_1, \alpha_2)|_{C_i} - E_s N_0(1,1)|_{C_i} [dB] \qquad (1)$$

For the example set out above, figure 5 gives the result as equipotential lines. The region inside a closed line labeled x is the set of all α's that give perfomance better than a loss of xdB as compared to the uniform constellation. Comparing the solid lines for the AWGN with the dashed lines for the flat Rayleigh fading channel it is evident that signal constellations performing well under both channel conditions exist.

420

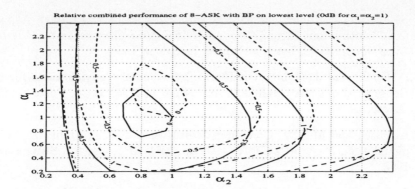

Fig. 5: Efficient signal constellations for $C_0 = 0.5$bit/symbol and
$C_{tot} = 2$bit/symbol (AWGN solid, flat Rayleigh fading dashed)

5. CONCLUSIONS

The behavior of non-uniform hierachical signal constellations using MLC
has been investigated under the AWGN and the flat Rayleigh fading channel.
It was found that BP together with an energetic separation of the levels to
be decoded is robust to channel variations. Additionally it was found that
the non-uniform signal constellations can be chosen such as to behave well
in both channels. Designing a hierarchical system special care has therefore
only to be taken for the levels that are to be decodable at the same SNR.
Combining the results of [9] with those of [10] we conclude that BICM should
be used on the these levels.

6. REFERENCES

[1] T. Cover, Broadcast Channels, *IEEE Trans. Inf. Theory*, IT-18, 2-14, 1972.

[2] H. Imai, and S. Hirakawa, A New Multilevel Coding Method Using Error Correcting Codes, *IEEE Trans. Inf. Theory*, IT-23, 371-377, 1977.

[3] J. Huber, Multilevel-Codes: Distance Profiles and Channel Capacity, *ITG Fachbericht 130*, pp. 305-319, Munich, Germany, 1996.

[4] J. Huber, and U. Wachsmann, On Set Partitioning Strategies for Multilevel Coded Modulation Schemes, *Proc. Mediterranean Workshop on Coding and Information Integrity*, p. 62, Palma de Mallorca, Spain, 1996.

[5] D. Schill, D. Yuan, and J. Huber, Efficient Hierarchical Broadcasting using Multilevel Codes, accepted for *Proc. IEEE ITW'99*, Metsovo, Greece, 1999.

[6] R. Fischer, J. Huber, and U. Wachsmann, Multilevel Coding: Aspects from Information Theory, *Proc. of IEEE Mini-Conference at GLOBE-COM'96*, pp.26-30, London, United Kingdom, 1996.

[7] D. Schill, and J. Huber, On Hierarchical Signal Constellations for the Gaussian Broadcast Channel, *Proc. IEEE ICT'98*, 34-38, Porto Carras, Greece, 1998.

[8] K. Fazel, and M. Ruf, Combined multilevel coding and multiresolution modulation, *Proc. of IEEE ICC'93*, pp. 1081-1085, Geneva, Switzerland, 1993.

[9] P. Schramm, Multilevel Coding with Independent Decoding on Levels for Efficient Communications on Static and Interleaved Fading Channels, *Proc. IEEE PIMRC'97*, 1196-1200, Helsinki, Finland, 1997.

[10] G. Caire, G. Taricco, and E. Biglieri, Bit-Interleaved Coded Modulation, *IEEE Trans. on Inf. Theory*, vol. 44, pp. 927-946, May, 1998.

Index